Public History in Poland

This volume presents various aspects of public history practices in Poland, alongside their historical development and theoretical reflections on public history.

Despite a long tradition and variety of forms of public history, the very term "public history", or literally speaking "history in the public sphere", has been in use in Poland only since the 2010s. This edited collection contains chapters that focus on numerous practices and media forms in public history including historical memory, heritage tourism, historical re-enactments, memes and graphic novels, films, archives, archaeology and oral history. As such, the volume brings together the Polish experiences to wider international audiences and shares Polish controversies related to public history within the academic discourse, beyond media news and politically engaged commentaries. Furthermore, it sheds crucial light on the developments of collective memory, historical and political debates, the history of Poland and East-Central Europe and the politics of post-World War II and post-communist societies.

Authored by a team of academic historians and practitioners from the field, *Public History in Poland* is the perfect resource for students from a variety of disciplines including Public History, Heritage, Museum Studies, Anthropology and Archaeology.

Joanna Wojdon is an associate professor at the Institute of History, University of Wrocław, Poland, member of the Steering Committee of the International Federation for Public History and chair of the Commission for Public History of the Committee of Historical Sciences of the Polish Academy of Sciences.

Global Perspectives on Public History
Edited by Dr. Kristin O'Brassill-Kulfan, Rutgers University

This series explores the work of public historians and the contested his-tories they engage with around the world. Authored by both scholars and practitioners, volumes focus on cases where complex histories and diverse audiences meet and examine public representations of history. The series aims to link professional discussions of different historical methodologies with broader dialogues around commemoration, preservation, heritage, and interpretation in diverse geographical, cultural, social, and economic contexts. The co-existence of both global and regionally specific volumes in the series highlights the wide range of innovative new projects and ap-proaches on offer. These books will provide students, researchers, and prac-titioners with new case studies and helpful analytical tools to confront the (mis)representations of history they encounter in their work and as members of twenty-first century communities.

Contested Commemoration in U.S. History
Diverging Public Interpretations
Edited by Melissa M. Bender and Klara Stephanie Szlezák

Public in Public History
Edited by Joanna Wojdon and Dorota Wiśniewska

Public History in Poland
Edited by Joanna Wojdon

Public History in Poland

**Edited by
Joanna Wojdon**

Routledge
Taylor & Francis Group

NEW YORK AND LONDON

First published 2021
by Routledge
605 Third Avenue, New York, NY 10158

and by Routledge
2 Park Square, Milton Park, Abingdon, Oxon, OX14 4RN

Routledge is an imprint of the Taylor & Francis Group, an informa business

Library of Congress Cataloging-in-Publication Data
Names: Wojdon, Joanna, 1973- editor, author.
Title: Public history in Poland / edited by Joanna Wojdon.
Description: New York : Routledge, 2021. | Series: Global perspectives
on public history | Includes bibliographical references and index. |
Identifiers: LCCN 2021031310 | ISBN 9780367761646 (hardback) |
ISBN 9780367761677 (paperback) | ISBN 9781003165767 (ebook)
Subjects: LCSH: Public history—Poland. | Collective memory—
Poland. | Historical museums—Poland. | Memory—Political
aspects—Poland. | Monuments—Political aspects—Poland. |
Poland—History—Philosophy.
Classification: LCC DK4155 .P83 2021 | DDC 943.8—dc23
LC record available at https://lccn.loc.gov/2021031310

ISBN: 978-0-367-76164-6 (hbk)
ISBN: 978-0-367-76167-7 (pbk)
ISBN: 978-1-003-16576-7 (ebk)

DOI: 10.4324/9781003165767

Typeset in Times New Roman
by codeMantra

Contents

vi *Contents*

Tables

Contributors

Anna Borkiewicz has a BA in History (2014) and an MA in Public History (2016) from the University of Wroclaw. Her research interest is history in popular culture. She has previously published papers on history-related internet memes. Awarded a MEXT scholarship, she is currently researching history in manga comic books at Nagoya University, Japan.

Lucyna Harc is an assistant professor at the Institute of History, University of Wrocław, a representative of the University of Wrocław at the International Centre for Archival Research, and since 2020 deputy director of the State Archives in Poland. She co-edited a series *Cuius regio? Ideological and Territorial Cohesion of the Historical Region of Silesia (c.1000–2000)*, vol. 1–5 (Wrocław, 2013–2015).

Ewa Jabłońska-Stefanowicz is an assistant professor at the Institute of Library and Information Science at the University of Wrocław from 2008. She started her professional career at the PWN Publishing Group. Her main research interests are modern publishing and Polish book market. She is the author of textbooks on information technology as well as scholarly articles and entries in *Encyklopedia książki* [Book Encyklopedia] (Wrocław, 2017).

Łukasz Kamiński is an assistant professor at the Institute of History, University of Wrocław, president of the Platform of the European Memory and Conscience and former president of the Institute of National Remembrance (2011–2016). His publications include six volumes on the history of the Solidarity movement, co-edited with Grzegorz Waligóra (Warszawa: IPN, 2010).

Marta Kurkowska-Budzan is Professor of History at Jagiellonian University in Krakow. Her area of expertise is the cultural history of twentieth-century Poland, heritage studies and the methodology of historical research. Her recent publications cover topics in cultural history of sports in Poland under the communist regime and oral history methodology.

Rafał Stobiecki holds the chair of History of Historiography and Auxiliary Sciences of History at the Institute of History of the University of Łódź. His areas of interest include Polish historiography of 1944–1989 in Poland and in exile, and Russian and Soviet historiography of the nineteenth and twentieth centuries. His recent publications include *Historiografia PRL: Zamiast podręcznika* (Łódź: Wydawnictwo UŁ, 2020).

Piotr Trojański is an associate professor at the Institute of History and Archival Studies of the Pedagogical University of Kraków. He specializes in twentieth-century Jewish history and Holocaust education in Poland and serves as an academic advisor for the International Centre for Education about Auschwitz and the Holocaust at the Auschwitz-Birkenau State Museum. He is also vice-chairman of the European Association for Holocaust Studies and a member of the Polish delegation to the International Holocaust Remembrance Alliance.

Paweł Ukielski is an assistant professor at the Institute of Political Studies, Polish Academy of Sciences, Warsaw. He is the deputy director of the Warsaw Rising Museum (2004–2014 and since 2016). His publications include *Aksamitny rozwód. Rola elit politycznych w procesie podziału Czechosłowacji* [The velvet divorce. The role of political elites in the division of Czechoslovakia process] and *Pamięć Polski, pamięć sąsiadów. Pamięć Europy* [Memory of Poland, memory of neighbors. Memory of Europe].

Przemysław Wiszewski is Professor of Medieval and Modern History at the Institute of History, University of Wrocław. His research interests focus on the past of heterogeneous societies in Europe, social cohesion of medieval societies, regional history of Silesia, and political and social history of Central Europe. Together with Nora Berend and Przemysław Urbańczyk he co-authored the monograph *Central Europe in the High Middle Ages: Bohemia, Hungary and Poland c.900–c.1300* (Cambridge: Cambridge University Press, 2013). Recently he published *Memories in Multi-Ethnic Societies: Cohesion in Multi-Ethnic Societies in Europe from c. 1000 to the Present, I* (Turnhout: Brepols, 2020).

Joanna Wojdon is an associate professor at the Institute of History, University of Wrocław, where she is also a chair of the Department of Methodology of Teaching History and Civic Education, and a coordinator of MA program in Public History. She is a member of the Steering Committee of the International Federation for Public History and chair of the Commission for Public History of the Committee of Historical Sciences of the Polish Academy of Sciences. Her recent publications include *Textbooks as Propaganda. Poland under Communist Rule. 1944–1989* (Routledge, 2018); *Communist Propaganda at School. Reading Primers of the Soviet Bloc. 1949–1989* (Routledge, 2021); and *Public in Public History*, edited together with Dorota Wiśniewska (Routledge, 2022).

Filip Wolański is an associate professor at the University of Wrocław, a cultural historian specializing in Polish travel history and education, as well as preaching and social communication. His research focuses mainly on the first half of the eighteenth century.

Anna Izabella Zalewska is an associate professor at the Institute of Archaeology and at the Institute of History, Maria Curie Skłodowska University of Lublin. She is a member of the Advisory Board of Outreach and Education of the Organisation for the Prohibition of Chemical Weapons. Her publications include contributions to memory studies, landscape studies, heritology, pro-social and socialized archaeology of contemporaneous times, public history, historiography, communication, museology, material-discursive practices with the engagements and agency of the material, written and non-material remains of the recent past, and methodology.

Anna Ziębińska-Witek is an associate professor at the Institute of History, Maria Curie-Sklodowska University of Lublin. Her recent publications include *Historia w muzeach. Studium ekspozycji Holokaustu* (2011) and *Muzealizacja komunizmu w Polsce I Europie Środkowo-Wschodniej* (2018). She has been awarded a Kościuszko Foundation Grant (United States Holocaust Memorial Museum, Washington, DC, 2002) and a Fulbright Grant (Princeton University, 2005/2006).

Piotr Zwierzchowski is Professor of Film Studies and Director of the Institute of Culture Studies at Kazimierz Wielki University of Bydgoszcz, Poland. He is President of the Polish Society for Film and Media Studies. He has published several books on the history of Polish cinema. Currently, together with Marek Haltof, he is writing *Screen as Battlefield: Confronting the Past in New Polish Cinema* for Bloomsbury.

Introduction

Public History in Poland

Joanna Wojdon

The concept of public history was introduced in Poland in the 2010s. In scholarly literature it was first used by Robert Traba in a footnote of his article devoted to the concept of applied history.[1] The article had originated from Traba's conference paper rooted predominantly in the German academic discourse, and the footnote stated that as time passed the author would not insist on using the term "applied history," but would rather choose "public history," or in the Polish translation "history in the public space."

Already before the text was published, the first MA program in public history had been launched at the University of Wrocław. Developed independently from Traba's projects, based on American models and consulted with Theodore Karamanski and his colleagues from Loyola University in Chicago, it adopted the same Polish translation of "public history," i.e., history in the public space.[2] The issue of translation returned on various occasions, for example, when the first academic textbook on public history in the Polish language was to be published in 2018,[3] and when the Commission for Public History of the Committee of Historical Sciences of the Polish Academy of Sciences was to be created in 2020.[4]

As is discussed below, humanities in Poland have a long tradition of serving to protect the national heritage, including the Polish language. Thus, on the one hand, using the English name without translation, as happened in Italy for example, did not seem potentially to facilitate the acceptance of this emerging field or (sub)discipline in academia. Some discussants even referred to the provisions of the bill on the Polish language[5] which obliges public institutions, including the educational ones, to teach in the Polish language (unless under provisions of special regulations) and to use the Polish names/labels. On the other hand, the literal translation, *historia publiczna*, evoked rather negative connotations, either with prostitution (like a public house) or with something primitive or unsophisticated. This would not make the introduction of public history into academic or popular discourse any easier. Last but not least, "history in the public space" is broad enough to refer to history as historical research and the publicly presented results thereof, as well as to history understood as the past or memory of the past and its material and non-material presence in the public spaces. It

DOI: 10.4324/9781003165767-1

corresponds with the ways in which public history has functioned in Poland for many years before it began to be theoretically conceptualized.

Despite the fact that the texts in this volume refer mostly to the post-Second World War developments, Polish practices of public history existed long before that. For example, some of the oldest pieces of literature in the Polish language, written in the sixteenth century, refer to historical topics.[6] Development of Polish academic historiography in the nineteenth century was hindered by the limitations imposed by the partitioning empires: Russia, Prussia and Austria. Literature,[7] music and fine arts served as carriers of historiographical narratives instead and promoted certain visions of the past: either a glorious one, seen as a counterbalance to the depressing reality, or that of a suffering nation. They were addressed mostly to the educated part of the public, originating from the higher classes of the society who were forming the intelligentsia. One of the goals of the intelligentsia, however, was to "enlighten" the lower strata,[8] including in terms of forming their national identity, based on the awareness of their shared past. Émigré poets dreamed of reaching uneducated audiences with their patriotic messages.[9] Secret Polish language and history classes as well as reading and common rooms with Polish literature were established with the purpose of enlightening the public. Mass rallies were organized in Warsaw in 1860 to commemorate the 30th anniversary of the November uprising of 1830. Those commemorative practices eventually resulted in the new anti-Russian insurrection of 1863.

When liberated from the ethnic policies of Austro-Hungary at the turn of the nineteenth and twentieth centuries, Poles seized the opportunity to commemorate Polish historical events officially. Paintings by Jan Matejko, director of the Academy of Fine Arts in Kraków, concentrated on famous battles, treaties and other significant events, often from the distant past.[10] Critics keep pointing to numerous mistakes and deliberate distortions that he made for symbolic or esthetic reasons, but the general public was captured by his interpretations and has been treating them almost as ancient photographs even today. He also authored an iconic collection of portraits of the Polish kings, reproduced in school textbooks up to the present. The panorama painting of the battle of Racławice against the Russian army during the Kościuszko uprising of 1794 by the team of Wojciech Kossak and Jan Styka was commissioned to commemorate its centennial in the city of Lwów (Lvov/Lviv/Lemberg).[11] The unveiling of the Grunwald monument in Kraków in 1910 for the quincentennial of the battle fought with the Teutonic Knights brought together participants from all parts of the partitioned Poland, as well as representatives of the Polish diaspora from places as distant as Chicago, Illinois and Buffalo, New York.[12]

Therefore, similar to other European countries, artists were involved in promoting certain interpretations of history. They took on the role of public historians in this important period when national heroes, holidays, myths and symbols were selected that subsequently have been shaping collective memory for decades. Those representatives of the intelligentsia were reaching the Polish public and trying to counterbalance the national narratives of the partitioning powers, in particular Russia and Germany, who would prefer the history of Poland to fall into oblivion.

When Poland regained independence in 1918, its new authorities paid a great deal of attention (and resources) to its own politics of history, even though they were not using this term, which was only coined in the early twenty-first century. The national anthem was adopted based on the song of the Polish Legions formed within the Napoleonic army at the end of the eighteenth century and which referred to the earlier wars.[13] Surviving veterans of the January Uprising of 1863 enjoyed privileges and reverence, alongside the former combatants of the military units under the command of Marshal Józef Piłsudski (but not necessarily of his political opponents who had also participated in the struggles for Poland's independence). The 1920 Battle of Warsaw against the Red Army gained particular prominence as the one that had not only saved Warsaw from Soviet subjugation but had also protected the world from the spread of the Bolshevik revolution. Historical commemorations, as well as heated debates related to the past, shaped the public life of the Second Polish Republic of 1918–1939 and were continued in exile where political divisions still had historical roots, strengthened by the divergent interpretations of the then most recent political and military developments.

Public history practices could be observed in the Polish territories even during the Second World War, especially in Warsaw under German occupation, when the underground scouting movement engaged in commemorating national anniversaries by hanging Polish flags on public buildings, in painting national symbols on walls and in other public places, or in removing the German plaque from the monument of Nicolaus Copernicus.[14]

A strong national dimension (rather than individual, local or global), as well as an imperative to take a position regarding the state and its policies, can be still observed in Polish public history, as the chapters in the first part of this book clearly indicate. They analyze the "top-down" approach to public history, that is history developed "for the public" or even delivered "to the public," with the expectation that the public will accept the message and engage in propagating it further.

At the same time, the first four chapters illustrate that the interpretations of the recent developments in public history and the politics of history in Poland can be poles apart. They agree on the choice of events that constitute the turning points and of flagship institutions of "top-down" public history, but not on the assessment of their activities nor of the general course of events. As editor, I deliberately decided not to seek consensus or compromise but to allow divergent perspectives to be included, opinions and arguments to be expressed, especially because, as in case of other chapters, some of them come from academia, others from the practitioners in the field and some authors play or used to play a double role. Coming from the field of history education, I have always favored what Robert Stradling called "multiperspectivity,"[15] allowing readers to form their own opinions or, what is no less important, to recognize and understand divergent viewpoints and place them in broader contexts that may reach beyond the authors' (or editor's) knowledge.

The last two chapters of the first part of the book, as well as those included in the second part, devoted to the relations between public history and historical research, pay a lot of attention to the changes that took place in Poland under communist rule and after the transition to democracy. They start by noting the attempts of the post-war communist regime to monopolize historical narratives delivered to the Polish public. At the same time, they look for grassroots activities that were undermining the monopoly of the regime, not always with the aim of overthrowing it, but rather of finding a way to nurture natural interests (as in the case of oral or local history presented in this volume by Marta Kurkowska-Budzan and Przemysław Wiszewski to gain public support (the case of archaeology characterized by Anna I. Zalewska), or to fulfil public needs (the case of archives discussed by Lucyna Harc) or obligations (as in the case of the former concentration camps presented by Piotr Trojański). They prove that neither propaganda nor repressions managed to prevent bottom-up historical practices beyond the system control, although their development was not always safe and easy. More research on independent public history under communism is certainly required. It included, among others, the *"samizdat"* publishing movement that produced and distributed hundreds of books, periodicals and other publications (such as postcards, stamps, calendars, posters) beyond the control of the censorship office,[16] a significant part of which referred to history. Commemorations of forbidden heroes and anniversaries (e.g. the Battle of Warsaw of 1920 on August 15, the May 3 Constitution of 1791, or Poland's Independence regained symbolically on November 11, 1918), historical lectures for and historical research by amateurs who have rejected the state monopoly on historical truth and even history-related jokes all contributed to the counternarratives that were making the official top-down public history increasingly difficult to handle. The role of the Catholic Church as a public history institution in both the nineteenth and twentieth centuries deserves special attention, though thus far this aspect of its activities seems to be neglected in academic scholarship.

The collapse of the communist regime, symbolically assigned to the year 1989, brought not only an almost immediate end of political limitations, but also opened up multiple new opportunities that also benefitted public history: from freedom in travelling abroad and free access to ideas, to growing economic strength (all the difficulties notwithstanding) and accessibility of new technologies. Thus, on the one hand, the "top-down" public history seemed to take a step back, with the popularity of the notions such as "the end of history"[17] or "We split away the history of our recent past with a thick line"[18] – yet another issue of consensus between the authors of the four initial chapters of this book. On the other hand, however, as the subsequent six chapters illustrate, significant progress was made in developing grassroots public historical initiatives, done **with** the public and **about** the public. Many endeavors, up to that point hidden and illegal, were officially recognized, continued and developed. Some profited from material and social capital accumulated in the difficult times of the "People's Republic of Poland," while others emerged from scratch as a reaction to new ideas and new opportunities. Yet others had to shift their attention towards the public(s) whom they had so far largely ignored (as illustrated in the example of archives by Lucyna Harc) – a trend not uncommon after the collapse of the communist system in the fields located very far from public history, such as commerce, services or public institutions.

All had to face new challenges, including the economic hardships of the free market economy. As the chapters by Ewa Jabłońska-Stefanowicz and Piotr Zwierzchowski argue, historical books and historical films managed to retain considerable public interest. Popular historical magazines proliferated. While they are not discussed in this book, they followed the patterns discussed on the grounds of history education within the project European History Crossroads as Pathways to Intercultural and Media Education (EHISTO).[19] Detailed analyses of trends and changes in this area of public history would require a team of researchers from various social backgrounds and political options since these publications have become strongly politicized and their interpretations can be no less contrasting than the ones regarding the museums from the chapters by Paweł Ukielski and Anna Ziębińska-Witek in this volume.[20]

The last part of the book deals with public history as entertainment and its forms developed **by** the public, or at least with the active participation of the public. Historical tourism, with special emphasis placed on dark tourism, is discussed earlier by Piotr Trojański in the chapter devoted to memorial sites. It has recently become a research area per se.[21] Historical reenactments, presented in this volume by Filip Wolański, have shown both continuity (as some of the most popular manifestations of this movement have their roots in the 1970s) and change, but first and foremost considerable growth despite some controversies, also political in nature. Moreover, they have become a field of intensive studies in Poland and internationally (with Polish input visible both in terms of topics covered and of researchers engaged),[22] so that discussions on this aspect of public history could result in yet another parallel chapter. Public controversies have also been evoked by such grassroots activities as history-related graffiti (recently also commissioned by some state-sponsored institutions), murals, stickers, so-called "patriotic clothes," and other memorabilia, which, unfortunately, remain on the margins of academic research in public history.[23] Discussions on Wikipedia, its development, reliability and drawbacks are not specific to Poland, although their individual topics may be.[24] The same can be said about online discussions in social media or in the comments in online journals and newspapers.[25]

Thus, the public can be understood not only as readership, audience, visitors or other recipients, but also as actors, initiators, creators and producers who are not professionally trained as historians.[26] The division between public historians and their public becomes blurred at times. Are film directors, who are not historians but who deal with historical topics, public historians? What about the authors of literary fiction set in the past? Or members of a music band whose lyrics reflect a certain period of history as if they were created then?[27] In any case, more studies on public history done within the realms of literature, music or fine arts would be more than desired. In this volume they are represented by cinema characterized by Piotr Zwierzchowski and by the phenomenon of the "Polandball" internet memes analyzed by Anna Borkiewicz.

As for more passive forms of history-related entertainment, Polish comic books have been included only cursorily in this latter chapter though their numbers have grown exponentially. Unlike in some other countries, however, in Poland they do not have a longer tradition and did not gain considerable popularity in the twentieth century. The ones developed recently are mostly didactical in nature, with educational and political goals dominating over engagement and entertainment.[28] The same can be said about video games if compared to board games. History-related "serious" computer games were developed in Poland already in the 1990s. However, as a rule, their educational aspects killed any pleasure of playing and thus they proved to be rather counterproductive in reaching the goal of attracting young people to history. Therefore, it is hard to regard them as effective examples of public history. Board games, on the contrary, however vintage they may seem, not only turned out to be a commercial success but also set new trends of spending free time in both private and public settings. The most successful of them, *The Queue* (*Kolejka*) serves as a case study to discuss these and other aspects of board games as a form of public history in the last chapter of this book.

The concept of public history has been introduced in Poland on several levels: in research projects and scholarly publications, through the practices of institutions (grassroots and state-sponsored) and in the study programs at the universities. Public history practices still outperform theoretical reflections, and the term "public history" is not as widely recognized and used in academic or popular discourse as I would expect or desire it.

The number of public history classes or teaching modules within academic history programs is growing. Full new programs are emerging. The MA program at the University of Wrocław originated from the discussions on the ongoing problems with dropping enrollment to the MA program in history and the poor perspectives of its graduates on the job market. Due to the striking similarities with the situation in the United States of the 1970s that we were teaching about in our US history classes, we decided to follow the American solutions. Other universities have identified similar difficulties and even adopted similar solutions (to place more emphasis on practical skills and social interactions, and on digital forms of research, preservation and presentation) but for various reasons have been reluctant to use the name "public history." Instead, there is "animation of social memory" at University of Warmia and Mazury in Olsztyn, historical tourism, or preservation of historical heritage at other universities, all of which encompass various aspects of public history.

The Institute of National Remembrance (IPN), regarded as the first institution to implement the new "politics of history" and initiate large-scale state-sponsored history-related activities addressed to the general public, characterized in this volume by Łukasz Kamiński, developed them under the label of "public education," not public history, however.

Flagship Polish institutions of public history are new history museums (presented in detail in this volume by Paweł Ukielski and Anna Ziębińska-Witek, as well as by Rafał Stobiecki) – to the degree that during the last General Congress of Polish Historians in 2019, the panels in the section of "public history" were devoted exclusively to the discussions about history museums.

The book *Historia w przestrzeni publicznej* referred to the concept of Barbara Franco, also used in this volume, of public history as the history for the public, by the public, with the public and about the public.[29] In the introduction to that volume, aimed at bringing the international ideas of public history into the Polish academic discourse and practices, I wrote that we can regard as public history any history that is done outside academia and school at least to the "extent in which those two institutions play their traditional role of the transfer [of knowledge] from professionals to professionals and from teachers-masters to students-pupils." I also added that

> in effect, public history can be seen as a patchwork rather than a coherent entity [...] with diversity, polyphony and openness to multiple needs, voices and experiences being its distinctive features. It is a sui generis umbrella that encompasses research and activities from various other subdisciplines, such as history didactics, museum studies, cultural heritage, social archives, oral history, heritage tourism or visual history.[30]

Today, I would also add memory studies and studies on the politics of history, at least.

The Polish problems with and debates on the essence of public history have never been specific for Poland only. Rather they are parallel to the ongoing international discussions where, despite its 40 years of existence, public history still lacks one precise definition, epistemology or methodology, and the International Federation for Public History has recently rejected any attempts to present one universal approach to public history, opting instead for noting a variety of public history practices, e.g. in the form of a tree developed by Thomas Cauvin.[31] Since the concept of public history was imported to Poland from abroad and, moreover, simultaneously from multiple sources – although numerous case studies discussed in this volume prove that the practices of public history have been deeply rooted in the Polish traditions – its Polish proponents and commentators have become immediately engaged in the existing international debates. Their presence is still visible and recognizable there, with the University of Wroclaw appearing as the most active Polish academic center in this area. Its Willy Brandt Center for German and European Studies is a co-founder and co-publisher of the *Public History Weekly*, an electronic blog-journal published by DeGruyter.[32] The Public History Summer School, organized annually since 2018, used to bring together about 50 participants face-to-face from all over the world, and over 200 in its online pandemic edition in 2020 and 2021.[33] It is organized under the auspices of the International Federation for Public History. Other public history-related conferences at the University of Wrocław included *Public in Public History* within the framework of a Jean-Monnet Network "Applied Contemporary European History" coordinated at the University of Jena,[34] and "Migrations in the Public Space," the annual meeting of the Committee for Migration Research of the Polish Academy of Sciences in 2019. These are the reasons why the authors affiliated with the University of Wrocław are somewhat overrepresented in this volume.

We realize that this collection of essays does not exhaust the topic of public history in Poland, but rather presents reflections on its selected aspects. Taking this into consideration, alongside the ongoing development of public history in Poland, we do hope that this will not be our last word.

Notes

1 Robert Traba, "Historia stosowana jako subdyscyplina akademicka. Konteksty i propozycje," in *Historia dziś. Teoretyczne problemy wiedzy o przeszłości*, ed. Ewa Domańska, Rafał Stobiecki, and Tomasz Wiślicz (Kraków: Universitas, 2014), 143–164.
2 Joanna Wojdon, "Do We Need Public History Study Programs?," *Public History Weekly* 4, no. 33 (2016).
3 *Historia w przestrzeni publicznej*, ed. Joanna Wojdon (Warszawa: PWN, 2018).
4 http://www.knh.pan.pl/index.php/lista-komisji-knh/156-komisja-historii-w-przestrzeni-publicznej, accessed May 15, 2021.
5 "Ustawa z dnia 7 października 1999 r. o języku polskim," *Dziennik Ustaw*, no. 90 (1999), 99.
6 Jacqueline Glomski, "Historiography as Art. Jan Kochanowski's Lyricorum libellus (1580)," in *Renaissance Culture in Context. Theory and Practice*, ed. Jean R. Brink and William F. Gentrup (Aldershot: Scolar Press, 1993), 145–154.
7 Cf. the novels by Henryk Sienkiewicz, the laureate of the Noble Prize in Literature 1905: *Quo Vadis* set in the Ancient Rome, or *Trilogy* recently translated into English by Wiesław S. Kuniczak, set in the seventeenth century Poland.
8 Jerzy Jedlicki, "Problems with the Intelligentsia," *Acta Poloniae Historica* 100 (2009): 15–30.
9 E.g. Adam Mickiewicz, *Pan Tadeusz*, first published in Paris in 1834.

10 Cf. Danuta Batorska, "The Political Censorship of Jan Matejko," *Art Journal* 51, no. 1 (1992): 57–63.

11 Jakub Zarzycki, "The Battle of Racławice – Wojciech Kossak, Jan Styka (in cooperation with other artists)," *culture.pl*, August 2020, accessed May 15, 2021, https://culture.pl/en/work/the-battle-of-raclawice-wojciech-kossak-jan-styka-in-cooperation-with-other-painters.

12 Anna D. Jaroszyńska-Kirchmann, "'Memories of Greatness:' American Polonia and the Rituals of National Commemorations before World War I." *Polish American Studies* 74, no. 1 (2017): 38; Andrew K. Wise, "Dr. Francis Fronczak and the Rhetoric of Polish Independence." *Rocznik Przemyski. Historia* 55, no. 3 (2019): 97.

13 *Mazurek Dąbrowskiego* (Poland Is Not Yet Lost).

14 Those actions are presented in the book by Aleksander Kamiński, *Kamienie na szaniec* – English language edition: *Stones for the Rampart; the Story of Two Lads in the Polish Underground Movement* (London: Polish Boy Scouts' and Girl Guides' Association, 1945).

15 Robert Stradling, *Multiperspectivity in History Teaching: A Guide for Teachers* (Strasbourg: Council of Europe, 2003).

16 Cf. Paweł Sowinski, Gwido Zlatkes, and Ann M. Frenkel, *Duplicator Underground: The Independent Publishing Industry in Communist Poland, 1976–1989* (Bloomington: Slavica Publishers, 2016).

17 Francis Fukuyama, *The End of History and the Last Man* (New York: Simon and Schuster, 2006).

18 The citation comes from the 1989 speech by Tadeusz Mazowiecki, the first post-communist prime minister of Poland.

19 Susanne Popp, Miriam Hannig, and Jutta Schumann, *Commercialised History: Popular History Magazines in Europe* (Frankfurt: Peter Lang, 2015).

20 An extremely critical approach towards abusing history by right-wing (not only history-related) magazines has recently been presented by Magdalena Saryusz-Wolska, "Abusing Public Visual History: The Current Right-Wing Press in Poland," *The Public Historian* 42, no. 3 (2020): 61–85. My anecdotal knowledge of the magazines from other sides of the political spectrum suggests that the right-wing press does not have a monopoly on this kind of abuse.

21 Armin Mikos von Rohrscheidt, *Historia w turystyce kulturowej* (Warszawa: PWN, 2018).

22 Vanessa Agnew, Jonathan Lamb, and Juliane Tomann, eds. *The Routledge Handbook of Reenactment Studies: Key Terms in the Field* (New York: Routledge, 2019).

23 Rafał Stobiecki, "Jak gadżety oswajają nas z przeszłością," *Polityka* no. 22, May 26, 2015.

24 Andrzej Zawistowski, "Historia w Wikipedii," in *Historia w przestrzeni*, 351–358.

25 Cf. Dorota Choińska, "Researching the Public(s) through Internet Readers' Comments. Case Study of the Cursed Soldiers in North-Eastern Poland," in *Public in Public History*, ed. Joanna Wojdon and Dorota Wiśniewska (New York: Routledge, 2021), 161–179.

26 Cf. Joanna Wojdon and Dorota Wiśniewska, eds., *Public in Public History* (New York: Routledge, 2021).

27 Cf. http://hanba1926.pl, accessed May 25, 2021.

28 Ewa Stańczyk, "'Long Live Poland!': Representing the Past in Polish Comic Books," *Modern Language Review* 109, no. 1 (2014): 178–198.

29 Barbara Franco, "Public History and Memory: A Museum Perspective," *The Public Historian* 19, no. 2 (1997): 66.

30 *Historia w przestrzeni.*

31 https://twitter.com/thomascauvin/status/1194283070062391296, last modified
    November 12, 2019, accessed May 15, 2021.
32 https://public-history-weekly.degruyter.com, accessed May 15, 2021.
33 https://publichistorysummerschool.wordpress.com, accessed May 15, 2021.
34 https://aec-history.uni-jena.de, accessed May 15, 2021.

Bibliography

Agnew, Vanessa, Jonathan Lamb, and Juliane Tomann, eds. *The Routledge Hand-
    book of Reenactment Studies: Key Terms in the Field*. New York: Routledge, 2019.
Batorska, Danuta. "The Political Censorship of Jan Matejko." *Art Journal* 51, no.
    1 (1992): 57–63.
Choińska, Dorota. "Researching the Public(s) through Internet Readers' Com-
    ments. Case Study of the Cursed Soldiers in North-Eastern Poland." In *Public in
    Public History*, edited by Joanna Wojdon and Dorota Wiśniewska, 161–179. New
    York: Routledge, 2021.
Franco, Barbara. "Public History and Memory: A Museum Perspective." *The Pub-
    lic Historian* 19, no. 2 (1997): 65–67.
Fukuyama, Francis. *The End of History and the Last Man*. New York: Simon and
    Schuster, 2006.
Glomski, Jacqueline. "Historiography as Art. Jan Kochanowski's Lyricorum libel-
    lus (1580)." In *Renaissance Culture in Context. Theory and Practice*, edited by Jean
    R. Brink and William F. Gentrup, 145–154. Aldershot: Scolar Press, 1993.
Jaroszyńska-Kirchmann, Anna D. "'Memories of Greatness:' American Polonia
    and the Rituals of National Commemorations before World War I." *Polish Amer-
    ican Studies* 74, no. 1 (2017): 27–51.
Jedlicki, Jerzy. "Problems with the Intelligentsia," *Acta Poloniae Historica* 100
    (2009): 15–30.
Kamiński, Aleksander. *Stones for the Rampart. The Story of Two Lads in the Polish
    Underground Movement*. London: Polish Boy Scouts' and Girl Guides' Association,
    1945.
Mickiewicz, Adam. *Pan Tadeusz*, first published in Paris in 1834.
Popp, Susanne, Miriam Hannig, and Jutta Schumann. *Commercialised History:
    Popular History Magazines in Europe*. Frankfurt: Peter Lang, 2015.
Saryusz-Wolska, Magdalena. "Abusing Public Visual History: The Current Right-
    Wing Press in Poland." *The Public Historian* 42, no. 3 (2020): 61–85.
Sowiński, Paweł, Gwido Zlatkes, and Ann M. Frenkel. *Duplicator Underground:
    The Independent Publishing Industry in Communist Poland, 1976–1989*. Bloom-
    ington: Slavica Publishers, 2016.
Stańczyk, Ewa. "'Long Live Poland!': Representing the Past in Polish Comic Books."
    Modern Language Review 109, no. 1 (2014): 178–198.
Stobiecki, Rafał. "Jak gadżety oswajają nas z przeszłością," *Polityka* no. 22, May
    26, 2015.
Stradling, Robert. *Multiperspectivity in History Teaching: A Guide for Teachers*.
    Strasbourg: Council of Europe, 2003.
Traba, Robert. "Historia stosowana jako subdyscyplina akademicka. Konteksty i
    propozycje." In *Historia dziś. Teoretyczne problemy wiedzy o przeszłości*, edited
    by Ewa Domańska, Rafał Stobiecki, and Tomasz Wiślicz, 143–164. Kraków: Uni-
    versitas, 2014.

"Ustawa z dnia 7 października 1999 r. o języku polskim," *Dziennik Ustaw*, no. 90 (1999), 99.

von Rohrscheidt, Armin Mikos. *Historia w turystyce kulturowej*. Warszawa: PWN, 2018.

Wise, Andrew K. "Dr. Francis Fronczak and the Rhetoric of Polish Independence." *Rocznik Przemyski. Historia* 55, no. 3 (2019): 97–116.

Wojdon, Joanna. "Do We Need Public History Study Programs?" *Public History Weekly* 4, no. 33 (2016).

Wojdon, Joanna, ed. *Historia w przestrzeni publicznej*. Warszawa: PWN, 2018.

Wojdon Joanna and Dorota Wiśniewska, eds. *Public in Public History*. New York: Routledge, 2021.

Zarzycki, Jakub. "The Battle of Racławice – Wojciech Kossak, Jan Styka (in co-operation with other artists)." *culture.pl*, August 2020. Accessed May 15, 2021. https://culture.pl/en/work/the-battle-of-raclawice-wojciech-kossak-jan-styka-in-incooperation-with-other-painters.

Zawistowski, Andrzej. "Historia w Wikipedii." In *Historia w przestrzeni publicznej*, edited by Joanna Wojdon, 351–358. Warszawa: PWN, 2018.

Websites

Applied European Contemporary History. Jean-Monnet Network. Accessed May 15, 2021. https://aec-history.uni-jena.de.

Cauvin, Thomas. Tweet on Twitter, last modified November 12, 2019. Accessed May 15, 2021. https://twitter.com/thomascauvin/status/1194283070062391296. Accessed May 25, 2021.

http://hanba1926.pl.

Komisja Historii w Przestrzeni Publicznej KNH PAN. Accessed May 15, 2021. http://www.knh.pan.pl/index.php/lista-komisji-knh/156-komisja-historii-w-przestrzeni-publicznej.

Public History Summer School in Wrocław. Accessed May 15, 2021. https://publichistorysummerschool.wordpress.com.

Public History Weekly. Accessed May 15, 2021. https://public-history-weekly.degruyter.com.

Part I
Public History and Politics

1 Public History and Politics of History

The Case of Poland in Central Europe: 1989–2015

Łukasz Kamiński

Communism, Opposition and the Past

Communist regimes placed great weight on the sphere of what we would today call the politics of history, which is the sum of actions taken with the aim of shaping collective memory. The communist party controlled historical research, access to archives, all publications, museums and the depiction of history in works of culture, such as movies or novels. Street names were changed, monuments were torn down and new ones erected. Some past events and their participants were sent into oblivion, some were distorted and others were glorified regardless of their real importance. A Marxist view of history was promoted, and "patriotic" legitimization of communist rule was not uncommon.[1]

The democratic opposition emerging in some countries from the mid-1970s had few tools to oppose these practices. In most cases, its actions were limited to occasional statements and publications in the few independent imprints.[2] Poland was an exception in this regard. The Polish opposition was able not only to fight words with words, but also to organize commemorative events (such as masses and demonstrations), lectures on history and even research independent of the communist authorities already in the second half of the 1970s. These activities were expanded after the Solidarity movement developed. In 1980–1981, history was openly debated (especially topics that had previously been omitted or falsified), uncensored books and brochures were published, and celebrations of anniversaries rejected by the communists were organized. Moreover, multiple new monuments were erected (some of them were even devoted to victims of communism), numerous exhibitions were organized and a project for the reform of the school curriculum in history was developed.[3] The martial law imposed in 1981 only partially limited these activities. History was one of the most important topics of independent underground publications. Documentation centers such as the Solidarity Archive or the Eastern Archive worked in conspiracy.[4] It can be said that in the 1980s, the Polish opposition implemented its own politics of history that served both to delegitimize the communist system (by recalling its crimes) and to build its own (and at the same time national)

DOI: 10.4324/9781003165767-3

identity by referring to particular elements of the past. The Catholic Church was an important ally in these actions by protecting and supporting many initiatives.[5]

After 1989

Paradoxically, this legacy prevented the state from implementing active historical policies in the first few years after the collapse of the communist system. On the one hand, the memory of the totalitarian aspirations of the pre-1989 governments created a resolve to reverse the practices, but on the other hand, many of the opposition activists (who at that point became prominent politicians) believed that the social awareness of history had already been improved by the earlier actions, and so they felt it unnecessary to conduct any significant projects in this sphere. Moreover, both political elites and the society were preoccupied by the problems caused by the political and economic transformation.

Under such circumstances, the activity of the state in the first years of the Third Republic of Poland was limited to legal matters – the traditional name of the country (*Rzeczpospolita Polska* – Republic of Poland, instead of The People's Republic of Poland) and the coat of arms were restored, most communist celebrations were abolished and pre-war ones re-established (Constitution Day on May 3 and National Independence Day on November 11), and the school history curriculum was changed. Actions were taken that could be considered an element of transitional justice – bills were adopted that allowed unlawful court sentences to be appealed and reparations to be paid to victims of some forms of repressions, as well as crimes designated as Stalinist (committed in 1944–1956) to be prosecuted. No new institutions dealing with history were created, however – only the names and ranges of competence of some of the existing ones were changed. The Chief Commission for Investigation of Hitlerite Crimes in Poland became the Chief Commission for Investigation of Crimes against the Polish Nation; the Museum of the History of Polish Revolutionary Movement and the Museum of Vladimir Lenin were transformed into the Museum of Independence; and the Institute of Political Studies was built on the foundation of the Institute of Socialist Countries of the Polish Academy of Sciences, in which a small team of historians led research on modern history.[6]

In the first years after the fall of the communist system, the field of public history was populated mostly by NGOs. A particular role was played by the KARTA Center, established in 1991 by a group of people previously engaged in publishing an underground journal of the same name. The Eastern Archive continued its work under the auspices of KARTA while the materials documenting the post-war history of Poland were collected in the Peerel Archive,[7] later renamed the Archive of Opposition. *Karta* became a quarterly journal educating about the history of the twentieth century in an engaging form. In 1997, the Center started organizing the *Historia bliska* (History at Hand) competition, encouraging young people to discover the stories of their surroundings, towns or families on their own. In 1997–2000, the KARTA Center also organized large historical exhibitions, presented both within and outside of Poland, devoted, among others, to the story of the opposition and resistance against totalitarian systems, the Solidarity movement and the fall of the communist system.[8]

Among the groups that contributed to the field of popularizing history was the Republican League with the first exhibition on the post-war armed resistance presented in 1993 and later expanded.

Some initiatives were undertaken by individuals, for example, the exhibition titled *Winni? Niewinni?* (Guilty? Innocent?) was an effect of the work of Krzysztof Szwagrzyk, who investigated the post-war staged trials and presented the judges and prosecutors involved in those practices. The scandal that arose out of the exhibition and attempts to block it under the pretext of protecting personal data brought this matter to public attention.[9]

Next to NGOs (including veteran associations), local governments were quite active in the 1990s. Soon after 1989 most of the toponyms connected to communism were changed and many monuments glorifying people, events and organizations tied to the old system were removed.[10] However, new monuments, reflecting the shift in the historical consciousness of the Poles, were erected mainly as a result of social initiatives, i.e., actions undertaken by associations, committees, veteran organizations, etc. State structures (like the Council for the Protection of Struggle and Martyrdom Sites) showed greater activity only in the construction of the war cemeteries in Charków (Kharkov), Katyń and Mednoye which opened in 2000.[11]

The lack of an active policy in the matter of dealing with the communist past, meager effects of investigations and numerous obstacles encountered by groups and individuals interested in these matters (ranging from lack of funding, through difficulties in accessing the archives, to lawsuits) increased the importance of this sphere in general politics. Appeals for a more active engagement of the government were made mainly with the slogan of decommunization, understood both as legal (the Czech experience was often referred to) and institutional changes (Germany and the Federal Commissioner for the Records of the State Security Service of the former German Democratic Republic, Der Bundesbeauftragte für die Unterlagen des Staatssicherheitsdienstes der ehemaligen Deutschen Demokratischen Republik (BStU), served as a pattern to follow here).[12] To some degree, which is hard to determine exactly today, these actions were also connected to the ongoing procedures of Poland's admission to the North Atlantic Treaty Organization (NATO) (especially matters of lustration) and to the European Union (accessibility of archives).

Institute of National Remembrance

Fulfilling the demands for a more active state engagement in matters of history and remembrance became possible after the parties which arose from anti-communist opposition (Solidarity Electoral Action and Freedom

Union) won the parliamentary elections in September 1997. However, their options were limited by the veto power of the post-communist President Aleksander Kwaśniewski, which was overridden only once – in the case of the act of December 18, 1998, on the creation of the Institute of National Remembrance – Commission for the Prosecution of Crimes against the Polish Nation (usually shortened to *Instytut Pamięci Narodowej*, or IPN). The Institute began actual operation in June 2000, after its first president (Leon Kieres) was elected. Other noteworthy actions in this period include active promotion of the history of Poland abroad, connected to the anniversaries in 1999 (60th anniversary of the outbreak of the Second World War and 10th anniversary of the fall of communism). For instance, the Ministry of Foreign Affairs presented the exhibition "End of Yalta 1945–89," prepared by the KARTA Center, in multiple countries. In 2000, the 30-year withdrawal period limiting access to documents of the communist party was abolished. At the same time, the idea of creating two new institutions – the European Solidarity Centre and the Polish History Museum – was born, both of which materialized in the following years.[13]

As it later turned out, the main breakthrough was the creation of IPN. In its original form, it comprised three main divisions:

- prosecutorial, whose job is to lead investigations on crimes committed in the period of 1939–1990[14] by functionaries of occupying states (Germany and the Soviet Union) and communist dictatorship (the term "communist crime" was also defined then);
- archival, whose job is to collect the documents of the widely understood security and repressions apparatus from the same period, and making them available to victims, researchers and journalists;
- Office of Public Education, which conducts research and popularizes its results.

As the creators of the act admitted, the first two divisions were considered the core of the institution, while the third one was supposed to fulfil supportive functions. It is visible in the text of the bill, where very little space is devoted to the matters of research and education. In reality, this latter division turned out to be not only equally important to the former two, but also the most visible to general public.[15]

It was widely expected that an independent institution taking over previously inaccessible documents of the communist Security Service would turn public attention to the matters related to its operations, and especially to the issue of secret collaborators. Meanwhile, the first case that IPN (successfully) dealt with was related to the Second World War.

The inauguration of the Institute's activities coincided with a great national debate around the case of Jedwabne, a small town in central Poland where the Poles were accused of participating in a pogrom of Jews in the beginning of July 1941. The case, brought to public attention by the book

Neighbors by Jan Tomasz Gross, shocked public opinion. IPN played a significant role in the debate, both by leading both an investigation and scholarly research, published in two volumes in 2002.[16]

The effects of IPN's activities (see below), the discussion about Jedwabne[17] and finally the opening and huge success of the Warsaw Rising Museum (see Paweł Ukielski's chapter in this volume) placed matters of history at the center of public debate in Poland. At the time, the term "politics of history" saw wider use. For many years discussions were centered on the term itself, but as Antoni Dudek has noted, its critics did not in fact reject the possibility of pursuing the politics of history but rather proposed its different, more liberal model.[18]

Regardless of disputes and controversies around the term itself (the analogous term "politics of memory" does not cause such strong feelings), politics of history does exist. It comprises decisions regarding matters such as school history curricula, museums, street names, monuments (erected and torn down), works of culture related to the past, as well as actions contained within the sphere of public history, such as exhibitions, murals, historical reenactments, scavenger hunts, etc. Paradoxically, the most stalwart defenders and the staunchest opponents of the term share the belief that politics of history belongs in the domain of the state. However, although the state has the most resources at its disposal, local governments, NGOs, religious organizations, informal social movements and sometimes even individuals are also actors in politics of history. Some, especially the state, may declare a lack of interest in pursuing it, but paradoxically it will still mean adopting a concrete stance – in this case, omission.

For many years, the IPN has been the most prominent entity designing and implementing politics of history in Poland. It is treated by some as the executor of the state's policy, however, until the amendment of the law in 2016, it enjoyed a significant degree of independence, and during the terms of the first three presidents, numerous conflicts and tensions with the governing authorities took place, leading to budget reductions, among others. Regardless of the disputes about the role and achievements (or failures) of IPN, it is worth noting that due to placing research and educational activities in the foreground, it has become involved in numerous public history projects. The statistical data below is presented as of 2015, since IPN has not published similar information later.

One of the most visible public history activities of the IPN are exhibitions. During the first 15 years of its existence, the Institute prepared a total of 453 exhibitions, most of which were presented multiple times (6,763 presentations, including 288 abroad).[19] Both the topics and forms varied: there were both indoor and outdoor exhibitions, made in various techniques where panels, multimedia and artifacts were used. Some exhibitions required thousands of square feet, while some were more humble, made for independent printing. In agreement with the statutory range of activity of IPN, they pertained mostly to the Second World War and the post-war communist dictatorship, however, other topics appeared occasionally, mostly connected to the early twentieth century.

In 2009, IPN published its first educational board game *Awans: Zostań marszałkiem Polski* ("Promotion: Become the marshal of Poland"), teaching about pre-war military ranks and particular heroes of the Second World War. In the following years, more such games appeared, but the success of the game *Kolejka* ("Queue," 2011), which shows the reality of the communist economy of the 1980s, was a breakthrough. Not only did it help popularize the concept of games presenting history, but it also increased the general interest in board games in Poland (see Joanna Wojdon's chapter in this book).

As time passed, the collective view of history has been increasingly shaped by various forms of digital education. The IPN started creating educational websites in greater numbers relatively late. The first website was created in 2006, on the 25th anniversary of the imposition of martial law. The idea was to combine popular texts, iconography, multimedia (historical recordings, witnesses' testimonies, documentaries) and digital publications. Until 2015, 30 websites, devoted to particular events, wider historical phenomena or prominent people have been created. Some are available in multiple languages. In 2015, four million visits to educational sites were noted, making them an educational tool of a far greater range than traditional exhibitions.[20]

Activities of IPN contain many other forms of popularizing history, fitting within the public history framework: historical rallies, reenactments, movie screenings, scavenger hunts, concerts, Oxford-style debates, etc. Altogether, in the first 15 years of its existence, IPN has organized 35,000 various educational activities. Its rich publishing record (1,794 publications up to 2015) contains books, scholarly and popular journals, as well as other forms, such as several comic books.[21] In the period of 2013–2016, a few dozen brochures from the "Namesakes of Our Streets" series were published, and then delivered to mailboxes of inhabitants of each street with the help of community organizations (mainly scouts). Regularly published press supplements also familiarized readers with history.[22] The music video recorded in 2013 for Kasia Malejonek's song *Jedna Chwila* ("One Moment"), based on the story of Danuta Siedzikówna, a 17-year-old paramedic murdered by the communist authorities in 1946, reached 850,000 views on YouTube.[23]

International Context

The success of IPN, visible especially in the areas of education and research, caused similar institutions to be created in some other countries of East–Central Europe to deal with their totalitarian past, while in some countries they existed beforehand in various forms.[24] Even though none of them fully mirrors IPN's structure, Polish inspirations are visible even in their names. In 2003, the Slovak National Memory Institute (*Ústav pamäti národa*) and in 2006, the Ukrainian Institute of National Memory (*Український*

Інститут Національної Пам'яті), began their activities. In Prague in 2007, during a parliamentary debate, the name of the newly created institution was changed from the Institute of National Memory to the Institute for the Study of Totalitarian Regimes (*Ústav pro studium totalitních režimů*). Finally, in 2014 in Hungary, the Committee of National Remembrance (*Nemzeti Emlékezet Bizottsága*) was established. As it seems, the Polish experience also had its part in the creation of the Institute for the Investigation of Communist Crimes in Romania in 2005, which currently functions as the Institute for the Investigation of Communist Crimes and the Memory of Romanian Exile, and in 2006 in the creation of the Committee for Disclosing the Documents and Announcing Affiliation of Bulgarian Citizens to the State Security and Intelligence Services of the Bulgarian National Army (*Комисия за разкриване на документите и за обявяване на принадлежност на български граждани към държавна сигурност и разузнавателните служби на българската народна армия*).

Most of these institutions, along with a few other organizations, became the founding members of the Platform of European Memory and Conscience (PEMC) in October 2011 in Prague, during the summit of the Visegrád Group. Currently it unites 63 organizations from 23 countries, with five more having candidate status. The creation of the PEMC was an effect of prolonged efforts from representatives of East–Central European countries after their accessions into the European Union in 2004 and 2007. The most important events leading to its creation were the Prague (2008) and Warsaw (2011) declarations, along with the European Parliament resolution of April 2, 2009 on European conscience and totalitarianism. Next to principal activities such as lobbying on the European level (including for the creation of a pan-European monument for the victims of totalitarianisms) and ongoing cooperation of member institutions, the PEMC also organizes scholarly conferences and educational actions. The most important of the latter include exhibitions (*Totalitarianism in Europe, Century of Martyrs, European Gulag*), the educational game *Across the Iron Curtain* (four language versions, two more in preparation) and a reader for high school students *Lest We Forget*, presenting the fates of particular people in the clash with totalitarian systems (nine language versions, two more in preparation).[25]

Next to the PEMC, which currently has six Polish members, IPN was also a founding member of the European Network of Official Authorities Dealing with Secret Police Files (2008). However, it does not show any greater activity other than yearly member meetings.[26]

The European Network Remembrance and Solidarity (ENRS) also plays a growing role in the discussions about the memory of the twentieth century. It was created in 2005 as an initiative of the Polish authorities but started its actual activities five years later. Currently, Germany, Slovakia, Romania and Hungary are members as well. The ENRS was created as a reaction to the initiative to create the Center against Expulsions in Berlin that posed the threat of having the fates of Germans after 1945 presented outside any broader historical context. Next to extremely important scholarly ventures (e.g. the conference cycles Genealogies of Memory and European Remembrance), the ENRS popularizes history both in traditional ways (e.g. "Sounds in the Silence" and "In Between?" projects, aimed at the youth; "After the Great War: A New Europe 1918–1923" and "Between Life and Death: Stories of Rescue during the Holocaust" travelling exhibitions) and online (Hi-storylessons.eu). The network actively promotes August 23 as the European Day of Remembrance for Victims of Totalitarian Regimes.[27]

Other Actors of Politics of History

Next to IPN and museums of various scale, the National Center of Culture (*Narodowe Centrum Kultury*, or NCK), the Adam Mickiewicz Institute (AMI) and the Pilecki Institute (PI) are important actors of politics of history in Poland, and are simultaneously institutions involved in public history projects.[28]

The NCK was created in 2002 from a few institutions whose roots dated back to communist Poland. In 2005, it was briefly made part of the AMI, but became an independent entity again in 2006. It is supposed to undertake cultural activities that "uphold and popularize national and state tradition" and "promote Polish national legacy as an important element of European cultural legacy." Both those spheres reflect the two basic dimensions of politics of history – internal (serving to form identity) and external (building an international image). The NCK has been engaged in multiple public history projects (exhibitions, concerts, historical shows, social campaigns) and financed many more that were organized by other entities (counties, local governments, NGOs). In agreement with the mission of the institution, many of its activities encourage seeking ways to present the past with the language of culture.[29]

The AMI was created in 2000 with the primary goal of popularizing Polish culture abroad. It attained its current shape in 2006, and at the same time "popularizing knowledge about Poland and its pluralistic (in national, linguistic, ethnic, religious dimensions) cultural legacy in the international environment" was added as the second point on its list of tasks.[30] In the most recent version of its by-laws, the point was characteristically changed so at the present time (2021), the Institute is to develop projects connected to "popularizing knowledge about Poland and its cultural legacy abroad" and "events of significant importance for Poland and celebrations of important anniversaries." However, the role of the AMI in the Polish politics of history in recent years seems to be limited, as at the moment only two out of its ten "megaprojects" pertain to the past (other than strictly to the sphere of cultural heritage). The first one deals with the "golden age" of the First Republic of Poland (sixteenth century and first decades of the seventeenth century) while the second relates to regaining independence in 1918 and 1989 (with the role of Solidarity).[31]

In 2016, the Minister of Culture and National Heritage established the Witold Pilecki Center for Totalitarian Studies. One of the basic tasks of the Center was to digitize and publish online the evidence for crimes committed during the Second World War, taken from archives of IPN. In 2017, a bill was introduced on the creation of an Institute of Solidarity and Courage, which would deal with commemorating and honoring (with state decoration) people who had helped the citizens of Poland (victims of communist, Nazi and other crimes) in 1917–1990. Due to the problems with launching the operation of this institution (called the Polish Yad Vashem), it was soon joined with the Center for Totalitarian Studies and named the Witold Pilecki Institute of Solidarity and Courage. In practice, the name Pilecki Institute is used, and the previous forms of activity still prevail. Among them are exhibitions, the project "Called by name," detailing the stories of Poles murdered for helping Jews during the Second World War, "educational walks," and film showings. The PI also uses social media to popularize history. In 2019, a branch in Berlin was created, with the primary goal of familiarizing the German public with Polish history.[32]

Next to various public institutions, there are multiple NGOs dealing with popularizing history. Their number has increased significantly in recent years.[33] They engage in a huge variety of actions – from creating exhibitions (traditional and online), organizing history fairs and scavenger hunts, through collecting witnesses' testimonies and digitizing private archives, to creating museums and erecting monuments. Recently, street and field races have become an increasingly prevalent form of popularizing history, mainly organized by NGOs (to a lesser degree by local governments and state institutions). There are races dedicated to virtually all major events from the twentieth-century Polish past, although many fewer runs are dedicated to events from more distant times. Independence Runs have the longest tradition (sometimes dating back to the 1990s). They are organized in hundreds of places on November 11, the anniversary of regaining Poland's independence in 1918. Another example is the Wolf's Track run, organized on March 1, the National Day of the Memory of the Cursed Soldiers.[34] In 2020, it was organized in over 300 locations with 75,000 participants.[35] Sometimes the organizers limit themselves to historical references and memorabilia (e.g. t-shirts, hats, pins), but often the historical part is much broader, with exhibitions and historical publications made available.

Another recent phenomenon are historical reenactment groups who take part in many events related to the popularization of history (see the chapter by Filip Wolański in this volume). In 2016, there were at least 458 active and 129 inactive (in the perspective of the year preceding the study) historical reenactment groups with about 10,000 people engaged. The number of performed historical reenactments has risen by roughly 2.5 times in comparison to 2011. The majority (79.2%) of interviewed spectators of selected reenactments have stated that they are primarily educational.[36]

The rising involvement of NGOs in the popularization of history is possible thanks to the increase in available resources. The most important fund providers are the state and state-controlled companies. The first larger program sponsored by the Ministry of Culture and National Heritage was called "The Patriotism of Tomorrow." It was launched in 2006 and was operated by the National Centre of Culture until 2009 when the Polish History Museum was put in charge. About 1,100 projects were subsidized with a total sum of 24 million PLN (ca. 5.5 million EUR) by 2020.[37] Even larger sums have been allocated for the multiyear program "The Independent," related to the centennial of regaining independence in 1918. Over 240 million PLN was used to finance projects of various entities (public and NGOs).[38] Competitions for history-related projects are organized by the NCK, Ministry of Foreign Affairs, Office for War Veterans and Victims of Oppression, and some local governments. Many state-owned and state-controlled companies have established their own foundations to support NGOs, and since 2016 the popularization of history has been one of the main supported areas. Spreading knowledge about history is also one of the basic tasks of the Polish National Foundation, which was established near the end of 2016 and has an enormous budget for grants.[39] On a lesser scale, Polish NGOs have benefitted from the *Europe for citizens* program (financing stream "Remembrance"), placed for 2014–2021 in the European Union's budget.

The historical boom is also visible in the press market. While in the 1990s only two journals popularizing history were functioning (the monthly *Mówią Wieki* (Centuries Speak) established in 1958, and *Karta* established in 1991), in the next decade the situation changed radically. First, the *IPN Bulletin* was created (2001), and in 2012–2016 the magazine *Pamięć.pl* (Memory.pl) was published. Soon afterwards, historical sections were created in nearly all weekly journals, and since 2005 new titles started appearing – both tied to existing magazines and brand new. At the moment, at least 20 nationwide titles are published,[40] including *Ale Historia* (What a History) weekly supplement of *Gazeta Wyborcza*, one of the fiercest critics of the concept of politics of history.

The dispute about politics of history as a concept is slowly dying out. At the same time, a heated conflict about the form of politics of history pursued since 2015 by the new government is rising. The divisions, along with the activities of new institutions (especially IPN and museums) and rising conflicts of memory with other nations have caused a true explosion of public interest in history in Poland. It has resulted in a significant development of public history, not only quantitative, but also qualitative. In some areas (e.g. exhibitions and museums), the Polish model has become an inspiration to others.

Notes

1 Tadeusz Rutkowski, *Nauki historyczne w Polsce 1944–1970. Zagadnienia polityczne i organizacyjne*, (Warszawa: Wydawnictwo UW, 2007); Joanna Wojdon, *Textbooks as Propaganda. Poland under Communist Rule, 1944–1989*

(New York: Routledge, 2018), 108–120; Marcin Zaremba, *Komunizm, legity-mizacja, nacjonalizm. Nacjonalistyczna legitymizacja władzy komunistycznej w Polsce* (Warszawa: Trio, 2005).

2 Peter Hallama and Stephan Stach, eds, *Gegengeschichte Zweiter Weltkrieg und Holocaust im ostmitteleuropäischen Dissens* (Leipzig: Leipziger Universitätsver-lag, 2015).

3 Magdalena Mikołajczyk, *Jak się pisało o historii... Problemy polityczne powo-jennej Polski w publikacjach drugiego obiegu lat siedemdziesiątych i osiemdziesią-tych* (Kraków: Księgarnia Akademicka, 1998); Zbigniew Osiński, *Nauczanie historii w szkołach podstawowych w Polsce w latach 1944–1989. Uwarunkowania organizacyjne oraz ideologiczno-polityczne* (Lublin: UMCS, 2010), 210–214; Rafał Stobiecki, *Historiografia PRL. Zamiast podręcznika* (Łódź: Wydawnictwo Uni-wersytetu Łódzkiego, 2020), 166–168, 189–199.

4 Zbigniew Gluza, *Odkrycie Karty. Niezależna strategia pamięci* (Warszawa: Ośrodek KARTA, 2012), 97–110; Patryk Pleskot, *Góry i teczki. Opowieść człow-ieka umiarkowanego. Biografia mówiona Andrzeja Paczkowskiego* (Warszawa: IPN, 2019), 202–217.

5 Next to making churches and other locations available for independent lectures, a significant role was played by the possibility of putting memorial plaques in churches, to remind about people, organizations and events omitted from the official narrative. This phenomenon is still undescribed. An exceptionally large initiative was the sanctuary devoted to "Fallen in the East," created in 1984 in the St. Charles Borromeo church in Warsaw. Small plaques, placed on the outside wall of the church around a cross, commemorated about a thousand people – murdered in Katyń and other places, deported, etc. The initiator of this project, Father Stefan Niedzielak, was murdered in January 1989 by "unknown perpetrators," most likely functionaries of the communist Security Service.

6 Antoni Dudek, *Historia polityczna Polski 1989–2005* (Kraków: Znak, 2007), 75; Andrzej Grajewski, "Balast po komunizmie. Instytucjonalne rozliczenie ko-munizmu w krajach Europy Środkowej – opis struktur oraz okoliczności ich powstania," *Pamięć i Sprawiedliwość* 22, no. 2 (2013): 174–175; Rafał Habielski, "Przeszłość w sferze publicznej i życiu kulturalnym 1989–2005 (obszary zaint-eresowań, interpretacje, nośniki)," in *Historycy i politycy: polityka pamięci w III RP* ed. Paweł Skibiński, Tomasz Wiścicki and Michał Wysocki (Warszawa: DiG, 2011), 84.

7 "Peerel" is a neologism coming from the PRL acronym meaning Polska Rzecz-pospolita Ludowa (Polish People's Republic).

8 Gluza, *Odkrycie Karty,* 133–22; "Sprawozdanie za rok 2004," 2–3, accessed March 20, 2021, https://karta.org.pl/sites/default/files/uploads/sprawozdanie_merytoryczne_za_2004.pdf. Cf. the chapter by Marta Kurkowska-Budzan in this volume for more details on the role of KARTA.

9 "Wystawa pokazująca sędziów i prokuratorów stalinowskich narusza ochronę danych osobowych," *Gazeta Wyborcza*, October 28, 1998.

10 The process has not been finished, it encompassed about two-third of the cases. In 2015, over a thousand Polish streets still had communism-related names, there were also a few hundred monuments and plaques (mainly devoted to the Red Army). In April 2016, a bill was passed to resolve this matter, but in some cases discussions are still ongoing (sometimes in court). See Joanna Kałużna, "Dekomunizacja przestrzeni publicznej w Polsce – zarys problematyki," *Środ-kowoeuropejskie Studia Polityczne*, no. 2 (2018): 157–158, 162–164.

11 Jolanta Adamska, "Charków 1940–2000," accessed March 15, 2021, https://katyn.miejscapamieci.gov.pl/page/strona-glowna/artykuly/charkow.php; Adamska, "Katyń Miednoje 1940–2000," accessed March 15, 2021, https://katyn.miejscapamieci.gov.pl/page/strona-glowna/artykuly/katyn-miednoje.php.

12 See e.g.: *Dekomunizacja i rzeczywistość* (Warszawa: Amarant, 1993); Bronisław Wildstein, *Dekomunizacja, której nie było* (Kraków: Księgarnia Akademicka, 2000).

13 Dudek, *Historia polityczna*, 371–372; Gluza, *Odkrycie Karty*, 226–227; http://fcs.org.pl/o-fundacji/, accessed March 15, 2021.

14 As a result of the amendment in 2016, the beginning of the period has been moved to 1917. At the same time, the number of divisions increased from four (in 2007 the Lustration Office was created) to seven. The Office of Public Education divided into the Historical Research Office and the National Education Office, the Office of Search and Identification and the Office for Commemorating the Struggle and Martyrdom were created, the latter replacing the separate Council for the Protection of Struggle and Martyrdom Sites, which has existed since the decline of communism.

15 Łukasz Kamiński, "Instytut Pamięci Narodowej," in *Historia w przestrzeni publicznej*, ed. Joanna Wojdon (Warszawa: PWN, 2018), 92–95.

16 Dariusz Libionka, "Debata wokół Jedwabnego," in *Następstwa zagłady Żydów. Polska 1944–2010*, ed. Feliks Tych and Monika Adamczyk-Garbowska (Lublin: UMCS, 2011), 742, 751, 765–767.

17 The discussion was not only about the crime in Jedwabne, the role played by Poles, matters of guilt, etc., but was also transformed into a fundamental argument about the vision of history which the state should promote (in school education, museums, IPN's activity, etc.). The title of Andrzej Nowak's article "Westerplatte or Jedwabne" became a symbol of the division between the proponents of "heroic-martyrological" (as Paweł Machcewicz has called it) narration and advocates for a critical outlook on the past. See the chapter by Rafał Stobiecki in this volume for details and developments of this debate.

18 Antoni Dudek, "Historia i polityka w Polsce po 1989 roku," in Skibiński, Wiścicki and Wysocki, *Historycy i politycy*, 35. See also: Paweł Machcewicz, *Spory o historię 2000–2011* (Kraków: Znak, 2012), 9–21.

19 All statistical data presented in this part are taken from the summary statement published by IPN in 2015 (https://ipn.gov.pl/pl/dla-mediow/komunikaty/12091,15-lat-Instytutu-Pamieci-Narodowej-w-liczbach.html, accessed March 16, 2021).

20 IPN, *Informacja o działalności Instytutu Pamięci Narodowej Komisji Ścigania Zbrodni przeciwko Narodowi Polskiemu w okresie 1 stycznia 2015 r. – 31 grudnia 2015 r.* (Warszawa: IPN, 2016), 98–100, accessed March 19, 2021, https://ipn.gov.pl/pl/o-ipn/informacje-o-dzialalnos/24307,w-okresie-1-stycznia-2015-r-31-grudnia-2015-r.html.

21 https://ipn.gov.pl/pl/publikacje/komiksy, accessed March 20, 2021.

22 https://ipn.gov.pl/pl/publikacje/periodyki-ipn/dodatki-historyczne-do, accessed March 20, 2021.

23 https://www.youtube.com/watch?v=QvqLy88OPJ4, accessed March 20, 2021.

24 Since 1992, the Genocide and Resistance Research Centre of Lithuania (*Lietuvos gyventojų genocido ir rezistencijos tyrimo centras*) has operated in Lithuania, and since 1997, the Historical Archives of the Hungarian State Security (*Állambiztonsági Szolgálatok Történeti Levéltára*, originally with a different name) has operated in Hungary. Since 2000, the National Council for the Study of the Securitate Archives (*Consiliul Național pentru Studierea Arhivelor Securității*) has operated in Romania. The latter two institutions are mainly archival and their educational and research activities are limited.

25 https://www.memoryandconscience.eu/, accessed March 20, 2021. All above mentioned documents are available on this website, too; Laure Neumauer, *The Criminalisation of Communism in the European Political Space after the Cold War* (London – New York: Routledge, 2019), 199–204.

26 Rafał Leśkiewicz and Pavel Žaček, eds. *Handbook of the European Network of Official Authorities Dealing with Secret Police Files* (Prague: Institute for the Study of Totalitarian Regimes, 2013).
27 https://enrs.eu/, accessed March 21, 2021; Rafał Rogulski, "Europejska Sieć Pamięć i Solidarność – sposób na realizowanie międzynarodowej polityki pamięci," in Wojdon, *Historia w przestrzeni*, 105–109.
28 Of course, the list could be extended with the network of Polish Institutes subject to the Ministry of Foreign Affairs, Office for War Veterans and Victims of Oppression, National Institute of Heritage, Book Institute, Centre for Polish-Russian Dialogue and Understanding, and National Archives. See: Marek Mutor, "Praktyka polityki historycznej a instytucje," in Wojdon, *Historia w przestrzeni*, 86–87, 89.
29 www.nck.pl, accessed March 20, 2021.
30 https://bip.mkidn.gov.pl/media/download_gallery/index75fd.pdf, accessed March 20, 2021.
31 https://iam.pl/pl, accessed March 20, 2021.
32 https://instytutpileckiego.pl/en/?setlang=true, accessed March 20, 2021.
33 Available data does not allow us to determine precisely how many of the 100,000 active foundations and associations deal with history. However, taking into consideration that about 13% of them deal with education and 14% with culture and art, we can assume that a few thousands of them deal with various aspects of the past. Data from ngo.pl, accessed March 20, 2021.
34 The term refers to soldiers of the post-war anti-communist underground (1944–1956). This phenomenon was brought out of oblivion largely by the IPN. Using this part of history by state authorities since 2015 is another part of the debate around Polish politics of history. See the chapter by Rafał Stobiecki in this volume.
35 https://tropemwilczym.org, accessed March 20, 2021.
36 *Grupy rekonstrukcji historycznych – działania oddolne na rzecz krzewienia kultury narodowej. Raport z badań* (Warszawa: NCK, 2016), 3, 25, accessed March 20, 2021, https://www.nck.pl/upload/attachments/318583/Grupy-rekonstrukcji-historycznych-raport-z-badan.pdf.
37 https://muzhp.pl/pl/c/1532/patriotyzm-jutra, accessed March 20, 2021; *Patriotyzm jutra. Program operacyjny Ministra Kultury i Dziedzictwa Narodowego* (Warszawa: MKiDN, 2006).
38 *Program wieloletni Niepodległa na lata 2017–2022* (Warszawa, 2018), 106, accessed March 20, 2021, https://niepodlegla.gov.pl/wp-content/uploads/2020/06/PW-Niepodleg%C5%82a-sierpie%C5%84-2018-3.pdf.
39 https://www.pfn.org.pl/, accessed March 20, 2021.
40 Author's calculations.

Bibliography

Adamska, Jolanta. "Charków 1940–2000." Accessed March 15, 2021. https://katyn.miejscapamieci.gov.pl/page/strona-glowna/artykuly/charkow.php.
Adamska, Jolanta. "Katyń Miednoje 1940–2000." Accessed March 15, 2021. https://katyn.miejscapamieci.gov.pl/page/strona-glowna/artykuly/katyn-miednoje.php.
Dekomunizacja i rzeczywistość. Warszawa: Amarant, 1993.
Dudek, Antoni. "Historia i polityka w Polsce po 1989 roku." In *Historycy i politycy: polityka pamięci w III RP*, edited by Paweł Skibiński, Tomasz Wiścicki and Michał Wysocki, 33–57. Warszawa: DiG, 2011.
Dudek, Antoni. *Historia polityczna Polski 1989–2005*. Kraków: Znak, 2007.

Gluza, Zbigniew. *Odkrycie Karty. Niezależna strategia pamięci*. Warszawa: Ośrodek KARTA, 2012.

Grajewski, Andrzej. "Balast po komunizmie. Instytucjonalne rozliczenie komunizmu w krajach Europy Środkowej – opis struktur oraz okoliczności ich powstania." *Pamięć i Sprawiedliwość* 22, no. 2 (2013): 153–182.

Grupy rekonstrukcji historycznych – działania oddolne na rzecz krzewienia kultury narodowej. Raport z badań. Warszawa: NCK, 2016.

Habielski, Rafał. "Przeszłość w sferze publicznej i życiu kulturalnym 1989–2005 (obszary zainteresowań, interpretacje, nośniki)." In *Historycy i politycy: polityka pamięci w III RP*, edited by Paweł Skibiński, Tomasz Wiścicki and Michał Wysocki, 83–107. Warszawa: DiG, 2011.

Hallama, Peter, and Stephan Stach, eds. *Gegengeschichte Zweiter Weltkrieg und Holocaust im ostmitteleuropäischen Dissens*. Leipzig: Leipziger Universitätsverlag, 2015.

IPN. *Informacja o działalności Instytutu Pamięci Narodowej Komisji Ścigania Zbrodni przeciwko Narodowi Polskiemu w okresie 1 stycznia 2015 r. – 31 grudnia 2015 r.* Warszawa: IPN, 2016.

Kałużna, Joanna. "Dekomunizacja przestrzeni publicznej w Polsce – zarys problematyki." *Środkowoeuropejskie Studia Polityczne*, no. 2 (2018): 157–171.

Kamiński, Łukasz. "Instytut Pamięci Narodowej." In *Historia w przestrzeni publicznej*, edited by Joanna Wojdon, 92–96. Warszawa: PWN, 2018.

Leśkiewicz, Rafał and Pavel Žaček, eds. *Handbook of the European Network of Official Authorities Dealing with Secret Police Files*. Prague: Institute for the Study of Totalitarian Regimes, 2013.

Libionka, Dariusz. "Debata wokół Jedwabnego." In *Następstwa zagłady Żydów. Polska 1944–2010*, edited by Feliks Tych and Monika Adamczyk-Garbowska, 733–774. Lublin: UMCS, 2011.

Machcewicz, Paweł. *Spory o historię 2000–2011*. Kraków: Znak, 2012.

Marek Mutor, "Praktyka polityki historycznej a instytucje." *Historia w przestrzeni publicznej*, edited by Joanna Wojdon, 83–91. Warszawa: PWN, 2018.

Mikołajczyk, Magdalena. *Jak się pisało o historii … Problemy polityczne powojennej Polski w publikacjach drugiego obiegu lat siedemdziesiątych i osiemdziesiątych*. Kraków: Księgarnia Akademicka, 1998.

Neumauer, Laure. *The Criminalisation of Communism in the European Political Space after the Cold War*. London – New York: Routledge, 2019.

Osiński, Zbigniew. *Nauczanie historii w szkołach podstawowych w Polsce w latach 1944–1989. Uwarunkowania organizacyjne oraz ideologiczno-polityczne*. Lublin: UMCS, 2010.

Patriotyzm jutra. Program operacyjny Ministra Kultury i Dziedzictwa Narodowego. Warszawa: MKiDN, 2006.

Pleskot, Patryk. *Góry i teczki. Opowieść człowieka umiarkowanego. Biografia mówiona Andrzeja Paczkowskiego*. Warszawa: IPN, 2019.

Program wieloletni Niepodległa na lata 2017–2022. Warszawa, 2018.

Rogulski, Rafał. "Europejska Sieć Pamięć i Solidarność – sposób na realizowanie międzynarodowej polityki pamięci." In *Historia w przestrzeni publicznej*, edited by Joanna Wojdon, 105–109. Warszawa: PWN, 2018.

Rutkowski, Tadeusz. *Nauki historyczne w Polsce 1944–1970. Zagadnienia polityczne i organizacyjne*. Warszawa: Wydawnictwo UW, 2007.

"Sprawozdanie za rok 2004." Accessed March 20, 2021. https://karta.org.pl/sites/default/files/uploads/sprawozdanie_merytoryczne_za_2004.pdf.

Stobiecki, Rafał. *Historiografia PRL. Zamiast podręcznika.* Łódź: Wydawnictwo Uniwersytetu Łódzkiego, 2020.

Wildstein, Bronisław. *Dekomunizacja, której nie było.* Kraków: Księgarnia Akademicka, 2000.

Wojdon, Joanna. *Textbooks as Propaganda. Poland under Communist Rule, 1944– 1989.* New York: Routledge, 2018.

Wojdon, Joanna, ed. *Historia w przestrzeni publicznej.* Warszawa: PWN, 2018.

"Wystawa pokazująca sędziów i prokuratorów stalinowskich narusza ochronę danych osobowych." *Gazeta Wyborcza.* October 28, 1998.

Zaremba, Marcin. *Komunizm, legitymizacja, nacjonalizm. Nacjonalistyczna legitymizacja władzy komunistycznej w Polsce.* Warszawa: Trio, 2005.

Websites

http://fcs.org.pl/o-fundacji/. Accessed March 15, 2021.

https://bip.mkidn.gov.pl/media/download_gallery/index75fd.pdf. Accessed March 20, 2021.

https://enrs.eu/. Accessed March 21, 2021.

https://iam.pl/pl. Accessed March 20, 2021.

https://instytutpileckiego.pl/en/?setlang=true. Accessed March 20, 2021.

https://ipn.gov.pl/pl/publikacje/komiksy. Accessed March 20, 2021.

https://ipn.gov.pl/pl/publikacje/periodyki-ipn/dodatki-historyczne-do. Accessed March 20, 2021.

https://muzhp.pl/pl/c/1532/patriotyzm-jutra. Accessed March 20, 2021.

https://ngo.pl. Accessed March 20, 2021.

https://niepodlegla.gov.pl/wp-content/uploads/2020/06/PW-Niepodleg%C5%82a-sierpie%C5%84-2018-3.pdf. Accessed March 20, 2021.

https://tropemwilczym.org. Accessed March 20, 2021.

https://www.memoryandconscience.eu/. Accessed March 20, 2021.

https://www.nck.pl. Accessed March 20, 2021.

https://www.pfn.org.pl/. Accessed March 20, 2021.

https://www.youtube.com/watch?v=QvqLy88OPJ4. Accessed March 20, 2021.

2 Towards the Ideal Vision of the Twentieth-Century Polish History

On the Post-2015 Polish Politics of History

Rafał Stobiecki

I. Introduction

Politics of history can be analyzed and commented on from various perspectives:[1] focusing on its institutional dimension or its current political role as a soft power, on building social capital with the use of historical arguments, or on mutual relations between the politics of memory and historiography. The approach proposed in this chapter corresponds with the concept of public history, or as it is often referred to in the Polish language: "history in the public sphere." As Joanna Wojdon has noted, "history" in the term of "history in the public sphere" refers to "both narratives about the past and the traces of the past and its material and non-material symbols."[2] The major change of the place of history in culture or in the intellectual toolbox of a modern human is happening now. Having been part of a culture based on words for centuries, today, more and more frequently, it is based on images. Having been dominated by the principles of rational exploration of the world, it now tends to refer to emotions. These same phenomena also determine how history is present in the public sphere. I will focus on the contents of the politics of history inaugurated in Poland in 2015 by the double victory of the right-wing political parties in the parliamentary and presidential elections, and will also discuss the activities of the institutions of the Polish state.

This chapter is based predominantly on textual sources, with some references to audiovisual materials.[3] The leading questions to be addressed are: what image of the history of Poland emerges from the enunciations of the proponents of the new politics of history? What sources does it refer to? What are its main components? And last but not least, to what extent does it change or challenge earlier visions of the national past?

II. "Patriotism of Tomorrow"

Law and Justice's coming to power in 2015 did influence the politics of history in its broad sense. It was created by the politicians, journalists and historians whose ambition was to reconstruct fundamentally the narrative

DOI: 10.4324/9781003165767-4

of the history of Poland in the twentieth century. The symbolical beginning took place on December 17, 2015 in Juliusz Słowacki Theater in Kraków where Andrzej Nowak, professor of history at Jagiellonian University, in his keynote speech called for breaking with the "pedagogy of shame" and instead, for appreciating the historical achievements of Poland and the Polish people. The very notion of a "pedagogy of shame" was not new, as it had already appeared in the right-wing discourse earlier. Its authorship has been attributed to the journalist Bronisław Wildstein. Another journalist, Michał Karnowski, argued that "pedagogy of shame" was

> an attempt to diminish drastically the self-esteem of the Poles by depriving us of pride of the past, particularly the one that related to the struggle and martyrdom of the Second World War. The period, when our fathers and forefathers said NO to two godless, pagan totalitarianisms: the German and the Soviet one, the period of heroism and sacrifice.[4]

Nowak himself explained that "it is not about compiling the bill of wrongs but about starting an honest discussion on our common past." In another speech, this time in the palace of Belweder in Warsaw, by invitation of President Andrzej Duda, Nowak proposed four specific areas of Polish achievements to be promoted: (1) histories of Polish war heroes (but also the sufferings of the Polish victims); (2) achievements of Polish culture and science; (3) achievements of Polish Christianity; and (4) republicanism whose symbol was (is?) the love for freedom.[5]

The post-2015 changes have been rooted, however, in the earlier debates. Already at the beginning of the millennium in the conservative and right-wing circles, critical voices were addressed towards the liberal part of the political scene which tried to observe the principle that "the democratic authorities cannot rule what is the valid truth about the past."[6]

The sources of those controversies are best illustrated by two issues. Chronologically, the debate on the book *Neighbors* by Jan Tomasz Gross came first.[7] The second, less known, is the "belated" polemics of conservative authors, Dariusz Gawin and Dariusz Karłowicz, with the famous essay published in 1981 by Jan Józef Lipski, one of the leaders of democratic opposition, *Dwie ojczyzny dwa patriotyzmy (Uwagi o megalomania narodowej i ksenofobii Polaków)* [Two fatherlands, two patriotisms (Remarks on national megalomania and xenophobia of the Poles)].

The challenges of the Polish state at the beginning of the twenty-first century caused the Polish conservative circles to reflect on the new model of Polish patriotism which was subsequently named "the Patriotism of Tomorrow."[8] Its main principles were rooted in denying the model of "critical patriotism" proposed by Lipski that combined the distrust towards any form of megalomania and xenophobia with the Evangelical rule of love and forgiveness, thus eliminating any possibility of entangling the categories of collective interest in egoism. According to Gawin:

The politics of history in this perspective comes under total supremacy of ethics and becomes an area not of construction of collective identity, but of rejecting in a process of painful autopsychomachia any potential of sin, immanently ascribed to community and to political sphere.[9]

The arguments of Karłowicz went in a different direction. He claimed that Lipski and his followers in their thinking of Polish patriotism hit what the author called "the axiological memory," understood as "the canon of values inscribed in collective imagination which is a kind of community's spiritual constitution."[10] From this point of view, excessive criticism of the national past discredits this axiological sphere and, therefore, attacks the community's foundations and leads to tribalism of collective memory.

The new formula of reading the category of patriotism, mentioned above, has become a useful argument for those who rejected any version of national past based on criticism, either on axiological or ideological grounds.[11] It paved the way to reopening the nineteenth-century patterns of attitudes and choices, and to the return of ideas that accentuated the uniqueness of the Polish experience in Europe. It was no coincidence that the brochure promoting the idea of creating the Polish History Museum (the second most prominent endeavor of the politics of history, after the Warsaw Rising Museum) stated that:

> The activities of the Museum should emphasize what was exceptional, special, fascinating in the history of Poland. For Poland is the country of one of the longest lasting republican and parliamentary traditions in Europe, the country where civic freedoms were developed, where religious tolerance reached an exceptional level in the early modern period, the country of the original culture and customs.[12]

The thesis of the strong connections between the contemporary patriotism, Christianity and the Catholic church also referred to the patterns of the nineteenth century. To cite a researcher connected with the Kraków-based conservatively inclined journal *Arcana*:

> It is high time to realize what point we are in. It is time to make a thorough balance sheet of the past. This necessity is a duty of the day. In no way can we rely on the assistance of the West in this regard. There, they know even less about the present-day condition than we do, and they lag behind us significantly in returning to normalcy and to principles. We have to reject and radically negate all the left-wing tradition, starting from Jacobinism. For this tradition and this mentality contradicts our identity – Catholic, Christian, Polish, national, but also Latin, Western. It is the urgent and unconditional imperative [...] We will not be liberated intellectually, morally nor, therefore, politically, as long as we fail to fully realize what enslaves us. We will not find the road to the future unless we thoroughly discern the ideological debris of the present day.[13]

The concept of patriotism proposed by the supporters of the right-hand side of the political scene in most cases referred to the narrowly understood nationalism, based either on a simple dichotomy: "us" vs "them" at its extreme, or on specific paternalism towards "the alien" in its milder version.

In general, the goal of the supporters of the new politics of memory of the early twenty-first century was to bring back the pride in the national past and, no less importantly, to reinterpret select threads of Polish history. Those notions were applied to both the distant past and contemporary history. The proponents of changes declared that the negative stereotype of the first Polish Republic should be discontinued, while "true heroes who have been placed in the garbage heap of history for seventy years and where they were still kept in the last fifteen years" should be brought to the fore.[14]

Liberal circles criticized both the vision of the "Patriotism of Tomorrow" presented above and the strongly acclaimed necessity to revise the image of the national past. They pointed to numerous weaknesses and limitations of both. Some historians tried to oppose the affirmative vision of the national past with critical patriotism, non-antagonism and respecting the subjectivity of others. The critics objected to attempts to unify the worldview and to introduce some "catechismal kind of memory, common for everyone."[15] They preferred the patriotism referring to the nation as a category of political or civic, but not ethnic community. Their activities proved to be ineffective, however.

From today's perspective, one can risk the conclusion that Robert Traba was correct in noting that the success of the "new politics of history"

> uncovered the illusion that the Poles had left the national-romantic circle, the heroic myth of their own history. The resistance of critical formation of politicians and politically engaged professional historians did not generate an alternative historical narrative communicative enough to reach wider circles of the society.[16]

In this way, a void emerged which allowed the activities initiated at the beginning of the twenty-first century be continued.

III. *The Unconquered*

By 2015, the "conservative" or "right-wing" model of the politics of history with accompanying historical narratives had not reached the mainstream public debate, with the exception of a short period of the Law and Justice government of 2005–2007. In 2021, the situation is entirely different. The views characterized above turned out to be just a prologue of the fundamental changes. Before our eyes, a new image of the history of Poland in the twentieth century has been created, which fulfills the needs of the authorities in a model way. One can have an impression that the vision of the history "dreamt by the generations of Poles" has come true under the rule of the United Right (i.e., the coalition of the Law and Justice party and its political allies). This is a story with a clear moral overtone, and with the ambitions of agency in order to change the social reality. I understand the ideal vision of the history of Poland as the image of the national past that (1) makes the Poles feel proud; (2) cures them of various inferiority complexes rooted in history; and (3) re-roots the history of Poland in the history of Europe, with Poland presented not as a peripheral/backward nation/state, but as an indispensable part of the Western civilization for centuries.

One spectacular exemplification of this concept is *The Unconquered*, a four-minute animated film of 2017, depicting the history of Poland from the outbreak of the Second World War up to the regaining of sovereignty. Thanks to the support of the Institute of National Remembrance (or IPN) and due to the fact that it was broadcast on public television more than once, its audience must have reached millions. One of the goals of this project was to promote Polish history abroad. Its message corresponds with the romantic culture code of Poland as the Christ of Nations, defender of freedom and Christianity. The story, the ethnocentric character of which is emphasized by the excessive use of "we," appreciates the military struggles in which the Poles are

> always an innocent victim. Lonely, abandoned, in spite of any adversities heroically defending the highest values. There are always some 'others' to blame for their sufferings and failures (Russians, German, treacherous West). The steadfast struggle has been eventually rewarded, and after a fifty-year war Poland is resurrected.[17]

IV. The Ideal Past and Its Myths

Let us look more closely at this ideal vision of the national past, and identify its distinctive features and the convictions on which it is based. The authorities use it not only to make the Polish people proud of their history again, but sometimes also to set peculiar rules of history specific only to the Poles and secure them an appropriate place in world history.

First, the vision is very axiologically loaded and purposefully refers not so much to common sense as to emotions. The history of Poland becomes a kind of collective "morality play" where the Poles choose between good and evil, between condemnation and salvation. It is a story where language both constitutes the cognition and imposes meanings, interpretations and images of the past, promotes values and lays out attitudes.[18] Its offensive, activist message can be found in many statements. In this way, an "innocent" and "neutral" "patriotism of tomorrow" imperceptibly becomes the "patriotism of struggle" where not only popularization of history but also the control over people's historical knowledge is at stake. Jan Żaryn, one of the key promoters of the "new politics of history," in an interview by no coincidence entitled "To stop a lie," when asked "What is the most urgent task in the program of renovating the country?" replied:

Without any doubt we have a problem with the opinion-forming elite. It should transmit the Polish cultural code to young generations. Unfortunately, the People's Republic of Poland created its own counter-code, with rejection, contempt, lies and Bolshevik-like boorish behavior. This anti-code is, unfortunately, still present in Poland today. This is a pain.

Similar emphases appeared in the statement by Filip Musiał who claimed that the Polish mentality is still "contaminated" by "the Soviet imperial narrative" and "the first cause of the historical schizophrenia is the lack of clear definition [...] of what the 'People's' Poland was and how we treat it, whom the Polish elites served and how we judge their service today."[19]

The "patriotism of struggle" is accompanied by one more specific version of patriotism, "the patriotism of national catastrophes" – associated with national uprisings (the Warsaw Uprising), wars (the Yalta agreement), battles (the Polish campaign of September 1939), etc. – forged with the blessing of the Polish church into prospective victory (*gloria victis*). The air crash (or assassination, for some) in Smolensk in 2010 is also placed into this sequence of events.

The analyzed discourse, paradoxically, at times resembles communist "newspeak"[20] and, applying the findings of Marek Woźniak, two types of words can be identified therein: "canonic" or "key" words and "operational" words.[21] The latter "fulfill the meanings/intentions" of the former and make the ideas of the key words concrete. The key words are "freedom," "pride," "dignity," "heritage" and "memory" (the latter four with an indispensable adjective "national"). They belong to the realm of sacred words which cannot be confronted with the reality. The "operational" words include, e.g., "Cursed Soldiers," "Poles – The Righteous among Nations," "the victims of the Communist security apparatus" and "anti-communist opposition leaders in the era of communist rule."

Negative aspects of the dichotomous vision of the world, which is clearly present in the ideal story of the Polish past, are expressed by such key words as "betrayal," "eternal enemy" and "communist evil," and operational words such as "red elites," "(post)Communists" and "collaborators."

For the sake of brevity, only two examples will be briefly analyzed here. The proponents of "the new politics of history" are particularly keen on the notion of "liberty." Janusz Kurtyka (president of the IPN in 2005–2010) emphasized its role as allegedly belonging inherently to Polish history:

> our Polish cultural circle, with its original input into civilization, can be symbolized by the word 'liberty'. The word and its content have been equally important for the noble nation of the first Polish republic, for the contemporary Polish nation consolidated in the captivity of the nineteenth century, and for the Polish people throughout the twentieth century – from the struggle for regaining Poland's independence (1914–1921) up until the revolution of Solidarity and its 'long march' (1980–1989).[22]

In this sense, to use the words of Michał Łuczewski, the ideal vision of the Polish past is constructed by the "narrative of ethos" where, at particular times, freedom turns out to be a feature that defines the history of Poland from the earliest until the most recent times and "the struggle for it, all discontinuities and discrepancies of the Polish past notwithstanding, eventually brings back to them the continuity and compatibility."[23]

United Right's coming to power is often presented as a toilsome process of regaining "real" freedom, lost after 1945 but also "appropriated" by the "post-communist elites" after 1989. According to this concept, the postwar history of Poland can be divided into three periods: (1) 1945–1989 – the communist rule, or de facto the Soviet occupation; (2) 1989–2015 – the post-totalitarian or post-communist rule, based on the distorted historical consciousness; (3) from 2015, the victory of the pro-independent movement which aims at "rejecting the heritage of the communist state."[24] This is not only a new periodization but also a profound reinterpretation of the contemporary history of Poland. The Round Table talks of 1989 (i.e., negotiations between the Communist party and representatives of the democratic opposition) are marginalized and presented as "an agreement between a part of the opposition with the communist forces." The axis of this type of thinking is formed by a specific tension "between freedom and captivity."

Another key word in the ideal vision is "betrayal." Andrzej Nowak has emphasized, for example, that

> The West has betrayed the Poles numerous times, Napoleon not only failed to reconstruct Poland after partitions but he sent the Polish soldiers to kill the African slaves fighting for freedom on Haiti. During the November and January uprisings we counted on [Western] help but we received mostly warm words. The fundamental betrayal of the West, however, was Yalta: the pact between the Western allies and Stalin, where they gave him the rule over the whole of Eastern and Central Europe, Poland included.[25]

Similarly to the discussion on liberty, the argument about "the evil West, constantly betraying Poland" has a two-fold dimension.[26] It refers to the past, again making Poland "an innocent victim" of the conspiracy of the mighty of this world. It roots the thinking of the Poles back in the clichés of the so-called Second Great Emigration of the post-WWII period where the Yalta conference was referred to as "one of the most shameful international gatherings," the symbol of "raising the cynicism and depravation to the rank of the laws regulating international relations."[27] At the same time, commentators of Nowak's book have commented on its present-day message as a warning against closer ties with the West, in particular, with the European Union. Thus, the syndrome of "betrayal" has been reincorporated into the inventory of Polish fears and complexes and has reinforced the aversion to ideas "alien" to the Polish identity.

Second, strongly articulated polonocentrism is another fundamental feature of the "new politics of history."[28] The massive attack on the creators of the Museum of the Second World War can serve as a proof of this argument. The very idea of the museum and its core exhibition was first criticized by Jarosław Kaczyński himself, leader of the Law and Justice party. Kaczyński called the museum "a peculiar gift from [then prime minister of Poland] Donald Tusk to Angela Merkel" and added that it corresponds with the German politics of history.[29] The Ministry of Culture and National heritage commissioned a review of the core exhibition. The authors of the review accused Paweł Machcewicz and his team of creating a museum that was not Polish but "European" or "cosmopolitan."[30] Żaryn wrote:

> The authors, in my opinion, made a strategic choice in which the Polish point of view on the history of the Second World War was overwhelmed by some pseudo-universal version of the world history. The war and its results have become a collective protagonist. [...] It seems that the Museum of the Second World War in Gdańsk should present the Polish story of the tragedy of 1939–1945 and of its long-lasting consequences (material, political, in the collective memory of the Poles, etc.). In other words, the museum is for the world, but it tells about Poland and Poles – who we are and why we are like this: freedom loving, Catholics, patriots, etc. – and first and foremost proud of our history.[31]

The unequivocally polonocentric point of view can be found in many other press statements, books and museum projects, both completed and in progress. The centenary of regaining Poland's independence did not serve as an opportunity to emphasize the processual dimension of history. One could infer that independence broke out suddenly in November 1918 and was predominantly an achievement of the Poles, a kind of a "miracle" with no clear reason. The centenary version of the history did not mention the role of the First World War, of the simultaneous defeat of the three partitioning powers or of the Russian revolution. One could also gain an impression that no one but the Poles were celebrating independence in 1918 – Lithuanians, Latvians, Estonians, independent Czechoslovakia, Yugoslavia and Finland seem to have been forgotten, despite the fact that they have mostly been Poland's neighbors, then and now. Little has been written on the aspirations which Ukrainians and Belarusians voiced towards the end of the war and which partially materialized.

Newly opened history museums also care mostly about national pride and marginalize the international context of the Polish past. The Ulma Family Museum of the Poles Saving Jews in Markowa, opened in 2016, can serve as one example,[32] and the Museum of the Cursed Soldiers in Ostrołęka, inaugurated by the representatives of the highest state authorities on March 1, 2019 as another.[33] The last (so far) symbolic act in this sphere, reaching beyond the feeling of pride, was the state support for the Roman Dmowski and

Ignacy Jan Paderewski Institute of Heritage of National Thought founded in February 2020.[34]

"The new politics of history" tries to change the historical imaginary, symbolic sphere and "time" and "space" by announcing "new holidays." They often refer to the tradition of martyrdom during the Second World War, e.g., March 1 was proclaimed as the "Day of the Cursed Soldiers" while July 11 as "National Day of Remembrance of Victims of Genocide perpetrated by Ukrainian nationalists on the citizens of the Second Republic of Poland."[35] Yet another tool of this politics is the changing of street names and names of other objects in the public sphere, done according to the provisions of the so-called de-communization bill. The bill, introduced in 2016, was aimed at removing from the public sphere information on "persons, organizations, events or dates that symbolize communism or another totalitarian system."[36] Closer to everyday life, the changes of the historical imaginary can be observed in the historical memorabilia, including the so-called patriotic clothes, the popularity of which extends beyond young people. The motifs of hussars (seventeenth-century Polish cavalry), the symbols of "Fighting Poland" from the Second World War (the so-called anchored P), the slogans "God–honor–fatherland," "Death to the enemies of fatherland" and "Red is Bad" are reproduced on t-shirts, hoodies, bags, scarves and other pieces of clothing.[37]

Last but not least, the issue of redefining the concept of Polishness after 2015 should not be omitted. Its new version incorporates anti-communist and national–Catholic tradition. The construction of the new pantheon of national heroes began already in the 1990s. It referred first to the tradition that combined romantic patriotism and Catholic heritage, mentioning directly or indirectly the nineteenth-century nationalist stereotype of a Catholic Pole as a model to follow. The national–Catholic tradition generates two types of heroes. One is a saint, defender of Faith, epitomizing Christian values and sensitive towards the needs of the poorest, while at the same time being a patriot and a faithful son of the fatherland. Rev. Ignacy Skorupka, the hero of the Polish-bolshevik war of 1920 can serve as an example of this category. The second type is an activist of the struggle for independence, typically a soldier who sacrifices his life to save the fatherland, who usually refrains from politics but emphasizes his ties with religion and the Church. These virtues were represented by General Józef Haller during the war for independence of 1918–1921. Both types of heroes represent the same set of virtues, presented as being nationwide, overcoming any class or party divisions. It refers to the historical tradition that denies any conflicts. Originally, it lacked any female heroes (except for the Catholic saints) who appeared only in 2018 when, within the framework of the public discussion on the events of 1918, for the first time the women's input in regaining Poland's independence was appreciated at such a scale. Periodicals, internet portals, books and other anniversary publications by and large presented the female heroes of the irredentist movement from the pre-1914 period and the first female members of the Polish parliament of 1919, but also the female activists of the anti-communist movement of the Second World War period and post-war years.

The process of changing the national pantheon that had begun already before 2015 was two-fold. On the one hand, it was enhanced but on the other hand, its members were carefully selected. The vision of "Polishness" was, thus, both inclusive and exclusive. The "Cursed Soldiers"[38] have become the repositories of the new version of patriotism, with their idealism, heroism and determination.[39] Przemysław Czarnek, then in charge of Lublin voivodship (in 2021 the Minister of Science and Education) called the Day of the Cursed Soldiers "the day of regaining the dignity of the Polish state."[40] The anti-communist struggle of the Cursed Soldiers is more and more often incorporated into the popular insurgent tradition dated back to the Polish uprisings of the nineteenth century. It has been even called "the anti-communist uprising" lasting from 1944 till 1963 [sic], which is historically doubtful to say the least.[41] Uneasy facts from the biographies of some of the "Cursed Soldiers," who committed crimes against the civilian (including the Jewish) population, are at the same time tabooed or marginalized.[42] Such "nuances" notwithstanding, the Cursed Soldiers have been firmly rooted in the public sphere in the form of monuments, murals and street names, and in popular music. They have been presented in numerous documentaries, theatrical performances, books and articles, and have become icons of contemporary pop culture, with all the positive and negative results thereof. Even the clubs of soccer fans refer to the Cursed Soldiers.

In 2017, soldiers of the National Armed Forces and National Military Union, right-wing military formations from the WWII period, were added to the new historical imaginarium by the proponents of the "new politics of history." In his letter to the participants of special observances at the Tomb of the Unknown Soldier in Warsaw, President Andrzej Duda emphasized that the members of the nationalist wing of the Polish resistance movement were most valuable fighters for the liberation of Poland from the power and terror of both occupants.[43] Letters in a similar vein were addressed to the veterans of the National Armed Forces by Jarosław Kaczyński, leader of the Law and Justice party, and Marek Kuchciński, marshal (president) of Sejm, the lower chamber of the Polish parliament. Prime Minister Mateusz Morawiecki during his visit in Munich laid flowers on the graves of the soldiers of the Holy Cross Mountains Brigade (*Brygada Świętokrzyska*) of the National Armed Forces. The Brigade, which operated in 1944–1945, did not recognize the Polish Underground State and its authority, and numerous sources prove that it collaborated with German Nazis and murdered Polish communists and Jews. In 1945, according to the provisions of an agreement with German forces, it was evacuated to Czech territories.

Apologetic and hagiographic features of the image of the "Cursed Soldiers," created by the IPN and other state institutions, received a positive welcome by some, especially young people. A student of my colleague's class at the Institute of History, University of Łódź, told him that all the honest Poles after 1945 either emigrated or joined the armed resistance – thus, anyone engaged in the post-war reconstruction should be regarded as the communists' collaborator. The fact that the Cursed Soldiers have been promoted by IPN in school education, with numerous lesson scenarios, exhibitions, workshops, history and art competitions, films, excursions and field trips, also plays in favor of their popularity.[44] Some pupils, however, especially those who do not share right-wing political views, tend to call it "cursiostities." Some historians have noted that the fascination with the soldiers of anti-communist resistance leads to the marginalization of the achievements of the Home Army and Polish Underground State, i.e., the mainstream participants of the Polish resistance movement.[45] The public discourse on history largely lacks the left-wing tradition. Whoever refuses to share the abovementioned right-wing views is accused of being unpatriotic and excluded from the national community.[46]

Third, the ideal vision of the Polish past is strongly mythologized, i.e., myths are created and used deliberately, with the intention of socializing the community, in this case, in line with the goals of the "new politics of history."[47] This kind of mythologization is regarded as a necessary but insufficient condition for any community to survive, for it gives it the feeling of Anthony Giddens' "ontological security" in the sense of a lived, common history. Myths, however, are steeped in ambivalence. We need them for they give sense to our past, but on the other hand, they close us to others and make the dialogue about the past difficult, both within one national community and with "others."

Historiography differs from myth in dealing with three categories: values, truth and time.[48] Both historiography and myth tend to ascribe some values to the events they examine. In the realm of myth, however, the values are dichotomous, any gradation disappears and the events are precepted through the lens of the perpetual confrontation of "good" versus "evil." As for the truth, historiography usually engages in long-term arduous research that results in a narrative that, in the researcher's opinion, best reflects the past reality. Myth, to cite the literature of the subject, "does not establish the truth, but it contains and preaches it. It is given and as such is not to be discussed or verified."[49] Last but not least, historiography, its multiple connections with the present times notwithstanding, generally deals with the past time. Myth, on the contrary, refers to the idea of "eternal return" – the mythical time is the eternal present time.[50]

In a moment when the myth replaces critical reflection on the past, the phenomenon of "the true history" arises. In the statements of the proponents of the "new politics of history," examples of this way of thinking can be found in abundance. The myth of the "true history" originates from the social need of "domesticating" the knowledge of the past, making it an important and at times, decisive argument in ideological, political or religious debates. On the declarative level, reappreciation of history is the ultimate goal. It is to be achieved by clearing the image of the national past from the pieces that are for some reasons assessed negatively. The "true" history, according to its supporters, should serve as a foundation of the national re-birth of the Poles from the traumatic experiences under both totalitarian systems. A clear reference to the world of values is made by ascribing to them certain elements of the national past. Everything "good" in Polish history is related to Catholicism, Christianity and Nation, while all "evil" is related to left-wing, especially communist, values. It therefore comes as no surprise that the supporters of the "new politics of history" regard the history of the "People's Poland" (1944–1989) as the "history of occupation" where constant confrontation was taking place of evil, alien and totalitarian authorities with good, imbued with the ideas of resistance, enslaved society. Filip Musiał has noted: "The Soviet aggression of 1944 was a fact. The sooner we start call-ing things by names, the sooner will we be able to accept the **coherent** (em-phasis R.S.) narrative of the most recent Polish past."[51] In the vision of this past, the predilection to adjudicate on the truth, which should be obvious for everyone, can be observed. Historians have a special role to play, espe-cially those who perceive themselves as the "curators of the national values" or "secular chaplains who preach the historical truth."[52] In the myth of the "true" history, understood by the supporters of the "new politics of history," traditional understanding of history as a moral lesson has been revitalized. When no conflict can exist between the past world and a historian, "truth" and "values" become synonyms. The value decides on what is "true." The image of the past becomes an arena of confrontation of axiological systems, and thus, an ideological dispute. Whatever belongs to the set of values repre-sented by a participant of the public debate becomes "true."

Finally, mythologization takes the form of escape from history into the world of the mythical present time. As a prominent historian of the nineteenth-twentieth century, Andrzej Chwalba wrote,

> In the 19th century history used to carry mythologized contents, cre-ated for use by the emerging nationalism. In order to build nations, made-up stories were referred to. [...] However, promoting those myths and legends in the times of no real threat, can lead to propaganda.[53]

In this optics, history has little in common with what actually happened, but rather reflects the view of what "it should be like," according to the political, religious or worldview principles of its interpreters. It remains in the realm of propaganda rather than common social capital.[54] It becomes what Um-berto Eco used to call creating reality "more real than reality itself."[55] As a result, it becomes less and less comprehensible for an outside observer.[56]

V. Conclusions

The analysis of the content popularized by the creators of the "new politics of history" leads to the following, probably provisional conclusions.

First, it suggests that a deeper reflection is necessary on the issue mentioned by Aleksander Smolar: "Does our freedom also comprise the past? Can the past be a matter of free choice? Can we make up everything? Who are we? Where do we come from?" The borders of the image of the past become an issue. To continue with the remarks by Smolar: "if manipulating the past is regarded as a manifestation of freedom not only on an individual level, then there is no past, everything is possible."[57] Quite ironically, the proponents of the "new politics of history" do not take their own role. Notwithstanding their support, for the most part, of a quite traditional vision of history, they step into an extremely post-modernist approach where everyone can create their own narrative in a totally arbitrary way. In their views, the "new politics of history" disturbingly tends to resemble a historical utopia – an ideal image of the past, with a clearly marked conflict of an absolute "good" and "evil," with model heroes who should become role models to be followed by the subsequent generations.

Second, the ideal vision of the Polish past brings us back to the pre-Weber era of the humanities. It rejects Weber's categories of rationality and secularization and the aim of "disenchanting" the world. The proponents of this new vision want the world of Polish history to be "enchanted back" and to be made into a magic place of the particular condensation of national feelings, self-contained and liberated from outside influences. In their view, the historiosophical curse cast on Poland should be rejected and erased from memory.

Third, in the history modelled in this way, the truth is a matter of faith and the facts are what the majority is willing to believe in.[58] Will they believe? We will probably learn this over the course of time. Then we will also see the results of this "historical engineering" with the use of "socialization by the past."

Notes

1 The literature on the Polish politics of history, also in the context of European disputes, is quite rich. In the Polish language, two monographs deserve particular attention: Rafał Chwedoruk, *Polityka historyczna* (Warszawa: PWN, 2018) and Michał Łuczewski, *Kapitał moralny. Polityki historyczne w późnej nowoczesności* (Kraków: Ośrodek Myśli Politycznej, 2017). Cf. also Valentin Behr, "The Writing of the 'Political" History of Communism in Poland," https://halshs. archives-ouvertes.fr/halshs-01021644, accessed January 15, 2021; Behr, "Histoire du temps présent et politique en Pologne," *Les Cahiers Sirice* 21, no. 2 (2018): 121–137; Jan Pomorski, "What Is 'Politics of History" Concerning Poland's Raison d'etat," *Institute of National Rememberance. Review* no. 1 (2019): 37–60; Kornelia Kończal and Joanna Wawrzyniak, "Provincializing Memory Studies: Polish Approaches in the Past and Present," *Memory Studies* 11, no 4 (2018): 391–404; Jo Harper (ed.), *Poland's Memory Wars: Essays on Illiberalism* (New York – Budapest: CU Press, 2018).
2 Joanna Wojdon, "Czym jest Public History?," in *Historia w przestrzeni publicznej*, ed. Joanna Wojdon (Warszawa: PWN, 2018), 14.
3 For the perspective of iconosphere, see Magdalena Saryusz-Wolska, "Publiczne konstruowanie historii. Przeszłość w prawicowej ikonografii," *Teksty Drugie* no. 6 (2016): 325–346.

4 Michał Karnowski, "Pedagogika wstydu nie działa? Wielkie badania 'w Sieci' pokazują, jak kruche są podstawy prób przerobienia Polaków," wpolityce.pl, December 30, 2014, https://wpolityce.pl/historia/227719-pedagogika-wstydu-nie-dziala-wielkie-badania-w-sieci-pokazuja-jak-kruche-sa-podstawy-prob-przerobienia-polakow, accessed January 20, 2021. Jarosław Kaczyński spoke in a similar vein in 2012. For critical remarks on such an approach, see Jakub Majmurek, "Pedagogika wstydu, której nigdy nie było," August 6, 2016, https://oko.press/pedagogika-wstydu-ktorej-nigdy-bylo/, accessed January 21, 2021.

5 Adam Sosnowski, "Trzy wybitne dzieła, czyli inauguracja nowej polityki historycznej. Na sali Szczerski, Gliński, Kolarski... i marszałek Piłsudski," December 18, 2015, http://wpolityce.pl/polityka/275550-nasza-relacja-trzy-wybitne-dziela-czyli-inauguracja-nowej-polityki-historycznej-na-sali-szczerski-glinski-kolarski-i-marszalek-pilsudski, accessed January 21, 2021.

6 Andrzej Walicki, "Sprawiedliwość na pasku polityki," *Przegląd Polityczny* no. 40/41 (1999): 33.

7 Jan T. Gross, *Neighbors: The Destruction of the Jewish Community in Jedwabne, Poland* (Princeton: Princeton University Press, 2001).

8 In 2009, a research program of the emerging Polish History Museum was named "Patriotism of Tomorrow."

9 Dariusz Gawin, "O pożytkach i szkodliwości historycznego rewizjonizmu," *Pamięć i odpowiedzialność*, ed. Robert Kostro and Tomasz Merta (Kraków-Wrocław: Ośrodek Myśli Politycznej, 2005), 20.

10 Dariusz Karłowicz, "Pamięć aksjologiczna a historia," in Kostro and Merta, *Pamięć*, 35.

11 Cf. Rafał Stobiecki, "Historians Facing Politics of History," in *Past in the Making* ed. Michal Kopeček (Budapest – New York: CEU Press, 2008), 179–196.

12 Muzeum Historii Polski, *Odkryć historię– zrozumieć wolność* (Warszawa: MHP, 2006), 16.

13 Tomasz Wituch, "Narodowy bilans XX wieku," *Arcana*, no. 2 (1999): 25. Cf. also contributions of Jan Żaryn, Andrzej Nowak, and Marek Jurek in the debate "Polska polityka historyczna," *Biuletyn Instytutu Pamięci Narodowej* no. 5 (2006): 2–3, 7–8, 11.

14 Andrzej Nowak in "Polska polityka historyczna," *Biuletyn Instytutu Pamięci Narodowej* no. 5 (2006): 28.

15 Andrzej Walicki, "O liberalizmie, wspólnocie i historii. Rozmowa Łukasza Gałeckiego z Andrzejem Walickim," *Przegląd Polityczny* no. 75 (2006): 26.

16 Robert Traba, "Polityka wobec historii: kontrowersje i perspektywy," *Teksty Drugie* no. 1–2 (2010): 303.

17 https://www.youtube.com/watch?v=M7MSG4Q-4as, accessed January 21, 2021. Rafał Wnuk, "'Niezwyciężeni' czyli folk-history po polsku," http://ohistorie.eu/2018/07/17/niezwyciezeni-czyli-folk-history-po-polsku/, accessed January 20, 2021. Wnuk points out several instances of adulteration in the movie which were later used by the new director of the Museum of the Second World War in Gdańsk to replace the original film (https://streamable.com/yelt1, accessed January 21, 2021) at the exit of the core exhibition. Cf. the chapter by Anna Ziębińska-Witek in this volume.

18 Marek Woźniak, "SŁOWO jako narzędzie kreowania i zawłaszczania przeszłości w dyskursie/dyskursach publicznych," *Almanach Historyczny* 22 (2020): 303–323.

19 *"Powstrzymać kłamstwo. Rozmowę przeprowadzili J. i M. Karnowscy,"* wSieci, September 21, 2015.

20 Michał Głowiński who specialized in the analysis of newspeak has noticed that the goal of newspeak is not to present facts and events, but to set the limits of acceptable interpretations and commentaries, as well as to impose meanings and values. One of the basic rules of such newspeak allows the creation of a

fictitious world and treats it as if it were real. Michał Głowiński, *Rytuał i demagogia* (Warszawa: Open, 1992), 18–19.

21 Woźniak, "SŁOWO," 309.

22 Janusz Kurtyka in Marek Jurek, Andrzej Nowak, Arkadiusz Rybicki, Piotr Skibiński, Janusz Kurtyka, and Jan Żaryn. "Polska polityka historyczna [debata]." *Biuletyn Instytutu Pamięci Narodowej* 5 (2006): 17. Remarks of A. Nowak and J. Żaryn in this publication contain similar accents.

23 Łuczewski, *Kapitał moralny*, 240.

24 Filip Musiał, "Wybór tradycji. Między wolnością a posttotalitaryzmem," *Biuletyn Instytutu Pamięci Narodowej* no. 1–2 (2017): 7–19. Cf. Marek Chodakiewicz, *Międzymorze* (Warszawa: 3S Media, 2016).

25 "A. Nowak o pierwszej zdradzie Zachodu," *Gazeta Wyborcza*, December 8, 2016. Cf. discussion between Jan Pomorski and Andrzej Nowak: Jan Pomorski, "Appeasement jako ostrzeżenie. Rozważania o historiografii i polityce historycznej. (Wokół Pierwszej zdrady Zachodu Andrzeja Nowaka)," *Dzieje Najnowsze* 49, no. 3 (2017): 269–298; Andrzej Nowak, "Czy w politycznej historii jest miejsce na kategorię 'zdrady'?" *Dzieje Najnowsze* 49, no. 3 (2017): 299–312.

26 I disregard two issues here. First, the notion of "betrayal," due to its axiological dimension, should not be part of academic history. Second, such a view on "betrayal" is a manipulation which presumes that a subjective relation exists, accompanied by the consciousness of betraying or being betrayed. Cf. Pomorski, "Appeasement."

27 R.P [Piestrzyński], "Przekleństwo złego czynu," *Orzeł Biały* no. 7 (1955), cited in Jan Lencznarowicz, "Wyobrażenia konferencji jałtańskiej w dyskursie emigracji po II wojnie światowej," in *Jałta. Rzeczywistość, mit, pamięć*, edited by Sławomir Łukasiewicz (Warszawa: IPN, 2019), 236.

28 Błażej Brzostek has recently used the term "autochtonism" in a similar context, meaning the "focusing on vernacular cultural patterns, conviction of their intrinsic meaning and neglecting imported patterns". Błażej Brzostek, "Nachodźców zatopić!", *Wolna Sobota. Magazyn Wyborczej*, January 23–24, 2021.

29 Cf. his statment for Radio Maryja of July 28, 2017, accessed July 30, 2017, http://www.radiomaryja.pl/infomacje/u-nas-j.kaczynski-obecna-sytuacja-odwrocenia-warunkiem-ze-bedziemy-razem.

30 Łuczewski, *Kapitał*, 233–237; Paweł Machcewicz, *Muzeum* (Kraków: Znak, 2017), 207–221. In a special letter, Timothy Snyder and Andrzej Nowak have protested against the museum closure. Cf. Timothy Snyder, "Poland vs History," *New York Review of Books*, May 3, 2016.

31 Jan Żaryn, "Recenzja wewnętrzna: Program funkcjonalno-użytkowy wystawy głównej. Muzeum II Wojny Światowej w Gdańsku," accessed October 27, 2020, www.muzeum1939.pl/object.php/act/sho/oid/ddb2639b93aea6fe19bddd01aab694ce.

32 Cf. chapter by Anna Ziębińska-Witek in this volume.

33 https://muzeumzolnierzywykletych.pl/, accessed January 20, 2021.

34 Biographies and achievements of the proponents of the Institute indicate that its formation paves the way towards full rehabilitation of Polish national thought, including the ideas and activities related to the Polish version of fascism of the late 1930s. Jan Żaryn is acting director of the Institute.

35 The Day of Poland's Baptism was also introduced to be celebrated on April 14.

36 The action was not entirely successful. E.g. in Warsaw, The Supreme Administrative Court invalidated the decision to change the names of 44 streets that, according to IPN, "symbolized or propagated communism." Piotr Osęka, a historian who served as an expert in this case, questioned the interpretation of the term "communism" by the law as being too one-sided and used to eradicate a large part of the left-wing political tradition from the public space. He claimed that "only the people directly engaged in the establishment of institutions of

the post-war totalitarian state on the managerial positions can be regarded as symbols of communism," https://archiwumosiatynskiego.pl/wpis-w-debacie/ipn-chcial-skonfiskowac-pamiec-ta-ekspertyza-obronila-ulice-warszawy-przez-szalona-dekomunizacja/, accessed January 23, 2021.

37 Cf. Rafał Stobiecki, "Jak gadżety oswajają nas z przeszłością," *Polityka* no. 22, May 26, 2015.

38 Leaders of the anti-communist underground movement had emerged in the public discourse and in city spaces already in the 1990s. The term "Cursed Soldiers" was coined by Jerzy Ślaski as the title of his book published in 1996 (Jerzy Ślaski, *Żołnierze Wyklęci* (Warszawa: Rytm, 1997). Cf. Rafał Wnuk, "Wokół mitu żołnierzy wykłetych," *Przegląd Polityczny*, October 8, 2016, accessed January 20, 2021, http://przegladpolityczny.pl/wokol-mitu-zolnierzy-wykletych-rafal-wnuk/; Ewa Bacia, "The Phenomenon of Banished Soldiers in Polish Schools as an Example of the Politics of Memory," *Journal of Social Science Education* 18, no. 1 (2019): 13–31; Kornelia Kończal, "The Invention of the 'Cursed Soldiers' and Its Opponents: Post-war Partisan Struggle in Contemporary Poland," *East European Politics and Societies and Cultures* 20, no. 10 (2019): 1–29.

39 Cf. Adam Dziurok, Marek Gałęzowski, Łukasz Kamiński and Filip Musiał, *Od niepodległości do niepodległości: historia Polski 1918–1989* (Warszawa: IPN, 2010).

40 Natalia Wiślińska, "Partia Razem oburzona udziałem wojewody lubelskiego w marszu ONR. 'Doskonale wczuł się w retorykę nienawiści,'" *wMeritum.pl*, February 27, 2017, accessed February 20, 2020, http://wmeritum.pl/partia-razem-oburzona-udzialem-wojewody-lubelskiego-marszu-onr-doskonale-wczul-sie-retoryke-nienawisci/173774.

41 In 1963, the last "cursed soldier", Józef Franczak (Lalek) died. In 2016, his bust was unveiled in Jordan park in Kraków in the pantheon of prominent Poles.

42 Cf. "Polska pamięć i duma. 'Żołnierze wyklęci' – między historią popkulturą a polityką dyskusja," *Więź*, no. 3 (2016): 7–27 (in particular remarks by R. Wnuk); Mariusz Mazur, *Antykomunistycznego podziemia portret zbiorowy 1945–1956. Aspekty mentalno-psychologiczne* (Warszawa: Bellona, 2019).

43 http://wiadomosci.onet.pl/kraj/listy-od-dudy-i-kaczynskiego-do-kombatantow-nsz/nysef0g, September 16, 2017, accessed January 20, 2021.

44 The topic "Polish anti-communist underground (1944–1956), Fates of the 'cursed soldiers'" was one of the proposals. According to the data from the Łódź division of IPN, it became the most popular one and schools chose it 120 times in the years 2010–2014. I do not have more recent data but one can presume that its popularity even increased. Cf. Rafał Stobiecki. "Polityka historyczna a edukacja szkolna we współczesnej Polsce. Kilka uwag do dyskusji," in *Historia i pamięć. Studia i szkice historiograficzne*, ed. Joanna Kolbuszewska and Rafał Stobiecki (Łódź: Wydawnictwo Uniwersytetu Łódzkiego, 2016), 179–190.

45 "Polska pamięć i duma..." (particularly remarks by Wnuk); Andrzej Friszke (interviewed by Jacek Nizinkiewicz), "Samobójcza polityka historyczna PiS," *Rzeczpospolita*, September 10, 2017.

46 Attacks on J. T. Gross can serve as an example, when the Polish League against Defamation (Fundacja Reduta Dobrego Imienia) requested for Gross to be deprived of the Knight's Cross of the Order of Merit of the Republic of Poland that he had received from President Kwaśniewski. The Foundation argued that "Anti-Polish propagandist activity of Jan Tomasz Gross [...] leads to diminishing Poland's international position, hinders Polish diplomatic activities and, most importantly, Gross has been slandering Poland and the Poles for years in international media by ascribing the responsibility for the Holocaust to us," accessed January 21, 2021, https://historia.wprost.pl/531316/gross-straci-panstwowe-odznaczenie-prezydent-poprosil-msz-o-opinie.html. Ultimately, Gross was not deprived of the medal.

47 Jan Pomorski, "Polityzacja/mitologizacja historii, czyli w czym neuronauka (i metodologia) może pomóc badaczowi historii najnowszej," *Teoria@historia*, no. 4 (2017): 17 (together with the discussion with the author).
48 I refer to the findings of Andrzej F. Grabski, "Historiografia – Mitotwórstwo – Mitoburstwo," in *Historia. Mity. Interpretacje*, ed. Alina Barszczewska-Krupa (Łódź: Wydawnictwo Uniwersytetu Łódzkiego, 1996), 29–62.
49 Grabski, "Historiografia," 30.
50 Mircea Eliade, *Sacrum – mit – historia* (Warszawa: PIW, 1970), 112.
51 Filip Musiał, "Podbój zwany wyzwoleniem," *Biuletyn Instytutu Pamięci Narodowej* no. 1–2 (2017): 200.
52 Rafał Stobiecki, "Rola historyka we współczesnym świecie," *Europa*, no. 2 (2005): 8–10; Brzostek, *Nachodźców*.
53 Andrzej Chwalba (interviewed by Janusz Majcherek), "Czy wystarczy prawda historyczna," *Przegląd Polityczny*, no. 75 (2006): 65.
54 Pomorski, "Polityzacja/mitologizacja."
55 Cited after *ibid.*, 40.
56 This issue was raised by Friszke, "Samobójcza polityka:"

> Today, politics of history is a [political] parties' mess which must be totally incomprehensible abroad, and in Poland it serves to exclude various communities and traditions [...] it is an attempt to re-formulate national traditions and values in order to create myths in most drastic way.

57 Aleksander Smolar, "Bezpieczne miejsce," *Gazeta Wyborcza*, October 15–16, 2016.
58 These are paraphrased words of a leading ideologist of contemporary Russian euroasianism Alexandr Dugin. Cited after Martin Šimečka, "Wrogowie prawdy," *Gazeta Wyborcza*, April 23–24, 2017.

Bibliography

"A. Nowak o pierwszej zdradzie Zachodu," *Gazeta Wyborcza*, December 8, 2016.
Bacia, Ewa. "The Phenomenon of Banished Soldiers in Polish Schools as an Example of the Politics of Memory." *Journal of Social Science Education* 18, no. 1 (2019): 13–31.
Behr, Valentin. "Histoire du temps présent et politique en Pologne." *Les Cahiers Sirice* 21, no. 2 (2018): 121–137.
Behr, Valentin. "The Writing of the 'Political' History of Communism in Poland." Accessed January 15, 2021. https://halshs.archives-ouvertes.fr/halshs-01021644.
Brzostek, Błażej. "Nachodźców zatopić!" *Wolna Sobota. Magazyn Wyborczej*, January 23–24, 2021.
Chodakiewicz, Marek. *Międzymorze*. Warszawa: 3S Media, 2016.
Chwalba, Andrzej (interviewed by Janusz Majcherek). "Czy wystarczy prawda historyczna." *Przegląd Polityczny* no. 75 (2006): 64–68.
Chwedoruk, Rafał. *Polityka historyczna*. Warszawa: PWN, 2018.
Dziurok, Adam, Marek Gałęzowski, Łukasz Kamiński and Filip Musiał. *Od niepodległości do niepodległości: Historia Polski 1918–1989*. Warszawa: IPN, 2010.
Eliade, Mircea. *Sacrum – mit – historia*. Warszawa: PIW, 1970.
Friszke, Andrzej (interviewed by Jacek Nizinkiewicz). "Samobójcza polityka historyczna PiS." *Rzeczpospolita*, September 10, 2017.
Gawin, Dariusz. "O pożytkach i szkodliwości historycznego rewizjonizmu." In *Pamięć i odpowiedzialność*, edited by Robert Kostro and Tomasz Merta, 1–29. Kraków – Wrocław: Ośrodek Myśli Politycznej, 2005.
Głowiński, Michał. *Rytuał i demagogia*. Warszawa: Open, 1992.

Grabski, Andrzej F. "Historiografia – Mitotwórstwo – Mitoburstwo." In *Historia. Mity. Interpretacje*, edited by Alina Barszczewska-Krupa, 29–62. Łódź: Wydawnictwo Uniwersytetu Łódzkiego, 1996.

Gross, Jan T. *Neighbors: The Destruction of the Jewish Community in Jedwabne, Poland.* Princeton: Princeton University Press, 2001.

Harper, Jo, ed. *Poland's Memory Wars: Essays on Illiberalism.* New York – Budapest: CU Press, 2018.

Jurek, Marek, Andrzej Nowak, Arkadiusz Rybicki, Piotr Skibiński, Janusz Kurtyka, and Jan Żaryn. "Polska polityka historyczna [debata]." *Biuletyn Instytutu Pamięci Narodowej* 5 (2006): 2–33.

Karłowicz, Dariusz. "Pamięć aksjologiczna a historia." In *Pamięć i odpowiedzialność*, edited by Robert Kostro and Tomasz Merta, 35–41. Kraków – Wrocław: Ośrodek Myśli Politycznej, 2005.

Karnowski, Michał. "Pedagogika wstydu nie działa? Wielkie badania 'w Sieci' pokazują, jak kruche są podstawy prób przerobienia Polaków," last modified December 30, 2014. Accessed January 21, 2021. https://wpolityce.pl/historia/227719-pedagogika-wstydu-nie-dziala-wielkie-badania-w-sieci-pokazuja-jak-kruche-sa-podstawy-prob-przerobienia-polakow.

Kończal, Kornelia and Joanna Wawrzyniak. "Provincializing Memory Studies: Polish Approaches in the Past and Present." *Memory Studies* 11, no. 4 (2018): 391–404.

Kończal, Kornelia. "The Invention of the 'Cursed Soldiers' and Its Opponents: Post-war Partisan Struggle in Contemporary Poland." *East European Politics and Societies and Cultures* 20, no. 10 (2019): 1–29.

Lencznarowicz, Jan. "Wyobrażenia konferencji jałtańskiej w dyskursie emigracji po II wojnie światowej." In *Jałta. Rzeczywistość, mit, pamięć*, edited by Sławomir Łukasiewicz, 231–247. Warszawa: IPN, 2019.

Łuczewski, Michał. *Kapitał moralny. Polityki historyczne w późnej nowoczesności.* Kraków: Ośrodek Myśli Politycznej, 2017.

Machcewicz, Paweł. *Muzeum.* Kraków: Znak, 2017. The English edition: *The War that Never Ends. The Museum of the Second World War in Gdańsk.* Berlin: DeGruyter, 2019.

Majmurek, Jakub. "Pedagogika wstydu, której nigdy nie było," last modified, August 6, 2016. Accessed January 21, 2021. https://oko.press/pedagogika-wstydu-ktorej-nigdy-nie-bylo.

Mazur, Mariusz. *Antykomunistycznego podziemia portret zbiorowy 1945–1956. Aspekty mentalno-psychologiczne.* Warszawa: Bellona, 2019.

Musiał, Filip. "Podbój zwany wyzwoleniem." *Biuletyn Instytutu Pamięci Narodowej,* no. 1–2 (2017): 198–200.

Musiał, Filip. "Wybór tradycji. Między wolnością a posttotalitaryzmem." *Biuletyn Instytutu Pamięci Narodowej* no. 1–2 (2017): 7–19.

Muzeum Historii Polski. *Odkryć historię – zrozumieć wolność.* Warszawa: MHP, 2006.

Nowak, Andrzej. "Czy w politycznej historii jest miejsce na kategorię 'zdrady'?" *Dzieje Najnowsze* 49, no. 3 (2017): 299–312.

"Polska pamięć i duma. 'Żołnierze wyklęci' – między historią popkulturą a polityką dyskusja." *Więź* no. 3 (2016): 7–27.

Pomorski, Jan. "Appeasement jako ostrzeżenie. Rozważania o historiografii i polityce historycznej. (Wokół Pierwszej zdrady Zachodu Andrzeja Nowaka)." *Dzieje Najnowsze* 49, no. 3 (2017): 269–298.

Pomorski, Jan. "Polityzacja/mitologizacja historii, czyli w czym neuronauka (i metodologia) może pomóc badaczowi historii najnowszej." *Historia@Teoria* 2, no. 4 (2017): 15–42.

Pomorski, Jan. "What is 'Politics of History' Concerning Poland's Raison d'etat." *Institute of National Rememberance. Review* 1 (2019): 37–60.

Saryusz-Wolska, Magdalena. "Publiczne konstruowanie historii. Przeszłość w prawicowej ikonografii." *Teksty Drugie* no. 6 (2016): 325–346. Cf. Saryusz-Wolska, Magdalena. "Abusing Public Visual History: The Current Right-Wing Press in Poland." *The Public Historian* 42, no. 3 (2020): 61–85.

Šimečka, Martin. "Wrogowie prawdy." *Gazeta Wyborcza*, April 23–24, 2017.

Ślaski, Jerzy. *Żołnierze Wyklęci*. Warszawa: Rytm, 1997.

Smolar, Aleksander. "Bezpieczne miejsce." *Gazeta Wyborcza*, October 15–16, 2016.

Snyder, Timothy. "Poland vs History." *New York Review of Books*, May 3, 2016.

Sosnowski, Adam. "Trzy wybitne dzieła, czyli inauguracja nowej polityki historycznej. Na sali Szczerski, Gliński, Kolarski… i marszałek Piłsudski," last modified December 18, 2015. Accessed January 21, 2021. http://wpolityce.pl/polityka/275550-nasza-relacja-trzy-wybitne-dziela-czyli-inauguracja-nowej-polityki-historycznej-na-sali-szczerski-glinski-kolarski-i-marszalek-pilsudski.

Stobiecki, Rafał. "Historians Facing Politics of History." In *Past in the Making*, edited by Michal Kopeček, 179–196. Budapest – New York: CEU Press, 2008.

Stobiecki, Rafał. "Jak gadżety oswajają nas z przeszłością." *Polityka*, no. 22, May 26, 2015.

Stobiecki, Rafał. "Polityka historyczna a edukacja szkolna we współczesnej Polsce. Kilka uwag do dyskusji." In *Historia i pamięć. Studia i szkice historiograficzne*, edited by Joanna Kolbuszewska and Rafał Stobiecki, 179–190. Łódź: Wydawnictwo Uniwersytetu Łódzkiego, 2016.

Stobiecki, Rafał. "Rola historyka we współczesnym świecie." *Europa* no. 2 (2005): 8–10.

Traba, Robert. "Polityka wobec historii: kontrowersje i perspektywy." *Teksty Drugie* no. 1–2 (2010): 300–319.

Walicki, Andrzej. "Sprawiedliwość na pasku polityki." *Przegląd Polityczny* no. 40/41 (1999): 12–33.

Walicki, Andrzej and Łukasz Gałecki. "O liberalizmie, wspólnocie i historii. Rozmowa Łukasza Gałeckiego z Andrzejem Walickim." *Przegląd Polityczny* no. 75 (2006): 20–30.

Wiślińska, Natalia. "Partia Razem oburzona udziałem wojewody lubelskiego w marszu ONR. 'Doskonale wczuł się w retorykę nienawiści." *wMeritum.pl*, February 27, 2017. Accessed February 20, 2020. http://wmeritum.pl/partia-razem-oburzona-udzialem-wojewody-lubelskiego-marszu-onr-doskonale-wczul-sie-retoryke-nienawisci/173774.

Wituch, Tomasz. "Narodowy bilans XX wieku." *Arcana*, no. 2 (1999): 20–25.

Wnuk, Rafał. "'Niezwyciężeni' czyli folk-history po polsku." Accessed January 20, 2021. http://ohistorie.eu/2018/07/17/niezwyciezeni-czyli-folk-history-po-polsku/. July 17, 2018.

Wnuk, Rafał. "Wokół mitu żołnierzy wyklętych." *Przegląd Polityczny*, October 8, 2016. Accessed January 20, 2021. http://przegladpolityczny.pl/wokol-mitu-zolnierzy-wykletych-rafal-wnuk.

Wojdon, Joanna. "Czym jest public history?" In *Historia w przestrzeni publicznej*, edited by Joanna Wojdon, 11–16. Warszawa: PWN, 2018.

Woźniak, Marek. "SŁOWO jako narzędzie kreowania i zawłaszczania przeszłości w dyskursie/dyskursach publicznych." *Almanach Historyczny* 22 (2020): 303–323.

Żaryn, Jan. "Recenzja wewnętrzna: Program funkcjonalno-użytkowy wystawy głównej Muzeum II Wojny Światowej w Gdańsku." Accessed October 27, 2020. www.muzeum1939.pl/object.php/act/sho/oid/ddb2639b93aea6fe19bddd01aab694ce.

Żaryn, Jan, Andrzej Nowak, and Marek Jurek in the debate "Polska polityka historyczna." *Biuletyn Instytutu Pamięci Narodowej* no. 5 (2006): 2–34.

Weblinks

https://archiwumosiatynskiego.pl/wpis-w-debacie/ipn-chcial-skonfiskowac-pamiec-ta-ekspertyza-obronila-ulice-warszawy-przez-szalona-dekomunizacja/. Accessed January 23, 2021.

https://historia.wprost.pl/531316/gross-straci-panstwowe-odznaczenie-prezydent-poprosil-msz-o-opinie.html. Accessed January 21, 2021.

https://muzeumzolnierzywykletych.pl. Accessed January 20, 2021.

http://wiadomosci.onet.pl/kraj/listy-od-dudy-i-kaczynskiego-do-kombatantow-nsz/nysef0g, September 16, 2017. Accessed January 20, 2021.

http://www.radiomaryja.pl/infomacje/u-nas-j.kaczynski-obecna-sytuacja-odwrocenia-warunkiem-ze-bedziemy-razem. Accessed July 30, 2017.

Movies

The Unconquered, https://www.youtube.com/watch?v=M7MSG4Q-4as
https://streamable.com/yelt1

3 New Historical Museums in Poland

Paweł Ukielski

Introduction

The date July 31, 2004 marks a milestone in Polish historical museology as the day when the Warsaw Rising Museum was opened. It was not only the first museum created in Poland after regaining independence and freedom of speech in 1989, but it was created in an extremely short period of time, already managing to build its "trademark" and raise great expectations before the solemn opening. The expectations have been met – since the very beginning, the Museum is amongst the most visited places in Poland and has also been declared to be one of the greatest attractions in Warsaw according to polls.[1] It proposed a revolutionary approach to the way in which history is presented, as the first narrative and interactive museum in Poland, more focused on storytelling than on presenting objects. This change was accompanied by the shift from visitor-observer to visitor-participant paradigm, which proved to be a concept broadly accepted by the public.[2]

In the following years, a significant increase in interest in museums, and in particular in historical ones, has been reported in Poland. The number of visitors to Polish museums in the years 2004–2019 has risen by almost 130%, for the first time breaking 40 million annually (17,505,000 and 40,200,000, respectively). The increase of the number of visitors in historical museums has been even more impressive, exceeding 170% (3,150,000 and 8,600,000 respectively).[3] At the end of 2019, there were 959 museums in Poland in comparison to 668 in 2004 (a 43% increase).[4]

What is more, museums have become a vital part of Polish public debate. New museum projects were broadly discussed and became the subject of popular interest even before their opening. This led some observers to the conclusion that Poland is "over-musealized" and the museums' density is too great. Statistical data does not confirm such an opinion – Poland lags behind most European countries. According to data quoted by Piotr Majewski, in 2014 an indicator presenting the number of museums per 100,000 inhabitants in Poland reached 2.22, while in Spain it was 3.20, in Lithuania 3.50, in Portugal 3.80, in Finland 6, in Croatia 6.6, in Latvia 7.30 and in Switzerland 14.[5]

DOI: 10.4324/9781003165767-5

This text will focus on "the big five," that is, the "five most important historical, narrative museums," according to Robert Traba, which include: Warsaw Rising Museum, Polish History Museum (under construction), Museum of the Second World War, POLIN Museum of the History of Polish Jews and European Solidarity Centre.[6] Those will serve as *pars pro toto*, as, according to Paweł Kowal, since 2004 "depending on how rigorous a definition to use, around 60 new narrative historical museums have emerged."[7]

The Roots

The moment when the Polish museological boom started was not a coincidence. To understand it better, one has to analyze several intertwining factors that determined the development of historical museums of a certain type in Poland. On the one hand, it has to be perceived in a broad context, both as a process in world museology (the appearance of new concepts shaped as a "new museology" idea[8]) and politics, including the politics of memory in other countries, particularly Germany and the Russian Federation. On the other hand, internal factors both of certain stagnation before 2004 and of a boom after that date have to be explained.

The last two decades of the twentieth century and the beginning of the third millennium mark a significant change in museology. Its general meaning can be defined as an expansion of museums' functions that now are expected to focus on social goals and visitors' needs rather than on perfecting museological forms or on objects only.[9] It was also combined with a modification of the image of museums from a passive institution towards a creative and stimulating one which connects and combines different activities, such as education, research or entertainment.[10] As a result, museums gained in importance in shaping the identity of different social groups or local societies and thus became more influential in public life. It was combined with a change in the role of artifacts on exhibition – it became still more immersed in the broad context, explained, enclosed in scenography. It arose from another tendency originating from the 1970s, that is, the increasingly common presence of objects of everyday use in exhibits. The new approach brought significant shifts – on the one hand towards a focus on "narrative strategy" rather than on the collection of objects, and on the other hand from the visitor's status of passive observer to active participant in the process of creation.[11] It was particularly visible in the new historical exhibitions of the 1990s and 2000s. Therefore, the new methodology was ready for the Polish boom.

Poland did not belong to the avant-garde of changes. They were discussed among museologists during the time when the communist regime was still collapsing and transformation had just begun. Thus, while it was not only

Polish museums which were mostly absent from the worldwide debate, Poland did not even create a single new and modern institution in the years 1989–2004 – that is, in the 15 years since regaining independence. Paweł Kowal presents a list of reasons to explain this situation:

1   A common trend of focusing on the future rather than on the past combined with the liberal conviction that authorities should minimize their influence on the presentation of history. It was strengthened by an "exhaustion with history" after years of communist propaganda (particularly during the martial law in 1981–1983).
2   A lack of possibility of agreement on a common historical canon between post-communist and post-Solidarity elites.
3   The financial weakness of the state (and self-governments) during the process of transformation from the command to the market economy.[12]

Those general factors can be complemented with an additional remark. The trend described in point (1) was present not only because of overwhelming communist propaganda before 1989, but also due to the special role of uncensored history in the resistance against the communist regime. Once it collapsed, this role was superfluous. In combination with the possibility of economic development and the building personal wealth (unattainable in communist times), this paved the way for pushing history outside the mainstream public debates.[13]

The decade of the 1990s created a paradigm which can be described with some popular catchwords of the time: "Let's choose the future" or "leave history to historians." This approach began to change at the end of the 1990s and in the early 2000s. The establishment of the Institute of National Remembrance in 2000 and its role in the debate over the Jedwabne massacre in the following years were the first symptoms of the shift. Another came with the so-called Rywin affair – the huge corruption scandal which not only broke the power of the post-communist party, but also revealed the backstage of Polish politics. It was clear evidence that a liberal model with the free market at its core had its limitations and was corrupted by informal relations between business and politics.[14]

In parallel, changes came in the surrounding world. The euphoria after the end of the Cold War with an "optimistic" conviction about the "end of history" was broken after September 11, 2001. From the Polish perspective, however, much more important were the new approach to history in Putin's Russia and the activities of Erika Steinbach's Federation of Expellees (*Bund der Vertriebenen* or BdV) in Germany. In the first case, it meant the gradual rehabilitation of Stalin, which turned to neo-Stalinist and imperialist politics of history in the following years.[15] In the latter one, it meant a significant shift in the way the German fate in the Second World War was presented, focusing on the suffering of Germans as co-victims, which raised fears in Poland of a possible "re-writing" of history.[16]

All the above-mentioned factors appeared in a very short period and thus their cumulative impact was multiplied. All the necessary components seemed to be there – both internal and external incentives as well as modern, well-developed methods. The last missing piece was the ignitor.

The Beginning – The Warsaw Rising Museum[17]

It is broadly agreed that the process of preparation and the solemn opening of the Warsaw Rising Museum was a turning point which initiated a new wave of narrative museums in Poland. The idea itself had been present in Polish public debate for decades, however, until the beginning of the twenty-first century such a museum did not emerge.[18] In 2002, the election for the mayor of Warsaw was won by Lech Kaczyński, who decided to make the creation of the Warsaw Rising Museum one of his flagship projects. In July 2003, he granted the site of the former tram power plant at 28 Przyokopowa Street in Wola district as the site of the Museum and appointed Jan Ołda-kowski as Plenipotentiary for the construction of the Museum.[19]

From the very beginning, the basic concept of its creators assumed the establishment of a modern institution that would set new trends in Polish historical museology. It was to present a narrative exhibition, broadly using modern technological achievements and breaking the stereotype of a museum as a boring place. To achieve the goal, it was decided to shift the approach from a visitor-observer to visitor-participant paradigm, [20] and six main target groups were defined. Those were: children; students of primary, middle and high schools as well as university students; the insurgent community, veterans and their families; tourists, both from Poland and abroad, and in particular Poles from abroad; students, researchers and ordinary people whose focus of interest is modern Polish history; and soldiers on active service.[21]

To strengthen the participatory approach, from the very beginning the museum was being created with an "open curtain" – the public was broadly informed by the media about the progress of works, ideas and preparations. This was accompanied by several public actions of which the public collection of memorabilia was the most important. It was held between November 9 and 11, 2003 and within those three days, several hundred people (insurgents and their families) came to donate about 2,000 exhibits. All those efforts resulted in a growing interest in the emerging institution – the public's expectations increased and "circles of loyalty" emerged. The first visible effects were reported already in December 2003. According to a poll conducted then, the Warsaw Rising Museum had become number one on the "must see" list of more than a dozen percentage of respondents, even though it had not yet come into being.[22]

The atmosphere created in this way was huge capital, but also a great challenge for the museum team appointed as a result of public competition: Mirosław Nizio – interior designer; Jarosław Kłaput – computer graphic designer; and Dariusz Kunowski – theatrical scenographer. Using the diversity of their competences, experience and skills, they created modern narrative exhibitions which used state of the art multimedia on the one hand, and many original artifacts and photographs on the other. Scenography created a unique atmosphere, while diverse means of interaction were aimed at stimulating the visitors. All those means caused the public actively to be involved in their visits – every single visitor could decide which topics to examine more deeply, which route to choose and what to focus on.[23]

The official opening of the Warsaw Rising Museum took place on July 31, 2004, on the eve of the 60th anniversary of the Rising. It was a culmination of the broad program of anniversary celebrations that had been prepared by the same team who created the institution itself and its exhibition. The events were quite diverse in nature and targeted very different social groups in order to reach as broad an audience as possible. The museum opening turned out to be a huge success, proved by long queues of visitors and extensive media coverage. Other anniversary celebrations had a different, much more ceremonial character.[24]

The concept of entrusting the anniversary celebrations to the museum team corresponded with the idea of the institution that went far beyond a mere collection of artifacts and exhibitions. Starting with the initial program document worked out in August 2003, the museum's creators continually emphasized that it should be a social, educational and cultural polyphonic center that would deliver diverse activities to its public and be present in the public debate.[25] The museum thus became a kind of a "cultural hub," organizing concerts and theatrical performances, debates and sporting events, educational projects and location-based city games, and promoting civil society. Shortly after opening, the museum established its branch, the Stefan Starzyński Institute, which focuses on contemporary Warsaw, its identity, dynamic development, architecture, urbanistic character, culture and diversity.[26] The flagship of the Institute is the "Innocent Sorcerers" Warsaw Festival which has taken place in November every year since 2006. The Warsaw Rising Museum also became a cultural producer – it has issued more than ten music albums, dozens of books and even two feature films.[27]

In the years 2004–2019, the Warsaw Rising Museum was among the most popular and most attractive cultural institutions in Poland. In that period, there was never a significant decrease in audience, in 2019 reaching 754,102 visitors of exhibitions and events organized by the Museum, of which 517,802 had visited the permanent exhibition in the main hall.[28] Temporary exhibitions abroad were seen by 241,133 people. The museum organized 1,267 lessons for students of all ages (from initial years of primary schools to high schools) with an audience of 30,983 people.[29]

The ignitor did its job. The Warsaw Rising Museum and its success have encouraged other local governments as well as the Ministry of Culture to create more museums that adopt similar methodologies of presentation.

The Boom

The Warsaw Rising Museum was opened just three months after Poland's accession to the European Union. It proved that large investments in culture were not only possible but also profitable. After joining the EU, the financial possibilities in Poland increased, as European funds were available and the country's economy was developing rapidly. Both local and central authorities have appreciated the social impact of the museums[30] (and – more broadly – of the institutions of culture) as well as their positive impact on the city's or region's trademark and attractiveness for tourists.[31]

An idea for establishing a museum devoted to the history of Polish Jews had emerged even prior to the project of the Warsaw Rising Museum. The direct incentive for the concept came from the opening of the United States Holocaust Memorial Museum in Washington, D.C. in 1993. It inspired the Association of the Jewish Historical Institute of Poland to propose an exhibition which would eventually develop into a museum devoted to the history of Jews in Poland. In 1994, the authorities of the city of Warsaw assigned an area for the future institution – it was to be placed in the heart of the Muranów district where a pre-war Jewish quarter and later the Warsaw ghetto had been located.[32]

The idea of the museum was to present in a narrative way the thousand-year history of Jews in the Polish territories. In the years 2000–2004, Event Communications, a London-based company, prepared the "Masterplan" – the general concept of the exhibition. In 2005, the museum was formally established as an institution curated by three organizations: the Association of the Jewish Historical Institute of Poland, the City of Warsaw and the Ministry of Culture and National Heritage. It was the first museum in Poland to be established on the basis of private-public partnership. In the same year an architectural contest was announced and the proposal by a Finnish architect, Rainer Mahlamäki, was chosen. In 2011, Nizio Design International took over from Event Communications the task of designing and producing the permanent exhibition.[33]

The POLIN Museum opened in 2014.[34] Its aim is to present the multidimensional history of the Jews in the Polish territories. Creators of the exhibition have underlined that their goal was to avoid being limited to a "Shoah museum" only. As they define it: it is "de facto the first 'museum of Polish history' that covers the entire thousand years of Poland's existence," and it is "Polish history told through the prism of Jewish experience, a slanting look from the side, a history of Poland that is not a national history."[35]

From the methodological point of view, it constitutes a typical case of a narrative exhibition, where the story, not the collection, is the starting point. Such a decision was made not only due to trends or the long history to cover, but also due to the lack of artifacts. It is often presented as one of the main factors in the choice of a narrative approach, which itself had started with the Museum of the Jewish People opened in Tel Aviv in 1978.[36]

The general scheme of the permanent exhibition is based on four basic axes outlined in the Masterplan: the Polish and European timeline, turning points, chronological-thematic galleries and galleries of the Jewish cultures.[37] The team of curators has also developed a set of metahistorical rules and narrative methods:

- the most important period in the history of Jews in the Polish territories is the entire millennium;
- the history of the Polish Jews is not a mere footnote to Polish history, but is an integral part;
- the Polish Jews have created (according to Moshe Rosman) a culture "definitely Jewish and distinctly Polish;"
- a broad spectrum of mutual relations should be presented that should contain: coexistence and rivalry, conflicts and cooperation, separation and integration;
- "defensive history" should be avoided;
- historical apologetics should be abandoned;
- teleology of the Shoah (conviction that the Holocaust was an inevitable end of Polish Jews) should be avoided;
- "materialization" of history has to be addressed in the face of the lack of original items.[38]

From the beginning, the POLIN Museum enjoyed recognition and popularity in Warsaw. In the first five years (2014–2019) after the opening, its audience reached 1.8 million visitors of the core exhibition with dozens of thousands of visitors to each temporary exhibition prepared in the museum. In 2019, it organized 1,330 workshops for pupils reaching approximately 30,000 participants. It also became a cultural center, offering a broad variety of activities – music, literature, theatre plays, movies, etc.[39]

The most important social action of the museum is the Daffodils Campaign, held annually on the anniversary of the Warsaw Ghetto Uprising. The first edition was organized before the museum opening, in 2013, in cooperation with the Warsaw Rising Museum.[40] In the seventh edition, in 2019, 2,500 volunteers distributed 150,000 paper daffodils in the streets of Warsaw. The campaign was joined by 1,200 schools and libraries from all over Poland.[41] What is even more important, the campaign created a well-recognized symbol of the Ghetto Uprising, the daffodil – a bunch of these flowers were laid every year under the Monument to the Ghetto Heroes by Marek Edelman, one of the Warsaw Ghetto Uprising commanders.[42]

Another strong museum center emerged in Gdańsk, or more broadly – the Tri-City metropolitan area on the Baltic Sea coast, including the cities of Gdańsk, Gdynia and Sopot. In the short period of 2014–2017, three museums were opened there – the European Solidarity Centre (*Europejskie Centrum Solidarności*, ECS) in Gdańsk (2014), [43] the Emigration Museum in Gdynia (2015) [44] and the Museum of the Second World War in Gdańsk (2017).[45]

The first idea to commemorate the unique role of the Solidarity movement in the process of the dissolution of the communist regime and the
collapse of the bipolar world came in the late 1990s. Initially, it was an
unspecified concept of a rather conservative museum, however, in the following years, marked by the opening of the Warsaw Rising Museum, it
evolved towards a more complex center that would both commemorate
the recent past and help build a contemporary culture of democracy. The
new institution of ECS was established in November 2007 in cooperation
with the city of Gdańsk, the Pomerania voivodship, the Ministry of Culture
and National Heritage, the Solidarity trade union and the Foundation
Solidarity Centre.[46]

The seat of the museum was placed in the former Gdańsk Shipyard area,
the historical location where the Solidarity movement had emerged in 1980.
It is located in a newly constructed building, designed by the FORT architectural studio – a rusty, modern facility, which refers to the industrial history of the neighborhood.[47] Only within recent years has the neighborhood
changed, since the whole area has become visited as a kind of a cultural
center. Its historical value was appreciated and in December 2017, after a
decision of the General Conservator of Heritage, Prof. Magdalena Gawin,
it has been listed on the national heritage register.[48]

When creating the exhibition, the Centre's team referred to the ongoing
debate of whether to focus on artifacts or on photographs, films and multimedia in the narrative line of the museum. It was decided that a "middle
way" would be the best solution, and therefore each of the seven main chapters of the exhibition has its own language of communication. While the
first hall, covering the story of the mass strikes in August 1980 is based on
exhibits, including the original table with the 21 demands of the workers on
strike (listed on the UNESCO heritage list), the sixth one, devoted to the
revolutions of 1989 in other countries of Central Europe, uses multimedia
almost exclusively.[49]

Similar to other newly established museums, the European Solidarity Centre also does not focus on the exhibitions only. As its director, Basil Kerski,
stresses: "it is also a centre for dialogue regarding the modern world. ECS
is a place where history meets the future, in line with our mission: 'Learn
from history, and decide upon the future'."[50] During the first five years of
its functioning, the Centre had 4,342,099 visitors, of whom 1,003,028 visited
the permanent exhibition.[51] Those numbers, of which less than a quarter of
the audience goes to the main exhibition, have proven a mass participation
in other events organized by the Centre.

In parallel with the ECS, the Museum of the Second World War was being
prepared. Its creators from the very beginning stressed the complementarity
of both institutions, as well as the complementarity of their project with
other newly established Polish museums. They assumed that the emerging
European Solidarity Centre would: "present not only the history of the
Solidarity movement, but also other opposition movements in Poland and

East-Central Europe and to some extent also the history of communism."
Thus, they stated that the Museum of the Second World War did not need
to include the post-war period in its exhibition as "where the narrative line
of the Museum of the Second World War ends, it will be taken on by the
European Solidarity Centre."[52] They also declared that some aspects of the
war itself might be presented only briefly, as they constituted the core of
exhibitions of other museums.

The museum was formally established on September 1, 2008 by Prime Minister Donald Tusk, who appointed his plenipotentiary, Prof. Paweł Machcewicz as the museum's director. The exhibition, which opened in March 2017,
focuses on the fate of people – civilians, soldiers, POWs, inmates of concentration camps or forced labor. The military as well as political dimension of
the war are presented in a very limited way and have been declared by its
creators as supplements to the main axis of the narrative. According to the
creators of the museum, such perspective "brings a deeply pacifist message,"
and should cover five main threads: the total nature of the conflict, everyday
life, ethnic conflicts and cleansings, resistance, and forced migrations.[53]

The concept proposed by Machcewicz and museum's deputy director Piotr
M. Majewski opened a heated and emotional debate, which also raised criticism, mostly concerning "not considering the Polish perspective," and the
limited presentation of the political, military and diplomatic part of the story.
The conflict moved to the political level and resulted in a merge of the Museum
of the Second World War with Westerplatte and the War of 1939 Museum,
which was a formal opportunity to dismiss Paweł Machcewicz from the post
of director. On April 6, 2017 (soon after the opening of the museum), he was
replaced by Karol Nawrocki. The new director started to introduce changes
in the exhibition which became the subject of a lawsuit from predecessors.
The court decided that one out of 17 changes should be reversed.[54]

Changes introduced by the new leadership, although raising a lot of emotions, did not alter the exhibition substantially, they were rather amend-
ments to the narrative line. The museum is eagerly visited – in 2019, the main
exhibition's audience reached 487,674 people, about 10,000 pupils participated in 446 lessons and dozens of events are held every year.[55]

The last of the "big five," the Polish History Museum, was still under
construction in the spring of 2021. The first idea came in 2000, and it was
later developed as a concept of the Museum of Freedom, but the institution was finally established in 2006 under the name of Polish History Museum.[56] Three main threads were defined being as most important for the
Museum: the history of Polish freedom (both independence of the Polish
state and political freedom within Poland), identity and its changes (starting
with the baptism of a Slavic country of Polans in the tenth century, through
the republic of many nations and religions, up to contemporary national
consciousness), and everyday life with economic and social changes in the
Polish territory.[57]

Robert Kostro, the director of the museum defined three main challenges for the creators of the main exhibition to overcome:

- The size and the scale of the project. The exhibition must cover more than 1,050 years of history, the story without a "one-way dramaturgy" that includes both dynamic moments and less intensive everyday life, or intellectual debates which are hard to visualize. Therefore, it cannot present one linear story with an introduction, development and conclusion. Instead, it must present many different narrative lines.
- The diversity of the collection needed and the difficulties with gathering it. While trying to keep the balance between objects, scenography and multimedia, the museum has attempted to collect exhibits to fill the future exhibition. This has been done in cooperation with many institutions, through both purchases and acquisition of memorabilia from individuals.
- Diversity of expectations and numerous controversies over Polish history. The aim of the museum is to be a meeting place and a center of dialogue, therefore it cooperates with experts from different environments, preparing an exhibition that would not be a "didactic reader," but rather a story to open new horizons. Contrary to common stereotypes, history does not cause division, and objects and sources are not controversial.[58]

The exhibition will be organized into six galleries: Poland of the Piasts and the Jagiellonians (from the beginning of the state to 1573), the Old Republic (1573–1795), Under the Partitions (1796–1914), Independent Poland (1914–1939), Fighting Poland (1939–1945) and Poles against communism (1945–1990).[59] Construction work started on July 6, 2018[60] and the opening of the permanent exhibition is expected in spring 2023.[61]

Aware of potential difficulties on different levels, the leadership of the museum decided to be active in numerous fields from the very beginning. Multiple temporary exhibitions were organized in attractive locations both in Poland and abroad, which gathered a large audience and received several awards. Educational projects, research and international cooperation have been developed. All these experiences are useful in the process of the preparation of the main site and permanent exhibition.[62]

Conclusions

The museums presented in this chapter are only the "tip of the iceberg," taking into consideration the rapid development of this sector of Polish museology. Some other important institutions that were established after 2004 should be mentioned here: the new exhibition of the Chopin Museum in Warsaw (2010), Rynek (Marketplace) Underground in Kraków (2010),

Oskar Schindler's Enamel Factory (2010), the new exhibition of the John Paul II Museum in Wadowice (2014), the Emigration Museum in Gdynia (2015), the new site and exhibition of the Silesian Museum in Katowice (2015), the permanent exhibition "Wrocław 1945–2016" in the Depot History Centre in Wrocław (2016), the Ulma Family Museum of Poles Saving Jews in World War II in Markowa (2016), the Pan Tadeusz Museum of National Ossoliński Institute in Wrocław (2016) and the Centre of Dialogue Upheavals in Szczecin (2016).

The opening of the Warsaw Rising Museum introduced a new type of a museum and exhibitions, thus changing the previous attitude to historical museums in Poland. The notions of a "narrative museum" or "interactive museum" were newly introduced into the public debate, resulting not only in a desire to follow the Warsaw Rising Museum's pattern, but also to use the same categories in other emerging projects. It has caused an extension of the semantic meaning of those notions as well as intensive discourse among specialists of different fields on their essence. Various definitions,[63] theories and counter-theories appear and arguments around them are heated at times.[64]

As well, the content of particular exhibitions is a matter for numerous debates and even quarrels. The dispute, sometimes very emotional, is ongoing on several levels, engaging experts, intellectuals, journalists and politicians. The political dimension of the argument is the most controversial and raises the most criticism. As Paweł Kowal has rightly noted, historical museums are separated from politics by only the shortest distance, and while they would never have been created without politicians and their democratic decisions, politicians' influence on them can lead to the shifting of political conflicts to museums,[65] as has happened in several situations. The case of the Museum of the Second World War was probably the most spectacular, but it is not the only one. In 2007, the then Speaker of Sejm (lower chamber of the Polish parliament), Bronisław Komorowski, tried to force Jan Ołdakowski, director of the Warsaw Rising Museum, to resign – otherwise he claimed that his parliamentary mandate would be terminated. However, in the end, Komorowski decided not to fulfil his threat.[66] In 2019, the Minister of Culture and National Heritage, Deputy Prime Minister Prof. Piotr Gliński, did not appoint Prof. Dariusz Stola for a second term as director of the POLIN Museum, although Stola had won the competition for the post. Gliński accused him of engaging in politics.[67] Political decisions also influenced delays in the development of the Polish History Museum.

Modern historical museums arouse both public interest and heated debates. The museum boom was visible for 15 years (2004–2019). However, the coronavirus pandemic has changed the rules – museums were closed for months and could not reach the "pre-pandemic" numbers of visitors in the periods when they could be open. Will this be a long-term change? Only time will tell.

Notes

1 According to a survey, in 2019, the Warsaw Rising Museum was declared to be among the main sights and attractions of Warsaw by 37% of domestic and 36% of foreign tourists. It also ranked third among the largest tourist attractions among domestic visitors – 21% of them indicated the Warsaw Rising Museum. Cf. *Tourism in Warsaw. Report 2019*, 18, accessed February 3, 2021, https://mediabank. warsawtour.pl/documents/1098.
2 Cf. Paweł Ukielski, "Warsaw Rising Museum – on, with and for Participatory Public," in *Public in Public History*, ed. Joanna Wojdon and Dorota Wiśniewska (New York: Routledge, 2021), 22.
3 Data according to the Main Statistical Office in Poland. Cf. *Kultura w 2019 r./ Culture in 2019* (Warszawa – Kraków: GUS, 2020), 70, accessed February 1, 2021, https://stat.gov.pl/obszary-tematyczne/kultura-turystyka-sport/kultura/kultura-w-2019-roku,2,17.html; *Kultura w 2004 r.*, 129, accessed February 1, 2021, https://stat. gov.pl/obszary-tematyczne/kultura-turystyka-sport/kultura/kultura-w-2004-r-,2,2. html?pdf=1.
4 Ibid.
5 Piotr Majewski, "Słowo wstępne," in *Muzea w Polsce. Raporty na podstawie danych z projektu "Statystyka muzeów" (2013–2015)*, ed. Katarzyna Skomorucha-Figiel and Katarzyna Andrzejkowicz (Warszawa: Narodowy Instytut Muzealnictwa i Ochrony Zbiorów, 2016), 9.
6 Robert Traba, "Epoka muzeów? Muzeum jako medium, muzeum jako mediator," in *I Kongres Muzealników Polskich*, ed. Michał Wysocki (Warszawa: Narodowe Centrum Kultury, 2015), 47.
7 Paweł Kowal, "Społeczny, cywilizacyjny i polityczny kontekst polskiego *boomu* muzealnego," in *Muzeum i zmiana. Losy muzeów narracyjnych*, ed. Paweł Kowal and Karolina Wolska-Pabian (Warszawa – Kraków: Universitas and Muzeum Powstania Warszawskiego, 2019), 43.
8 Peter Vergo, *Introduction to The New Museology* (Chicago: Reaction Books, 1989).
9 Kowal, "Społeczny," 37.
10 Dorota Folga-Januszewska, "Muzea w Polsce 1989–2008," *Muzealnictwo* 50 (2009): 29.
11 Monika Heinemann, „Między Wschodem a Zachodem: pytanie o specyfikę narracji muzealnej w Europie Środkowej i Wschodniej," in *Historia Polski od-nowa. Nowe narracje historii i muzealne reprezentacje przeszłości*, ed. Robert Kostro, Kazimierz Wóycicki and Michał Wysocki (Warszawa: Muzeum Historii Polski, 2014), 46–47.
12 Kowal, "Społeczny," 33–36. For details see the chapter by Łukasz Kamiński in this volume.
13 Paweł Ukielski, "Koniec 'końca historii.' Muzea narracyjne w nowym myśleniu o przeszłości," in *Muzeum i zmiana*, 80.
14 Ukielski, „Koniec," 84.
15 Cf. Wojciech Materski, *Od cara do „cara." Studium rosyjskiej polityki historycznej* (Warszawa: ISP PAN, 2017), 235–300.
16 Cf. Jan Rydel, *Polityka historyczna w Republice Federalnej Niemiec. Zaszłości, idee, praktyka* (Kraków: Wydawnictwo Naukowe Uniwersytetu Pedagogicznego, 2011), 251–284.
17 Some information in this chapter is based on the author's memory, as the author was a member of the preparatory team and has been deputy director since the very beginning of the Warsaw Rising Museum.
18 More about the prior attempts to create the museum: Paweł Ukielski, "Historia pewnego muzeum," *Mówią Wieki*, Special issue 1 (2006): 68–71.

62   *Paweł Ukielski*

19 Ukielski, "Koniec," 85.
20 More on the topic of the public in the Warsaw Rising Museum: Ukielski, "Warsaw Rising Museum," 21–39.
21 Jan Ołdakowski and Paweł Kowal, in cooperation with Joanna Bojarska and Lena Dąbkowska-Cichocka, "Podstawowe założenia programowe i organizacyjne Muzeum Powstania Warszawskiego w Warszawie ul. Przyokopowa 28" (Warszawa, 2003), 9; in the author's collection.
22 *Polityka historyczna. Historycy – politycy – prasa,* ed. Agnieszka Panecka (Warszawa: Muzeum Powstania Warszawskiego, 2005), 272.
23 Ukielski, "Warsaw Rising Museum," 26–28.
24 *Księga prasowa Muzeum Powstania Warszawskiego,* vol. II, ed. Anna Kotonowicz, Marcin Roszkowski and Ewa Ziółkowska (Warszawa: Muzeum Powstania Warszawskiego, 2004).
25 Jan Ołdakowski, "Dlaczego powstają muzea historyczne narracyjne," in *Muzeum i zmiana,* 74.
26 "Oddziały Muzeum," Warsaw Rising Museum, last modified July 28, 2020, accessed August 27, 2020, https://www.1944.pl/artykul/oddzialy-muzeum,4515.html.
27 For more about the cultural activity of the Warsaw Rising Museum see Ukielski, "Warsaw Rising Museum," 30–31; Karolina Wolska-Pabian, "Nowe zadania muzeów narracyjnych na przykładzie Muzeum Powstania Warszawskiego," in *Muzeum i zmiana,* 97–100.
28 I present data for 2019, as numbers from 2020 are non-representative due to the COVID-19 pandemic.
29 All data is according to the annual report for 2019, in author's collection.
30 The above can be illustrated with an anecdote: two former mayors of Warsaw, Paweł Piskorski and Wojciech Kozak, were present at the solemn opening of the Warsaw Rising Museum. Looking at the crowd and feeling the atmosphere, Piskorski asked Kozak: "Wojtek, actually, why didn't we do this?" Piotr Legutko, *Jedyne takie muzeum. Odzyskana pamięć o Powstaniu Warszawskim* (Kraków: Znak, 2014), 151–152.
31 Basil Kerski, „Europejskie Centrum Solidarności (ECS) w Gdańsku. Muzeum Solidarności w połączeniu z instytucją wspierającą kulturę obywatelską," in *Muzeum i zmiana,* 121.
32 Barbara Kirshenblatt-Gimblett, "Inscenizowanie historii. Muzeum Historii Żydów Polskich Polin," in *Muzeum i zmiana,* 103.
33 Ibid., 103–104.
34 POLIN Museum of the History of Polish Jews, accessed February 21, 2021, https://polin.pl/en.
35 Kirshenblatt-Gimblett, "Inscenizowanie historii," 105.
36 Heinemann, "Między Wschodem," 47–48.
37 Kirshenblatt-Gimblett, "Inscenizowanie historii," 107–111.
38 Ibid., 111–113.
39 All data taken from: *POLIN Museum of the History of Polish Jews. Annual Report 2019* (Warsaw: POLIN, 2020); accessed February 21, 2021, https://www.polin.pl/system/files/attachments/RAPORT_POLIN_2019_final_WEB_22.07.2020.pdf.
40 "Zostań Wolontariuszem dwóch muzeów na czas obchodów 70. rocznicy Powstania w Getcie Warszawskim," Warsaw Rising Museum, last modified February 6, 2013, accessed February 21, 2021, https://www.1944.pl/artykul/zostan-wolontariuszem-dwoch-muzeow-na-czas-ob,3810.html.
41 *POLIN Museum of the History of Polish Jews. Annual Report 2019,* 40.
42 "Zostań Wolontariuszem."
43 European Solidarity Centre, accessed February 21, 2021, https://www.ecs.gda.pl/.

44 The Emigration Museum, accessed February 21, 2021, https://polska1.pl/en/home/.
45 Museum of the Second World War, accessed February 21, 2021, https://muzeum1939.pl/en.
46 Kerski, "Europejskie Centrum," 121–122.
47 Ibid., 122. Cf. Wojciech Targowski, "Architecture of the European Solidarity Centre Building," in *European Solidarity Centre Permanent Exhibition. Catalogue*, ed. Basil Kerski, Konrad Knoch, Jacek Kołtan and Paweł Golak (Gdańsk: ECS, 2015), 252–255.
48 "Historyczny zespół budowlany Stoczni Gdańskiej trafił do rejestru zabytków. To decyzja MKiDN!," *Gdańsk Nasze Miasto*, last modified, December, 14, 2017, accessed February 25, 2021, https://gdansk.naszemiasto.pl/historyczny-zespol-budowlany-stoczni-gdanskiej-trafil-do/ar/c1-4346925.
49 Kerski, „Europejskie Centrum," 122–123.
50 Basil Kerski, "European Solidarity Centre – a Meeting-Place for Citizens," in *European Solidarity Centre permanent exhibition*, 251.
51 "Raport roczny 2019," European Solidarity Centre, accessed February 26, 2021, https://ecs.gda.pl/library/File/media/ECSRAPORTROCZNY_2019.pdf
52 Paweł Machcewicz and Piotr M. Majewski, "Muzeum II Wojny Światowej. Zarys koncepcji programowej," in *Przegląd Polityczny* 91/92 (2008): 46.
53 Ibid., 48–50.
54 Jacek Wierciński, "Wyrok w sprawie zmian w wystawie Muzeum II Wojny Światowej. Obie strony twierdzą, że wygrały," *Dziennik Bałtycki*, October 15, 2020, accessed March 2, 2021, https://dziennikbaltycki.pl/wyrok-w-sprawie-zmian-w-wystawie-muzeum-ii-wojny-swiatowej-obie-strony-twierdza-ze-wygraly/ar/c1-15237433.
55 *Raport z działalności Muzeum II Wojny Światowej w Gdańsku za rok 2019* (Gdańsk: Muzeum II Wojny Światowej, 2020), 41, 61, accessed March 2, 2021, https://muzeum1939.pl/u/pdf/6dabc4785bbd57523d4f97357870749613779.pdf.
56 Robert Kostro, "Doświadczenie Muzeum Historii Polski," in *Muzeum i zmiana*, 126.
57 Ibid., 127.
58 Ibid., 128–129.
59 Muzeum Historii Polski, "Wystawa stała," accessed March 2, 2021, https://muzhp.pl/pl/c/2388/wystawa-stala
60 Muzeum Historii Polski, "Siedziba," accessed March 2, 2021, https://muzhp.pl/pl/c/1141/siedziba
61 Robert Kostro, "Program działania Muzeum Historii Polski w Warszawie na lata 2021-2027," 3, accessed March 2, 2021, https://bip.mkidn.gov.pl/media/docs/programy%20inst/20201221_Program%20dzia%c5%82ania%20MHP%20-%20akcept%20MKDNiS.pdf
62 Kostro, "Doświadczenie Muzeum Historii Polski," 127.
63 Cf. Paweł Kowal and Dorota Folga-Januszewska, "Definicja muzeum narracyjnego," in *Muzeum i zmiana*, 49–50.
64 Cf. Maria Kobielska, "Muzeum narracyjne – muzeum doświadczeniowe. Uwagi terminologiczne," *Teksty Drugie* no. 4 (2020): 15–36; and the chapter by Anna Ziębińska-Witek in this volume.
65 Kowal, "Społeczny," 32.
66 Iwona Szpala, "Komorowski odpuszcza Ołdakowskiemu," *Gazeta Wyborcza*, November 13, 2007.
67 "Gliński tłumaczy, dlaczego nie powołał Stoli na dyrektora Muzeum POLIN. 'Prowadził agresywną politykę,'" Gazeta.pl, accessed March 5, 2021, https://wiadomosci.gazeta.pl/wiadomosci/7,114884,25230855,glinski-tlumaczy-dlaczego-nie-powolal-stoli-na-dyrektora-muzeum.html.

64   *Paweł Ukielski*

Bibliography

"European Solidarity Centre. Accessed February 21, 2021. https://www.ecs.gda.pl/

Folga-Januszewska, Dorota. "Muzea w Polsce 1989–2008." *Muzealnictwo* 50 (2009): 18–46.

"Gliński tłumaczy, dlaczego nie powołał Stoli na dyrektora Muzeum POLIN. 'Prowadził agresywną politykę.'" *Gazeta.pl.* Accessed March 5, 2021. https://wiadomosci.gazeta.pl/wiadomosci/7,114884,25230855,glinski-tlumaczy-dlaczego-nie-powolal-stoli-na-dyrektora-muzeum.html

Heinemann, Monika. "Między Wschodem a Zachodem: pytanie o specyfikę narracji muzealnej w Europie Środkowej i Wschodniej." In *Historia Polski od-nowa. Nowe narracje historii i muzealne reprezentacje przeszłości*, edited by Robert Kostro, Kazimierz Wóycicki and Michał Wysocki, 45–56. Warszawa: Muzeum Historii Polski, 2014.

Kerski, Basil. "European Solidarity Centre – A Meeting-Place for Citizens." In *European Solidarity Centre Permanent Exhibition. Catalogue*, edited by Basil Kerski, Konrad Knoch, Jacek Kołtan and Paweł Golak, 250–251. Gdańsk: ECS, 2015.

Kerski, Basil. "Europejskie Centrum Solidarności (ECS) w Gdańsku. Muzeum Solidarności w połączeniu z instytucją wspierającą kulturę obywatelską." In *Muzeum i zmiana. Losy muzeów narracyjnych*, edited by Paweł Kowal and Karolina Wolska-Pabian, 117–124. Warszawa – Kraków: Universitas and Muzeum Powstania Warszawskiego, 2019.

Kirshenblatt-Gimblett, Barbara. "Inscenizowanie historii. Muzeum Historii Żydów Polskich Polin." In *Muzeum i zmiana. Losy muzeów narracyjnych*, edited by Paweł Kowal and Karolina Wolska-Pabian, 101–116. Warszawa – Kraków: Universitas and Muzeum Powstania Warszawskiego, 2019.

Kobielska, Maria. "Muzeum narracyjne – muzeum doświadczeniowe. Uwagi terminologiczne." *Teksty Drugie* no. 4 (2020): 15–36.

Kostro, Robert. "Doświadczenie Muzeum Historii Polski." In *Muzeum i zmiana. Losy muzeów narracyjnych*, edited by Paweł Kowal and Karolina Wolska-Pabian, 125–130. Warszawa – Kraków: Universitas and Muzeum Powstania Warszawskiego, 2019.

Kostro, Robert. "Program działania Muzeum Historii Polski w Warszawie na lata 2021–2027." Accessed March 2, 2021. https://bip.mkidn.gov.pl/media/docs/programy%20inst/20201221_Program%20dzia%c5%82ania%20MHP%20-%20akcept%20MKDNiS.pdf

Kotonowicz, Anna, Marcin Roszkowski and Ewa Ziółkowska, eds. *Księga prasowa Muzeum Powstania Warszawskiego*, vol. II. Warszawa: Muzeum Powstania Warszawskiego, 2004.

Kowal, Paweł. "Społeczny, cywilizacyjny i polityczny kontekst polskiego *boomu* muzealnego." In *Muzeum i zmiana. Losy muzeów narracyjnych*, edited by Paweł Kowal and Karolina Wolska-Pabian, 31–48. Warszawa – Kraków: Universitas and Muzeum Powstania Warszawskiego, 2019.

Kowal, Paweł and Dorota Folga-Januszewska. "Definicja muzeum narracyjnego." In *Muzeum i zmiana. Losy muzeów narracyjnych*, edited by Paweł Kowal and Karolina Wolska-Pabian, 49–50. Warszawa – Kraków: Universitas and Muzeum Powstania Warszawskiego, 2019.

Kultura w 2004 r. Accessed February 1, 2021. https://stat.gov.pl/obszary-tematyczne/kultura-turystyka-sport/kultura/kultura-w-2004-r-, 2,2.html?pdf=1

Kultura w 2019 r./Culture in 2019, Warszawa – Kraków 2020. Accessed February 1, 2021. https://stat.gov.pl/obszary-tematyczne/kultura-turystyka-sport/kultura/kultura-w-2019-roku, 2,17.html

Legutko, Piotr. *Jedyne takie Muzeum. Odzyskana Pamięć o Powstaniu Warszawskim.* Kraków: Znak, 2014.

Machcewicz, Paweł and Piotr M. Majewski. "Muzeum II Wojny Światowej. Zarys koncepcji programowej." *Przegląd Polityczny* no. 91/92 (2008): 46–51.

Majewski, Piotr. "Słowo wstępne." In *Muzea w Polsce. Raporty na podstawie danych z projektu „Statystyka muzeów" (2013–2015)*, edited by Katarzyna Skomorucha-Figiel and Katarzyna Andrzejkowicz, 9–10. Warszawa: Narodowy Instytut Muzealnictwa i Ochrony Zbiorów, 2016.

Materski, Wojciech. *Od cara do „cara." Studium rosyjskiej polityki historycznej.* Warszawa: Instytut Studiów Politycznych Polskiej Akademii Nauk, 2017.

Museum of the Second World War. Accessed February 21, 2021. https://muzeum1939.pl/en

Muzeum Historii Polski. "Siedziba." Accessed March 2, 2021. https://muzhp.pl/pl/c/1141/siedziba

Muzeum Historii Polski. "Wystawa stała." Accessed March 2, 2021. https://muzhp.pl/pl/c/2388/wystawa-stala

Ołdakowski, Jan. "Dlaczego powstają muzea historyczne narracyjne." In *Muzeum i zmiana. Losy muzeów narracyjnych*, edited by Paweł Kowal and Karolina Wolska-Pabian, 73–78. Warszawa – Kraków: Universitas and Muzeum Powstania Warszawskiego, 2019.

Ołdakowski, Jan and Paweł Kowal, in cooperation with Joanna Bojarska and Lena Dąbkowska-Cichocka, "Podstawowe założenia programowe i organizacyjne Muzeum Powstania Warszawskiego w Warszawie ul. Przyokopowa 28." Warszawa, 2003 (in author's collection).

Panecka, Agnieszka, ed. *Polityka historyczna. Historycy – politycy – prasa.* Warszawa: Muzeum Powstania Warszawskiego, 2005.

POLIN Museum of the History of Polish Jews. Accessed February 21, 2021. https://polin.pl/en

POLIN Museum of the History of Polish Jews. Annual Report 2019. Warszawa: POLIN, 2020. Accessed February 21, 2021. https://www.polin.pl/system/files/attachments/RAPORT_POLIN_2019_final_WEB_22.07.2020.pdf

Raport z działalności Muzeum II Wojny Światowej w Gdańsku za rok 2019. Gdańsk: Muzeum II Wojny Światowej, 2020. Accessed March 2, 2021. https://muzeum1939.pl/u/pdf/6dabc4785bbd57523d4f973578770749613779.pdf

"Raport roczny 2019." European Solidarity Centre. Accessed February 26, 2021. https://ecs.gda.pl/library/File/media/ECSRAPORTROCZNY_2019.pdf

Rydel, Jan. *Polityka historyczna w Republice Federalnej Niemiec. Zaszłości, idee, praktyka.* Kraków: Wydawnictwo Naukowe Uniwersytetu Pedagogicznego, 2011.

Szpala, Iwona. "Komorowski odpuszcza Ołdakowskiemu." *Gazeta Wyborcza*, November 13, 2007.

Targowski, Wojciech. "Architecture of the European Solidarity Centre Building." In *European Solidarity Centre permanent exhibition. Catalogue*, edited by Basil Kerski, Konrad Knoch, Jacek Kołtan and Paweł Golak, 252–255. Gdańsk: ECS, 2015.

The Emigration Museum. Accessed February 21, 2021. https://polska1.pl/en/home/

Tourism in Warsaw. Report 2019, 18. Accessed February 3, 2021. https://mediabank. warsawtour.pl/documents/1098.

Traba, Robert. "Epoka muzeów? Muzeum jako medium, muzeum jako mediator." In *I Kongres Muzealników Polskich*, edited by Michał Wysocki, 47–56. Warszawa: NCK, 2015.

Ukielski, Paweł. "Historia pewnego muzeum." *Mówią wieki*, special issue 1 (2006): 68–71.

Ukielski, Paweł. "Koniec 'końca historii'. Muzea narracyjne w nowym myśleniu o przeszłości." In *Muzeum i zmiana. Losy muzeów narracyjnych*, edited by Paweł Kowal and Karolina Wolska-Pabian, 79–90. Warszawa – Kraków: Universitas and Muzeum Powstania Warszawskiego, 2019.

Ukielski, Paweł. "Warsaw Rising Museum – on, with and for Participatory Public." In *Public in Public History*, edited by Joanna Wojdon and Dorota Wiśniewska, 21–39. New York: Routledge, 2021.

Vergo, Peter. *Introduction to the New Museology*. Chicago: Reaction Books, 1989.

Warsaw Rising Museum. "Oddziały Muzeum," last modified July 28, 2020. Accessed August 27, 2020. https://www.1944.pl/artykul/oddzialy-muzeum, 4515.html.

Warsaw Rising Museum. "Zostań Wolontariuszem dwóch muzeów na czas obchodów 70. rocznicy Powstania w Getcie Warszawskim," last modified February 6, 2013. Accessed February 21, 2021. https://www.1944.pl/artykul/zostan-wolontariuszem-dwoch-muzeow-na-czas-ob, 3810.html

Wierciński, Jacek. "Wyrok w sprawie zmian w wystawie Muzeum II Wojny Światowej. Obie strony twierdzą, że wygrały." *Dziennik Bałtycki*, October 15, 2020. Accessed March 2, 2021. https://dziennikbaltycki.pl/wyrok-w-sprawie-zmian-w-wystawie-muzeum-ii-wojny-swiatowej-obie-strony-twierdza-ze-wygraly/ar/c1-15237433

Wolska-Pabian, Karolina. "Nowe zadania muzeów narracyjnych na przykładzie Muzeum Powstania Warszawskiego." In *Muzeum i zmiana. Losy muzeów narracyjnych*, edited by Paweł Kowal and Karolina Wolska-Pabian, 91–100. Warszawa – Kraków: Universitas and Muzeum Powstania Warszawskiego, 2019.

4 Polish Historical Museums and Challenges of the Twenty-First Century

Anna Ziębińska-Witek

A quarter of a century after the collapse of communism, the societies of Central and Eastern Europe still have greater needs than the stable Western societies regarding self-identification and creation of integrative narratives, and therefore the presence of history in the public domain is very pronounced in this region. The function of legitimizing and interpreting the past for the museum public is performed among others by museums that shape the collective memory and historical consciousness of postcommunist national communities. I understand collective memory as ideas of their past shared by members of a social group while historical consciousness is an effective value-filled historical knowledge functioning within a given social group.[1]

In this context, historical exhibitions are representations of the past, since the range of their impact is far greater than cognitive, emotional or esthetic, but they also create meanings and guide the understanding of the represented historical phenomena and processes. It is at exhibitions, as part of the chronological and teleological narrative, that the difficult and inconvenient past is reworked in order to satisfy the contemporary needs for sense and orientation in the complex present, to evoke pride in one's own heritage as well as to present one's exceptional uniqueness.[2]

The Polish museum boom began after the political-system transformation, but the best conditions for this flourishing emerged only after 2004, when Poland's entry into the European Union and economic development enabled the implementation of new museum projects and applications for additional grants and funds. This coincided with a change in thinking about history and its use to shape a desired collective consciousness and remembrance. Directly after 1989, the state adopted a neutral stance with regard to shaping the historical consciousness of the Poles.[3] At the turn of the century, particularly in 2005–2007 and after 2015, when the rightist Law and Justice (*Prawo i Sprawiedliwość*) party assumed power, the liberal model gave way to conservative thinking. In the first place, criticism was leveled at the liberal assumption that the state should not be officially involved in promoting knowledge about historical events; instead, it was recognized that policymakers should openly support and develop patriotic attitudes.

DOI: 10.4324/9781003165767-6

This entailed the rejection of the critical examination of national history (the critical attitude was termed "the pedagogy of shame") and promoting instead a positive image of the community both in international contacts and for internal political purposes. With this change, a strong need appeared to discipline the narrative of the past in the public sphere.

Polish historical museums established after the political transformation are mainly strongly identity-based romantic-heroic exhibitions (e.g. the Warsaw Rising Museum in Warsaw, or the European Solidarity Center in Gdańsk). They also include the museums that clearly manipulate the past for short-term political purposes (e.g. the Ulma Family Museum in Markowa). Nevertheless, two critical museums were established, entirely consistent with the advanced trends in world museum practice (the POLIN Museum of the History of Polish Jews and the Museum of the Second World War in Gdańsk). All the above-mentioned institutions adapted to changes both with regard to museum architecture (new buildings are the result of international tenders participated in by architects from all over the world or are created through the revitalization of post-industrial structures) and to exhibition strategies.

The first signs of changes in the traditional art of exhibition appeared in Poland with the concept of "new museology," known in the West since the 1980s. The classic texts by Peter Vergo, Mieke Bal and Carol Duncan (with comments) were translated and introduced into general circulation in 2005.[4] Extremely significant in the context of popularizing the "new museology" was the work of Piotr Piotrowski (2011),[5] who, on the basis of new theories, created the concept of the critical museum as the third type of museum (alongside the museum-temple and museum-forum[6]). It would be open to the politico-social context, overtly involved in the problems of contemporary reality and its exhibitions would take controversial issues and problems of excluded groups into consideration. However, these assumptions were successfully implemented only to a negligible extent.

In Polish (as in the world) historical exhibitions, the category of "experience" spread, the main goal of "modern" exhibitions being to produce one. This was followed by the reconceptualization of the idea of authenticity. Original objects receded into the background, thus becoming mere tools to evoke emotional involvement as a priority and subjective experience. It was this effect rather than a historically legitimated artifact that became a "genuine thing" that museums wanted to have.[7]

Based on this foundation, the new Polish history museums widely adopted an exhibition model, termed narrative or interpretive, which meant the departure from exhibits (artifacts) occupying the central position towards constructing consistent narratives about the past. This freed the curators from limitations imposed by the lack of objects and gave them a powerful tool to mold historical consciousness. The term "interpretive" is misleading, however. Such exhibitions are not concerned with research oriented towards interpreting the past; they simply present a specific interpretation. I call them "fictionalized," because the construction is essentially based on the creation of an interesting story with underlying, selected historical facts. The emotional force of such narrative can be compared with the emotions evoked by a novel or film, which involves the process of projection-identification.[8] The change of exhibition strategies evolving towards the theatrical, the performative and the interactive, achieved through multimedia and simulation technologies, does not necessarily result in a pioneering character of the content of the newly emerging museum institutions. Technologically advanced solutions are no guarantee of the modernity of the whole exhibition, as they may as easily strengthen the well-known and tradition-rooted visions of the past, conceal ideological commitment or use old metaphors.

The Warsaw Rising Museum in Warsaw

The first and best known implementation of the narrative paradigm is the Warsaw Rising Museum (*Muzeum Powstania Warszawskiego*, MPW), opened on July 31, 2004. The exhibition is entirely devoted to the Home Army's insurrection against the German occupiers of Warsaw and (politically) against the Soviet Union. The operation that lasted from August 1 to October 2, 1944 ended in a spectacular defeat and the destruction of Warsaw; nevertheless, the uprising came to be regarded by many as one of the major events in Poland's history.[9] The Warsaw Rising Museum located in the revitalized building of the Warsaw power plant is one of the first in Poland to have abandoned the traditional treatment of artifacts in favor of paratheatrical forms, copies, sceneries and technologically advanced multimedia installations. The museum space, quiet and silent not long ago, was filled with sounds, monitors, objects, voices of witnesses and experimental installations, which ultimately produced an impression of a spectacular extravaganza very distant from the recently dominant practice of display cases full of original exhibits. The theatralization of the exhibition space enabled an entirely new contact with the past rather than reading an objectified historical narrative or visiting a (equally objectified) traditional museum exhibition, i.e., objects with captions and documents in glass cabinets. A theatrical performance about historical events was thus produced, a peculiar esthetic adaptation, in which the audience appear in the scenographic space and as in a drama, assume an extremely emotionally engaging role (in this case of actors-witnesses to the event). This modern form hides the shortcomings of the exhibition, however. The exhibition in the Warsaw Rising Museum expresses archaic messianic values and attributes positive qualities to war and suffering, thus belittling or even concealing the human cost of war operations. The audience fail to notice a different perspective of the Warsaw Uprising as one of the most tragic events in Polish history, which ended in defeat and claimed thousands of civilian victims.

The extremely attractive means of expression, however, convey an impression of the modern character of the whole exhibition – practically entirely distant from the tenets of "new museology" that focus on confronting the audience with difficult moments in national history and developing their ability for critical judgment. Instead, the Warsaw Rising Museum is becoming an exponent of Polish politics of memory which, Lech Nijakowski argues, should be perceived as an element of nationalistic processes. The scholar says

> the politics of memory is meant to strengthen one's own identity by reminding one of glorious events, by concealing crimes of the past, inventing traditions from scratch, and demonizing the role of strangers and enemies in history, but also by creating 'perennial' foes. The specificity of politics of memory depends on the cultural and civilization circle as well as on the state itself. On the one hand, the Polish politics of memory has universal characteristics but is very particularistic on the other, connected with the history of a nation that was under the yoke of partitions for 123 years.[10]

The exhibition in the Warsaw Rising Museum is a realization of the romantic idea of a national struggle for freedom at the cost of the greatest sacrifices and it is in this that it sees the exceptional uniqueness of Polish society compared with Europe and the world. Regardless of its debatable message, the Warsaw Rising Museum has achieved unusual financial and attendance success, materializing the desired image metamorphosis of museum institutions. Other institutions followed suit.

The European Solidarity Centre in Gdańsk

One of the major Polish museums that distinctly demonstrates the romantic-heroic vision of Poland's past is the European Solidarity Centre (*Europejskie Centrum Solidarności*, ECS) in Gdańsk, opened in 2014 on the thirty-fourth anniversary of the signing of the Gdańsk Agreement. It was one of the four agreements concluded with the communist government by the striking workers in 1980. Signed by Lech Wałęsa at the Gdansk Shipyard, it resulted in the establishment of self-governing trade unions that would be genuine representations of the working class. Under this paragraph, the Independent Self-Governing Trade Union "Solidarity" was officially registered.

The shape of the ECS building is to render both the "Solidarity spirit" and the industrial character of the surroundings, and to refer to the shipyard and ships. The façade is suggestive of a ship and is made of a special kind of steel causing the mass of the building to appear covered by rust. Wojciech Targowski, when referring to the ECS architecture, says "[...] its form can be interpreted in many ways and brings a sailing ship to mind, or rather the hull of a ship now under construction, or the stored metal sheeting prepared for its construction."[11] The building and the exhibition suggest that the work begun by the Solidarity trade union (a lonely ship on rough seas) demands continuation, that the Polish "liberation mission" is not yet complete.

The ECS exhibition is mainly concerned with the history of the Solidarity movement (it begins in 1980 and ends with the collapse of the communist system), which is extremely convenient from the perspective of the heroic and identity narrative. The earlier events (1945–1970) are confined to the symbolic dates of 1953, 1956, 1961 and 1968 which refer, symptomatically, to the acts of social disobedience and rebellions against communist rule. This has its justification because national identity and collective memory readily refer to such moments in history that enhance the positive self-image of a community, rejecting that which does not fit the heroic picture. The difficult and complicated communist period (especially with regard to social attitudes) was reduced and acquired unambiguous dimensions of the heroic past as presented in the European Solidarity Centre. The history of Solidarity goes together with the story here because that period was a truly romantic national uprising, morally motivated action in the name of superior values. The language that was then used to express anger was one of moral rightness,[12] which died out after the transformation. The ECS returns to this discourse, restoring the feeling of community at the same time.

By focusing only on the steadfast resistance and rebellion of large masses of society, the narrative omits the questions of wide adaptation of the Poles to the system, their causes and far-reaching consequences of those activities.[13] In this case, forgotten or rather consciously expunged is a set of social attitudes that Leszek Kołakowski simply called "the feeling of normalcy."[14] The majority of Poles adjusted themselves to the system, or for some time even had expectations of modernization of the country under socialist rule. During some periods the acceptance of the system was greater, during some lesser, but it cannot be validly argued that "Polish society" constantly fought against the Soviet enemy. Jerzy Eisler writes about the growing "mass membership" and "nationalization" of the Polish United Workers' Party, which in the late 1970s consisted of over three million members and candidates, i.e., almost 15% of the adult population, with many people joining not for ideological reasons but to prevent the blocking of their promotion, which could not be awarded without party membership. Eisler also emphasizes the importance of the passage of time for the society's self-awareness: the successive generations found it easier to accept the system as their own as they did not know any other.[15]

The most important iconic objects in the ECS are the plaques with the demands of the strikers of 1980 and Gate no. 2 of the Gdańsk Shipyard which is outside of the building but constitutes an integral element of the narrative (the Gate can be seen from the windows of the exhibition rooms). These are the two objects that ideally carry out the ECS's mission, which intends to make the Solidarity movement a part of Europe's memory. They are large and recognizable in the world. The former feature is extremely important in the case of historical reconstructions of phenomena or processes, for which spectacular tangible evidence is difficult to find, while the existing artifacts are difficult to exhibit because they are entirely "ordinary." Such elements of the exhibition like helmets, tables from the BHP (Health and Safety) room where the Agreement was signed, time cards or the shipyard tools are not as attractive as valuable objects, their value being understood not so much as their financial worth as the uniqueness that makes an object an easy museum exhibit that can be interpreted at the cognitive or esthetic level.

The ECS is a romantic museum characterized by a predominance of emotional over intellectual factors, appealing to imagination, patriotism, political involvement in the struggle for freedom and independence, as well as showing the cult of heroes (in this case they are Lech Wałęsa and Pope John Paul II, whose pilgrimages to Poland were religious and political events). The fundamental ideal represented by the ECS is the immortality of the nation on condition of retaining its identity and the will to fight for survival. It is therefore not surprising that the ECS ascribes to the Solidarity movement, somewhat excessively, the positive changes in the mentality of Polish society: the movement was meant to be a "school of democracy," owing to which "millions" of Poles took part in public debate, it was the "time of tremendous activity, of calling meetings, rallies, incessant discussions, debates, and sessions."[16] The goal of the exhibition is to elevate the importance of national dignity. The language of the narrative is solemn, it refers to the categories of good and evil and to moral grounds. The narrative in the ECS places the story about heroic deeds with a moral message not only in the heroic history of Poland but, or perhaps first of all, of the world.[17]

In the case of the ECS, one can also speak of nation branding. The authors of the museum concept write openly about this,

> We wanted to show 'Solidarity' as a positive movement that impacted on the shape of contemporary Europe. We wanted to convey a simple message: it began in Poland, it began in Gdańsk. Another important objective – however banal and trivial it may sound or outrage others – was to promote the best Polish brand which is the 'Solidarity' movement.[18]

One of the essential elements of nation branding is to identify key issues and to show the rites, pictures and symbols that place a nation in a specific space and distinguish it from others. In the case of national identity, branding denotes the process of attribution of exceptional identity to a community by emphasizing certain (positive) significances and myths as well as ignoring others. This process is supported by the state's policy and is aimed for Poland to stand out in the globalized world and bring economic benefits from tourism, investments, creation of jobs, etc. Branding can be a highly effective strategy for achieving them, while the "commercial" character of the term does not mean that practice cannot be a symbolic act, a representation of social and political reality.[19]

Jewish Museums

The political transformation became a distinct turning point, after which followed a multifaceted revival of the memory of Jews in Polish culture. First of all, memorial sites in the former Nazi German concentration and extermination camps were taken care of. Institutional questions were regulated, erroneous inscriptions on information plaques were corrected, archaeological and renovation work was undertaken, and new exhibitions and memorial facilities were designed and constructed. One of the most important exhibitions is the so-called Central Sauna in the Auschwitz-Birkenau Museum (2001), the new memorial at the Museum-Memorial Site in Bełżec (2004), and the new exhibition building and exhibition at the Museum and Memorial Site in Sobibór (2020). These exhibitions comply with the latest trends in martyrdom museology, personalizing victims and ensuring the historical fidelity of the exhibition. In all the authentic former-camp spaces, so-called remedial conservation rules have been applied since the 1990s, which involves only necessary supplements and it restricts interference in the authentic structure to a minimum.[20] This certainly makes open manipulation and ideologization more difficult than in modern-day narrative centers that are located in specially designed buildings with exhibitions prepared in accordance with presupposed assumptions.

The POLIN Museum of the History of Polish Jews in Warsaw

In 2013, owing to the trilateral agreement between the then Polish government, the Warsaw local government and a non-governmental organization (the Association of the Jewish Historical Institute of Poland), the POLIN Museum of the History of Polish Jews was opened. The building, designed by Rainer Mahlamäki and granted awards many times, was erected in the center of the former Jewish district, where the Germans had established a ghetto during the Second World War. The permanent narrative exhibition tells the history of the millennium-long presence of Jews in Polish territory. The exhibit emphasizes the positive elements of the common Polish-Jewish heritage but the authors did not omit the difficult and painful questions. Consequently, neither pogroms nor collaboration of a portion of the Polish society with the Nazis during the Second World War have been forgotten, which, as the right-wing politics of history assumes, is part of the "pedagogy of shame." However, I am not going to discuss the main exhibition because more important for the present article is that the POLIN Museum is an institution that continues to respond actively to current controversial problems. Such an attitude (extremely rare in Polish museums) conforms to the latest model of world museology called museum activism. This category, elaborated upon in the study by Robert Janes and Richard Sandell (2019), is based on the thesis that the development of contemporary museum practice should be based on ethical values, and should strive to achieve actual political, social and environmental changes. Janes and Sandell highlight the need for museums to abandon the attitude of seeming neutrality and to pro- mote the agency of the institution. In this vision, museums become institu- tions that should provide communities with tools of intellectual self-defense against manipulation and governance in the interest of dominant political or economic goals. Activism also denotes resistance, or, as Janes and San- dell understand it, the critical questioning and redefining of the status quo.[21]

Curators in Poland shun subjects of this kind because, as the example below shows, they may become the germs of many conflicts. On the 50th anniversary of the March 1968 events, the POLIN Museum of the History of Polish Jews prepared a temporary exhibition *Strangers at Home: Around March '68*. The show was accompanied by an educational program embrac- ing lectures, workshops, scholarly conferences and film shows. Using the ob- jects, pictures, documents and films of the period, the exhibition showed the Jewish experience of March 1968 in Poland and its consequences, especially the forced emigration of thousands of people. The anti-Semitic campaign launched by the then Polish government was presented in a broader context covering the political events of the Polish spring of 1968: rebellion of the young people at the University of Warsaw, the arousing of prejudices and resentments and the evolution of the communist dictatorship.[22]

In compliance with the assumed objectives, the exhibition referred to a universal experience: in this case to an existential fear associated with the loss of a sense of security. It presented a narrative of stigmatization, uproot- ing and exile, experienced by about 13,000 Polish Jews expelled from their homeland.[23] The exhibition also stressed the media hate campaign accom- panying those dramatic events. It showed a critical picture of Polish society, who in their majority remained passive towards acts of aggression directed against fellow citizens.

The exhibition, which is vital and rare in Polish historical presentations, was self-reflective. In the part called the *Railway Station: The Told Story* the audience could listen to witnesses talking about their experiences of March 1968. When preparing this section of the exhibition, the curators (Justyna Koszarska-Szulc and Natalia Romik) encountered a difficult situation when the objectified historical narrative did not match the living memory of the actors of history. By revealing their own perspective, the curators shared with the audience the dilemmas and problems connected with the substan- tive concept of the exhibition, showing its inside story. They abandoned the position of the omniscient authority, giving the public an opportunity to take a stance on the problem, whereby they fully satisfied the requirements of "new museology" and the critical museum.

From the standpoint of the paradigm of museum activism, the most im- portant point is that the curators made references to the current political situation. The fragment of the exhibition titled *Newspeak and Continua- tions* presented titles, headlines and excerpts from texts or tweets published mainly by the right-wing media in connection with the diplomatic conflict between Poland and Israel following the amendment to the law, pushed through by the Institute of National Remembrance, which provided for a fine or a penalty of imprisonment for persons who "accuse the Polish nation or Polish state of being responsible or complicit in the crimes committed by the Third German Reich."[24] This law, according to scholars, could easily be used against researchers studying the complicity of the Poles in the Holocaust of the Jews during the Second World War. The heated discussion that took place in the media revealed many anti-Semitic prejudices still present in Polish society.

The exhibition at the POLIN Museum allowed the audience to juxtapose two seemingly different situations that produced similar results. The anti-Semitic statements of 2018 strikingly resembled those from 50 years ago. By showing the dramatic results of passivity in the past, the exhibition confronted the audience with the contemporary problem of lack of response and inactivity towards the hate speech. The question of how a member of civil society should behave under similar circumstances had to be answered by every member of the audience themselves, while the museum, however, took an explicit stance on the issue, giving up any pretense of neutrality.

The significance and importance of the exhibition were swiftly noticed by policymakers. Both the exhibition and the accompanying conference, "Hate Speech," were commented on particularly in the right-wing media. Appearing on public television (TVP Info), Deputy Prime Minister and Minister of Culture and National Heritage Piotr Gliński accused the then Director of the POLIN Museum Dariusz Stola of profound political involvement. Prime Minister Mateusz Morawiecki suggested that the exhibition was a manifestation of anti-Polonism (Polonophobia), whereas March 1968 was a reason for pride for the Poles because of the anti-government rebellions of young people.[25] The discussion around the exhibition and its ultimate consequences (dismissal of the director[26]) once again confirmed that Polish history museums are not merely memorial or history sites but the institutions for the development of historical consciousness and setting the official and desirable canon of knowledge. Their function is to select and interpret the past for their audiences in a way that suits current political goals.

The Ulma Family Museum of Poles Rescuing Jews in Markowa

The culminating point of Polish politics of memory is the implementation of the idea of building a museum to commemorate heroic Poles rescuing Jews during the Holocaust. An example of such attitudes was the Ulma family in the Sub-Carpathian region. During the the Second World War, Wiktoria and Józef Ulma gave shelter to eight Jewish people: five men from Łańcut and their neighbor's two daughters with a child belonging to one of them. On March 24, 1944, following a denunciation by a Polish so-called navy-blue policeman (a member of the German-commanded auxiliary police composed of compulsorily drafted Polish pre-war police officers) Włodzimierz Leś, German gendarmes and navy-blue policemen arrived at Markowa from Łańcut. They murdered both the Jews and the Ulma couple as well as their six children. The Ulma Family Museum of Poles Rescuing Jews in Markowa was opened in 2016. President Andrzej Duda delivered a speech during the opening ceremony, and not long afterwards it became a place where the presidents of the Visegrad Group countries met, the intention being to give international publicity to the event.

The form of the museum building draws upon a peasant cottage (the Ulma house has not survived to the present), but it has been made of the material covered by Corten steel sheets that have become rusty, which shatters the sense of security and of the familiar. In front of the museum entrance there is a wall with the surnames of several hundred Poles who rescued Jews. The exhibition is largely multimedia-based although in its center there is a symbolic model of the Ulma house with realistically arranged space. Documents and photographs have also been collected and prominently displayed: they are devoted both to the history of the Ulma family and other people from the Sub-Carpathian region who had rescued Jews.

The ultimate effect of the museum experience is to convey to the visitors the impression of widespread Polish solidarity with the Jews during the Second World War and to arouse the feeling of national pride in such attitudes. Scholars studying this subject matter maintain, however, that the exhibition conceals many facts and documents that indicate the exceptional behavior of those who rescued Jews in the context of general indifference, aversion and complicity in murdering Jewish victims.[27] Jan Grabowski and Dariusz Libionka say:

> The Museum in Markowa tries to re-write the history of the Holocaust, which becomes here first of all the history of noble Poles coming to help the perishing, the principal axiom being the assumption of the innocence of our nation. For this kind of writing and exhibitions a high price is paid, however – that of concealing facts and misrepresenting historical evidence. (...) Passing over whole spheres of life under the Nazi German occupation, during which ill will and terror were prevalent, allows the visitors who watch and read to achieve complete comfort and to rid themselves of cognitive dissonance, which usually accompanies attempts to absorb 'difficult' history.[28]

The Museum of the Second World War in Gdańsk

The fiercest dispute in Poland over a historical exhibition arose in connection with the widely discussed content of the main exhibition in the Museum of the Second World War in Gdańsk (WWIIM) (opened in 2017). The spectacular building with its large (5000 m^2) underground exhibition space and its subject matter make this institution one of the major Polish history museums. The museum building is deliberately ambiguous. Its architects (Jacek

Droszcz and Bazyli Domsta) consciously avoided a direct comparison with war and literal forms. Ambivalence was to be the strength of the facility, opening it up for different interpretations. The form refers to a sinking ship, a crumbling building, a barrage, a precipice or a rocket sunk in the ground. The illuminated structure can be also associated with an ever-burning light. Jacek Droszcz said:

> The tower is a symbol of the future – it opens towards the Nowe Miasto [New Town] district in Gdansk. After the hardship of touring the museum, we have an opportunity to see the panorama of the rebuilt city. We wanted to create something universal. The same happened in the past: the city space was marked by such dominant characteristics – formerly they used to be church towers. We have built a contemporary tower. [...] Worth mentioning is also the square formed in front of the museum entrance. We have created a space where we can make a date or arrange to meet: this is of tremendous city-forming importance.[29]

The building appearance is disturbing to look at, it appears unstable and does not allow simple, optimistic interpretations.

The narrative of the WWIIM covers a long period in history (1933–1989) and refers not only to different periods but also to cultures (e.g. Japanese totalitarianism), which must have made it difficult to construct one consistent narrative line. The main content of the exhibition covers the Second World War. However, its authors found it important to show both its origin and long-term consequences. The exhibition opens with the presentation of the crisis of democratic systems after the First World War and the development of the first authoritarian regimes, and continues until 1989, also covering the postwar period and the time of the Cold War. The narrative is chronological, but some elements of the past reality are presented in an in-depth, problem-centered manner.

The agent of the narrative in the WWIIM is a collective one, yet these are not fighting heroes but civilian, often forgotten or marginalized victims. Since the 1980s, there has been a clearly visible change in war museology compared to earlier exhibitions that celebrated glorious national victories. The WWIIM in Gdańsk, speaking up for civilian victims of wars, shows death, which is difficult to assess positively and cannot be easily heroized. In other Polish museums thematically related to the Second World War (e.g. the Warsaw Rising Museum, the Home Army Museum in Kraków (2000), Katyń Museum in Warsaw (1993) or Pawiak Prison Museum in Warsaw (1965)), the prevailing subject matter is heroic, with the heroes dying in the name of universal values such as honor and freedom. They are the pride of the community, verging sometimes on megalomaniac proportions.[30] The defeated heroes are worshipped and held up as an example to be emulated, and their history often becomes part of a broader narrative – as the founding myth of the independent, revived community (as in the case of Home Army soldiers in the Warsaw Rising Museum).

In the WWIIM, the main enemy spreading terror and death is the war itself as a historical event rather than specific countries or nations (Germany or the Soviet Union). Extremely significant for the narrative here is to show the chain of circumstances that can lead to large-scale conflicts. These factors are more important than the persons of tyrants or dictators, to whom the narrative does not ascribe their traditional demonic role. Enemies are also the events that usually accompany war: hunger, corruption, collaboration, etc. Nor does the exhibition omit the long-term consequences of war: displacements, expulsions, devastation, failure to bring criminals to account, as well as the decades-long division of the world.

The exhibition concept in the WWIIM came in for harsh criticism from right-wing politicians and journalists. The main objection raised by representatives of the so-called new politics of history was the lack of a distinctly Polish narrative line and the "Polish viewpoint."[31] The expressed reservations were not about a deficit of information on the Polish war experience, because it constitutes the vast majority of the exhibition content, but about the absence of a special perspective of the museum message forming an identity narrative that could be a founding myth of the Polish nation. To some Polish journalists, politicians and historians, the affirmative war history (similar to nineteenth-century exhibitions devoted to the glory of the Polish Army) is still one of the fundamental elements forming the community and the feeling of pride in the national past and future. The right-wing journalist Piotr Semka, in his analysis of the WWIIM writes:

> Certainly, no one in their right mind will deny that war brings terror with it, but it is not accidental that we revere people that this war terror does not make passive, cowardly, and servile towards the invaders, or confined exclusively to fighting for their survival or possibly for their family. When talking about war, atrocities should not be concealed but emphasis should also be laid on the strengthening of characters, the ingenuity of resistance and social solidarity. And also on what has always fascinated people: the caliber of leaders, the quality of war tactics and courage on the battlefield.[32]

As a result of the growing conflict over the main exhibition[33], the authors of the original concept (the team headed by the Museum director, historian Paweł Machcewicz) were dismissed in 2017. The institution is now run by a new ministerial-appointed director, who has already carried out certain changes in the main exhibition that are meant to highlight the Polish war martyrdom and the Polish viewpoint. This conflict clearly reflects the clash of two models of history museum representation: affirmative (identity-based) and critical.

Identity museums share common problems because of the objectives set: provide a consistent narrative that will guarantee the continuation of national identity and popularize a formation narrative or sometimes even a founding one conforming to different senses of *raison d'état* and the positive image of the nation.[34] This requires making difficult choices because the history of each nation is full of moments that do not necessarily match the identity-based self-positive vision. An additional problem is the fact that at present history museums are also established on account of the rivalry between nations over which one is more "unique" or "advanced." Museums seek paths to "elevate" their own community to a higher status; consequently, they do not so much represent its history as combine it with diverse popular ideas: progress, change, modernity, or – which is the Polish case – with freedom.[35] Identity narratives adopt a specific moral position and test the ethical judgment of the visitors. They also seek ways to arouse specific empathy responses, a feeling of good and evil, justice or a feeling of being wronged. As a result of all these efforts, the authority of the institution should remain unchallenged, and the (national) ideas and objects/artifacts ("that speak for themselves") legitimize each other, which leaves the visitors with an impression that there is unquestionable and unmediated evidence in support of specific theses. The museum presents itself as the owner of national treasures and the place of dissemination of knowledge, an institution owing to which the nation's cultural attributes become tangible and visible. Visitors are expected to recognize the authority of the institution – "a trusted purveyor of national orthodoxy."[36]

The critical model accentuates the plurality of perspectives, finds forgotten actors of history and highlights difficult heritage rather than the glorious national legacy only. The WWIIM (in its original concept) is a unique institution in Poland and in the world. By showing the war as a phenomenon affecting all aspects of the lives of millions all over the world, the WWIIM has made the Polish perspective a part of mankind's universal experience. The authors have assumed that the histories of conflicts, exclusions, fights, domination, genocide and colonization are also elements of national histories. Such an attitude poses a challenge both to the institution and the audience; however, in the case of critical exhibitions, the relationship between the museum and visitors does not consist in being an arbiter in judging what is "objective history" or what should remain a permanent element of collective memory.[37]

Conclusions

The popularity of museums in the public sphere is influenced by the increasingly frequent perception of historical exhibitions as a reflection of the self-image of a nation, i.e., how specific communities want to be perceived "externally." Exhibitions are becoming sets of cultural patterns teaching a community how to identify itself, define and point out the "other," and create the "national" brand. Creating a "museum experience" makes an exhibition increasingly emotional, which is a vital element of public history.[38] This should not, however, hide other crucial goals of the latter: involvement of people in the processes of presentation and interpretation of the past should go hand in hand with promoting a critical look at one's own history. The public, encouraged to participate and involved in "history in the making," should become a self-aware historical subject.[39]

Public history uses historical research but it is not history for its own sake, i.e., it does not focus exclusively on academic, research objectives because it also embraces the needs of individuals, local groups and national communities or institutions.[40] Its essential functions were pertinently defined by Robert Traba as: the molding of historical imagination and acquisition of technical competencies, or the ability to categorize narratives about the past through critical analysis of diverse source material.[41] Traba insists that public history should preserve and take care of the balance between scholarly understood cultural history, historical knowledge and the emotional experiencing of the past, which (experience) may lead to the mythmaking, sentimentalizing or hypostatizing of history, or attributing to historical phenomena the importance of an intrinsic being rather than relational phenomena that can be criticized and redefined.[42] Museums as one of the public-domain media with the strongest impact on the imagination are in a particularly dangerous situation because they are perceived by many as the ideological apparatuses that reproduce hegemonic social and cultural norms. The fluidity and indeterminacy of links between the object and meaning[43] may cause exhibitions to become dangerous tools of manipulation, particularly in the case of the narrative model, in which sparse objects function as the scenery for coherent narrative, while the elements of drama and the application of other theatrical strategies make the narrative very convincing. The narrative model restricts the independent interpretive activity of the audience because it presents a readymade story. Polish narrative exhibitions organized in the twenty-first century have explicitly shown that, paradoxically, it is the traditional representation of history in museums, i.e., in general, objects (preferably authentic) with short descriptive texts about them as well as the minimal use of new technologies, that offer a larger margin of interpretive freedom, allowing the visitors to create their own narratives based on the artifacts displayed. In new museum theories, more important than technological advancements are modifications of attitudes towards the museum audiences, the transparency of curators' activities and a readiness to share with the public the authority and control over cultural inheritance. It is difficult to argue convincingly that a revolution in the above sense has taken place in Polish history museums. The change in exhibition techniques mostly serves to strengthen the power to give significance, the authority to represent and create official versions that become generally adopted, even commonsense views, and the authority to represent the social world and the past. Many a time, museum exhibitions turn into instruments of the politics of history and express specific visions of the world or a specific ideology. Curators not only refuse to share authority with the museum public but, on the contrary, they want to control it. For the museum, control means representing the society and its highest values. It is also the power to define an individual's position within this society.[44] This brings many problems with it because, even if historical exhibitions have never been neutral in terms of outlook, the high degree of ideologization may cause them to lose their greatest value: authority and social trust.

Notes

1 On the two definitions and their broad elaborations see *Modi memorandi. Leksykon kultury pamięci*, ed. Magdalena Saryusz-Wolska and Robert Traba (Warszawa: Wydawnictwo Naukowe Scholar, 2014), 346–351, 478–483.
2 I conducted large-scale studies in Central and Eastern European museums (in Poland, Lithuania, Latvia, Estonia, Hungary, the Czech Republic, Serbia, Romania and Germany) from 2014 to 2018. Cf. Anna Ziębińska-Witek, *Muzealizacja komunizmu w Polsce i Europie Środkowo-Wschodniej* (Lublin: UMCS, 2018).
3 Cf. Antoni Dudek, "Historia i polityka w Polsce po 1989 roku," in *Historycy i politycy: polityka pamięci w III RP*, ed. Paweł Skibiński, Tomasz Wiścicki, and Michał Wysocki (Warszawa: DiG and Muzeum Historii Polski, 2011), 33–57.
4 They were previously known in the narrow circle of museum theorists. Maria Popczyk, *Muzeum sztuki. Antologia* (Kraków: Universitas, 2005).
5 Piotr Piotrowski, *Muzeum krytyczne* (Poznań: REBIS, 2011).
6 Duncan F. Cameron, "The Museum, a Temple or the Forum," *Curator: The Museum Journal* 14 (1971): 11–24.
7 Hilde S. Hein, *The Museum in Transition. A Philosophical Perspective* (Washington, DC: Smithsonian Books, 2000), 66.
8 Anna Ziębińska-Witek, *Historia w muzeach. Studium ekspozycji Holokaustu* (Lublin: UMCS, 2011).
9 The most extensive study of the Warsaw Uprising in English-language literature is the book by Norman Davies, *Rising '44: The Battle for Warsaw* (London: Pan Macmillan, 2019).
10 Lech M. Nijakowski, *Polska polityka pamięci* (Warszawa: Wydawnictwa Akademickie i Profesjonalne, 2008), 19.
11 Wojciech Targowski, "Architektura budynku Europejskiego Centrum Solidarności," in *Wystawa stała Europejskiego Centrum Solidarności. Katalog*, ed. Paweł Golak, Basil Kerski, and Konrad Knoch (Gdańsk: ECS, 2014), 253.
12 Jadwiga Staniszkis *Antropologia władzy. Między traktatem Lizbońskim a kryzysem* (Warszawa: Prószyński i S-ka, 2009), 186–190.
13 Krystyna Kersten, *Między wyzwoleniem a zniewoleniem. Polska 1944–1956* (London: Aneks, 1993).
14 Leszek Kołakowski, "PRL – wesoły nieboszczyk?," *Tygodnik Powszechny*, February 12, 1995.
15 Jerzy Eisler, "Jakim państwem była PRL w latach 1956–1976?" *Pamięć i Sprawiedliwość* no. 2 (2006): 21–22.
16 Konrad Knoch "Solidarność i nadzieja," in *Wystawa stała*, 89–90. It is easy to observe, however, that in the present political discussions, the conflict about historical memory is still carried on, the Round Table talks of 1989 and the person of Lech Wałęsa being its most heated and controversial points. The rituals of laying flowers or paying homage at monuments are only the external manifestations of respect for the past, to which different groups attach different significance. The features like "traditional" Polish "love of freedom" or "civil society" can in practice be attributed only to a part of the community.

17 Jacek Kołtan writes in the ECS *Catalog*: "The Solidarity movement in Poland and peaceful revolutions in most Central and Eastern European countries are becoming part of the tradition of peaceful resolution of social and political conflicts." Jacek Kołtan, "Kultura pokojowych przemian," in *Wystawa stała*, 245.

18 Jarosław Szymański and Beata Szymańska, "Powstawanie wystawy stałej," in *Wystawa stała*, 259.

19 Melissa Aronczyk, "New and Improved Nations. Branding National Identity," accessed August 1, 2020, www.culturaldiplomacy.org/academy/content/articles/events/nationbranding/participant-papers/New-And-Improved-Nations_-_Melissa-Aronczyk.pdf.

20 Rafał Pióro and Witold Smrek, "Materialne świadectwa zbrodni," *Pro Memoria* no. 27 (2007): 64–65. Cf. the chapter by Piotr Trojański in this volume.

21 Robert R. Janes and Richard Sandell, "Posterity Has Arrived: The Necessary Emergence of Museum Activism," in *Museum Activism*, ed. Robert R. Janes and Richard Sandell (London and New York: Routledge, 2019), 1, 6.

22 Dariusz Stola, "Pół wieku po marcu," in *Obcy w domu. Wokół marca'68* (Exhibition catalog), ed. Justyna Koszarska-Szulc and Natalia Romik (Warszawa: Polin, 2018), 8–9.

23 Justyna Koszarska-Szulc and Natalia Romik, "Obcy w domu," in *Obcy w domu*, 15.

24 The law was voted through but the penalty of imprisonment was ultimately withdrawn, https://www.wprost.pl/swiat/10135410/izraelski-dziennik-polska-wycofuje-sie-z-kontrowersyjnej-ustawy-o-holokauscie-rezygnujac-z-kary-wiezienia.html, accessed December 5, 2020.

25 https://www.gazetaprawna.pl/artykuly/1109591,premier-marzec-68-powinien-byc-powodem-do-dumy-dla-polakow-ktorzy-walczyli-o-wolnosc.html, accessed December 5, 2020.

26 In 2020, Dariusz Stola lost the directorship of the POLIN Museum. Minister Gliński, against the decision of the competition committee, never appointed Stola for the second term. The exhibition was not the only sore point in the relations between the Ministry and the Museum director, who had earlier protested against the amendment of the Institute of National Remembrance law mentioned in this chapter.

27 Emmanuel Ringelblum, *Polish-Jewish Relations during the Second World War*, ed. Joseph Kermish, translated from Polish Dafna Allon, Danuta Dąbrowska and Dana Keren (Evanston: Northwestern University Press, 1992); Barbara Engelking and Jacek Leociak, *The Warsaw. Ghetto: A Guide to the Perished City*, trans. Emma Harris (New Haven: Yale University Press, 2009); *Dalej jest noc. Losy Żydów w wybranych powiatach okupowanej Polski*, ed. Barbara Engelking and Jan Grabowski (Warszawa: Centrum Badań nad Zagładą Żydów, 2018); Jan Grabowski, *Na posterunku. Udział polskiej policji granatowej i kryminalnej w zagładzie Żydów* (Wołowiec: Czarne, 2020).

28 Jan Grabowski and Dariusz Libionka, "Markowa. Żydowska śmierć, polska wina, wspólny strach," *Gazeta Wyborcza*, last modified December 9, 2016, accessed Decebmer 29, 2018, http://wyborcza.pl/magazyn/7,124059,21097043,markowa-zydowska-smierc-polska-wina-wspolny-strach.html.

29 "Co o swoim projekcie Muzeum II Wojny Światowej mówią architekci z pracowni KWADRAT," accessed January 12, 2020, https://archirama.muratorplus.pl/architektura/co-o-swoim-projekcie-muzeum-ii-wojny-swiatowej-mowia-architekci-z-pracowni-kwadrat,67_4832.html.

30 Jan M. Piskorski, "Od kultu herosów do adoracji ofiar. Przemiany w kulturze pamięci," *Więź* 53, no. 2/3 (2010): 5.

31 Cf. the chapter by Rafał Stobiecki in this volume.

32 Piotr Semka, "Muzeum II Wojny Światowej. Analiza Piotra Semki," *Rzeczpospolita*, last modified August 15, 2016, accessed February 2, 2020, www.rp.pl/Plus-Minus/308119920-Muzeum-II-Wojny-Swiatowej-Analiza-Piotra-Semki.html.

33 The history of the establishment of the WWIIM, the concept of the main exhibition and the conflict with its final consequences have been described by the former director and founder of the Museum and are presented in Paweł Machcewicz, *The War that Never Ends. The Museum of the Second World War in Gdańsk* (Berlin: De Gruyter, 2019).

34 Minister of Culture and National Heritage Piotr Gliński openly admitted this while opening the Ulma Family Museum of Poles Rescuing Jews in Markowa: "I want to state clearly that the Polish Government will continue to build and co-found museums important for Polish memory, for Polish identity, for the Polish present." Cf. Magdalena Mach, "Minister Gliński w Markowej: 'Muzeum ważne dla polskiej racji stanu,'" *Gazeta Wyborcza,* last modified June 23, 2017, accessed June 26, 2017, http://rzeszow.wyborcza.pl/rzeszow/7,34962,22001128,minister-glinski-w-markowej-muzeum-wazne-dla-polskiej-racji.html.

35 On the comparison of national museums cf. *National Museum Making Histories in a Diverse Europe*, accessed May 20, 2017, http://liu.diva-portal.org/smash/get/diva2:573632/FULLTEXT01.pdf.

36 *National Museum Making Histories.*

37 Cf. *Challenging History in the Museum: International Perspectives*, ed. Jenny Kidd, Sam Cairns, and Alex Drago (London: Routledge, 2016).

38 Stephen E. Weil, *Rethinking the Museum and Other Meditations* (Washington, DC: Smithsonian Institution Press, 1990).

39 Jerome de Groot, *Consuming History. Historians and Heritage in Contemporary Popular Culture* (London and New York: Routledge, 2009), 3–4.

40 Hilda Kean, "Introduction," in *The Public History Reader*, ed. Hilda Kean and Paul Martin (London and New York: Routledge, 2013), xiv–xvi.

41 Robert Traba, "Pożyteczność uczenia się z historii. Historia stosowana: między 'History Sells' a 'Public History,'" in *Historie wzajemnych oddziaływań*, ed. Robert Traba (Berlin – Warszawa: Oficyna Naukowa, 2014), 91–92.

42 Traba, "Pożyteczność," 83.

43 Hein, *The Museum in Transition*, 54–60.

44 Carol Duncan, *Civilising Rituals* (Routledge: London 1995), 8.

Bibliography

Aronczyk, Melissa. "New and Improved Nations. Branding National Identity." Accessed August 1, 2020. www.culturaldiplomacy.org/academy/content/articles/events/nationbranding/participant-papers/New-And-Improved-Nations_-_Melissa-Aronczyk.pdf

Cameron, Duncan F. "The Museum, a Temple or the Forum." *Curator: The Museum Journal* 14 (1971): 11–24.

"Co o swoim projekcie Muzeum II Wojny Światowej mówią architekci z pracowni KWADRAT." Accessed January 12, 2020. https://archirama.muratorplus.pl/architektura/co-o-swoim-projekcie-muzeum-ii-wojny-swiatowej-mowia-architekci-z-pracowni-kwadrat, 67_4832.html.

Davies, Norman. *Rising '44: The Battle for Warsaw.* London: Pan Macmillan, 2019.

Dudek, Antoni. "Historia i polityka w Polsce po 1989 roku." In *Historycy i politycy: polityka pamięci w III RP*, edited by Paweł Skibiński, Tomasz Wiścicki and

Michał Wysocki, 33–57. Warszawa: Wydawnictwo DiG and Muzeum Historii Polski, 2011.

Duncan, Carol. *Civilising Rituals*. London: Routledge, 1995.

Eisler, Jerzy. "Jakim państwem była PRL w latach 1956–1976?" *Pamięć i Sprawiedliwość* 10, no. 2 (2006): 11–23.

Engelking, Barbara, and Jacek Leociak. *The Warsaw. Ghetto: A Guide to the Perished City*. Translated by Emma Harris. New Haven: Yale University Press, 2009.

Engelking, Barbara, and Jan Grabowski, eds. *Dalej jest noc. Losy Żydów w wybranych powiatach okupowanej Polski*. Warszawa: Centrum Badań nad Zagładą Żydów, 2018.

Grabowski, Jan. *Na posterunku. Udział polskiej policji granatowej i kryminalnej w zagładzie Żydów*. Wołowiec: Wydawnictwo Czarne, 2020.

Grabowski, Jan, and Dariusz Libionka. "Markowa. Żydowska śmierć, polska wina, wspólny starch," last modified December 9, 2016. Accessed Decebmer 29, 2018. http://wyborcza.pl/magazyn/7,124059,21097043,markowa-zydowska-smierc-polska-wina-wspolny-strach.html.

Hein, Hilde S. *The Museum in Transition. A Philosophical Perspective*. Washington, DC: Smithsonian Books, 2000.

Janes, Robert R., and Richard Sandell. "Posterity Has Arrived: The Necessary Emergence of Museum Activism." In *Museum Activism*, edited by Robert R. Janes and Richard Sandell, 1–21. London – New York: Routledge, 2019.

Kersten, Krystyna. *Między wyzwoleniem a zniewoleniem. Polska 1944–1956*. London: Aneks, 1993.

Kidd, Jenny, Sam Cairns, and Alex Drago, eds. *Challenging History in the Museum: International Perspectives*. London: Routledge, 2016.

Knoch, Konrad. "Solidarność i nadzieja." In *Wystawa stała Europejskiego Centrum Solidarności. Katalog*, edited by Paweł Golak, Basil Kerski, and Konrad Knoch, 84–121. Gdańsk: ECS, 2014.

Kołakowski, Leszek. "PRL – wesoły nieboszczyk?" *Tygodnik Powszechny*, February 12, 1995.

Kołtan, Jacek. "Kultura pokojowych przemian." In *Wystawa stała Europejskiego Centrum Solidarności. Katalog*, edited by Paweł Golak, Basil Kerski, and Konrad Knoch, 244–249. Gdańsk: ECS, 2014.

Koszarska-Szulc, Justyna, and Natalia Romik. "Obcy w domu." In *Obcy w domu. Wokół marca'68. Estranged: March '68 and Its Aftermath*, edited by Justyna Koszarska-Szulc and Natalia Romik, 2–7. Warszawa: Polin, 2018.

Mach, Magdalena. "Minister Gliński w Markowej: 'Muzeum ważne dla polskiej racji stanu,'" last modified June 23, 2017. Accessed June 26, 2017. http://rzeszow.wyborcza.pl/rzeszow/7,34962,22001128,minister-glinski-w-markowej-muzeum-wazne-dla-polskiej-racji.html.

Machcewicz, Paweł. *The War that Never Ends. The Museum of the Second World War in Gdańsk*. Berlin: De Gruyter, 2019.

"National Museum Making Histories in a Diverse Europe." Accessed May 20, 2017. http://liu.diva-portal.org/smash/get/diva2:573632/FULLTEXT01.pdf.

Nijakowski, Lech M. *Polska polityka pamięci*. Warszawa: Wydawnictwa Akademickie i Profesjonalne, 2008.

Pióro, Rafał, and Witold Smrek. "Materialne świadectwa zbrodni." *Pro Memoria* no. 27 (2007): 63–66.

Piotrowski, Piotr. *Muzeum krytyczne*. Poznań: REBIS, 2011.

Piskorski, Jan M. "Od kultu herosów do adoracji ofiar. Przemiany w kulturze pamięci." *Więź* 53, no. 2/3 (2010): 5–21.

Popczyk, Maria. *Muzeum sztuki. Antologia.* Kraków: Universitas, 2005.

Ringelblum, Emmanuel. *Polish-Jewish Relations during the Second World War*, edited by Joseph Kermish, translated from Polish by Dafna Allon, Danuta Dabrowska and Dana Keren. Evanston: Northwestern University Press, 1992.

Saryusz-Wolska, Magdalena, and Robert Traba, eds. *Modi memorandi. Leksykon kultury pamięci.* Warszawa: Scholar, 2014.

Semka, Piotr. "Muzeum II Wojny Światowej. Analiza Piotra Semki," *Rzeczpospolita.* Last modified August 15, 2016. Accessed February 2, 2020. www.rp.pl/Plus-Minus/308119920-Muzeum-II-Wojny-Swiatowej-Analiza-Piotra-Semki.html.

Staniszkis, Jadwiga. *Antropologia władzy. Między Traktatem Lizbońskim a kryzysem.* Warszawa: Prószyński i S-ka, 2009.

Stola, Dariusz. "Pół wieku po marcu." In *Obcy w domu. Wokół marca'68. Estranged: March '68 and Its Aftermath*, edited by Justyna Koszarska-Szulc and Natalia Romik, 8–11. Warszawa: Polin, 2018.

Szymański, Jarosław, and Beata Szymańska. "Powstawanie wystawy stałej." In *Wystawa stała Europejskiego Centrum Solidarności. Katalog*, edited by Paweł Golak, Basil Kerski, and Konrad Knoch, 256–259. Gdańsk: ECS, 2014.

Targowski, Wojciech. "Architektura budynku Europejskiego Centrum Solidarności." In *Wystawa stała Europejskiego Centrum Solidarności. Katalog*, edited by Paweł Golak, Basil Kerski, and Konrad Knoch, 252–255. Gdańsk: ECS, 2014.

Ziębińska-Witek, Anna. *Muzealizacja komunizmu w Polsce i Europie Środkowo-Wschodniej.* Lublin: UMCS, 2018.

Ziębińska-Witek, Anna. *Historia w muzeach. Studium ekspozycji Holokaustu.* Lublin: UMCS, 2011.

https://www.gazetaprawna.pl/artykuly/1109591,premier-marzec-68-powinien-byc-powodem-do-dumy-dla-polakow-ktorzy-walczyli-o-wolnosc.html. Accessed December 5, 2020.

https://www.wprost.pl/swiat/10135410/izraelski-dziennik-polska-wycofuje-sie-z-kontrowersyjnej-ustawy-o-holokauscie-rezygnujac-z-kary-wiezienia.html. Accessed December 5, 2020.

5 The Role of Memorial Sites in Public History

The Case of Auschwitz State Museum

Piotr Trojański

Auschwitz Memorial and Its Historical and Cultural Landscape

In Poland, the Auschwitz Memorial has been the subject of considerable social, media and political interest for years. Some researchers even claim that the entire martyrdom museology in Poland today is dominated by this institution in the socio-political dimension. Therefore, in this article, the museum will be treated as a case study for the purposes of discussing the problem contained in the title. In reference to Pierre Nora's concept of *lieux de memoire* it will be presented as a multidimensional memorial site, with both topographical connotations and metaphorical meaning.

The social reception of this memorial site is influenced by its historical and cultural landscape, one of the most important elements of which is the history of KL[1] Auschwitz. The camp was established at the beginning of the Second World War in April 1940 and until its end it played a very important role in the system of German Nazi concentration camps. Until early 1942, it was a concentration camp where mainly Polish political prisoners were held, and later it also became a center for the extermination of European Jews, who ultimately accounted for 90% of its victims. People deported to Auschwitz came from over 20 European countries, which imparted an international character to it. Historians estimate that 1.3–1.5 million people were deported to Auschwitz and at least 1.1 million of them were murdered. Jews constituted the largest group of victims, estimated at ca. one million. Approximately 70,000 ethnic Poles, 21,000 Sinti and Romani people, 14,000 Soviet prisoners of war and about 12,000 representatives of other national and social groups also died at Auschwitz. This particular ethnic, national and social mosaic of victims made the camp a symbol of martyrdom of various groups of victims of Nazi terror and genocide. Another significant distinguisher thereof was the fact that throughout most of its existence in the system of death camps, KL Auschwitz had two functions, i.e., it was both a concentration camp and a center for immediate extermination of Jews. In addition, it was also a large camp complex, which consisted of two main sub-camps (KL Auschwitz II-Birkenau and KL Auschwitz III-Monowitz)

DOI: 10.4324/9781003165767-7

and approximately 40 smaller sub-camps. The bodies of KL Auschwitz victims were initially buried in mass graves, and then burned in pits, on pyres and in crematorium furnaces, five of which were located within the camp grounds. Their ashes were thrown into the nearby Soła and Vistula rivers or into the ponds in the vicinity, they were scattered over the fields as fertilizer, or buried in nearby terrain depressions and marshes. Today, therefore, this place is not only a museum, but also – and for some primarily – a huge cemetery, where the ashes of more than a million people murdered there are buried.

The historical and cultural landscape of Auschwitz was also shaped by the post-war history of the post-camp memorial site, on which the Auschwitz-Birkenau State Museum was established in 1947. Immediately after liberation, Soviet and Polish military units were stationed in this area, where they established two internment camps for German prisoners of war, *Volksdeutsche*,[2] and Polish activists from the anti-communist underground. By 1947, some of the camp buildings of the former Auschwitz camp had been legally demolished or plundered. During this period, the Birkenau camp area was also the scene of numerous acts of profanation of human ashes carried out by people seeking valuable items hidden there or left behind by murdered prisoners. This was combatted by former Auschwitz prisoners, who were sent to the site of the former camp in April 1946 by the Ministry of Culture and Art in order to create the foundations of the future museum.

The museum was created over a period of two years in the atmosphere of nationwide discussions on what should be done with the post-camp site: preserve it for posterity or perhaps "tear it down and plow it up" – as some postulated.[3] Ultimately, the first option prevailed and the State Museum in Oświęcim was officially established on July 2, 1947. It consisted of two parts: the museum and the so-called reservation. The first one was located on the site of the former Main Camp (KL Auschwitz I), where the buildings and most of the camp infrastructure had survived. The main exhibition, which to this day remains the main route for visiting the museum, was set up in the former prisoners' barracks. It is complemented by the so-called national exhibitions, opened from the beginning of the 1960s, which present the fate of the victims of Auschwitz before their deportation to the camp.[4] A decision was made that the second part of the museum, which consisted of the remains of the former Auschwitz II- Birkenau camp, remain intact, so that its authenticity would stimulate visitors' reflection. The only permissible interference in this space was the erection of monuments there.

In both parts of the museums, the ruins of the crematoria and gas chambers that the Germans had blown up before leaving the camp were important elements of the landscape of the memorial site. One of them (Crematorium 1) in the main camp was rebuilt after the war to show visitors what it looked like. It should be emphasized that the then conceptual assumptions of the museum have survived to this day. The only significant change was the opening in 2001 of a permanent exhibition of the family photographs

of Jews from Będzin deported to Auschwitz, which was located in the former Baths building in Birkenau. Both on the site of the former main camp
and Birkenau, sightseeing routes with information boards presenting short
descriptions and photographs from the time of the camp's existence have
been marked out. In addition, in 2009, a historical railcar was placed on
the unloading ramp at Birkenau, intended to symbolize the mass depor-
tations of Hungarian Jews in 1944. In turn, on the grounds of the former
Auschwitz I, the gallows used for hanging the camp commandant Rudolf
Höss, sentenced to death by the Supreme National Tribunal in Warsaw in
1947, were reconstructed.

The Auschwitz Memorial is not only a broad area with preserved elements
of the former camp infrastructure and the cemetery with the ashes of the
murdered prisoners. These are also tens of thousands of items having special
character, significance and symbolism. This extensive historical collection
connected with human suffering includes primarily personal belongings
left by the deportees, prisoners' items (shoes, suitcases, pots, prostheses, or-
thoses, striped uniforms, prayer shawls) and camp-related objects. Many of
the latter provide evidence of primitive living and unhygienic conditions,
hunger, as well as attempts to maintain humanity behind the barbed wires
of Auschwitz. The Museum's collections also include objects related to the
extermination process and the SS crew, i.e., the perpetrators of these crimes.

A special position in the Museum's collections is reserved for the world's
largest and most exceptional collection of works of art connected with KL
Auschwitz. It consists of approximately 2,000 works of art created by prisoners. These were created in an official manner, that is, commissioned by
the SS officers (among others, in the so-called Camp Museum) and also
covertly.

Meanwhile, camp documents, the majority of which were produced by
the camp administration, are collected and preserved in the museum archives, which were established in 1957. These archival documents are mainly
connected with the history of KL Auschwitz and originate from the period
of its functioning.

Only a very small part of the evidence of the crimes described above is on
display in the museum exhibitions and represents an important element of
the historical and cultural landscape of the Auschwitz Memorial. Over the
years, some of these artifacts have even become an icon of the camp, and
for some people also a "special tourist attraction," attracting numbers of
visitors. These are primarily stacks of suitcases, shoes, glasses and piles of
hair remaining after the deported prisoners. The main gates leading to the
Auschwitz and Birkenau camps also hold iconic significance. Particularly
the first one with the inscription *"Arbeit macht frei,"* which was replaced
by a duplicate after its much-publicized theft in 2009. At some point in the
future, the original inscription will be displayed in the new main exhibition.
Another iconic landmark of Auschwitz is the unloading ramp located at

Birkenau, which, accompanied by a freight wagon, has become an indispensable part of the post-camp space.

Various forms of commemoration can be found on this site, such as monuments erected from the very beginning of the museum's existence, mainly on the grounds of the former KL Birkenau. The first one was established in 1948 close to the remains of Crematorium II in Birkenau and was devoted to the Jews murdered there. The second one was most likely established a year later and placed near the side entrance to the Museum and commemorated the soldiers of the Red Army – the liberators of Auschwitz. Another one was a relatively small monument commemorating the victims of Auschwitz, unveiled in 1955 on the site of the Birkenau. After 12 years it was replaced by the International Monument to the Victims of Fascism. This imposing monument, unveiled in 1967, continues to form the main element of Birkenau landscape to this day. During the following years, other smaller forms of commemoration also started to appear on the museum site. Among them, particular attention should be paid to the monument dedicated to the Romani victims, which was unveiled in 1973 on the grounds of the former so-called "Gypsy family camp" in Birkenau.

Another category is the handful of commemorative plaques located on the walls or on the inside walls of the buildings in Auschwitz I (the former prisoner blocks). They commemorate important historical events in the history of the camp (e.g. the first attempt at gassing people) or famous persons who were murdered in Auschwitz. On the external wall of block No. 27 there is, for example, a memorial plaque commemorating four Jewish women who were executed for helping in the organization of the revolt of *Sonderkommando* prisoners. In block No. 11, in turn, in the starvation cell, there is a memorial plaque commemorating St. Maksymilian Kolbe, who died as a martyr in 1941. In this cell there is also a special candle donated by Pope John Paul II during one of his pilgrimages to Auschwitz. There is a relatively small number of commemorative plaques at the Auschwitz Museum compared to other post-camp commemorative sites. The reason behind this is the approach of the museum's administration, which treats this form of commemorative practices with caution. A similar approach is adopted by them with respect to the display of religious symbols in the post-camp exhibition area, thus wanting to prevent any conflicts over religious forms of commemoration which took place on the Museum grounds at the turn of 1980s and 1990s.[5]

Martyrological Museums as Memorial Sites

Museums were established in Poland on the sites of former concentration camps starting from the first years following their liberation. This stemmed primarily from the fact that the communist government recognized them as a potential propaganda tool used to create the memory of the Second World

War, which then played an extremely important role in the legitimization of the new socio-political order.

Throughout the period of the Polish People's Republic, the term "martyrological museum" was used to describe memorial sites related to the Second World War.

The 1999 Act on the Protection of Former Nazi Death Camps refers to some post-camp sites as "Genocide Monuments." This category includes the following institutions: Monument to Martyrdom in Oświęcim; Monument to Struggle and Martyrdom in Majdanek; the "Stutthof" Museum in Sztutowo; Gross-Rosen Museum in Rogoźnica; the Mausoleum of Struggle and Martyrdom in Treblinka; the Martyrdom Museum-Camp in Chełmno on the Ner river; the Museum of the Former Death Camp in Sobibór; and the Former Death Camp in Bełżec.

In order to present the full picture of the memorial sites in Poland, one should also mention smaller museums of regional importance, which were also established on the former camp sites. These are, among others: the Martyrdom Museum in Żabikowo or the KL Plaszow Museum. Despite the fact that, compared to other countries, the number of martyrdom museums in Poland is relatively high (24), it must not be forgotten that they were established only in places where the Nazis committed the greatest crimes during the Second World War. The remaining approximately 2,000 minor places of murder and execution were commemorated only in the form of a monument, a stone, a commemorative plaque or an obelisk. All of them – in accordance with the nomenclature being in force in Poland – are treated in the same way, i.e. – as monuments of martyrdom.

Many sites of the former concentration and extermination camps have lost their original appearance over the years; therefore, the term "historical site" is used increasingly often to emphasize their specific character. Generally speaking, the term refers to specific topographic sites where historical events took place, but their current shape refers to them more symbolically than literally.

Tasks of Museums in the Post-Camp Space

The tasks and functions of museums operating in the post-camp space have received a statutory definition in Poland. They can be defined as: commemorating the victims of the camp; protecting their sites, buildings and other material evidence; collecting, conserving and sharing related collections; as well as documenting and presenting their history.[6] Some researchers argue that this catalogue does not exhaust all the possibilities of in situ memorial museums. One of them is Tomasz Kranz, a well-known researcher on this subject in Poland and the director of the Museum at Majdanek. In his opinion, the statutory tasks and functions of the post-camp memorial sites should be expanded. The premise for this is – as he claims – the polymorphism of martyrdom museums and the related multidimensionality, which should be perceived both in material and symbolic categories. Bearing in mind their material dimension, these museums are cemeteries, historical sites and monuments. On the other hand,

> as museum institutions, they play the role of the objects of historical culture, which they shape primarily in the cognitive area through research, publishing and educational activity. As in situ remembrance museums, they also perform symbolic functions resulting from the historical and symbolic meanings assigned to them and the role they play in the politics of history and the culture of remembrance at the regional and national, sometimes also international, levels. The multitude of functions, meanings and symbols means – according to Kranz – that the former camps transformed into museums can be considered to be spaces containing many memorial sites.[7]

Although one of the important constitutive elements of in situ memorial museums is the authentic crime site, these museums are not only cemeteries reminding of dramatic events. These are also institutions that present historical exhibitions. "That is why museums-camps not only maintain and transmit memory, but also co-create it."[8]

> The activity of the museums themselves in the field of promotion, visitor service and social communication is [also] not without significance in this regard. What is meant here is social media and various types of marketing campaigns, which de facto serve the purpose of raising the awareness of and communicating tourist values of the museum institutions which manage historical sites, if not of the historical sites themselves.[9]

Martyrdom Museums in the Politics of History

In Poland, martyrdom museums have a state-owned character, which means that they are not only established, but also indirectly dependent on politicians. Therefore, government authorities often use them to articulate their political interests. They do so by influencing the shape of exposition and forms of commemoration. As a consequence, these activities may lead to the instrumentalization of remembrance. The flagship example of such practices was the Auschwitz-Birkenau State Museum, where the process of imparting a political message to remembrance began with its establishment and, in principle, continues today, although its intensity level and some forms may differ.

The first period in the history of the museum was characterized by the coexistence of three unequally stressed narratives and memory symbols associated with them, which in various arrangements and hierarchies of symbolizing the past were manifested throughout its subsequent history. The first narrative is the national vision of Auschwitz as the place of the martyrdom of the Polish nation. Whereas the second narrative is the vision of Auschwitz as the place of exterminating Jews.[10] The third narrative appeared in the Stalinist period when Auschwitz became the basic element of communist propaganda (anti-German, anti-American, anti-Western) not only legitimizing its power, but also serving to implement short-term political goals.[11] In the mid-1950s, the ideological narrative was abandoned, just as was the Jewish one. Instead, a new narrative emerged, in accordance with which Auschwitz became a site of international martyrdom.

In the 1960s, Auschwitz was a model example of Polish suffering, the perpetrators of which were no longer the fascists, but – just as immediately after the war – Germans. The political symbolism was weakened, and the significance of Auschwitz was shifted from a universalist and social class-related one to a national one. The falsification of the history of the former camp at that time consisted mainly in emphasizing the martyrdom of the Polish nation, while concealing the fact that the majority of the camp victims were Jews. The lack of a clear connection between the victims of Auschwitz and the Jews was a symptom of the process of Polonization and internationalization of the camp victims, which was common at that time.

In order to demonstrate that Auschwitz is primarily a site of Polish and international martyrdom, people deported to the camp were presented at museum exhibitions and in public discourse mainly in terms of their country of origin. In this way, the Jews, the main victims of the camp, were treated as citizens of various European countries and not as a separate ethnic or national category.

The symbolic culmination of this specific internationalist politics of memory was the 1967 unveiling of the International Monument to the Victims of Fascism at the former Birkenau. At its feet there are 19 plaques with the text in the languages of the victims: "Four million[12] people suffered and died here at the hands of the Nazi murderers between the years 1940 and 1945." Thus, the text made it impossible to recognize who the main victims of Auschwitz were or how many of them really died. In addition, the first plaque was in Polish and the subsequent ones were arranged alphabetically, so that the plaques in Hebrew and Yiddish (*jidysz* in Polish), symbolizing Jews – the largest ethnic group of victims – were placed in the middle. This meant marginalization of Jewish victims.

In the 1970s, the policy of belittling the size and significance of the extermination of Jews at KL Auschwitz was continued. To cite Jonathan Huener, "Neither the State Museum nor Polish government ever explicitly denied that the vast majority of victims at Auschwitz were Jews. But this fact was not emphasized; nor did it designate Auschwitz in any distinctive way."[13]

A fundamental change in the perception of Auschwitz did not begin until the late 1980s, when Jewish symbolism of the camp reappeared on the premises of the museum. This was influenced by the process of "reconstructing"[14] and "recovering" the social memory of the Jews[15] observed throughout Poland, which in the case of Auschwitz took the form of a conflict over the crosses and the Carmelite convent located in the immediate vicinity of Auschwitz.[16]

The impulse for significant changes to the museum exhibition and the description of this historical site was supplied by the media debates about the history of the camp taking place in the mid-1990s. As a result, new plaques were placed at the monument in Birkenau with new estimates of the number of victims and information on Jews as the largest group. In the aftermath of these changes, at the end of the twentieth century the extermination of the Jews became one of the most important topics in the museum's message.[17]

The Auschwitz Museum in Historical Tourism

Since the very beginning, museums established on the former death camp sites have been a popular destination for individual and group trips of many Poles. The state authorities played an important role in this, and seeing the propaganda potential, they encouraged citizens to visit these sites in large numbers. Following these recommendations, visits to memorial sites were organized by factories and similar establishments, schools, universities, as well as social and political organizations. The most important in situ memorial museums, such as Auschwitz, Majdanek or Stutthof, where until the end of the 1960s, monumental memorials were erected, also became an integral part of visits by important foreign and state delegations. On the grounds of the martyrdom museums operating there, the authorities willingly organized various political gatherings, youth rallies, ceremonies and anniversary celebrations related not only to the history of the former camps, but also to the Second World War in general. During the Cold War period, they usually took the form of mass political rallies, during which speeches were made and anti-war slogans were chanted in support of the policy of the Polish communist government and the entire Eastern Bloc. These events were attended by tens or even hundreds of thousands of people who were brought in from all over the country to show the mass public support for state policy. The largest gatherings included the ceremonies of the opening of museums, consecutive round anniversaries of the outbreak and end of the Second World War, the liberation of the camps and the unveiling of the main monuments.

After the political transformation, the commemoration of the liberation of the camps became the most important anniversary commemorations, which take place annually on January 27 on the grounds of the former Auschwitz camp. In 2005, this day was declared International Holocaust Remembrance Day by the UN. In addition, some groups of victims (Poles and Roma) also organize their anniversary celebrations there on other dates.

Religious ceremonies are also organized at the site of the former camp memorials. The most significant and massive one was the Catholic mass celebrated by Pope John Paul II in Birkenau in 1979, attended by over 450,000 people. All these ceremonies show how varied the symbolism of Auschwitz was and still is and its multidimensional social significance.

Over the years, visits to the largest memorial sites have become a kind of tradition and an integral part of travelling around Poland, and a particular type of historical tourism has developed, referred to as memorial tourism or martyrological tourism. Today such tourism is understood as "a special type of cultural tourism involving travel of explorative or explorative-religious character to the sites which document and commemorate the suffering, pacification, martyrdom, Holocaust, or death of population."[18] The main destinations of this tourism are former concentration and extermination camps, ghettos, prisons, places of mass execution and death, together with cemeteries and monuments commemorating the persecution, suffering and death of the victims of Nazi genocide.

It is impossible to disregard the fact that such understood tourism to places of remembrance becomes an integral part of the globally noticeable phenomenon of travelling to places of remembrance associated with death, which commemorate a tragic event of the past. Therefore, in the literature on this subject, it can be associated with the dynamically developing dark tourism and thanatotourism. The first expression indicates tourist traffic connected with the phenomenon of death in the context of the place where human tragedy occurred and the memory of this event. The second one, in turn, concerns travelling motivated by the necessity of "contact" (real or symbolic) with death. It is important to highlight that two of the five categories of thanatotourism are related to the Second World War remembrance tourism in which we take particular interest. In accordance with its assumptions, the grounds of former death camps are perceived as broadly understood sepulchral spaces, which are associated with death and with many forms of worshipping the dead.[19]

Travelling to places documenting human suffering and death has always been, and continues to be, an important aspect of travelling and exploring various parts of the world. This stems from the fact that the very interest in death, in both individual and collective tragedies, has always fascinated man. Furthermore, all unfavorable and destructive events encourage people to contemplate and reflect on the fragility of human existence.

The analysis of the needs, motivation and behaviors of the tourists visiting the post-camp memorial sites allows, in the opinion of Sławoj Tanaś, for distinguishing at least two main categories of tourists: "cultural tourists" and "tourists by coincidence."[20] The first category characterizes a tourist who "in reality treats commemorative museums as tourist attractions and interferes with the visit in terms of a tourist excursion, but primarily seeks to broaden their knowledge, obtain new experience and develop their own interests."[21] Whereas the second one encompasses visitors who have been called "dark tourists," having difficulties with defining their expectations and concentrated on visiting the commemorative places from the perspective of their tourist attractiveness.[22]

The research undertaken by Jadwiga Berbeka, who has analyzed the behavior of tourists at the Auschwitz Memorial, provides some insights into this problem. This research was undertaken in 2011 among domestic and foreign tourists. Approximately half of the questionnaire respondents claimed that the visit to Auschwitz was actually part of a wider sightseeing program, which mainly included Kraków. Despite the fact that among the motivations for visiting Auschwitz given by the respondents of the survey the themes of exploration were predominant, for nearly 13% of them the motive was simple curiosity.[23] This demonstrates that Auschwitz is treated as a tourism product. And even though not all places of commemoration in Poland are perceived in a similar way, nevertheless the number of visitors is systematically increasing everywhere. For example, in the Auschwitz Museum the annual number of visitors has increased nearly five-fold over the last 20 years, from around half a million in 2001 to 2.3 million in 2019.

Such tendencies have their consequences highlighted by Tanaś, who observes that "tourist traffic may result in an excessive and inappropriate exploitation of their [memorial site] spaces, or even to its objectification and profanation."[24] Other consequences of mass tourism may also include a widespread musealization of post-camp places of commemoration, which gradually reduces their sacrum and transforms them into tourist spaces. Nevertheless, it is important not to forget that mass tourism in places of remembrance can also fulfil an explorative function. This is demonstrated when the perception of the visit changes over time, from the category of a simple tourist trip to an educational and emotional experience.[25]

The interest in trips to the places of remembrance associated with the Second World War (marked by death), which grows year over year, makes martyrological tourism an important part of historical tourism in Poland which contributes to its development and raises interest among the organizers and animators of education.[26] Therefore, martyrological tourism can also become an educational instrument for the future. This postulate is being implemented by the pedagogy of (the places of) remembrance, which has been recently developed dynamically also in Poland.[27]

It is not uncommon for tourists visiting memorials to become later involved in their activities. They are involved in collecting documentation and verifying historical accounts of particular memorial sites, in organizing events and exhibitions, in developing their own narratives and their attractive presentation in order to reach the widest possible audience with a desired, predetermined profile.[28] In many cases, the former prisoners of concentration camps also become involved and active, and even initiate the creation of museums/places of remembrance on the post-camp sites.

In Auschwitz, former prisoners not only established the foundations of the museum institution, but also protected the area, kept it safe from desecration and plundering of the remains of the camp. Afterwards, they were the first guides and trained their successors. They met people visiting this place, to whom they told stories about their experiences, offered their accounts of events and gave testimonies. In addition, they also established associations and patronage organizations (the so-called committees of former prisoners) that looked after the development of museum institutions, raised funds for their activities, built monuments and created exhibitions.[29]

The most famous of them was the International Auschwitz Committee, which was established in the early 1950s. It was on its initiative that the so-called national exhibitions began to be created from the beginning of 1960s and in 1967 the monumental International Monument to the Victims of Fascism was unveiled.[30] The International Council of the Museum was established in 1989, and later transformed into the International Auschwitz Council (IAC). The council was composed of a representative of the IAC and other prisoner organizations from Poland and abroad, who advised the Polish authorities and the management of the Auschwitz Museum in shaping the politics of memory and developing forms of commemoration. The activities of the Council had a direct impact on the new shape and development directions of the museum institution after the political transformation and, as a result, contributed to a change in the museum narrative at the Auschwitz Memorial.[31]

The Auschwitz Museum Today – New Functions and Social Memory

The fall of communism, Poland's opening to the world and the changes in the historical narrative about Auschwitz that took place in the last decade of the twentieth century provided an impulse for a new opening of the Auschwitz Memorial. The museum gradually began to change its character and, as a result, transformed from an institution that was a propaganda tool for implementing the politics of history of the communist regime, into a modern in situ memorial museum. In order to increase the Museum's ability to influence social awareness in Poland and worldwide, in 2005 the International Centre for Education about Auschwitz and the Holocaust was established within its structures to deal with education aimed at various groups of recipients. Apart from young people, its program offer is addressed to various professional groups, mainly teachers, journalists, lawyers, policemen, officials, soldiers and the prison service. To meet their expectations, the Museum offers various types of individual and group tours, with a guide and audio guide, the time and program of which can be adapted to individual needs. Recently, on account of the pandemic, extensive works have also been carried out to launch the possibility of virtual sightseeing. In addition, the Museum places great emphasis on the use of social media for the purposes of promotion and communication with visitors.

The results of the changes introduced at the Museum for almost three decades are reflected in the findings of sociological research on the collective memory of Poles about Auschwitz in the context of the Second World War. These studies show not only new tendencies, but also old cliches of remembrance, which are the result of its deliberate and long-term instrumentalization by the communist authorities. These studies confirm the decline in the perception of the former Auschwitz camp in terms of a symbolic Polish-Jewish remembrance conflict, which has been observed for years.[32] Auschwitz is still one of the most frequently mentioned elements of the Second World War. And although it is still recognized as the site of the genocide committed against Poles and Jews, it is slowly becoming an increasingly recognizable symbol of the Holocaust. At the same time, Poles also associate it mainly with the genocide that took place there and with the feelings of the victims of the camp and towards them. Auschwitz is also the Nazi camp from the Second World War which is best known to Poles. Next, the most frequently mentioned ones are: Treblinka, Majdanek and Stutthof. On the other hand, Bełżec and Kulmhof (Chełmno on Ner) appear relatively rarely.

Conclusions

Memorial sites in the post-camp space, also known as new-type historical museums, perform many socially and culturally important functions in Poland. They are not only guardians of the knowledge of the past and components of the culture of remembrance, but also subjects of historical communication and centers of social influence. Moreover, from the point of view of material culture, they are also cemeteries, relics and monuments, affecting not only the explorative but also the emotional sphere of visitors.[33]

Many of them conduct intensive scholarly, educational and popularizing activities, the effects of which go beyond the premises of the museum and enter the public space, both the immediate and the more distant one. They engage the public both as recipients and co-authors of their message. Nevertheless, in the public sphere, these museums are seen primarily as memorial sites, sometimes as "tourist attractions," addressed to the tourists who desire "extreme" experiences. On the other hand, they are treated to a much lesser extent as elements of contemporary culture and as entities creating it.

Notes

1 KL is the commonly used abbreviation for *Konzentrationslager*, the German word for "concentration camp."
2 People of German ancestry from occupied countries willing or consenting to Germanization.
3 See Jacek Lachendro, *Zburzyć i zaorać...? Idea założenia Państwowego Muzeum Auschwitz-Birkenau w świetle prasy polskiej w latach 1945–1948* (Oświęcim: Państwowe Muzeum Auschwitz-Birkenau, 2007).
4 Currently, there are ten so-called national pavilions with the following exhibitions: Polish, Russian, Jewish, Romani, Slovak, Czech, Hungarian, French, Dutch and Belgian. Two more are being prepared: Greek and Austrian.
5 Cf. Alan L. Berger, Harry James Cargas, and Susan E. Nowak, *The Continuing Agony. From the Carmelite Convent to the Crosses at Auschwitz* (Lanham: University Press of America, 2004).
6 Tomasz Kranz, "O społecznych znaczeniach muzeów w dawnych niemieckich obozach zagłady," in *Muzea martyrologiczne w Polsce i Niemczech.*

Pamięć – edukacja – turystyka, ed. Robert Traba, Katarzyna Woniak, Enrico Heitzer, and Günter Morsch (Warszawa – Berlin: ISP PAN, CBH PAN, 2018), 56–57.

7   Tomasz Kranz, "Majdanek – poobozowe lieu de memoire w przestrzeni miasta," in *Lubelskie miejsca pamięci w przestrzeni publicznej i edukacji*, ed. Mariusz Ausz, Joanna Bugajska-Więcławska, Dominika Staszczyk, Andrzej Stępnik, and Dariusz Szewczuk (Lublin: Instytut Historii UMCS, 2015), 113–114.

8   Kranz, "Krajobrazy pamięci – podmioty kultury," 37. Cf. James Young, *The Texture of Memory. Holocaust Memorials and Meaning* (New Haven: Yale University Press, 1993).

9   Tomasz Kranz, "Krajobrazy pamięci – przestrzenie turystyczne – miejsca edukacji. O współczesnych znaczeniach muzeów martyrologicznych," in *Turystyka w edukacji historycznej i obywatelskiej*, ed. Mariusz Ausz, Joanna Bugajska-Więcławska, Andrzej Stępnik, and Dariusz Szewczuk (Lublin: UMCS, 2017), 79.

10 Sławomir Kapralski, "The Role Played by the Auschwitz-Birkenau State Museum in Public Discourse and the Evolving Consciousness of the Holocaust in Polish Society," in *Jewish Presence in Absence: Aftermath of the Holocaust in Poland 1945–2010*, ed. Feliks Tych and Monika Adamczyk-Garbowska (Jerusalem: Yad Vashem, 2014), 605–633.

11 Jacek Chrobaczyński and Piotr Trojański, "Auschwitz and Katyn in Political Bondage: The Process of Shaping Memory in Communist Poland," in *Memory and Change in Europe. Eastern Perspectives*, ed. Małgorzata Pakier and Joanna Wawrzyniak (New York – Oxford: Berghahn Books, 2016), 255. See also: Zofia Wóycicka, *Arrested Mourning. Memory of Nazi Camps in Poland, 1944–1950* (Frankfurt am Main: Peter Lang, 2014).

12 The number of 4 million victims of KL Auschwitz was established in 1945 by the Extraordinary Soviet State Commission for the Investigation of the Crimes of German-Fascist Aggressors and was mandatory throughout the entire period of the Polish People's Republic.

13 Jonathan Huener, *Auschwitz, Poland, and the Politics of Commemoration, 1945–1979* (Athens: Ohio University Press, 2004), 29.

14 Michael Steinlauf, *Bondage to the Dead: Poland and the Memory of the Holocaust* (Syracuse: Syracuse University Press, 1997).

15 Cf. Piotr Forecki, *Reconstructing Memory: The Holocaust in Polish Public Debates* (Frankfurt am Main: Peter Lang, 2013).

16 Cf. Geneviève Zubrzycki, *The Crosses of Auschwitz. Nationalism and Religion in Post-Communist Poland* (Chicago: University of Chicago Press, 2006).

17 Kranz, „Krajobraz pamięci – podmioty kultury," 64.

18 *Turystyka martyrologiczna w Polsce na przykładzie Państwowego Muzeum Auschwitz-Birkenau*, ed. Jadwiga Berbeka (Kraków: Proksenia, 2012), 11.

19 Sławoj Tanaś, "Tourism 'Death Space' and Thanatourism in Poland," *Current Issues of Tourism Research* 3, no. 1 (2013): 25.

20 Sławoj Tanaś, "Tanatoturystyka – kontrowersyjne oblicze turystyki kulturowej," *Peregrinus Cracoviensis* 17 (2006): 95.

21 Wiesław Wysok, "Turyści w autentycznych miejscach pamięci na przykładzie Państwowego Muzeum na Majdanku," in *Turystyka w edukacji*, 242–243.

22 Katarzyna Stec, "Symbolika i znaczenie miejsc pamięci utworzonych na terenach byłych obozów koncentracyjnych i zagłady z perspektywy współczesnego młodego człowieka," in *Antysemityzm, Holokaust, Auschwitz w badaniach społecznych*, ed. Marek Kucia (Kraków: Wydawnictwo Uniwersytetu Jagiellońskiego, 2011), 44.

23 Berbeka, *Turystyka martyrologiczna*, 163–166.

24 Sławoj Tanaś, *Tanatoturustyka. Od przestrzeni śmierci do przestrzeni turystycznej* (Łodź: Wydawnictwo Uniwersytetu Łódzkiego, 2013), 151. See also: Sławoj Tanaś, "The Perception of Death in Cultural Tourism," *Turyzm* 18, no. 1 (2008) 51–63.

25 Katarzyna Stec, "Rola wizyty w muzeum – miejscu pamięci dla współczesnego młodego człowieka – doświadczenie edukacyjne czy turystyczne?," in *Auschwitz i Holokaust. Edukacja w szkole i miejscu pamięci*, ed. Piotr Trojański (Oświęcim: Państwowe Muzeum Auschwitz-Birkenau, 2014), 296.

26 Andrzej Stępnik, "Turystyka historyczna," in *Historia w przestrzeni publicznej*, ed. Joanna Wojdon (Warszawa: Wydawnictwo Naukowe PWN, 2018), 151.

27 Cf. *Pedagogika pamięci. O terorii i praktyce edukacji w muzeach martyrologicznych*, ed. Tomasz Kranz (Lublin: Państwowe Muzeum na Majdanku, 2018); *U podstaw pedagogiki pamięci Auschwitz i Holokaustu*, ed. Agata Czajkowska and Piotr Trojański (Oświęcim: Państwowe Muzeum Auschwitz-Birkenau, 2018).

28 Joanna Wojdon, "Turystyka historyczna jako element historii w przestrzeni publicznej (public history)," in *Turystyka w edukacji*, 69.

29 Cf. Zofia Wóycicka, "Ku wspólnej europejskiej pamięci? Międzynarodowy Komitet Oświęcimski i Buchenwaldzki w latach 1952–1989/90," in *Muzea martyrologiczne*, 109–121.

30 Cf. Piotr Trojański, *Auschwitz w okowach polityki. Międzynarodowy Komitet Oświęcimski w latach 1954–1970. Wybór dokumentów* (Kraków: Wydawnictwo Naukowe Uniwersytetu Pedagogicznego, 2019), 44–64.

31 Tomasz Cebulski, *Auschwitz po Auschwitz. Historia, polityka i pamięć. Wokół Państwowego Muzeum Auschwitz–Birkenau 1980–2010* (Kraków: Libron, 2016), 161–217.

32 Cf. Marek Kucia, "The Meanings of Auschwitz in Poland, 1945 to the Present." *Holocaust Studies. A Journal of Culture and History* 25, special issue no. 3 (2019), 220–247.

33 Tomasz Kranz, *Edukacja historyczna w miejscach pamięci. Zarys problematyki* (Lublin: Dialog i Współpraca, 2002), 38.

Bibliography

Berbeka, Jadwiga, ed. *Turystyka martyrologiczna w Polsce na przykładzie Państwowego Muzeum Auschwitz-Birkenau.* Kraków: Proksenia, 2012.

Berger, Alan L., Harry James Cargas, and Susan E. Nowak. *The Continuing Agony. From the Carmelite Convent to the Crosses at Auschwitz.* Lanham: University Press of America, 2004.

Cebulski, Tomasz. *Auschwitz po Auschwitz. Historia, polityka i pamięć. Wokół Państwowego Muzeum Auschwitz-Birkenau. 1980–2010.* Kraków: Libron, 2016.

Chrobaczyński, Jacek and Piotr Trojański. "Auschwitz and Katyn in Political Bondage: The Process of Shaping Memory in Communist Poland." In *Memory and Change in Europe. Eastern Perspectives*, edited by Małgorzata Pakier and Joanna Wawrzyniak, 246–263. New York – Oxford: Berghahn Books, 2016.

Czajkowska, Agata and Piotr Trojański, eds. *U podstaw pedagogiki pamięci Auschwitz i Holokaustu.* Oświęcim: Państwowe Muzeum Auschwitz-Birkenau, 2018.

Dorota Świtała-Trybek. "Turystyka miejsc pamięci – zwrot ku lokalności." In *Filozoficzne i społeczne aspekty sportu i turystyki*, edited by Jerzy Kosewicz, Eligiusz Małolepszy and Teresa Drozdek-Małolepsza, 253–264. Częstochowa: Akademia im. Jana Długosza, 2016.

Forecki, Piotr. *Reconstructing Memory: The Holocaust in Polish Public Debates.* Frankfurt am Main: Peter Lang, 2013.

Huener, Jonathan. *Auschwitz, Poland, and the Politics of Commemoration, 1945– 1979.* Athens, Ohio: Ohio University Press, 2004.

Kapralski, Sławomir. "The Role Played by the Auschwitz-Birkenau State Museum in Public Discourse and the Evolving Consciousness of the Holocaust in Polish Society." In *Jewish Presence in Absence: Aftermath of the Holocaust in Poland 1945–2010*, edited by Feliks Tych and Monika Adamczyk-Garbowska, 605–633. Jerusalem: Yad Vashem, 2014.

Kranz, Tomasz. *Edukacja historyczna w miejscach pamięci. Zarys problematyki.* Lublin: Dialog i Współpraca, 2002.

Kranz, Tomasz, ed. *Pedagogika pamięci. O terorii i praktyce edukacji w muzeach martyrologicznych.* Lublin: Państwowe Muzeum na Majdanku, 2018.

Kranz, Tomasz. "Krajobrazy pamięci – przestrzenie turystyczne – miejsca edukacji. O współczesnych znaczeniach muzeów martyrologicznych." In *Turystyka w edukacji historycznej i obywatelskiej*, edited by Mariusz Ausz, Joanna Bugajska-Więcławska, Andrzej Stępnik, and Dariusz Szewczuk, 71–90. Lublin: UMCS, 2017.

Kranz, Tomasz. "Krajobrazy pamięci – podmioty kultury obiekty turystyczne – przestrzenie edukacji." In *Muzea w poobozowych miejscach pamięci. Tożsamość, znaczenie, funkcje*, edited by Tomasz Kranz, 19–68. Lublin: Państwowe Muzeum na Majdanku, 2017.

Kranz, Tomasz. "Krajobrazy pamięci – przestrzenie turystyczne – miejsca edukacji. O współczesnych znaczeniach muzeów martyrologicznych." In *Turystyka w edukacji historycznej i obywatelskiej*, edited by Mariusz Ausz, Joanna Bugajska-Więcławska, Andrzej Stępnik, and Dariusz Szewczuk, 71–90. Lublin: UMCS, 2017.

Kranz, Tomasz. "Majdanek – poobozowe lieu de memoire w przestrzeni miasta." In *Lubelskie miejsca pamięci w przestrzeni publicznej i edukacji*, edited by Mariusz Ausz, Joanna Bugajska-Więcławska, Dominika Staszczyk, Andrzej Stępnik, and Dariusz Szewczuk, 113–128. Lublin: Instytut Historii UMCS, 2015.

Kranz, Tomasz. "O społecznych znaczeniach muzeów w dawnych niemieckich obozach zagłady." In *Muzea martyrologiczne w Polsce i Niemczech. Pamięć – edukacja – turystyka*, edited by Robert Traba, Katarzyna Woniak, Enrico Heitzer, and Günter Morsch, 55–72. Warszawa – Berlin: ISP PAN, CBH PAN, 2018.

Kranz, Tomasz, ed. *Pedagogika pamięci. O terorii i praktyce edukacji w muzeach martyrologicznych.* Lublin: Państwowe Muzeum na Majdanku, 2018.

Kubiszyn, Marta. "Działanie – przeżywanie – zaangażowane uczestnictwo. Pedagogika miejsc pamięci i edukacja o Zagładzie w wybranych projektach realizowanych na terenie Państwowego Muzeum na Majdanku w Lublinie." In *U podstaw pedagogiki pamięci Auschwitz i Holokaustu*, edited by Agata Czajkowska and Piotr Trojański, 95–120. Oświęcim: Państwowe Muzeum Auschwitz-Birkenau, 2018.

Kucia, Marek. "The Meanings of Auschwitz in Poland, 1945 to the Present." *Holocaust Studies. A Journal of Culture and History* 25, special issue no. 3 (2019): 220–247.

Lachendro, Jacek. *Zburzyć i zaorać…? Idea założenia Państwowego Muzeum Auschwitz-Birkenau w świetle prasy polskiej w latach 1945–1948.* Oświęcim: Państwowe Muzeum Auschwitz-Birkenau, 2007.

Stec, Katarzyna. "Rola wizyty w muzeum – miejscu pamięci dla współczesnego młodego człowieka – doświadczenie edukacyjne czy turystyczne?" In *Auschwitz i Holokaust. Edukacja w szkole i miejscu pamięci*, edited by Piotr Trojański, 51–64. Oświęcim: Państwowe Muzeum Auschwitz-Birkenau, 2014.

Stec, Katarzyna. "Symbolika i znaczenie miejsc pamięci utworzonych na terenach byłych obozów koncentracyjnych i zagłady z perspektywy współczesnego młodego człowieka." In *Antysemityzm, Holokaust, Auschwitz w badaniach społecznych*, edited by Marek Kucia, 37–54. Kraków: Wydawnictwo Uniwersytetu Jagiellońskiego, 2011.

Steinlauf, Michael. *Bondage to the Dead: Poland and the Memory of the Holocaust.* Syracuse: Syracuse University Press, 1997.

Stępnik, Andrzej. "Turystyka historyczna." In *Historia w przestrzeni publicznej*, edited by Joanna Wojdon, 149–156. Warszawa: PWN, 2018.

Tanaś, Sławoj. "The Perception of Death in Cultural Tourism," *Turyzm* 18, no. 1 (2008): 51–63.

Tanaś, Sławoj. "Tanatoturystyka – kontrowersyjne oblicze turystyki kulturowej." *Peregrinus Cracoviensis, z.* 17 (2006): 85–86.

Tanaś, Sławoj. *Tanatoturustyka. Od przestrzeni śmierci do przestrzeni turystycznej.* Łódź: Wydawnictwo Uniwersytetu Łódzkiego, 2013.

Tanaś, Sławoj. "Tourism 'Death Space' and Thanatourism in Poland," *Current Issues of Tourism Research* 3, no. 1 (2014): 22–27.

Trojański, Piotr. *Auschwitz w okowach polityki. Międzynarodowy Komitet Oświęcimski w latach 1954–1970. Wybór dokumentów.* Kraków: Wydawnictwo Naukowe Uniwersytetu Pedagogicznego, 2019.

Wojdon, Joanna. "Turystyka historyczna jako element historii w przestrzeni publicznej (public history)." In *Turystyka w edukacji historycznej i obywatelskiej*, edited by Mariusz Ausz, Joanna Bugajska-Więcławska, Andrzej Stępnik, and Dariusz Szewczuk, 59–70. Lublin: UMCS, 2017.

Wóycicka, Zofia. "Ku wspólnej europejskiej pamięci? Międzynarodowy Komitet Oświęcimski i Buchenwaldzki w latach 1952–1989/90." In *Muzea martyrologiczne w Polsce i Niemczech. Pamięć – edukacja – turystyka*, edited by Robert Traba, Katarzyna Woniak, Enrico Heitzer, and Günter Morsch, 109–121. Warszawa – Berlin: ISP PAN, CBH PAN, 2018.

Wysok, Wiesław. "Turyści w autentycznych miejscach pamięci na przykładzie Państwowego Muzeum na Majdanku." In *Turystyka w edukacji historycznej i obywatelskiej*, edited by Mariusz Ausz, Joanna Bugajska-Więcławska, Andrzej Stępnik, and Dariusz Szewczuk, 237–256. Lublin: UMCS, 2017.

Young, James. *The Texture of Memory. Holocaust Memorials and Meaning.* New Haven: Yale University Press, 1993.

Zubrzycki, Geneviève. *The Crosses of Auschwitz. Nationalism and Religion in Post-Communist Poland.* Chicago: University of Chicago Press, 2006.

6 National Pride and Echoes of Local Identity

Public History in Silesian Towns

Przemysław Wiszewski

The concept of public history does not function in the policies of local authorities managing towns and cities in Lower Silesia. However, this does not mean that the presence of history in urban space is spontaneous. On the contrary, as the examples presented in this chapter will show, the combination of the influence of national models of historical education and historical policies of individual Polish governments along with the decisions of local authorities after 1945 created a fairly coherent approach to creating an ideological message directed at people reading and experiencing towns' or cities' topographies as symbolical texts. Consistency does not mean that city authorities and citizens read various elements present in a settlement's space and refer to the past in the same way. Enriching urban spatial narrative in historical plots is a very broad topic, so in this chapter I focus on one particular problem – modes of building a network of meanings referencing to history in the space of selected urban centers in the Lower Silesia region after 1945.

I use the concept of mental maps, i.e., ideas of space specific to a person or a social group, ordered and valued according to the current needs of the owner. Their reconstruction makes it possible to analyze the diverse approach of their users to a space shared with others.[1] This differentiation of approaches to a meaning of shared space is related to the fact that individual entities pursue different goals in this space, have different cultural endowments (knowledge about the surrounding reality and the way it is perceived) and susceptibility to open or hidden ideological messages programmed by third parties. Mental maps change very dynamically, according to the needs and the current state of the mental equipment of their owners. The researcher can therefore capture their shape only at a given moment, without being sure that the presented image will be adequate in the long run.[2] This difficulty can be mitigated to some extent by tracking how elements recognizable to members of a given community appear in the common space, and then how their meanings change when their context – wider spatial narratives used to convey key values for the community – is gradually changing.[3]

The space that turns into a story by connecting symbolic points is shaped in a manner accepted by the community as a meeting place, an ideological

DOI: 10.4324/9781003165767-8

space shared by users. It is true that the public nature of this space has its limitations. As has been indicated above, a space containing references to the past as a stream of information interpreted by recipients, like any other type of text, may in detail have different meanings for each of the recipients. And yet the stability of the ideological meaning of public space, the spatial scene of community life, is of a special nature. Public space with its meanings is always between persons who have used it and read it. Public space connects these entities by the very essence of space, a place that is common per se for its users. This, in turn, is the source of the impact of the aforementioned network of spatial meanings on the participants of social life. We agree to them in order to have a chance to participate in relations with other users of this space. If so, what role does historical content play in this common space, shaping the worldview of the community members and at the same time being shaped by the very same community?

This question is of particular importance for border regions where the influences of different historical traditions intersect, especially in the period of development of strong nation states whose social cohesion is built on the basis of the domination of a centrally programmed national vision of history. For such a narrative about the past, multicultural, multi-ethnic border regions are a challenge, as they contest the explanatory validity of models focused on the history of nations as the only active subjects of history. In the case of contemporary Silesia, which is discussed in this chapter, the situation is even more difficult. Not only is it a region immersed in the history of Bohemia, Germany and Poland, but also with a tradition of its own autonomy in relation to the state organisms it was part of. Finally, after the end of the Second World War, an almost complete population exchange took place here. The previous German-speaking inhabitants, who had passed on local cultural traditions for hundreds of years, were displaced to Germany. Their place was taken by Polish-speaking newcomers from the pre-war areas of Poland occupied by the Soviet Union and from various regions that were parts of the Polish state after 1945. The region has become a new home for population groups representing various local cultures, and in part of various ethnic origins – especially after the forced settlement in Lower Silesia of Ukrainians displaced by force by the Polish authorities from the Bieszczady region bordering the Ukrainian Soviet Socialist Republic (Operation "Wisła," 1947–1950).[4]

This complicated situation of overlapping the existing cultural tissue, i.e., the material remnants of German-speaking Silesia, and many varieties of Polish regionalisms enriched by Jewish, Ruthenian, Ukrainian, Romanian, and other ethnic and national cultures brought by migrants, gives an opportunity to investigate to what extent the patterns of national interpretation of history, promoted by the Polish state authorities from 1945 to the present day, are the dominant forces shaping the symbolic space of cities? To what extent can regionalisms and local content modify this dominant trend? Searching for answers to these questions, I primarily use those ideologically significant elements of space that were permanently and relatively clearly programmed by their creators for recipients: local toponymy networks (street names mostly) and monuments.

I start my analysis by looking at the situation of Wrocław, the Lower Silesian metropolis and capital of the region. The city, as a center of power recognized before the year 1000, is today the capital of the voivodeship, one of the 17 basic administrative units of the Polish state, the center of the voivodeship self-government authorities and representatives of state authority in the region of Lower Silesia. The most important cultural institutions of the voivodeship are also located here. At present, it has an official population of 640,000. According to estimates of the consumption of municipal utilities, this number should be raised to around 825,000 inhabitants, including around 180,000 migrants and immigrants (mainly from Ukraine) unofficially staying in the city.[5] The significant nationwide political power of the city elites after 1989 enabled the processes of creating the city's own identity, to a large extent regardless of national trends. At the same time, as the dominant center in the region, Wrocław sets certain cultural and political fashions. The open question is whether the influential position of Wrocław is valid also in terms of creating a meaning of the public space? I will try to check it by comparing the content that dominates the Wrocław space with the situation in smaller urban centers. In their case, is the local identity with a historical background a strong element in shaping public space, and through it the building of regional or local identifications of its users?

I will examine these phenomena more closely through the examples of two cities of different sizes. The first is Oleśnica, a city located near Wrocław and at the same time having episodes of strongly marked separateness in its past. From the fourteenth century, it was the capital of a large principality bordering Poland. Until the end of the fifteenth century, the principality belonged to the Piast dynasty, from which the rulers of Poland descended, then the Czech Poděbrady dynasty, and from the mid-seventeenth century the German Württemberg and Wittelsbach dynasties, to pass into the hands of the Hohenzollerns at the beginning of the nineteenth century. The city then became the capital of the district (Kreis), and after 1945 it remained the main center of territorial units of the administrative division of Lower Silesia. The second city, Świerzawa, is a small town located in the mountainous south of the region. It has never played a significant political or economic role in the region. However, it was still an important center of local administration, and and a location of one of the most valuable architectural monuments of the region, strongly associated with the tradition of medieval Silesian princes from the Polish Piast dynasty.

Therefore, let us take a look at the space of Silesian cities, whose history offers a number of references to colorful characters, events and processes taking place in local contexts. Was their attractiveness sufficient to allow them to appear on mental maps designed for their inhabitants after 1945 by state and local authorities?

Wrocław: Geo-Cultural Identity
in the Face of National Stories

The incorporation of Silesia within the borders of Poland at the end of the Second World War was associated with the displacement of the remaining German inhabitants of the region. With them, local naming traditions and ideas about the city space disappeared. Radical ethnic change meant that it was necessary to carry out an equally radical change of topographical names. The new inhabitants not only used a different language than their predecessors, but also, after the years of cruel occupation, felt in the vast majority a profound aversion to the culture of the German language. Therefore, they expected a description of the urban space to be formulated in language and cultural categories that they would understand. Between May 1945 and May 1946, over 1,200 names of streets and squares in the city were changed, and most of the existing monuments were taken down. German signs and all kinds of inscriptions in public spaces were removed. Radical polonization, which continued in 1947, even led to the partial destruction of medieval and early modern buildings and tombstones in order to remove inscriptions in German. The changes to the names of streets and city squares introduced at that time were to emphasize clearly the relationship between Wrocław and the history of the Polish nation. All references to local traditions other than those related to the presence of Poles or people considered to belong to Polish history (the rulers of Silesia from the Piast dynasty) were removed from the public space. The changes were often of a clearly polemical nature. And so the bridge over the Oder called *Keiserbrück* was renamed Grunwald Bridge in reference to the decisive victory of Lithuanians and Poles over the Teutonic Order in the Battle of Grunwald (1410). In turn, the representative *Kaiser-Wilhelm Strasse* was renamed Silesian Insurgents Street to commemorate the Upper Silesians who fought in 1920–1921 in the course of three armed movements against the Germans for the annexation of Upper Silesia to Poland. Many names, especially in the Old Town, have retained their meaning and have only been translated into Polish. They were viewed as referring to medieval times, considered at that time to be related to the Polish stage of the city's history.[6]

The network of meanings that could be read from the urban space and was formed at that time clearly referred to the national model of Polish history. It also contained references to the current political context important to the authorities of the time (e.g. commemorating heroes of the international workers' movement and of communist parties with particular emphasis on the history of the Soviet Union). This particular set of street names was changing even before 1989 (e.g. Stalin Street was removed in 1957, Stalingrad Street was renamed Świdnicka Street – according to its historical meaning). The core process of removing from street names patrons referring to communist ideology and the history of the so-called communist states took place after 1989 and was essentially completed by 1994.[7] This process, however, did not change the fundamental tendency introduced in 1945–1946. If the patron of the given city space was a person or a historical event, the street names almost always referred to the national history of Poland. There were practically no references to the local history before Poland took control of the city.

From the second half of the 1990s, the city authorities began consistently to build a new image of Wrocław. The former "Piast capital of Lower Silesia," where, according to the communist propaganda slogan, "even the stones speak Polish," was to become a multicultural and multi-ethnic metropolis. The foundation of this picture was to be the complicated history of the city in which Czech, German and Polish cultures intertwined and created an original mixture. In this way, Wrocław was to be a unique place, distinguished from other Polish metropolises due to its exceptionally close and constant relationship with the history of the whole of Europe, especially Central Europe. The ideological manifesto and the foundation for this urban politics of history was the synthesis of its history by Norman Davies and Roger Moorhouse, commissioned by the city, under the significant title: *Microcosm: A Portrait of a Central European City.*[8] This attempt by the city authorities to connect Wrocław more closely with European history and to loosen the domination of the national model of Polish history was not clearly reflected in the urban toponymy. A great example is the name of one of the iconic city buildings, a hall built to a design by Max Berg. It was erected in the years 1911–1913 to commemorate the events related to the war against Napoleon by Prussia. On 17 March 1813, King Frederick William III, during his stay in Wrocław, issued a historic proclamation addressed to his subjects from all over the Kingdom of Prussia (*To my people – An Mein Volk*), which initiated a nationwide movement against Napoleon Bonaparte's domination in the Kingdom. As a consequence, the new building was renamed the *Centennial Hall*, commemorating the close relationship between Wrocław and Prussian and German nationalism. After 1945, the name was changed to *Hala Ludowa – People's Hall* in reference to the popular character of the new Polish state. It was only after the start of the above-described plan of rebuilding the city's brand at the turn of the twentieth and twenty-first centuries that efforts were made to return to the historic name of the hall. It did not meet with the widespread understanding of the Wrocław inhabitants, even of part of the city elite. As a result, both names are still in use. The best example of this is that although the building is officially called *Hala Stulecia – Centennial Hall*, it is managed by a municipal company – *Wrocławskie Przedsiębiorstwo Hala Ludowa* (People's Hall Enterprise in Wrocław).[9]

An accurate illustration of shaping the symbolic space of Wrocław through various trends in understanding history is the presence in the very center of the city of three monuments to: the Polish writer Aleksander Fredro; King Bolesław the Brave (992–1025); and a series of bronze plates creating the "history path" of the city. The first of them was originally unveiled in 1897 in Lviv which was then part of the Habsburg monarchy, but was considered a city culturally dominated by Poles, and was the Polish capital of the

Ruthenian part of the Polish-Lithuanian Commonwealth (until 1772). After the First World War, it was, next to Vilnius, the second most important city in the eastern provinces of Poland (the so-called *Kresy*). With the end of the Second World War, these lands were incorporated into the Soviet Union and the Polish population was relocated to the west. Many refugees from Lviv settled in Wrocław. The monument was also taken from Lviv in 1946, but was first moved to Warsaw, and only at the end of the Stalinist period, in 1956, was it relocated to Wrocław. It was placed in the Main Market Square in the place where the statue of the King of Prussia, Frederick William III, had previously stood. Younger generations of Wrocław residents do not remember about the monument of the Prussian ruler, while the statue of Fredro and the related story about the Lviv origin of the first Polish settlers in Wrocław became a local myth that shaped the sense of belonging of the inhabitants. In this way, Wrocław played for Poles the role of the second Lviv, removing its German identity. The peripheral identity of Germany's eastern frontiers has been replaced by the idea of the heritage of Poland's eastern periphery – at its new, western borders.

In 2007, a statue of Bolesław the Brave on a horse was erected on the city's representative street leading south from the Main Market Square. It took the place of a long-defunct monument to Emperor William I. Its meaning is quite unambiguous – while riding a horse, it looks west. This ruler had become famous since medieval times for his many years of wars with Emperor Henry II, growing in historical memory to be the first, victorious defender of Polishness against the aggression of Germany. Despite the fact that the pedestal is decorated with reliefs and inscriptions emphasizing the German-Polish reconciliation, this does not change the nationalist, aggressive meaning of the monument.

Finally, in 2011, 17 plates with dates and symbolic representations of the most important events in the history of the city were placed on one of the historic streets within the Old Town. The path started from 1000, the establishment of a bishopric in the settlement, and reached 1997, the date of the historic flood. There were four plates for the period of the "Polish" city – commemorating the population exchange in 1945, the emergence of the Solidarity movement in 1980, the so-called Eucharistic Congress in 1997 and the above-mentioned flood. Over the years, new plates were added to commemorate the European Football Championship (2012), the year of the European Capital of Culture (2016), and the World Games (2017). However, the growing number and subsequent devaluation of the importance of the events commemorated after 2000 did not obliterate the main ideas of the original authors of the path – after two records of the "Polish" beginning (1000, 1241) of Wrocław, there are 11 objects commemorating the history of the "German" city (1242, 1335, 1526, 1530, 1633, 1702, 1741, 1793, 1807, 1842, 1913).[10]

It is the clearest declaration of the new narrative of the city's history created by local government authorities – the history of the city as a whole, from the first traces of settlement to the present day, is to be the center and point of reference for all descriptions of the history of this space. The national context has been completely obscured by the history of the people who created the culture of this particular place.

The three ways of telling stories about the city in recent decades have been reduced to two – national and regional. The more complicated and politically difficult to maintain vision of Wrocław as the replacement capital of the Polish eastern borderlands is pushed into the background. In the ideological dispute about the meaning of space and the identity of its inhabitants, a balance between regional and national has been maintained in Wrocław for years. However, this is not a typical situation for smaller towns in the region.

Oleśnica – The History of the Nation Overwhelming the Local Past

In the space of contemporary Oleśnica the most valuable symbolic statements were concentrated within the topography of the Old Town. However, due to the relatively small size of the city, interesting monuments referring to history can also be found on its outskirts. Finally, the network of streets covering the city, not as extensive as in the case of Wrocław, allows for a more precise ranking of particular types of patrons. As well, this has been done because it is easier to grasp the "interpretation field" in which individual signs are placed, i.e., a set of contexts created by the surrounding elements of space with socially assigned meanings. When writing about the presence of threads related to history in the urban space of Oleśnica, one can apply a classic, dualistic spatial valorization scheme to the scale of the city – the historic center, the most prestigious space, in which administrative and cultural life is concentrated, and zones of lower prestige. It is complemented by an indication of the enclaves of attention and prestige in peripheral spheres: the surroundings of churches and public administration buildings, and communication routes of significant importance to the city. In the "interpretative field" understood in this way, one can try to capture the practices of controlling the narrative of space through the names of streets, public buildings and the presence of monuments.

The analysis brings ambiguous results. On the one hand, the most important, historic element of the city is the Castle, the existence of which is closely related to the activities of the Czech Dukes of Oleśnica, Jan and Charles II of the Poděbrady family. However, this fact is not particularly emphasized in the names of the Castle or its vicinity. The occasional information boards show mainly the merits of other dynasties ruling the town (the Piasts, Württemberg and Hohenzollern). In the Old Town, we can find a number of street names with a double historical meaning: related to the historical nomenclature dating back to the period before 1945 and those relating to historical phenomena and figures applied after 1945. The former undoubtedly build a story about the continuity of the urban community's culture over the centuries, disregarding ethnic contexts. The latter emphasize almost without exception the connection of urban space with the national, Polish culture and historical tradition. Here were recalled the heroes of Polish political history (Jan Kiliński, Romuald Traugutt, Wały Jagiellońskie streets) or culture (Jan Matejko and Bolesław Prus streets). Nevertheless, we can also find here references to local history (Jan Sinapius Street, commemorating the baroque historiographer of Silesia associated with the city). In the immediate vicinity of the Old Town, though somewhat off the beaten track of the most important urban routes, there is an extensive Park named after the Dukes of Oleśnica (without specifying which dynasty). The tendency to emphasize Polish national history is growing in zones of lower prestige – here we can find *Wojska Polskiego*/Polish Army Street, the central communication route of the city; *Armii Krajowej*/the Home Army (Polish resistance army during the the Second World War) Street; and *3 Maja* (the date of the establishment of the Polish first constitution in 1791) Street; Polish writers: Jan Kochanowski, Mikołaj Rej, Henryk Sienkiewicz, Stefan Żeromski; political leaders: Bolesław Krzywousty, Józef Haller, Stanisław Maczek; politicians: Ignacy Paderewski, Ignacy Daszyński, Bolesław Limanowski; scholars: Maria Skłodowska-Curie, Mikołaj Kopernik, etc. This Polish pantheon of political and cultural heroes is rarely disturbed by references to regional or local history. As early as 1991, on the occasion of the first wave of street name changes, the one dedicated to Jerzy Bock, a Polish-speaking Protestant poet from Oleśnica was introduced.[11] It is significant, however, that this street is only a short link between two major streets dedicated to Polish, romantic heroes of culture – Sienkiewicz and Chopin. Among public buildings, it is worth mentioning in the context of space narrativization the Primary School No. 1 and Junior High School No. 1, both named after the dukes of Oleśnica. This is one of the few institutions that refer to local history in their name. Other schools received as their patrons personages from the national circle of heroes (Jan Kiliński, Juliusz Słowacki, Roman Dmowski, John Paul II, Janusz Korczak, Maria Skłodowska-Curie, Polish Nobel Laureates, and Polish Travelers and Explorers).[12]

The analysis of both the history of monuments in Oleśnica and the information they convey to the public shows the chronological layering of stories that were attempted to be attributed to these monuments and their groups by authorities.[13] Among the local monuments, the most frequently mentioned in literature (travel guide books, folders popularizing local history) are those with an indisputable historical value. First of all, is the so-called Golden Wedding column, unveiled in 1791 and commemorating the eponymous wedding anniversary of Carl Christian Erdmann Württemberg and his wife Maria Sophia Wilhelmina. Currently, the renovated column remains a sign suggesting to the recipients the historic splendor of the city. The lack of original medallions and inscriptions detailing the genesis of the monument makes it difficult to read its meaning more precisely.

Thus it is largely open to the recipient's interpretation. The next monument, the Victory Column, unveiled in 1873 to celebrate the victory of Prussia over France and the establishment of the united German Empire, has a similar character now. Before 1945, on its pedestal there were plates with inscriptions depicting the history of the city as a purely German society. They were taken down after 1945 and replaced in 1964 by their Polish version, celebrating the 1000th anniversary of Poland, the Piast history of the city, and its return to the Motherland (Poland) after the end of the Second World War. However, after 1989, these were also removed and replaced with plates that were devoid of any inscriptions.[14] As a result, the visually attractive monument is difficult to perceive and understand for an average recipient, who has to write in its content all by himself. And as in the case of the Golden Wedding Column, he/she has to consider it simply as a monument, a trace of the interesting, though unclear past of the city. This general reference is all the easier as both monuments are located in the historic Old Town, emphasizing past glory and the contemporary dignity of the city.

The pedestal of the monument of Emperor Frederick III was reused. Before 1939, this Hohenzollern was commemorated not only as the owner of the Castle, but also as the honorary head of Oleśnica's Dragoons Regiment No. 8. After 1945, the monument underwent a number of changes, removing not only the figure, but also part of the pedestal. Figures of Soviet and Polish soldiers were placed on the new pedestal in 1950, and the monument itself became the Monument of Gratitude to the Soviet Army and the Polish Army. The occasional inscription was removed after 1989, while the figures on the pedestal have survived the turmoil of history so far. The monument is located near the former center of Oleśnica, at the central point of the City Park (Henryk Sienkiewicz Park). It is difficult to say to what extent its content is legible today. It is more likely that for the younger generation it becomes a historical sign, which is attributed with meanings transferred from the narrative of older people, or as a generally understood reminder of old times.

The last monument, the genesis of which dates back to Prussian times, is the former statue of Chancellor Otto von Bismarck, officially unveiled in 1899. Even before the end of the Second World War, the figure was removed from the pedestal and melted down for military use. In 1963, a bust of Fryderyk Chopin was placed on an empty pedestal in front of the Oleśnica music school. The monument still commemorates this composer today, standing in front of the music school at the intersection of Church Street and Jan Matejko Street.[15]

An obelisk commemorating the peace ending the Austro-Prussian war in 1866, peripherally located within the city's topography, has also changed its meanings. The peace treaty was important for the then Prussians, because it opened the way to the reunification of Germany. For the inhabitants of Oleśnica, the war was of particular importance, because during this conflict the local dragoon regiment fought in key battles and suffered heavy losses. After 1945, as part of the Polonization of the so-called Recovered

Territories (Silesia, Pomerania and Masuria), the markings commemorating the original message were removed from it. In 1960, a decision was made to use it as the Monument to the Union of Fighters for Freedom and Democracy (that is, Poles fighting or repressed during the Second World War). It performed this function until the end of the political system of the time, only to change its destiny once again, though not so radically, in the wake of political changes. From then on, it became the Monument to the Veterans, in accordance with the inscription on the plaque ("For veterans and political prisoners – the society of the Oleśnica region"). It is striking that the columns of Oleśnica are treated as elements of the city's cultural heritage and only occasionally take part in creating elements of the city's political life. On the other hand, the Monument to Veterans is used as a space conducive to demonstrating patriotic feelings, or at least encouraging pro-state declarations as part of the celebration of national holidays, despite the fact that the monument, erected in the newly developed urban areas at the end of the nineteenth century, is today located outside the very center of Oleśnica. Its special place in the local liturgy of national holidays results from the fact that in the city's topography it promotes memories that are uniquely close to the state's historical narrative.

Two new monuments have been erected opposite the place where the Monument to Veterans stands, that is at Veterans Square, next to the Church of Our Lady of Mercy. One is dedicated to Pope John Paul II, the other commemorates Polish prisoners in Siberia. In the first case, we are dealing with a figural representation of the pope, in the second – with a stone with an appropriate inscription. The whole set contains a very clear, symbolic message that creates a clear vision of the place of Poland and Poles in history (fighters for freedom against Germans and Russians, always faithful to the Christian Roman Church). But – let us emphasize once again – this project is located far from the city center. Meanwhile, in 2003, a monument commemorating the suffering of Poles deported to Siberia after 1939 was unveiled in the central point of the city, next to the Basilica (main church of the city) and near the Castle, next to the Golden Wedding Column. The plaques on it, with their representations, suggest that it commemorates the broadly understood suffering of Poles at the hands of the troops and officials of Soviet Russia.[16] In 2015, the meaning of the monument was expanded with another element added to it, resembling the original one, but with a changed meaning and symbolism. While the first was to symbolize the mountain (Golgotha) with the shadow of the Cross, the second symbolized a plane's fin. It was dedicated to the Smolensk catastrophe, in which Lech Kaczyński, President of the Republic of Poland died. According to the narrative popularizing the political movement associated with him (the Law and Justice party led by his twin brother, Jarosław), the plane crash was a planned attack by the Russians. As a result, the interconnected elements interpret the meanings contained in each part of the monument and create a clear vision of the latest history of Poland as a tragic battleground between good (Poles) and evil (Russians).

In 1976, the Monument of the Second Polish Army was built, whose troops were stationed in Oleśnica during the siege of Wrocław in 1945. The monument was erected at *Wojska Polskiego*/Polish Army Street far from the city center, but near the place where there once stood a monument commemorating the second military unit of the Prussian army associated with Oleśnica, Rifle Battalion No. 6.

In 1972, one of the most original monuments in Poland was unveiled – the so-called Monument to the Space Age. In a concrete basin just outside the medieval city walls, three stylized spheres standing on three cones were placed. The occasional inscription hung on the remains of the city walls read: "On April 12, 1961, the first man, Yuri Gagarin, set off from the territory of the Soviet Union to conquer the skies. Honor and glory to the heroic conquerors of space." Today, there is no inscription on the wall behind the monument, only the naming tradition has remained. This one is evolving, as in the memory of the contemporary generation there are common names referring to the shape of spheres and troughs, without reference to the intended purpose of commemoration.[17]

In the context of all the above-mentioned symbolic manifestations of values important to the founders, the monument unveiled in 2007 is intriguing. A simple stone situated on a low plinth carries a plaque with an inscription in German and Polish: "The past in memory becomes part of the present. As a tribute to past generations. Residents of Oleśnica 2007." The intention of the creators was to commemorate the German inhabitants of the Oleśnica buried in the local cemeteries (hence the location of the monument on Cemetery Street, away from the city center). However, the inscription itself expresses a much broader content, emphasizing the importance not so much of recalling memories of lost times, but of actively creating the present.

In Oleśnica, the living tissue of toponymy and points affirming the values important to the city elite unambiguously emphasize the most important narratives related to the idea of the Polish nation, leaving local history far behind. It is the history of the Poles that is emphasized as a value that creates the bonds of the urban community. Regional and local issues appear, but only as elements that ennoble the community – the Polish national community, an element of which is the community of Oleśnica. The efforts of some local elites to emphasize local and regional content in the urban space (Jan Sinapius Street, the growing concern to restore the original shape of both monumental columns), which have been visible during the last three decades, have not yet been clearly reflected in the narrative told by the surroundings.

Świerzawa – National History and Local Past

Świerzawa is a small town in the south of Lower Silesia. After 1945, due to a lack of inhabitants, it lost its town rights, and only regained them again in 1984. It is the capital of the commune, and in 2011, it had 2,428 citizens, while in 2019, it had 2,249 citizens.[18] The choice of this town as the subject of this study is dictated by its peripheral location in relation to the center of the region, but also by the fact that it has an important historical object, the cultural importance of which exceeds the present-day economic or administrative importance of the settlement. It is the Romanesque church of St. John, one of the oldest in Silesia. Originally, it was associated with the neighboring village of Sędziszów, and for a long time served as the parish church of the town of Świerzawa. Today it is located on the outskirts of the city and is exhibited in tourist materials as the main attraction of the city.[19] On the other side of Świerzawa, in the neighboring village of Stara Kraśnica, one of the most beautiful baroque palaces in this part of Silesia was located – the court of the von Schliewitz family erected in the 1720s.[20] In addition to these two monuments, the historic space of the town is constructed by the preserved historical layout of buildings with a spindle-shaped square and a Gothic parish church located in its corner. Historic buildings in the town were not dominated in the urban landscape by modern additions built after 1945.

The main communication axis of Świerzawa is divided into sections consisting of streets whose names refer to the specific geographic location of the town, its topographic layout or characteristic building elements: *Dworcowa*/Railway Station Street, *Młyńska*/Mill's Street, Złotoryjska Street, Jeleniogórska Street. The last two street names refer to the names of two neighboring cities towards which these streets lead. All quoted names were translations of the German toponymy found in 1945 by Polish settlers (*Bahnhofstrasse, Mühlenstrasse, Goldbergerstrasse, Hirschbergerstrasse*). Thus, on the map taken over by the Polish authorities from local officials in 1945–1946, new names of the main streets of the town were introduced, without erasing the existing, German ones.[21] Over time, however, the scope of the interference of Polish inhabitants in the layer of the existing toponymy has increased. Today, the market square in the center of the town is called *Wolności*/Freedom Square. The remaining streets are dominated by those related to the political and cultural heroes of Polish history (T. Kościuszko, A. Mickiewicz, W. Reymont streets). A few refer to economic activity (*Spółdzielcza*/Cooperative's, *Rolnicza*/Agricultural streets). The name of the Castle Square, the translation of the pre-war *Burgplatz,* is related to the history of the city. It is located in the place where researchers from the nineteenth century located the medieval Piast castle. In this case, we are dealing with a monument that no longer exists and it is not known if it ever actually existed.[22] On the other hand, the name *Plac Najświętszej Marii Panny/* Holy Virgin Mary Square, although connected with the name of the parish church situated on it, does not refer to the local historical content. In the period before 1945, the space in front of the church was not marked by a separate name. The name was introduced in 2009 at the request of the local Roman Catholic Parish by a resolution of the town's Council. The application specifies the intention of the interested parties, the parish priest and the faithful collaborating with him, i.e., strengthening the impact of the city parish church on the perception of the surroundings by the residents.[23] The emphasis was placed on extracting the religious component of the urban space, overshadowing any reference to the history of the town.

Preserved monuments, including the Church of St. John, located today at Dworcowa Street, despite the importance they had for the cultural identity of the town, did not exert enough influence on the imagination of the community to guarantee them an imprint in the local toponymy. The exception was the aforementioned "virtually" existing Piast castle. Its evocation had deep political roots. It referred to the vision of the past of Silesia supported by the Polish authorities before 1989. The castle was supposed to be the creation of the Piast prince of Świdnica, Bolko – I or II, notwithstanding. Each of them was attributed a special relationship with Polishness at the time of the expansion of German culture and Czech political influence in the region of Silesia. The memory of the castle was to prove the Polish medieval roots of the town. Even if the castle no longer existed in the city, the name of the square was a constant reminder of the ethnic side of the town's genesis – and this despite it being, in fact, only a translation of the German version of toponymy, functioning long before 1945.

The names of the streets in Świerzawa emphasize the national identity of the inhabitants exceptionally strongly (references to national writers and heroes recognized as canonical for Polish culture), and completely ignore the history of Silesia. Moreover, the location of these communication routes, which commemorate the locality, is quite random and does not emphasize the value of local history in the public space. The exception is the central *Wolności*/Freedom Square. However, the term itself does not indicate the context of the creation of the name, which, without any further specification, evokes an abstract value – freedom – in isolation from local history. The earlier version of the name – *Plac Wyzwolenia*/Liberation Square – clearly indicated the historical roots of the community's founding myth: the liberation in 1945 of the western territories of Poland from German occupation. Let us repeat – such a mythologized narrative in the times of the Polish People's Republic was reinforced by the very central location of the square. Today's name of the square – *Wolności*/Freedom Square – is quite unclear for the common audience. For whose freedom is it about? After all, urban space does not at all affirm universal values. So what remains is the freedom the Poles gained after 1989 as opposed to the "liberation" of the city in 1945. Even this context, however, is unclear in general reception.

In this situation, it may come as a surprise that an element referring to its medieval history has been exposed in the town's space. In the official narrative about the town's past, an important role from the nineteenth century was played by the person of Bolko I, duke of Świdnica and Jawor, founder of the town. And although today you will look in vain for a street or square dedicated to him in Świerzawa, a statue of Prince Bolko stands proudly on the border of the town with the village of Stara Kraśnica.[24] The sculpture was created during the Second World War by sculptor Fritz Richter-Elsner. Its formation and form were then to prove the strength of the Germanic spirit in Silesia. The initiative of the foundation of the monument was supported by the Gauleiter of Silesia, Karl Hanke. Ultimately, the figure was not assembled before the capitulation of the Third Reich. Initially, the new Polish authorities were very interested in erecting a monument to symbolize the Piast character, i.e., the Polishness of these lands. However, while the translation of the name of Castle Square was easy, the funds for the symbolic investiture of the monument were short. For communist activists, the idea of the patronage of the medieval ruler over the town was not very attractive either. Parts of the statue deteriorated, the figure of the prince lost its head, raised arm and sword. In the 1980s, it was finally decided to get rid of the troublesome sculpture. The president of the Agricultural Production Cooperative saved it from the literal dustbin of history. However, it had to wait until 2009 for renovation and setting it in a more exposed place. Thanks to the initiative of the local elite, the statue was restored. The figure regained the missing parts, a new pedestal was created (the original had been lost) and after blessing, it was placed at the intersection of Adam Mickiewicz and Jeleniogórska Streets. The headquarters of the Agricultural Production Cooperative was located nearby, whose last president and later mayor of Świerzawa, Józef Kołcz, took care of the renovation of the monument. It is worth emphasizing this location, because it reflects a kind of play of meanings between the public character of this monument and the privatization of the entire activity, which was important for the narrow elite of the town (the fundraising for the renovation of the monument was supported by only 25 people out of over 1,200 adult inhabitants of the town).[25] At the same time, it was this "private" group that took care of the public dimension of the monument's meaning. On the pedestal of the monument there is the inscription: "To the founder of the town – the inhabitants." This symbolic declaration indicates the willingness to constitute a sign of remembrance of the person of the town's founder – a sign that was to be permanently rooted in the urban space and imagination of the inhabitants thanks to the material form of the monument.

History functions in the space of the town in an uncoordinated and inconsistent way. The national narrative about the past has overshadowed regional and local content. It is difficult to read a well-thought-out message, a synthetic narrative using the past to influence current recipients of the town's space. Rather, the town's landscape is the result of historical clashes and ideological compromises, overlapping layers of past and present ideologies. Temporarily significant elements (the so-called liberation of the Western Lands) crumble after 1989 within a specific ideological dialogue with the political needs of contemporary authorities. But those elements of the past that permanently correspond to the sense of the national identity of the inhabitants have remained untouched. A very small group of the town's elite is interested in building a local identity based on local history. History does not create a compact narrative in Świerzawa's space, but rather a set of randomly connected elements aspiring to the role of signs of memory at a given moment, for a small audience.

The vision of history present today in the space of the town largely functions in accordance with the narratives created in 1945–1989. History is a pragmatically used component. The multitude of goals and ideological programs inscribed in space makes it difficult to talk about the potential impact of the national, regional or local past on the recipient. We should remember, however, that the national pride of Poles (of cultural heroes), as well as local pride (of the ancient roots of the town), recorded in space at different times, do not have to be consistent with themselves in both toponymy and the minds of its recipients. History is a carrier of these emotions, but the artifacts it produces can take over the functions of transmitting additional content, sometimes radically different from the one encoded at the time of their creation (as in the case of the statue of Bolko I). Context and social and political needs determine the perception of space and the reading of historical narratives it contains.

Conclusions

In none of the cities we are interested in, has local history played a decisive role in shaping the space-scene that has had an ideological impact on the inhabitants. It was of greatest importance in Wrocław in connection with the consciously implemented re-branding of the city identity. Initiated and stimulated by the local authorities, the assimilation of ethnically different cultural heritage by the inhabitants of Wrocław finds its bottom-up certification in initiatives documenting the remains of the German-speaking culture in the city. An example may be the initiative "Breslau is looking from under the plaster," the participants of which documented and put on the map of contemporary Wrocław all German inscriptions from before 1945 preserved in the public space (mainly signs, advertisements).[26] This corresponds to the tendency to strengthen the historical identity of the metropolis, which may or may not be associated with national identification (as in the case of metropolises and capitals, including historical ones, in Poland it is clearly visible in the example of Krakow).[27] With regard to the Polish western borderlands, the correlation of locality and nationalism is difficult due to geopolitical and ethnic changes implemented in 1945, especially in view of the strong tendency toward state centralization, as also expressed in a set of ideas about the past propagated by the central authorities in the public space. As a result, in Wrocław the content referring to the national identity still plays a more important role than the elements referring to the local past of the city before 1945. It is even more pronounced in smaller towns, where the traditions of the dominant national identification of the inhabitants persist. It is visible in the names of streets and the display of monuments. The genesis and content of the monuments, which clearly indicated the complex, multi-ethnic and multicultural space of the cities, were not explicitly suggested to recipients (as in the example of Oleśnica). Nevertheless, it is also clear that local actors, cultural and political leaders, play a huge role in shaping this landscape of meanings intended for local audiences. The example of Świerzawa and the restoration of the Bolko I monument show that the privatization of communal historical memory may lead to actions against the dominant, nationalistic tendency. In achieving their goals, including building their prestige, local actors contesting the existing power relations may refer to local content when those narratives related to national identification are dominated by the local establishment.

In view of the clear lack of stability and coherence of memory threads in space, however, we can only draw a sketch of the memory maps contained in permanent elements of towns' toponymy. This map is determined (despite everything) in our case by the emphasis on national identity. Apart from Wrocław, the idea of local identity as being valuable for local society is suggested in a timid manner, has a rather pragmatic dimension and has not yet been consolidated as a clearly readable phenomenon in space. It is hard to resist the impression that local history is invoked mainly in ad hoc contexts, sometimes with the hope of making it a commodity supporting the economic development of the community (cultural tourism). Local history emphasizing the diversity of the past is not seen (yet?) as the creator of social cohesion in the local urban communities of Silesia. This is despite the fact that the value of local memory as a link and animator of social activity is commonly emphasized in contrast to the destructive influences of ideologies associated with power of a broader nature, destructive for social cooperation.

Undoubtedly, this is due to the specific history of the region after 1945. Poles replacing the displaced Germans were looking for a justification for their presence here and found it in relation to the history of the entire nation, because it was the history of Poland that brought them to Silesia from various parts of their motherland. Local history will become relevant over time only for those who have already been born on this land. Thus, history in the public space of Silesian cities is not only dominated by national models of the past. Its core is a pragmatic description of space through references to the geographical location, local administrative institutions and significant buildings treated ahistorically as orientation signs. It is undoubtedly not a "world without history." However, history was brought here primarily "from the outside," by forces of the national past.

Notes

1 Cf. Kevin Lynch, *Image of the City* (Cambridge, MA: MIT Press, 1960), 1–13 (he used the general term "mental image"), a summary of reflection on the topic written by Peter Gould and Rodney White, *Mental Maps* (Harmondsworth: Penguin 1974, 2nd edition: 1986), see also short polemic Elspeth Graham, "What is a Mental Map?," *Area* 8, no. 4 (1976): 259–262.

2 Reflections presented by Antonio García García, "An Everyday Living Herit-age Landscape. Reading Public Space as a Complete and Complex Expression of the Contemporary City. Applications Based on Andalusia Cases," *Ri-vista: Ricerche per la progettazione del paesaggio* 18, no. 1 (2020): 214–237 are a great introduction to the discussion on interpretative limitations and perspectives opened by a synthetic view of the city space as a multidimensional system of meanings programmed and read by residents (especially pp. 217–225).

3 A fine example of the dynamics of changes in the meanings of "heritage" in the capitals of national states is Ankara and the changes in the shape and signifi-cance of the Gençlik Park space over the last 90 years. The works undertaken in this area were always aimed at restoring the "original" shape and meanings of the space, but in practice "renovation" always meant programming new content, basically without contact with the inhabitants, in accordance with the will of the central or local authorities, Müge Akkar Ercan, "'Evolving' or 'Lost' Identity of a Historic Public Space? The Tale of Gençlik Park in Ankara," *Journal of Urban Design* 22, no. 4 (2017): 520–543, esp. 538–540.

4 Joanna Nowosielska-Sobel, Grzegorz Strauchold, and Przemysław Wiszewski, *Permanent Change. The New Region(s) of Silesia (1945–2015)* (Wrocław: Wy-dawnictwo eBooki.com.pl, 2015) (*Cuius regio? Ideological and Territorial Cohe-sion of the Historical Region of Silesia (c. 1000–2000)*, vol. 5); accessed May 15, 2021, https://www.bibliotekacyfrowa.pl/dlibra/publication/78119/edition/76597.

5 Piotr Pawliczek, *Sytuacja demograficzna województwa dolnośląskiego w 2019 r. / Demographic Situation of Dolnośląskie Voivodship in 2019* (Wrocław, Urząd Statystyczny we Wrocławiu, 2020), 16, accessed May 15, 2021, https://wroclaw. stat.gov.pl/files/gfx/wroclaw/pl/defaultaktualnosci/756/1/14/1/ludnosc_2020.pdf; https://www.wroclaw.pl/portal/raport-o-stanie-wroclawia-za-rok-2019, accessed May 15, 2021.

6 See Maria Wagińska-Marzec, "Wokół zmian nazewnictwa ulic na Ziemiach Zachodnich i Północnych po 1945 r. Wybrane aspekty, " *Rocznik Ziem Zachod-nich* 1 (2017): 395–398.

7 Kamila Kędziora, *Nazewnictwo ulic Wrocławia w latach 1945–1994* (Warszawa: IPN, 2012).

8 Norman Davies and Roger Moorhouse, *Microcosm. A Portrait of a Central Eu-ropean City* (London: Jonathan Cape, 2002).

9 https://halastulecia.pl/kontakt/, accessed May 15, 2021.

10 Joanna Wojdon, *Thinking about Multiethnicity* (Warszawa: Centrum Edukacji Obywatelskiej, 2020), 32–33; Joanna Wojdon, *Using Commemorative Practices to Teach That History Is a Constructed Narrative* (Antwerp: Evens Founda-tion, 2021), 11, accessed May 15, 2021, https://www.euroclio.eu/wp-content/ uploads/2021/02/SEH-Using-commemorative-practices.pdf.

11 Wojciech Mrozowicz and Przemysław Wiszewski, *Oleśnica od czasów najdawnie-jszych po współczesność* (Wrocław: Atut, 2006), 256–257.

12 See https://www.e-oswiata.olesnica.pl/#7, accessed May 15, 2021.

13 See http://www.olesnica.pl/sm/olesnica-informacje/pomniki-olesnickie, ac-cessed May 15, 2021.

14 Mrozowicz and Wiszewski, *Oleśnica*, 233 (phot. 123), 257.

15 *Ibid.*, 234.

16 *Ibid.*, 257.

17 *Ibid.*, 234–235.

18 Małgorzata Ruchniewicz and Przemysław Wiszewski, *Życie w dolinach. Dzieje Świerzawy i okolic* (Wrocław: Wydawnictwo eBooki.com.pl, 2015) (Series: *His-toria obok. Studia z dziejów lokalnych*, vol. 1), 403–415, accessed May 15, 2021, http://www.bibliotekacyfrowa.pl/Content/78273/Zycie_w_dolinach_Dzieje_ Swierzawy_i_okolic.pdf).

19 On the main website of the town: http://www.swierzawa.pl/asp/kosciol-sw-jana-i-sw-katarzyny,325,,1, accessed May 15, 2021.
20 Ruchniewicz and Wiszewski, *Życie w dolinach*, 84, 174, 213–214.
21 Joanna Nowosielska-Sobel, Grzegorz Strauchold, and Przemysław Wiszewski, *Gmina Świerzawa. Atlas materiałów i źródeł historycznych* (Wrocław: Wydawnictwo eBooki.com.pl, 2015), 76–77, accessed May 15, 2021, https://www.bibliotekacyfrowa.pl/dlibra/publication/80111/edition/78294/content.
22 Ruchniewicz and Wiszewski, *Życie w dolinach*, 53.
23 Resolution of the Świerzawa Town and Commune Council, September 30, 2009, no. XXXIII, accessed May 15, 2021, http://www.swierzawa.pl/data/download/old/uchwaly/f2cb76e8bca0.pdf.
24 Rainer Sachs, "Bolko redivivus. Pomnik Bolka I lwówecko-jaworskiego w Świerzawie i jego historia," *Szkice Legnickie* 32 (2011): 149–162.
25 *Ibid.*, 162n14.
26 https://www.facebook.com/spodtynkupatrzybreslau/, accessed May 15, 2021.
27 Cf. Brian Graham, "The Past in Europe's Present: Diversity, Identity and the Construction of Place," in *Modern Europe. Place, Culture, Identity*, ed. Brian Graham (London, Arnold, 1998), 19–49; Matylda Wdowiarz-Bilska, "Identity of the City. Example of Cracow," *International Multidisciplinary Scientific Conference on Social Sciences & Arts. SGEM* 5 (2018): 85–92.

Bibliography

Akkar Ercan, Müge. "'Evolving' or 'Lost' Identity of a Historic Public Space? The Tale of Gençlik Park in Ankara." *Journal of Urban Design* 22, no. 4 (2017): 520–543.
Davies, Norman, and Roger Moorhouse. *Microcosm. A Portrait of a Central European City*. London: Jonathan Cape, 2002.
García García, Antonio. "An Everyday Living Heritage Landscape. Reading Public Space as a Complete and Complex Expression of the Contemporary City. Applications Based on Andalusia Cases." *Ri-vista: Ricerche per la progettazione del paesaggio* 18, no. 1 (2020): 214–237.
Gould, Peter, and Rodney White. *Mental Maps*. Harmondsworth: Penguin, 1974, 2nd edition: 1986.
Graham, Brian. *The Past in Europe's Present: Diversity, Identity and the Construction of Place*. In *Modern Europe. Place, Culture, Identity*, edited by Brian Graham, 19–49. London: Arnold, 1998.
Graham, Elspeth. "What is a Mental Map?" *Area* 8, no. 4 (1976): 259–262.
http://www.olesnica.pl/sm/olesnica-informacje/pomniki-olesnickie. Accessed May 15, 2021.
http://www.swierzawa.pl/asp/kosciol-sw-jana-i-sw-katarzyny, 325,1. Accessed May 15, 2021.
https://halastulecia.pl/kontakt/. Accessed May 15, 2021.
https://www.e-oswiata.olesnica.pl/#7. Accessed May 15, 2021.
https://www.facebook.com/spodtynkupatrzybreslau/. Accessed May 15, 2021.
https://www.wroclaw.pl/portal/raport-o-stanie-wroclawia-za-rok-2019. Accessed May 15, 2021.
Kędziora, Kamila. *Nazewnictwo ulic Wrocławia w latach 1945–1994*. Warszawa: IPN, 2012.
Lynch, Kevin. *Image of the City*. Cambridge, MA: MIT Press, 1960.

Mrozowicz, Wojciech, and Przemysław Wiszewski. *Oleśnica od czasów najdawniejszych po współczesność.* Wrocław: Atut, 2006.

Nowosielska-Sobel, Joanna, Grzegorz Strauchold, and Przemysław Wiszewski. *Permanent Change. The New Region(s) of Silesia (1945–2015).* Wrocław: Wydawnictwo eBooki.com.pl, 2015. (Series: *Cuius regio? Ideological and Territorial Cohesion of the Historical Region of Silesia (c. 1000–2000)*, vol. 5). Accessed May 15, 2021. https://www.bibliotekacyfrowa.pl/dlibra/publication/78119/edition/76597.

Nowosielska-Sobel, Joanna, Grzegorz Strauchold, and Przemysław Wiszewski. *Gmina Świerzawa. Atlas materiałów i źródeł historycznych.* Wrocław: Wydawnictwo eBooki.com.pl, 2015. Accessed May 15, 2021. https://www.bibliotekacyfrowa.pl/dlibra/publication/80111/edition/78294/content

Pawliczek, Piotr. *Sytuacja demograficzna województwa dolnośląskiego w 2019 r. / Demographic Situation of Dolnośląskie Voivodship in 2019.* Wrocław, Urząd Statystyczny we Wrocławiu, 2020. Accessed May 15, 2021. https://wroclaw.stat.gov.pl/files/gfx/wroclaw/pl/defaultaktualnosci/756/1/14/1/ludnosc_2020.pdf.

Ruchniewicz, Małgorzata, and Przemysław Wiszewski. *Życie w dolinach. Dzieje Świerzawy i okolic.* Wrocław: Wydawnictwo eBooki.com.pl, 2015. (Series: *Historia obok. Studia z dziejów lo*kalnych, vol. 1). Accessed May 15, 2021. http://www.bibliotekacyfrowa.pl/Content/78273/Zycie_w_dolinach_Dzieje_Swierzawy_i_okolic.pdf).

Sachs, Rainer. "Bolko redivivus. Pomnik Bolka I lwówecko-jaworskiego w Świerzawie i jego historia." *Szkice Legnickie* 32 (2011): 149–162.

Świerzawa Town and Commune Council. Resolution of September 30, 2009, no. XXXIII. Accessed May 15, 2021. http://www.swierzawa.pl/data/download/old/uchwaly/f2cb76e8bca0.pdf.

Wagińska-Marzec, Maria. "Wokół zmian nazewnictwa ulic na Ziemiach Zachodnich i Północnych po 1945 r. Wybrane aspekty." *Rocznik Ziem Zachodnich* 1 (2017): 395–398.

Wdowiarz–Bilska, Matylda. "Identity of the City. Example of Cracow." *International Multidisciplinary Scientific Conference on Social Sciences & Arts. SGEM* 5 (2018): 85–92.

Wojdon, Joanna. *Thinking about Multiethnicity.* Warszawa: Centrum Edukacji Obywatelskiej, 2020.

Wojdon, Joanna. *Using Commemorative Practices to Teach That History Is a Constructed Narrative.* Antwerp and Copenhagen: Evens Foundation and Euroclio, 2021. Accessed May 15, 2021. https://www.euroclio.eu/wp-content/uploads/2021/02/SEH-Using-commemorative-practices.pdf.

Part II
Public History and Research

7 Oral History in Poland

Marta Kurkowska-Budzan

Introduction

It is the latter half of the 1960s, the period of spontaneous, grassroots activity for the equality and empowerment of social life, when oral history entered the stage in the Western world as a systematic program and undertaking. England saw then the formation of a self-education movement known as "History Workshops." These workshops brought together students and leftist academics in a search for a way to "rewrite" – metaphorically, but also much more literally – history. That is, they aimed to unveil what had been silenced in the dominant historical narrative.[1] In this current, there also originated the idea of presenting history from the point of view of humanity's experience. What defined oral history at its outset was not merely the fact of applying a certain method, but a deliberate shift in balance – rooted in the ethical and socio-political demands – from written documents to individual oral narratives of persons representing social groups which had up to that moment been deprived of the opportunity to develop their own interpretation of the past. It was a coup against the ideal of history as the study of a closed past performed from a distance. Oral history is the history of the living here and now, it is the past recreated in the present, its terms specified by the present. Furthermore, oral history involves a participatory and in many cases compensatory history, being at its core public, albeit even before 1978 when "public history" came to be defined.[2]

The Awkward Question of Beginnings

In the Polish official historiography of the time, the dominant role – resulting from the political situation – was attributed to Marxist-Leninist historical materialism. Thus, the Polish historians of that period – stuck in these "methodological shackles," as some like to see it, or merely assuming that perspective, as others do – devoted their attention to the so-called "oppressed" classes: workers and peasants,[3] people who had not had an opportunity to write their own history and thus received "public defenders." Concurrently, the symbolic stage of history was either entirely purged of the aristocracy,

DOI: 10.4324/9781003165767-10

the landed gentry, to some extent the burghers, and of course the manufac-
turers, or these groups were exclusively portrayed as the forces of evil. The
policy of the communist authorities in Poland at the same time did have
some nationalistic undertones, as manifested in the exclusion of ethnic minorities from the textbook history the history of twentieth-century Poland.

Set by the political authorities, giving the underprivileged classes the leading
role on the stage of history was subsequently carried out by the state system of
educational and cultural institutions: state schools, continuing education institutions, and state-supervised youth associations and organizations, such as
scouting. These performed educational undertakings which encompassed, for
instance, meetings with witnesses of history (scouting storytelling meetings,
"evening gatherings," meetings with veterans), interviews and the recording
of local history (of course, only to the extent allowed by available technology).
On the basis of the knowledge of the activity profile of the aforementioned organizations, syllabi, textbooks, organizational guidelines for tourists and educational events (such as, for instance, historical treks), it can be ascertained
that the dominant motif of meetings and interviews was the experience of the
Second World War, as well as that of local history, tradition and folklore. This
optimistic image has to be balanced by an awareness that these projects were
run under the auspices of an authoritarian state.

Paul Thompson in *The Voice of the Past* describes the methods of financing social projects during the 1970s in the UK and the USA. From the outset, state institutions provided funding for such social undertakings in the
UK, whereas in the USA these were supported by local business enterprises.
The author admitted that: "the influence of sponsorship can be one reason
why oral history is not necessarily an instrument for change." That is why
in practice oral history

> is based on awakening people's consciousness and strengthening pride
> in their own experience and identity, rather than radically challenging
> their attitudes ... it can give back to the people who made and experi-
> enced history, through their own words, a central place.[4]

Thompson recognized the idea of the democratization of history in the
"memoir competitions" held on a mass-scale in communist Poland by
research institutions, libraries and periodicals.[5] The sociologists who organized these undertakings gave the authors of life stories a sense of belief
that their historical experience was important and that they were able to
"contribute to the writing of history."[6] On the other hand, however, the archives of these competitions provide emphatic evidence that the organizers
controlled, and in a way censored, these compositions.[7]

In the 1970s, Polish academic historians also developed an awareness
of the potential of autobiographical oral accounts, which they referred
to – in line with the sociological tradition – as "evoked primary sources."[8]

Their stance resulted largely from the fact that historians studying the history of twentieth-century Poland had at the time very limited access to archives, particularly regarding the development of the People's Republic of Poland, and also the Second World War. One of them, Tomasz Strzembosz, an archivist and historian of the Second World War, took upon himself the burden of collecting the oral accounts and memoirs already taken down in the 1960s.[9] Years later, he wrote:

> To the task of gathering accounts I owe the privilege of having met hundreds of interesting, unusually valuable persons and of having learned more – I came to understand their point of view, their beliefs and emotions, ... I learned to listen to what they have to tell me, not necessarily in the arid domain of facts. What they see as **really important** [emphasis original], what is "their truth," and what they wished to tell a historian... These meetings also taught me to value highly and respect the simple folk, the low-ranked soldiers of the underground, and at the same time the co-originators of the crucial actions, the **creators of history** [emphasis original]. I learned to look at historical events through their eyes, to feel them with my heart. Thanks to these conversations, no longer I was a "clerk," an intellectual coldly looking down on "historical processes."[10]
>
> The joy that truth may be revealed, having been condemned to absolute oblivion by "the rulers of this world," and by the passage of time ...; the secret further protected by the "littleracy" or inability to write down the events by eye-witnesses; ... I was happy to be the catalyst helping it come to light ...[11]

In the above few sentences, the author who never referred to the oral history-oriented literature, happened to express the key concepts thereof.

The ideas of oral history emerged in Poland at the same time as they did in Western countries. They inspired the period's educational and cultural undertakings in line with the official narrative of history. The then slogan about "the leading role of the working people of cities and villages" would all too often be taken up mechanically by historians; thus, it soon became an object of ridicule. Concurrently, this very slogan provided numerous opportunities of empowerment to entire communities and individuals. In both a symbolic and a literal sense, the further from Warsaw, the greater was the chance for such projects actually to be authentic. In spite of a top-down narrative, the grassroots initiatives were suffused with local content and brought about specific dimensions and results. At the same time, the slogan excluded other social groups. As a result, what occurred in the historical writing and in the public space was not only exclusion, but also secondary victimization by being pushed into oblivion, as in the case of the victims of the communist regime or of Jews (after 1968).[12]

Rewriting Poland

Oral history above all performs a social role. Thompson writes that "its impact depends upon the spirit in which it is used."[13] That is why, due to the difficulties faced when trying to determine the "spirit" of the undertakings of the 1960s and 1970s in Poland, the contemporary "founding myth" of Polish oral history indicates the late 1980s as its beginning. It was a peculiar period when the communist regime made attempts at reforms, but had already gone into decline. This was the time when the process of "freeing history from ideological and political constraints"[14] was under way.

In the 1980s, Tomasz Strzembosz had already amassed vast experience in oral history research. At the time, this charismatic academic teacher held a seminar whose participants went on joint field trips.[15] Strzembosz had for a long time been involved in the independent scouting movement and enjoyed much authority among numerous dissident groups. It was these communities who in 1987 initiated a campaign to collect testimonies about the history of Polish citizens in the East (i.e., in the territories occupied by the Soviet Union during the Second World War, and in the territories annexed by the USSR by the decision of the Yalta and Potsdam Conferences), and of the military underground in post-war Poland. Memories of groups excluded from the official history were tape-recorded or written down. Already then, it was consistent with the current of broader changes in the public discourse, as well as the straightforward political transitions which commenced in 1989. After 1989, Strzembosz served as the Vice-President of the Academic Council of the Eastern Archive, as the collection established as a result of this civic action came to be called. Initiated in Warsaw, it turned into a nation-wide social movement coordinated by Zbigniew Gluza, who became the head of a non-governmental organization popularly known as the KARTA Center.

Even though 1989 serves as its symbol, the "Great Transformation" in Poland had not been accomplished immediately. Aside from the political and economic changes, an important dimension of the transformation process are the shifts in the symbolic fabric of social life, and symbolic transformations are, by definition, extended in time. At its first stage, the obelisks in honor of the Red Army and Lenin monuments were taken down, monoliths commemorating the "champions of communism" were removed, and the names of streets and squares were changed.[16] The scores with material commemoration were settled rapidly. The subsequent stage encompassed the changes in the public discourse. As phrased by one socially engaged writer and activist: the intention was to "rewrite Poland."[17] The deliberate fallacies and omissions of many facts about twentieth-century history by the until-then official historical narrative, and thus the exclusion of the experiences of masses of people from it, led to an outbreak of simultaneously spontaneous and state-organized movement of the "restoration of memory." In a 1989 TV interview, Gluza said: "These are the last years when we are able to restore that deliberately expunged past together with the witnesses of those events.

Our contemporaneity has become a great challenge. But our past is an even greater one."[18] The KARTA Center was at the forefront of the movement. They indicated the topics to be documented and the methods of performing it, with a strong emphasis placed upon the interviews. The phenomena at the center of the subsequent projects of the KARTA pertained to the experience of twentieth-century totalitarianism in the territories belonging to Poland currently as well as before the Second World War. Starting with its first projects, the KARTA Center concurrently took upon itself the archiving of the recordings and other materials, including photographs, memoirs and family memorabilia. Thereby, it simultaneously became a rapidly growing first community archive in Poland. Already in the 1990s, the KARTA Center had become a "historical conglomerate," and in 1991, a periodical of the same name was established to "give voice to the witnesses of history."[19] Between 1992 and 1997, Alicja Wancerz–Gluza and other collaborators of the KARTA Center appeared in another medium – they created reportages and historical programs broadcast on the public television station. In the latter half of the 1990s, as an important form of the Center's public activity, competitions for school students were developed, and accompanied with a broadly conceived advisory campaign for teachers. Annual competitions, under the motto *Historia Bliska* (History at Hand) promoted the independent research work of youths within their local community.

In their journal, KARTA pursued the then-common notion of "putting history straight," associating it closely with particular historical content, with the interview as a method and with the ethical imperative of historical activity. In 1991, in the second issue of the monthly, Gluza wrote:

> The experience of our century cannot be "relegated to archives." (...) We ought to be stimulated to research the recent history not only by reason, but most of all by our moral sense. One has merely to acknowledge how many of us carry with them through their lives the burden of the past, these people are maimed, mentally scarred, aching; they had been deprived of their right to speak for decades – and it is their only chance to rid themselves of that burden. How many of them only now are able – having overcome great difficulties – to try to speak out. It is predominantly to them, the witnesses of history, that we would like to offer the pages of *Karta*. We, the editors, will be ready to listen, to get to know, and to record what they have to say.[20]

Thanks to *Karta*, the witness of history has since the 1990s been the central notion in public oral history in Poland. Furthermore, it should be added that the word "witness" is predominately used in Polish in the context of institutions of the judiciary. The associations of the word include such expressions as: credible or unreliable, false or true testimony. During that special period, when there was a burning issue of "putting history straight" but there was a scarcity of traditional sources and what remained was memory, the situation seemed somewhat reminiscent of the early years after the Second World War when citizens gave their testimonies before the Chief Commission for Investigation of Hitlerite Crimes in Poland, which were then used, among others, in the trials of war criminals. In the 1990s, the "testimony" was given against the official historiography safeguarding the totalitarian regime, but not against the functionaries of that regime. The opportunity to provide "testimony" was intended as a mitigation of the harm done in the symbolic sphere, as a therapy, and as a collective therapy, as well. Nevertheless, the number of witnesses of history remained limited due to the fact that through the projects of documentation and publications, a certain counter-history was being established. That is why the prevalent themes in the aforementioned activities of the KARTA Center during the 1990s pertained to political history. Even if a published instance of a memoir, or a competition topic referred to, say, everyday life, it was situated in the chronology outlined by the "great politics," such as: "during the Stalinist era," or "during martial law." No new thematic fields were sought. Consequently, such a practice ended up defining Polish oral history as a primarily political history.

Much like in Western countries two decades earlier, oral history in Poland was of a compensatory nature, though the recompense involved different groups of people: mainly those oppressed for political reasons, and hence oftentimes having origins in the intellectual and cultural elites. Oral history was aligned with an almost universal social tendency; furthermore, it did not enter into conflict with what was happening in the official historiography after 1989.

Healing the *Genius Loci*

The subject that was distorted in the official historical publications of the previous era through the use of various euphemisms, and consistently suppressed in the public narrative, one that required historians' attention after 1989, was the extermination of Jews. For public history, it proved to be a topic requiring longstanding work and local activity, for it largely concerned local identities. In Sejny and in Lublin – a pair of cities whose cultural identity had been brutally annihilated by the war, the Holocaust and the subsequent politics of oblivion – the early 1990s saw the development of initiatives that mark the other current of Polish oral history. These are: the Center "Borderland of Arts, Cultures and Nations" (*Ośrodek "Pogranicze – sztuk, kultur, narodów"*) and the "Grodzka Gate – NN Theatre" Center (*"Brama Grodzka – Teatr NN"*). Both institutions were established by artists with their roots in the renowned alternative theatres of the 1970s; therefore, their activity from the outset resisted being classified, much like the projects they carried out that eluded the definitions of either a "theatrical performance" or a "museum exhibition." Another thing they have in common is the effort they made to heal the "spirit of the place," injured by the war, with the participation of the local community. These both started from informal groups, spontaneous artistic work, profoundly embedded in the context of the place and its history. Over time, both transformed into municipal and regional institutions of culture, financed largely by the local government.

Tomasz Pietrasiewicz, Director of "Grodzka Gate – NN Theatre" Center, wrote:

> If we regard "memory" and "place" as categories basic for human's existence in time and space, "presence" can be interpreted as a fundamental dimension of identity of the individual set in a specific spatial-historical reality. "Memory – Place – Presence" – a program realized by the Grodzka Gate – NN Theatre Center in Lublin since 1992 envisages the reconstruction of identities and bonds connecting local communities by referring to the memory of the place.[21]

The artists and cultural animators who set up the center in Sejny regard their role in the local community in a similar vein. Particular attention should be paid to the fact that they work in a small community, mainly with children and young people who are involved in their projects from the beginning until the end, as was the case with the production of "The Chronicles of Sejny," staged in 2000. The youth recorded the testimonies of older residents and developed the iconography; young actors took to the stage in a performance according to their own script, while beforehand they created a diorama of their town, which they used as an element of the stage design. The performance of "The Chronicles of Sejny" was neither a one-off nor a seasonal event; it is a constantly renewed memory work. Another generation of young people uses the stage to speak about the stories of the Polish, Jewish and Lithuanian inhabitants of Sejny. "These are not stories they read in some books, these are stories they heard in person, the stories they asked for themselves," explained one of the co-founders of the Borderland Center, Bożena Szroeder.[22] A reviewer of the book *The Chronicles of Sejny* (another result of the project)[23] presented his reflection that aptly describes the activity of both the Borderland Center, and "Grodzka Gate – NN Theatre" Center:

> Such actions foster constructive responses: shared responsibility for one's community, creative attitude towards one's own space. When one rebuilds their own town as if from the scratch, trying not to overlook anything or anyone, it will never become alien to us. It may be called a form of socio-therapy, or simply – being rooted.[24]

The discussed centers deserve credit for the restoration of the identity of places, local communities and groups on the basis of engaging and reaching beyond the standard forms of artistic and cognitive practices (all lasting elements of Polish oral history) of public history. They were the first to demonstrate that oral history may constitute artistic material without compromising the overarching idea of such projects, that of empowering their narrators. They provided encouragement to attempt similar undertakings for all those – the youth, small local associations, artists – for whom history appeared to have been locked away in solely educational or scholarly forms. They were able to introduce into oral history an ever-greater ethical value, and, importantly, in the nation-wide fervor accompanying the restoration of the "true history" during the 1990s, and subsequently the nation's memory, they made it impossible to forget about Jews once again, as well as about other ethnic and religious minorities.

Guarding the Nation's Memory

Since 2005, when the conservative Law and Justice party won the parliamentary elections, a public debate was carried out over the subject of the image of Poland's most recent history and the so-called "Polish politics of history." The idea was expressed explicitly in a book titled *Memory and Responsibility*.[25] The authors called for an "axiological remembrance," defined as "a record impressed in the collective imagination of a canon of values, which is a type of spiritual constitution of the community – a canon usually dressed in a costume of historical events."[26] As the authors wrote, a central place in the history of the Polish political community belongs to the idea of freedom, and its message is Poland's greatest contribution to the heritage of Europe that has to be recognized by a wide audience, and not only in Poland. That is the reason why they demand that the history of the Polish struggle for independence be cultivated in social memory: the nineteenth-century uprisings, the fending off the Bolshevik assault in 1920, the Home Army during the Second World War and the Warsaw Uprising of 1944, the anti-communist struggle between 1956 and 1976, as well as the Solidarity movement in the 1980s. But what should also be important for contemporary Poles is bringing awareness to and reminding people of the experience of being deprived of freedom, as represented, for instance, by the fate of Poles under the Soviet and Nazi occupation, or their life under the communist regime.

Oral history became an attractive instrument in public history steered according to the tenets of the above politics of memory, which has been implemented in Poland over the past 15 years. Institutions with an actual nationwide scope of influence, involved in creating oral history projects and promoting this very method, are the Institute of National Remembrance (*Instytut Pamięci Narodowej*) and the Warsaw Rising Museum (*Muzeum Powstania Warszawskiego*).

Opened for visitors in 2004, the Museum is considered one of the best Polish museums and serves as a model for numerous undertakings within public history. In 2014, the Archive of Oral History was established at the Museum to collect accounts of the insurgents and involve young volunteers in conducting the recordings. In the mission statement and the activity of the Museum, a powerfully accentuated trait is that of trans-generational co-operation and, often very practical, even daily, assistance to the insurgents, as they are members of the oldest generation. What Polish oral history owes to the Warsaw Rising Museum is the idea for such projects also to be a platform of constant, tangible, humanitarian assistance for the witnesses of history, who in light of the economic situation in Poland are oftentimes among the poorest groups, because of their old age and the paucity of their retirement pension. Additionally, the example set by the Museum demonstrated that oral history constitutes an important element of a museum narrative. Today, it could prove a difficult task if one wanted to find a museum in Poland whose field of interest includes the twentieth century without it benefitting from oral history to at least a small degree.

The Institute of National Remembrance promotes oral history in nation-wide and local historical competitions and online activities, including the testimonies of members of the anti-communist resistance released as audio-books. Much like in the era of the People's Republic of Poland – the Institute holds tourist and educational events: treks in the footsteps of heroes, during which the participants have a chance to meet witnesses of history. When organizing those events, the Institute is keen to cooperate with various local associations. Thanks to such forms of public history, according to a local branch of the Institute in Bydgoszcz:

> we are able to provide new opportunities for the integration of the local community, as well as to popularize everyday research and educational activity of the Institute of National Remembrance. Thereby, we often-times discover elements of history forgotten or clouded in our memory, as well as the heroes thereof, and restore the good name they so deserve. All that in the spirit of fair sports competition, which fosters the forma-tion of patriotic attitudes.[27]

Nationwide, especially in minor towns, the intense activity of the Institute in the public space and the imposition of a limited set of themes led to the narrowing, already at the level of perception, of what a historical experience consists of, and who can be a witness of history. The witnesses of history are in a way nominated by the official discourse at the service of the politics of memory. Despite the fact that three decades have passed since the political transformation, the Institute cultivates revolutionary ardor, the belief that "the fight against communism" and the ideological distortion of history is still ongoing.

Among the institutions that have made a significant contribution to the development of Polish oral history, the "Remembrance and Future" Center (*Ośrodek "Pamięć i Przyszłość"*) in Wrocław should be mentioned. The Center was established in 2007 as a local state-run institution, and cur-rently is co-financed by the state and municipal self-government. Besides its regular museum activities focused on the post-war history of the so-called

Western Territories of Poland and on the local history of the "resistance of Polish society to the communist dictatorship," the Center has initiated several undertakings of nationwide scope. Since 2010 it has published the interdisciplinary academic journal *Wrocławski Rocznik Historii Mówionej* (*Wrocław Yearbook of Oral History*) which is a major forum of oral history in Poland. The journal integrates both academic and non-academic communities, animates discussion and introduces new research ideas, including methodology topics.[28] The Center promotes oral history amongst students, offering incentive scholarships for those who take up research based on interviews. One of the Center's latest research and educational projects is a good example of the way the institution works. As part of the anniversary project on the occasion of the centennial of Poland regaining independence, 100 interviews with 100-year-olds were conducted. The project was a highly challenging effort engaged in cooperative research with people and oral history institutions from all over the country. Despite its formally local character, the Center has played an important role in integrating Polish oral historians.

A long-term independent forum of integration has been the Polish Oral History Association or POHA (*Polskie Towarzystwo Historii Mówionej*) founded in 2009 in Kraków by a group of academic researchers, journalists and writers, the representatives of KARTA, Grodzka Gate-NN Theatre and the "Artifacts" Association. The mission of POHA is to connect and support practitioners in their work of ethically collecting and sharing oral histories.[29] In 2020, POHA established an ongoing partnership with the Center of Social Archives, an institution run cooperatively by the state and the KARTA Foundation.

Community Archives and Contemporary Emancipations

What was discussed above, and the examples of organizations I have provided, constitute, as indicated in the introduction, the lasting elements of Polish oral history. New organizations and projects that are developed tend to take them as their model. The last decade rapidly accelerated the development of communication technology – an obviously global trend. In Poland, it has been accompanied by the increase in society's wealth, and also by the intensification of civic activity with a concurrent aggravation of political divisions. Not only is the young generation now a community of consumers, it is also one of activists.

I would like to point out two phenomena which I associate with the above situation:

1   The notion of grassroots, participatory, identity-oriented oral history has gone beyond the form of projects based on traditional interviews, and has found itself in the downright rapid current of community archives.[30]

The growing social interest in grassroots activities for the protection of cultural heritage has been observed since 2012. On the one hand, it resulted from a success – the growing number of materials collected in various projects, the maintenance of which oftentimes proved debilitating for the financial means and competences of their initiators. Greater access to digitalization technologies and the expert support from the KARTA Center, which was the first to recognize the needs stemming from the rapid growth of oral history collections, led to the establishment of a network of archives and local libraries. In 2015, the legal status and the relationship between community and state archives was finally determined. Community archives were granted a set of state-of-the-art tools for cataloging and sharing their records.[31] The situation encourages the public to venture upon new oral history projects, to digitalize and share documents and memorabilia, and to focus on new historical themes. The archiwa.org database, documenting the current state of community archives in Poland, provides the information that as of 2021, their total number stood at 612. From a 2017 report on social archives, we learn that the majority of social archives are established in small towns with fewer than 100,000 inhabitants (with a large proportion of those towns with a population under 20,000). Close contacts among the members of small communities and their awareness of having to protect their own history themselves are among the key causes of this state of affairs. Community archives are most of all created by non-governmental organizations (59% of the entities listed in the archiwa.org database), but also by local self-governments (31%) and private persons (8%). The remaining 2% include corporations and trade unions.[32]

2   The young generation of activists has recognized the need to document their work and the history of their communities.

The political activity of the generation of today's youth, oftentimes a reaction to the ideological expansion and politics of the conservatives, has led to their self-organization around identity politics. It bore fruit first in the form of historical projects, such as the "Oral History of the LGBT+ Community" initiated in 2016 by the Lambda Association, and *QueerStoria: Czasopismo społeczno-historyczne Archiwum Lambdy* (first issue 2018/2019).[33] Furthermore, experts in social archives evermore frequently call for the documentation of the activity of NGOs, which started to be established in Poland as genuinely non-governmental institutions only after 1989. Whereas keeping an archive of traditional documents in the case of many often short-lived organizations may have been a challenging and cumbersome task, nowadays with the ease of access afforded by advanced technologies and the digitalization and sharing of records, it serves as an encouragement to undertake such efforts. It also provides an opportunity to take down and consolidate one's own history.

Conclusion

The first appearance of the idea of oral history in Poland can be traced to the same period when it emerged in the Western countries, that is, to the early 1970s. It was carried out in what can be split into two currents: the one curated by the state, within the framework of the official historical narrative (school education, scouting, educational tourism), and the independent one, in the dissident communities. Both currents would leave behind the elements of a legacy still present today. During the period of political transformation, the KARTA Center emerged from the groups within the democratic opposition. The Center has become the model of an NGO, imitated with regard to their methods of creating records, their archiving and their publishing activity. The KARTA Center was to provide the conceptual apparatus and the themes that would prove congruent with the lofty deeds of "restoring the memory," and "setting history straight." The period also determined the fact that in Poland it is now seen as only natural that oral history goes hand in hand with the official historiography. The Warsaw-based KARTA Center has exerted a nationwide influence, whereas the artistic communities on the periphery would develop their own modus operandi within the local context. Their proposals to coalesce anew the fractured local identities proved crucial for the extremely topical issues regarding the unwanted heritage of the Second World War. The era of the "Polish politics of memory" has now lasted for over 15 years. Without any considerations of its leftist roots, oral history has been adapted to the political needs of such organizations as the Institute of National Remembrance and other state-funded institutions. The process of the "restoration of memory" has been continued; however, its range of topics came to be restricted. In spite of the great power wielded in the public sphere by the state institutions, oral history resisted being channeled in a single direction. Small, independent undertakings reflecting the ideas of participatory elaboration of history continue to emerge and are developed thanks to the younger generation either under the banner of social archives, or solely in the digital space of the Internet.

This research was financially supported by the National Science Centre of Poland (project number 2015/19/B/HS3/01761). The proofreading of the text was financed by Jagiellonian University in Krakow (program ID.UJ: POB Heritage).

Notes

1 Dennis Dworkin, *Cultural Marxism in Postwar Britain: History, the New Left and the Origins of Cultural Studies* (Durham, NC: Duke University Press, 1997); Kynan Gentry, "Ruskin, Radicalism and Raphael Samuel: Politics, Pedagogy and the Origins of the History Workshop," *History Workshop Journal* 76 (Autumn 2013): 187–211.

2 Robert Kelly, "Public History: Its Origins, Nature, and Prospects," *The Public Historian* 1 (1978): 16–28.
3 Rafał Stobiecki, *Historiografia PRL* (Łódź: Wydawnictwo Uniwersytetu Łódzkiego, 2020), 161.
4 Paul Thompson, Joanna Bornat, *The Voice of the Past. Oral History* (Oxford: Oxford University Press, 2017), 3.
5 From 1945 to 1976, about 1,050 competitions were organized, and in total about 300,000 people took part in them, Krzysztof Kosiński, "Pamiętnikarstwo konkursowe jako źródło historyczne," *Polska 1944/45–1989. Studia i Materiały* 6 (2003): 135, http://w.rcin.org.pl/Content/59624/WA303_79123_B155-Polska-T-6-2004_Kosinski.pdf.
6 Thompson, *The Voice of the Past*, 16.
7 Kosiński, "Pamiętnikarstwo konkursowe," 139–140.
8 Krystyna Kersten, "Relacje jako typ źródła historycznego," in *Pamiętnik X Powszechnego Zjazdu Historyków Polskich w Lublinie 17–21 września 1968 r. Referaty plenarne. Sekcje VII-XI*, ed. Antoni Mączak (Warszawa: Polskie Towarzystwo Historyczne, 1968), 316–329.
9 Tomasz Strzembosz, *Odbijanie i uwalnianie więźniów w Warszawie 1939–1944* (Warszawa: PWN, 1972); Tomasz Strzembosz, *Akcje zbrojne podziemnej Warszawy 1939–1944* (Warszawa: PIW, 1978); Tomasz Strzembosz, *Oddziały szturmowe konspiracyjnej Warszawy 1939–1944* (Warszawa: PWN 1979); Tomasz Strzembosz, ed., *Ludność i cywilna w Powstaniu Warszawskim. Pamiętniki, relacje, zeznania* (Warszawa: PIW, 1974).
10 Tomasz Strzembosz, "Z przygód historyka polskiej konspiracji wojskowej 1939–1945," in *Ojczyzna i wolność. Prace ofiarowane Profesorowi Janowi Ziółkowi w siedemdziesiątą rocznicę urodzin*, ed. Anna Barańska, Witold Matwiejczyk, and Ewa Ziółek (Lublin: Towarzystwo Naukowe KUL, 2000), 684.
11 Strzembosz, "Z przygód historyka," 708–709.
12 Cf. the chapter by Piotr Trojański in this volume.
13 Thompson, *The Voice of the Past*, 3.
14 Piotr Wandycz, "Historiography of the Countries of Eastern Europe: Poland," *American Historical Review* 97, no. 4 (1992): 1011. Cf. the chapter by Łukasz Kamiński in this volume.
15 Janusz Marszalec, *Spotkanie poświecone pamięci profesora Tomasza Strzembosza. Warszawa 17 listopada 2004*, accessed March 1, 2021, https://ipn.gov.pl/pl/aktualnosci/612,Spotkanie-poswiecone-pamieci-prof-Tomasza-Strzembosza-Warszawa-17-listopada-2004.html.
16 Ewa Ochman, *Post-Communist Poland – Contested Pasts and Future Identities* (London: Routledge, 2013).
17 Leszek Szaruga, *Dochodzenie do siebie. Wybrane wątki literatury po 1989 roku* (Sejny: Wydawnictwo Fundacji Pogranicze, 1997).
18 Zygmunt Gluza, *Odkrycie Karty: Niezależna Strategia Pamięci* (Warszawa: Ośrodek KARTA, 2012), 113.
19 Gluza, *Odkrycie Karty*, 113.
20 Gluza, *Odkrycie Karty*, 133–134.
21 Marta Kubiszyn, "Historia nie-mówiona," *Scriptores* 2, no. 28 (2003): 91.
22 *Kroniki Sejneńskie. Następne pokolenie*, accessed March 1, 2021, https://www.youtube.com/watch?v=l8AA3PNerUA.
23 *Kroniki sejneńskie*, ed. Bożena Szroeder (Sejny: Fundacja Pogranicze, 2001).
24 Jerzy Kandziora, "Miasteczko zbudowane na nowo," *Tygodnik Powszechny*, December 2, 2001, accessed March 1, 2021, http://www.pogranicze.sejny.pl/miasteczko_zbudowane_na_nowo_jerzy_kandziora_quottygodnik_powszechnyquot_02122001,355-1,11936.html.

136 *Marta Kurkowska-Budzan*

25 *Pamięć i odpowiedzialność*, ed. Robert Kostro, and Tomasz Merta (Kraków – Wrocław: Ośrodek Myśli Politycznej, 2005).
26 Dariusz Karłowicz, "Pamięć aksjologiczna a historia," in *Pamięć i odpowiedzialność*, ed. Robert Kostro and Tomasz Merta (Kraków – Wrocław: Ośrodek Myśli Politycznej, 2005), 31.
27 https://edukacja.ipn gov.pl/edu/obeu/bydgoszcz/rajd, accessed February 22, 2021.
28 https://www.wrhm.pl/wrhm, accessed March 7, 2021.
29 http://pthm.pl, accessed March 7, 2021.
30 *Archiwistyka społeczna. Diagnoza i wyzwania* (Warszawa: Fundacja Ośrodka KARTA, 2017).
31 *Archiwistyka społeczna. Poradnik* (Warszawa: Fundacja Ośrodka KARTA, 2012), accessed March 1, 2021, https://ksiegarnia.karta.org.pl/wp-content/uploads/2017/11/Archiwa_spoleczne_podrecznik.pdf
32 https://archiwa.org, accessed March 1, 2021.
33 http://lambdawarszawa.org, accessed March 1, 2021.

Bibliography

Archiwistyka społeczna. Diagnoza i wyzwania. Warszawa: Fundacja Ośrodka KARTA, 2017.
Archiwistyka społeczna. Poradnik. Warszawa: Fundacja Ośrodka KARTA, 2012. Accessed March 1, 2021. https://ksiegarnia.karta.org.pl/wp-content/uploads/2017/11/Archiwa_spoleczne_podrecznik.pdf.
Dworkin, Dennis. *Cultural Marxism in Postwar Britain: History, the New Left and the Origins of Cultural Studies.* Durham, NC: Duke University Press, 1997.
Gentry, Kynan. "Ruskin, Radicalism and Raphael Samuel: Politics, Pedagogy and the Origins of the History Workshop." *History Workshop Journal* 76 (Autumn 2013): 187–211.
Gluza, Zygmunt. *Odkrycie Karty: Niezależna Strategia Pamięci.* Warszawa: Ośrodek KARTA, 2012.
Kandziora, Jerzy. „Miasteczko zbudowane na nowo." *Tygodnik Powszechny*, December 2, 2001. Accessed March 1, 2021. http://www.pogranicze.sejny.pl/miasteczko_zbudowane_na_nowo_jerzy_kandziora_quottygodnik_powszechnyquot_02122001,355-1,11936.html.
Kaźmierska, Kaja, and Jarosław Pałka. *Żołnierze Ludowego Wojska Polskiego.* Łódź: Wydawnictwo Uniwersytetu Łódzkiego, 2018.
Kelly, Robert. "Public History: Its Origins, Nature, and Prospects." *The Public Historian* 1 (1978): 16–28.
Kersten, Krystyna. "Relacje jako typ źródła historycznego." In *Pamiętnik X Powszechnego Zjazdu Historyków Polskich w Lublinie 17–21 września 1968 r. Referaty plenarne. Sekcje VII–XI.* Edited by Antoni Mączak. Warszawa: Polskie Towarzystwo Historyczne, 1968.
Kosiński, Krzysztof. "Pamiętnikarstwo konkursowe jako źródło historyczne." *Polska 1944/45–1989. Studia i Materiały* VI (2003): 135. Accessed March 1, 2021. http://w.rcin.org.pl/Content/59624/WA303_79123_B155-Polska-T-6-2004_Kosinski.pdf
Kostro, Robert, and Tomasz Merta. *Pamięć i odpowiedzialność.* Kraków – Wrocław: Ośrodek Myśli Politycznej, 2005.

Kroniki Sejneńskie. Następne pokolenie. Accessed March 1, 2021. https://www. youtube.com/watch?v=l8AA3PNerUA.

Kubiszyn, Marta. "Historia nie-mówiona." *Scriptores* 2, no. 28 (2003): 91–105.

Marszalec, Janusz. "Spotkanie poświecone pamięci profesora Tomasza Strzembosza. Warszawa 17 listopada 2004." Accessed March 1, 2021. https://ipn. gov.pl/pl/aktualnosci/612,Spotkanie-poswiecone-pamieci-prof-Tomasza-Strzembosza-Warszawa-17-listopada-2004.html.

Ochman, Ewa. *Post-Communist Poland – Contested Pasts and Future Identities.* London: Routledge, 2013.

Stobiecki, Rafał. *Historiografia PRL.* Łódź: Wydawnictwo Uniwersytetu Łódzkiego, 2020.

Strzembosz, Tomasz. *Odbijanie i uwalnianie więźniów w Warszawie 1939–1944.* Warszawa: PWN, 1972.

Strzembosz, Tomasz, ed. *Ludność i cywilna w Powstaniu Warszawskim. Pamiętniki, relacje, zeznania.* Warszawa: PIW, 1974.

Strzembosz, Tomasz. *Akcje zbrojne podziemnej Warszawy 1939–1944.* Warszawa: PIW, 1978.

Strzembosz, Tomasz. *Oddziały szturmowe konspiracyjnej Warszawy 1939–1944.* Warszawa: PWN 1979.

Strzembosz, Tomasz. "Z przygód historyka polskiej konspiracji wojskowej 1939–1945." In *Ojczyzna i wolność. Prace ofiarowane Profesorowi Janowi Ziółkowi w siedemdziesiątą rocznicę urodzin.* Edited by Anna Barańska, Witold Matwiejczyk, and Ewa Ziółek, 681–709. Lublin: Towarzystwo Naukowe KUL, 2000.

Szaruga, Leszek. *Dochodzenie do siebie. Wybrane wątki literatury po 1989 roku.* Sejny: Wydawnictwo Fundacji Pogranicze, 1997.

Szroeder, Bożena, ed. *Kroniki sejneńskie.* Sejny: Fundacja Pogranicze, 2001.

Thompson, Paul, and Joanna Bornat. *The Voice of the Past. Oral History.* Oxford: Oxford University Press, 2017.

Wandycz, Piotr. "Historiography of the Countries of Eastern Europe: Poland." *American Historical Review* 97, no. 4 (1992): 1011–1025.

Websites

Centrum Archiwistyki Społecznej. Accessed 1 March 2021. https://archiwa.org.

Instytut Pamięci Narodowej. Oddział w Bydgoszczy. Accessed 22 February 2021. https://edukacja.ipn.gov.pl/edu/oben/bydgoszcz/rajd.

Polskie Towarzystwo Historii Mówionej. Accessed 7 March 2021. http://pthm.pl.

Stowarzyszenie Lambda. Accessed 1 March 2021. http://lambdawarszawa.org.

Wrocławski Rocznik Historii Mówionej. Accessed 7 March 2021. https://www. wrhm.pl.

8 Polish Archives

Old and New and Their Role as Public History Institutions

Lucyna Harc

Archival Landscape in Poland

The archival network in Poland, with the key role played by the state archives, was shaped in the interwar period. However, after 1945, the archival network underwent a major reconstruction. In the communist period, resembling other areas of state activity, state archives had a strongly centralized nature. Their dominant role resulted from the dismantling of many previously existing entities that had their own historical archives. They were also focused on the arrangement of historical materials and the control of processes related to the creation of documentation and the preservation of collections, especially institutional ones. Access to archives in the reading rooms of state archives was subject to specific regulations, and in the case of citizens of other countries, it required the consent of the General Director of State Archives as the central administrative authority in archival matters. On the other hand, since the 1960s, state archives have been participating in the celebration of anniversaries and popularizing their own holdings by organizing exhibitions, lectures or publishing popular science publications. However, these activities did not receive public awareness, unlike similar initiatives undertaken by museums and libraries. Consequently, one of the legacies of communism, apart from the centralized structure, remained the broader public's perception of archives as institutions difficult to access by members of the general public.

Significant changes in the archival landscape in Poland began to take place as a result of the political and systemic transformations in the country that took place after 1989. The network of state archives still plays the most important role in the contemporary organization of archives in Poland. It consists of three central archives located in Warsaw. They contain archival materials from offices and organizations operating on a national scale, as well as resources from outstanding personalities and the most renowned families and houses of merit for the history of Poland. Apart from them, there are 30 regional archives located in larger Polish cities. Additionally, some of them have their branches located in 39 smaller towns in Poland. State archives of a regional nature accumulate, preserve, arrange

DOI: 10.4324/9781003165767-11

and provide access to archival materials created by local authorities and state offices, judicial institutions and local governments, educational institutions and organizations, medical centers, churches and religious associations, social organizations and industrial enterprises. They also offer collections belonging to the most important Polish families and houses until the end of the Second World War, including the files of their land estates, the personal papers of private individuals and regional collections. These are mostly materials from the nineteenth and twentieth centuries, although there also exist archives with holdings dating back to the Middle Ages, namely state archives in Gdańsk, Kraków, Poznań, Szczecin and Wrocław.[1]

Since the beginning of the 1990s, the role and activity of the historical archives of the Roman Catholic Church have been becoming more significant. These archives often contain holdings dating back to the early Middle Ages. Church archives, like state archives, apart from accumulation and preservation, are also obliged to provide access to their own historical resources.[2] Other churches and religious associations that survived the communist period or those that started operating in Poland after 1989 also began to create their archives. With the restoration of self-government in Poland, municipal archives reappeared in 1990, and after 1999 archives belonging to the self-government at the *powiat* and voivodeship level were also reactivated.[3]

The decision to resolve the communist period with its security apparatus led to the establishment of the Institute of National Remembrance – the Commission for the Prosecution of Crimes against the Polish Nation, which took place on January 19, 1999. Under the act, this unit took over documents related to the tragic fate of Poland and Poles in the twentieth century. Among them, there are materials created in the years 1944–1990 by communist special services and by civil and military state security agencies.[4]

From the very beginning, the Institute dealt with the wide-ranging popularization of its own research and educational activities, addressed to various age and social groups. It was the Institute of National Remembrance that disseminated online and outdoor exhibitions in Poland. It also has a wide range of publications (traditional and electronic) addressed to various social and age groups, with varying degrees of preparation in the field of historical knowledge. As the first institution with archival holdings, the Institute of National Remembrance introduced board games to the educational offer,[5] and joined the organization of city games.

After 1989, a new movement also emerged that concentrated on the accumulation, preservation, arrangement and description of the archival heritage of a wide variety of social organizations, groups interested in local or regional history, and the memory of selected aspects of the past. At the beginning of the twenty-first century, the term "social archives" began to spread in Poland. It was used to describe archival collections, often created in a spontaneous, collective, environmental and *pro bono publico* manner, collected by social organizations, including veterans, associations and foundations, whose activities focus on commemorating the past and the present with future generations in mind. Often, support for local initiatives is offered by cultural institutions operating locally or regionally, primarily libraries or less frequently, regional museums.

The growing number of social archives, of which there are now around 600, were dispersed for a long time. The KARTA Center Foundation began instigating and combining grassroots initiatives as early as the 1990s. The Foundation itself commemorates history, especially that of the twentieth century, dedicating special attention to individuals, both outstanding and distinguished for the history of Poland, and lesser known people who were collecting resources documenting everyday life and events from the recent past.[6] The KARTA Center, promoting the idea of social archivistics for many years, pointed to the need to coordinate the activities of institutions and non-governmental organizations collecting archives, as well as the need to guarantee financial support from the Polish state for this type of initiative. In 2002, the Council of Social Archives was established by the Ministry of Culture and National Heritage. The next step was the launch of a shared website for social archives – archiwa.org. At the beginning of 2020, on the initiative of the KARTA Center Foundation, which runs the largest social archive in Poland, and the Minister of Culture and National Heritage, the Center of Community Archives was established. Its tasks include supporting and developing the movement of social archives, assistance in preserving collections through training, workshops and increasingly popular webinars, providing free tools for creating electronic inventories and launching a website for sharing information about historical materials scattered in social archives all over the country.[7]

Finally, it is also worth noting the existence of private archives. These include not only personal and family archives, but also archives belonging to legal persons (including entities conducting economic activity, i.e., enterprises, production and service plants, financial institutions). Throughout the entire period of operation of business entities, but also associations, foundations, parties and trade unions, the documentation they gather is kept and managed by the owner. In the event of the termination of activity, the General Director of State Archives, as the central government administration body in Poland responsible for shaping the national archival resource, makes the decision for the state to take over a part of the documentation viewed as archival materials and to send it to the indicated state archives. In this case, it is crucial to define the role and significance of the entity that produced the documentation in economic or social life, or in the field of culture or education, regardless of whether the entity's activity spanned the entire country or was regional or local in nature. Being included as archival materials depends primarily on the values resulting from the content, but also the unique method of production or the original physical form.

Traditional Functions of Archives and Opening to the Public

The main functions of archives in Poland, as anywhere in the world, are invariably related to the acquisition, arrangement and description, preservation, protection and finally, providing access to archives, regardless of whether they are owned by the state or not. Some of these functions were performed internally for an extended period of time. The archives focused on ensuring the security of the collections of records by putting together the most valuable documentation, regardless of its physical form, placing it in safe storage areas protected against unauthorized access, and then by arranging archival units and preparing such recording tools that would provide information on the accumulated resource and ensure its integrity. For several decades now, we have seen the successively growing importance of functions performed externally, while concentrating on an increasingly defined and perceived public.[8] Especially since the beginning of the twenty-first century, it can be seen that directing the activities towards the widest possible popularization and accessibility of the holdings has brought a great, fundamental change. For many years, from the period after 1989 and the time of the political transformation, archives in Poland, unlike libraries, were still perceived as institutions difficult to access for non-researchers, mainly non-historians. Thanks to numerous top-down and bottom-up actions, this image, and above all the attitude of archives towards their visitors, is evolving. Additionally, as a result of the digital revolution, archives began to implement modern procedures, methods and technological solutions on a large scale, both for their own needs and for public functions.[9] The change is particularly visible in two areas: resource accumulation and accessibility.

Accumulation

Collections of archival materials stored in archives are overall documentation intended for permanent, perpetual storage. The accumulated archives may have a varied physical form. They may have been used in various historical periods, ranging from parchment and paper documents with or without seals, self-contained seals (most often wax, detached from documents), through registry books kept from the Middle Ages to the eighteenth century, files, correspondence, leaflets (such as posters or invitations), financial, statistical, technical, cartographic, geodetic documentation, photographs, films, microfilms, sound recordings, up to the latest type – electronic documents. The oldest materials, created before the conventionally adopted turning point (in Poland it is 1945, and recently it has even been moved to 1951), are treated as archives in their entirety.

When it comes to more recent documentation, produced in the last few decades, its classification as archival material is not determined by the manner of its production and its physical form. However, this criterion may be crucial in the case of unique methods of content registration, but above all the values resulting from the content. To become archives, documents need to contain important information and should constitute historical sources relating to the activity of the state and its institutions – both state- and local-government – as well as Poland's relations with other countries. They ought to provide information about political, social, economic, professional, religious life or about developments in science, culture, art, sport, etc. From the 1950s, one of the dominant topics in the discussions of archivists from around the world has been determining the principles of appraisal and selection of contemporary documentation due to its mass character and the inability to accumulate a more significant percentage of the created files due to the limited capacity of archival storage. Accumulating holdings in Poland, especially in state archives, over several post-war decades has concentrated on documentation produced by state institutions and the most important economic entities. Only 2%–10% of all the resulting documentation was selected for permanent storage. The task of selecting the most valuable testimonials of the functioning of the state and society in all their forms focused on two issues: identifying those public entities that could produce materials that were valuable from the point of view of future generations and history, and then on indicating the most valuable documentation from among all those produced by them. In Poland, these tasks continuously belong to the state archives and the supervisory functions that they perform.

However, for at least a dozen or so years, the area of interest related to the accumulation of archival resources has expanded. Several factors have caused the paradigm shift in this field. On the one hand, the emergence of the social archives movement in Poland has made it visible that there is considerable interest in regional and local history, as well as in the lives of "ordinary" people. Thus, the nature of the activity of social archives brought change to the approach of institutionalized archives, especially state archives. After years of narrowing the scope of their accumulation, they began to pay attention to fields that had previously remained outside of their interest. On the other hand, the state archives realized that in Poland after 1989, i.e., after the political transformation and privatization that covered most sectors of the economy, all non-state enterprises, private companies and institutions disappeared from the field of interest of state archives, in accordance with the applicable law. This meant a significant loss for future generations. Therefore, in recent years, state archives have begun to establish cooperation with entities and organizations from the non-state sector in order to secure and transfer the most valuable documentation to the state archives.

For the past decade, state archives have also been supporting social archives, recognizing their role in preserving archives related to many areas of social and cultural life, remaining beyond the current accumulation scope. In 2015, a special subsidy was established to finance, by means of selecting a limited number of applications and using the funds at the disposal of the General Director of State Archives, projects aimed at arranging, sharing and preserving archival materials included in the so-called non-state archival resource. The first event, aimed at supporting digitization activities, was concluded in 2016. In subsequent editions, a fixed amount of funds is given every year to the archives of associations, foundations and other public benefit organizations, as well as the archives of churches and religious associations for the conservation or arrangement and description of their archival collections. In 2020, 44 entities applied for this subsidy. Fifteen applications were selected as a result of the contest. Financing was granted, among others, to the Arton Foundation for archiving, processing and providing access to the archives of the avant-garde artist Paweł Kwiek, to the Main Board of the Association of Siberians for archiving and providing access to archival materials about people deported to Siberia, to the Monastery of the Discalced Carmelite Sisters in Kraków for the arrangement of their archives, and to the Archdiocesean Archives in Katowice for the conservation of seven record books dating back to the seventeenth–eighteenth century in Rybnik. In the five editions of the contest held between 2016 and 2020, grants were awarded to over 100 beneficiaries, and the total amount of funds transferred to them amounted to nearly five million PLN (over one million US dollars).[10]

When it comes to the process of accumulation, archives are becoming open to the public by taking materials from private collections, as long as they hold historical value. Entry into possession of family or personal collections through the state archives may occur through donations, deposits or, less frequently, purchases. However, the decision of choosing the institution that will receive the materials of private origin belongs entirely to the transferor or legal heirs of non-public collections, including family ones. The legacies of scientists or researchers are usually transferred to the archives of research institutions (like the Polish Academy of Sciences or individual universities and colleges). Collections accumulated by authors during their lives, such as those belonging to the field of culture, especially literature, usually go to the departments of manuscripts or everyday life documents located at the most important scientific libraries. Activists of the anti-communist opposition often donate their materials to the archives of the Institute of National Remembrance. Meanwhile, museums or municipal and district libraries, where a large percentage of Polish social archives operate, often receive collections of eminent people involved in the life of regions and towns. The Archives of Modern Records in Warsaw, in turn, conducts activities aimed at acquiring and arranging archival materials created by people and organizations related to underground and independence (anti-communist) activities, and those of the Polish diaspora. In the years 2004–2006, the Archives of the Independence Act and the Archives of the Polish Diaspora were combined into one branch of the Social Archives within the structure of the Archives of Modern Records. Sizable collections of photographs are, in turn, transferred by private collectors, or photographers and their heirs, to the National Digital Archives.[11]

In 2013, the State Archives cooperated with Polish Radio Program 1 to launch the campaign called "Become an archivist for your family." It resulted in a series of broadcasts encouraging people to look after collections and souvenirs kept in home archives and providing advice on how to maintain the collected documents. A competition for the most interestingly presented family archive was also announced. In its first edition, 87 applications were submitted, out of which nine best submissions were selected by a competition committee consisting of representatives of state archives and the Polish Radio. The winners talked about their collections on the Radio, and selected documents from their family archives were published.[12] The next step of the "Become an archivist for your family" action was the creation of a consultation point in each of the 33 state archives operating in Poland, providing help and support in the protection of home collections and souvenirs. In the following years, national and regional competitions were also organized. In 2020, the State Archives and Polish Radio Program I jointly organized an event called "My Archive 2020" to promote the cultivation of family collections. It was also accompanied by a competition with prizes.[13]

As part of the celebration of the 100th anniversary of Poland regaining independence, the General Director of State Archives, together with the Office of the "*Niepodległa*" ("Independent") Program, launched the "Independence Family Archives" project in 2019. It was addressed to people owning home collections of documents, sometimes ones that have been growing over many generations. The aim and the leading concept was to encourage the owners of family collections to share their knowledge with state archives in order to combine national and private history, and to highlight the role of unknown people, families and local communities in restoring Poland's independence. The campaign was summed up with a series of exhibitions and publications prepared by most of the state archives. Some of them received private archives donated by individual donors. Other people decided to prepare and donate only digital copies. At the end of 2020, a large open-air exhibition took place in Warsaw under the name of "A collective portrait of the families of the Second Polish Republic," summarizing the project, which was accompanied by a catalog published in print.[14] A guide for family archivists has also been prepared and made available online, explaining how to deal with family heirlooms in various forms (manuscripts, official documents, photos).[15]

On September 30, 2019, Archivist Day was celebrated in Poland for the first time. On this occasion, a training workshop entitled "Become an archivist for your family" was organized in each of the 33 state archives. In 2020, due to the COVID-19 pandemic, most archives prepared a large variety of online events on September 30, addressed to family archivists. By taking part in webinars, as well as stationary meetings in some of the archives, participants could broaden their knowledge about the methods of searching for ancestors, the rules of preparing a family tree, ways of storing family archives, and techniques for organizing and describing them. It was also possible to learn how to make digital copies to prevent damaging the originals, and archivists taught simple maintenance techniques that could be performed at home.[16]

In April 2020, state archives in Poland initiated the action of "Archives of the Pandemic A.D. 2020: Social Document Collection of the Coronavirus Pandemic (SARS-CoV-2)." Pointing to the social role of state archives as institutions that preserve memory, the General Director of State Archives appealed to private persons, associations, foundations, institutions, organizations, social communities and other interested parties to share their own experiences and reflections, recorded in both traditional and electronic documentation, creating records of the phenomenon of an epidemic in Poland right next to us, in everyday, social, cultural and professional life. They were asked to donate the originals or to enable the state archives to make digital copies of materials in the form of notes, diaries, journals, leaflets, photos, memes, blogs, vlogs, audio and video recordings, and other media types, or in the form of materials published on websites. Collected testimonies provided by individual donors, organizations and associations, as well as by the editorial offices of local newspapers and websites, constitute an invaluable resource documenting and illustrating the pandemic. At the same time, in mid-2020, there was a competition called *"O tempora, o mores!* Notes about the coronavirus pandemic A.D. 2020 taken by the family archivist." The best of the submitted works were selected and awarded in two age categories: prepared by children and youth up to 18 years of age, and by adults.[17]

Accessibility

The most traditional way of accessing archives is to order them to a reading room and read the content in person. Before 1989, such a direct method was subject to a number of restrictions, which were systematically simplified after the transformation that took place in Poland. One of the first steps was to waive the obligation for foreigners to get the permission of the General Director of State Archives to use the archives held in state archives, replacing this procedure with the approval granted by the director of a specific archive. The unification of the rules of access to archival materials in state archives, regardless of citizenship, was introduced on January 1, 2007. As a result, citizens of other countries do not have to apply for permission to see the files. However, in most archives in Poland (state archives, archives of the Institute of National Remembrance, church archives, archives of different institutions), being able to use the holdings still requires the interested person to fill in an appropriate application form, and then it is also necessary to place orders for selected archival units. Until recently, this required a personal visit to the archives. As part of opening themselves up to the public, most Polish archives have simplified their procedures, and introduced electronic applications and order forms, which facilitate and greatly accelerate ordering archival materials to the reading rooms. In order to meet the expectations of people who conduct personal searches in the reading rooms, since 2011, all state archives have permitted their visitors to photograph the archives with their own camera, which is free of charge and considered a non-invasive method. Some of the archives also make scanners available in their reading rooms for free.[18]

However, in order to share archival materials efficiently, it is necessary to expand the informativeness that the archives provide as institutions. For centuries, they preserved their resources by drawing up traditional, paper archival inventories. These basic inventory aids differed from each other in terms of the level of detail and appearance. Using them required a personal visit to the archives. The first step towards making information about one's own holdings more accessible was publishing book-based inventories of the most important and most valuable founds and collections of records, as well as publishing information and guides to the resources of specific archives in print. In Poland, the trend related to issuing various archival aids was clearly visible and alive from the 1970s to the beginning of the twenty-first century, and state archives played the leading role in it. The Institute of National Remembrance also published its printed information booklet in 2009.[19] In turn, printed aids were prepared for church archives by the Center for Archives, Libraries and Church Museums at the Catholic University of Lublin. However, the real qualitative change began in the 1990s. The first tool that proved helpful in reaching a wider audience with information about one's own holdings were websites, which were later surpassed by social media accounts.

The next step was the creation of online databases referring to the archival records. In Poland, state archives have the longest experience in creating tools that facilitate finding information about its holdings on the internet. In the mid-1990s, the first databases informing about fonds and collections of records kept in archives (the SEZAM Database – the Archive Holdings Record System) and electronic archival inventories (the IZA database – Archive Resource Inventories) began to be developed. Due to the growing number of people interested in the origins of their families and undertaking genealogical research, a separate database was created, containing information about the location of storage of civil status books and records (the PRADZIAD Database). In 2007, it was decided that several databases kept by state archives were to be merged. They were replaced by a single integrated system (Integrated Archive Information System – ZoSIA). The data it contains about fonds and collections of records, as well as individuals, is available via the "Search in Archives" website (szukajwarchiwach.gov.pl). Descriptions of archival materials are supplemented by growing numbers of their digital copies. In early 2021, there were over 48 million scans available. The ZoSIA system for creating descriptions presented in the "Search in Archives" service is made available free of charge by the General Director of

State Archives to church archives, associations, foundations, and scientific and cultural institutions.[20]

Other archives in Poland have also created their own online databases. For example, since 2012, the Institute of National Remembrance has been publishing its own archival inventories using their Digital Archive System. Due to the character of the collection (i.e., archival materials related to state security authorities and the prosecutor's department conducting investigations concerning, inter alia, communist crimes), not all descriptions contained in it are available online. The system has a module dedicated to digitization, but digital copies of archival materials are not published on the website due to the specific nature of the resource. The public inventory itself is available at https://inwentarz.ipn.gov.pl/#.

To serve the needs of social archives, a separate system was created (the Open Archiving System – OSA). It is a free application created on the initiative of the KARTA Center Foundation. The system became available in 2016. It is used to prepare descriptions of archival materials accumulated by non-governmental organizations and by individual collectors, which are then presented via a dedicated portal. OSA is currently run by the Center for Social Archives and is available at: https://osa.archiwa.org/.

Due to the scattered and decentralized mode of operation, the church archives were not compiled in a common IT system. Some of them use the KOHA database dedicated to libraries (e.g. Archdiocesan Archives in Poznań). Other archives of the Catholic Church often have fairly simple online catalogues for browsing the resources (e.g. Archdiocesan Archives in Gniezno, Archdiocesan Archives in Katowice, Diocesan Archives in Zielona Góra, Archives of Dominican Provinces in Poland). However, most church archives have not switched to electronic inventory tools, and the use of the resources still requires a personal visit to the archives, with prior consent to be able to access the archives.

In addition to access to record-keeping materials, the archives also undertook other activities aimed at presenting and making their own holdings available. There exists a long tradition of activity that revolves around the forms of promoting the resources, such as through the organization of exhibitions, conferences, lectures on topics related to the archives and anniversary events. For years, however, the archives were limited in this aspect to their own locations. As a result, the number of people who could be reached with the information was very limited. New ideas and solutions have been visible from the beginning of the twenty-first century. For years, open-air exhibitions organized by state archives or by the Institute of National Remembrance have taken place in the centers of Polish cities. While searching for a solution that would be closer to the public, the State Archives in Warsaw began presenting their own projects and exhibitions in large shopping centers. In ARCHIBUS, which has been driving for several years along the streets of Koszalin, city residents who are on their way to work or school can see thoroughly prepared and frequently changed exhibitions of archival materials, organized by the State Archives in Koszalin. In the summer of 2018 and 2019, photoplasticons, referring to those from the turn of the nineteenth and twentieth centuries, were installed in several Polish cities at popular tourist points. They presented vivid historical photographs of cities from the holdings of the National Digital Archives and individual state archives. Due to the prolonged pandemic that took place in 2020, the National Digital Archives, instead of organizing the next edition of the project and exhibition of photographs on the streets of Gdynia and Bydgoszcz, launched an online project called "Online Archive Photoplasticon."[21]

An excellent example illustrating how much the approach of archives to the public has changed in the field of popularizing the holdings is the series of events organized in the summer of 2020 for the 100th anniversary of the Battle of Warsaw that changed the course of the Polish-Bolshevik war in 1919–1920. On this occasion, numerous outdoor exhibitions were organized for the public. In Warsaw, in a representative part of the city, the General Directorate of State Archives cooperated with the Royal Łazienki Museum and embassies of several countries to prepare a special exhibition. It depicted the events of the Battle of Warsaw against the background of the situation in Central and Eastern European countries – Finland, Hungary, Czechoslovakia, Lithuania, Latvia, Estonia, Romania, Ukraine – and their way of achieving independence. It also showed the participation of American pilots from the 7th Fighter Squadron in the fight against the Bolshevik army. Several open-air exhibitions were prepared by the Archives of Modern Records in Warsaw in cooperation with the Union of War Invalids of the Republic of Poland, as well as the State Archives in Warsaw. The state archives in Kielce, Lublin, Łódź and Piotrków Trybunalski organized their own exhibitions to be presented in the centers of these cities. Due to the pandemic, numerous thematic exhibitions were also organized online. The project of the National Digital Archives called "1920/2020: The Animated Archive" enabled an entry into new interactions and connections with artistic circles that until then had not been connected with state archives. As a result of this, murals were created in Warsaw on the Vistula Boulevards and an installation was prepared – a work of art by Karolina Breguła, located in the place where in 1920 a branch of the Volunteer Women's Legion was stationed. Both projects were inspired by archival materials and were an artistic way of commemorating the Polish-Bolshevik war and the Battle of Warsaw 1920 in public space. In order to answer the needs of children and adolescents, an educational notebook was prepared, in which archival materials from the holdings of the State Archives in Lublin were used to tell about the participation of teenage soldiers in the Polish-Bolshevik war. In cooperation with groups of history re-enactors, the Archives of Modern Records created a short video published on the internet and YouTube, reminiscent of the Battle of Warsaw and promoting one more project – the multimedia thematic portal of the State Archives which can be found at www.1920.gov.pl. The story and the calendar of events were enriched with visual content, unique archival sources, photographs and maps, as well as a gallery of posters, and leaflets used by both sides of the conflict. This part was created in cooperation with the Archives of Modern Records and the Poster Museum in Wilanów.[22]

The classic formula has been enriched in recent years by the possibility of visiting the archives from behind the scenes, getting a glimpse into the warehouses, and ways of storing, securing and preserving archives in the archival conservation studios. Such events, accompanied by active participation from the public, are organized on the occasion of other events, for example, the Night of Museums, which has seen the involvement of the state, church, social and the Institute of National Remembrance's archives for many years. Since 2009, the Archive Picnic has been held in Warsaw every year at the beginning of June to celebrate International Archives Day. Most archives in Poland choose their own way of participating in the celebration of International Archives Day, and since 2019 the International Archives Week has been organized and coordinated by the International Council on Archives (#IAW2019, #IAW2020).[23] Most often, the events are centered around workshops that benefit from the participants' strong involvement and consist of activities such as creating a family tree, learning how to read old writings under the supervision of archivists and carrying out their own simple conservation of archives.[24]

Nowadays, it is easier to stay open and accessible to the public because of the dynamically growing popularity of electronic media, including social media, and information and promotional campaigns released with their help. In the year of the pandemic, state archives in Poland additionally joined the #stayhome campaign and gathered in one place their exhibitions (#stayhome and see the exhibition in the Archives), interesting collections (#stayhome and watch in the Archives) and educational materials (#stayhome and learn in the Archives).

An example of activities addressed to a specific target group of genealogists, especially beginners, is the creation of a special tab on the website of state archives containing instructions on searching for materials connected with the history of one's own family in archival holdings, as well as the publishing of informative guides in the form of brochures.[25] The result of cooperation with genealogical communities, including the Polish Genealogical Society and regional societies, was also the inclusion in the long-term plans of digitizing record books and resources from registry offices.

Another field that is being developed and targeted at the audience is educational activity. For years, the archives, observing the experience of museums, have been offering projects for children and young people. Archival lessons for students of all ages are the most popular solution and they are offered by all state archives.[26] Lessons and workshops for students and schoolchildren are also in the offerings of the Institute of National Remembrance.[27] It should be noted that there has been an evolution and a qualitative change in this field in recent years. Initially, archival lessons were prepared from the ground up and did not always correspond to the latest trends in teaching methodology. In order to meet the expectations of students and teachers and increase the quality and appeal of the educational offer prepared by the archives, the Archive Educators Forum was established in the form of a social initiative, organized from the ground up. As part of cyclically organized meetings and initiatives, participants exchange their experiences in preparing engaging and inspiring lessons in the history of their own family and the local community, region and country, in designing city and board games, and preparing educational aids.[28] Hoping to integrate the educators' community and exchanging experiences, the State Archive in Warsaw has for years been organizing a series of conferences, with the leading slogan being *Educare necesse est*. Recently, educational activities have been going beyond the circle of children and adolescents. They also reach adults, for whom workshops are prepared in the field of history, working with archival sources and preserving their own family archives. As a result, increasingly often and especially in smaller towns, archives become educational institutions on the one hand, and culture-forming ones on the other, as places where the public meets and experiences history. This is an important shift – due to the high competencies of archivists and the uniqueness of archival holdings, archives should be institutions that are naturally co-responsible for shaping the historical culture of societies.

The new way of thinking about the functions of archives connected with making them available and open to the public is visible in yet another aspect. In the last decade, the process of modernizing the archival infrastructure has begun in Poland. The new archives built in Białystok, Kraków or Rzeszów are adapted to the needs of people with disabilities. All the new buildings of the state archives contain exhibition spaces and rooms for lectures and conferences, and some of them, e.g., the building of the National Archives in Kraków, also contain rooms adapted for film screenings. Designing spaces for the public in new archives' buildings shows how important it has become for archives to provide access to and popularize the holdings.

Conclusions

There are two factors that have had a stimulating effect on, in particular, state archives and archives of large and important institutions operating in Poland. They affected the change in the perception of their tasks and the need to expand the areas of activity related to the public. The first factor was the establishment of the Institute of National Remembrance, while the second was the development of the social archive movement encouraging both passive and active participation of the public. As a result, the presence of most archives in public space has significantly expanded in recent years. The archives have also been opened to more diverse groups of recipients. New forms and methods of public activity have emerged as a response to social expectations and opportunities for cooperation with other institutions and individual recipients.

The change of perspective and raising the rank of activities aimed at the public is also evidenced by the organization of the discussion panel under the name of "Archives in public space" by the General Director of State Archives during the 20th General Congress of Historians in Lublin in September 2019. The discussion pointed to the achievements in the field of archives in the public space in recent years, but also to the challenges that archives in Poland still face.[29] The main challenge remains the simplification of accessibility, modernization of tools for using archives without the need to visit the archives, constant active involvement of the public in various forms of activity and efforts to change the socially entrenched image of archives as places unavailable to "ordinary" people.

Notes

1 Archiwa Państwowe, "Struktura organizacyjna," accessed February 20, 2021, https://www.archiwa.gov.pl/pl/o-nas/archiwa-pa%C5%84stwowe/struktura-organizacyjna.

2 Roland Prejs, "Organizacja i funkcjonowanie archiwów w domach zakonnych," *Archiwa, Biblioteki i Muzea Kościelne* 75 (2001): 139–151; Maria Dębowska, *Archiwa Kościoła katolickiego w Polsce. Informator* (Kielce: Wydawnictwo Jedność, 2002); Robert Kufel, "Powstanie archiwów kościelnych w Polsce. Zarys problematyki," *Adhibenda. Rocznik Archiwum Diecezjalnego w Zielonej Górze*, no. 1 (2017): 82; "Archiwa kościelne," Stowarzyszenie Archiwistów Kościelnych, accessed February 20, 2021, http://stowarzyszenie-archiwistow-koscielnych.pl/index.php/archiwa-koscielne/.

3 *Archiwa samorządowe w służbie mieszkańców i administracji publicznej. Referaty II Krajowego Sympozjum Archiwalnego 28–29 września 1999 r.*, ed. Jarosław Poraziński and Zbigniew Pustuła (Warszawa: Stowarzyszenie Archiwistów Polskich, 1999).

4 Jerzy Eisler, "Dzieje Archiwum Instytutu Pamięci Narodowej," in *Archiwa polskie wczoraj i dziś*, ed. Kazimierz Kozłowski and Władysław Stępniak (Warszawa: NDAP, 2012), 171–174; "O IPN," Instytut Pamięci Narodowej, accessed February 20, 2021, https://ipn.gov.pl/pl/o-ipn/24154,O-IPN.html. Cf. chapter by Łukasz Kamiński in this volume.

5 Cf. chapter by Joanna Wojdon in this volume.

6 *Ruch archiwów społecznych*, ed. Alicja Wancerz-Gluza (Warszawa: Ośrodek KARTA, 2014); Zbigniew Gluza, "Archiwa Ośrodka KARTA," in *Archiwistyka społeczna*, ed. Katarzyna Ziętal (Warszawa: Ośrodek KARTA, 2014), 27–35. Cf. "O nas," Ośrodek KARTA, accessed February 20, 2021, https://karta.org.pl/nas; and chapters by Łukasz Kamiński and Marta Kurkowska-Budzan in this volume.

7 Katarzyna Ziętal, "Wstęp," in *Archiwistyka społeczna*, ed. Katarzyna Ziętal (Warszawa: Ośrodek KARTA, 2014), 7–13; Archiwa społeczne, "Działalność," accessed February 20, 2021, https://archiwa.org/content/dzia%C5%82alno%C5%9B%C4%87.

8 Waldemar Chorążyczewski, "Zarys dziejów i charakterystyka archiwów państwowych," in *Archiwa polskie wczoraj i dziś*, ed. Kazimierz Kozłowski and Władysław Stępniak (Warszawa: NDAP, 2012), 182–183.

9 Lucyna Harc, "Współczesna archiwistyka," in *Historia w przestrzeni publicznej*, ed. Joanna Wojdon (Warszawa: PWN, 2018), 227.

10 Archiwa Państwowe, "Wspieranie działań archiwalnych 2020 – wyniki konkursu," accessed February 20, 2021, https://www.archiwa.gov.pl/

pl/aktualnosci/5213-%E2%80%9Ewspieranie-dzia%C5%82a%C5%84-archiwalnych-2020%E2%80%9D-wyniki-konkursu.

11 Harc, "Współczesna archiwistyka," 231–232.

12 *Archiwa rodzinne. Prace laureatów konkursu „Zostań rodzinnym archiwistą"* ed. Robert Górski et al. (Warszawa: NDAP, 2013); Archiwa Państwowe, "Archiwa rodzinne – nową publikacja," accessed February 20, 2021, https://www.archiwa. gov.pl/pl/582-%E2%80%9Earchiwa-rodzinne%E2%80%9D-nowa-publikacja.

13 Polskie Radio, "Moje Archiwum 2020," accessed February 20, 2021, https:// www.polskieradio.pl/447/8794/.

14 *Zbiorowy portret rodzin II Rzeczypospolitej,* ed. Anna Krochmal (Warszawa: NDAP, 2020); Archiwa Rodzinne Niepodległej, "Ogólnopolska wystawa 'Archiwa Rodzinne Niepodległej. Zbiorowy portret rodzin II Rzeczypospolitej," accessed February 20, 2021, https://archiwarodzinne.gov.pl/o-projekcie/ ogolnopolska-wystawa-archiwa-rodzinne-niepodleglej-zbiorowy-portret-rodzin-ii.

15 Archiwa Rodzinne Niepodległej, "Poradnik," accessed February 20, 2021, https://archiwarodzinne.gov.pl/domowe-archiwum/poradnik.

16 Archiwa Państwowe, "Dzień Archiwisty 2020 i warsztaty 'Zostań rodzin-nym archiwistą,'" accessed February 20, 2021, https://www.archiwa.gov.pl/pl/ aktualnosci/5256-dzie%C5%84-archiwisty-2020-i-warsztaty-%E2%80%9 Ezosta%C5%84-rodzinnym-archiwist%C4%85%E2%80%9D.

17 Grzegorz Mendykowski, "Archiwa państwowe w czasach pandemii," *Rocznik Kultury Polskiej,* (2020): 44–49; Archiwa Państwowe, "Archiwum Pandemii A.D. 2020," accessed February 20, 2021, https://www.archiwa.gov.pl/pl/ ucategorised/5165.

18 Archiwa Państwowe, "Warunki udostępniania zasobu archiwum," ac-cessed February 20, 2021, https://www.archiwa.gov.pl/pl/dla-uzytkownikow/ warunki-udost%C4%99pniania-zasobu-archiwum.

19 *Informator o zasobie archiwalnym Instytutu Pamięci Narodowej (stan na dzień 31 grudnia 2008 roku),* ed. Jerzy Bednarek and Rafał Leśkiewicz (Warszawa: IPN, 2009), accessed February 20, 2021, https://inwentarz.ipn.gov.pl/doc/informator. pdf.

20 Archiwa Państwowe, "Szukaj w Archiwach," accessed February 20, 2021, https:// www.szukajwarchiwach.gov.pl/.

21 Archiwa Państwowe, "Archiwalny Fotoplastikon Online," accessed Febru-ary 20, 2021, https://www.archiwa.gov.pl/pl/aktualnosci/5343-archiwalny-fotoplastikon-online.

22 Archiwa Państwowe, "Rok 1920 w Archiwach Państwowych," accessed Feb-ruary 20, 2021, https://www.archiwa.gov.pl/pl/aktualnosci/5222-rok-1920-w-archiwach-pa%C5%84stwowych.

23 International Council on Archives, "International Archives Week: 8–14 June 2020," accessed February 20, 2021, https://www.ica.org/en/international-archives-week-8-14-june-2020.

24 Archiwa Państwowe, "Międzynarodowy Dzień Archiwów 2019," accessed Feb-ruary 20, 2021, https://translate.google.pl/?hl=pl&sl=pl&tl=en&text=Mi%C4% 99dzynarodowy%20Dzie%C5%84%20Archiw%C3%B3w%202019%20& op=translate.

25 *Porady praktyczne dla osób planujących poszukiwania genealogiczne w Archiwum Głównym Akt Dawnych,* ed. Małgorzata Kośka (Warszawa: AGAD, 2020).

26 Archiwa Państwowe, "Warsztaty i lekcje archiwalne w archiwach państwowych," accessed February 20, 2021, https://www.archiwa.gov.pl/pl/aktualnosci/ 4957-warsztaty-i-lekcje-archiwalne-w-archiwach-pa%C5%84stwowych.

27 Instytut Pamięci Narodowej, "Z archiwum IPN lekcje i warsztaty," accessed February 20, 2021, https://edukacja.ipn.gov.pl/edu/lekcje-i-warsztaty/z-archiuwm-ipn-lekcje-i.

28 Hubert Mazur and Agnieszka Rosa, "Archiwa a publiczność," in *Historia w przestrzeni publicznej*, ed. Joanna Wojdon (Warszawa: PWN, 2018), 267–268; Forum Edukatorów Archiwalnych, accessed February 20, 2021, http://edukacjaarchiwalna.pl/.

29 Agnieszka Rosa, "O społecznych rolach archiwów we współczesnym dyskursie archiwalnym w Polsce na marginesie dyskusji panelowej 'Archiwa w przestrzeni publicznej," *Archeion* 120 (2019): 149–167, accessed February 20, 2021, https://www.archiwa.gov.pl/files/Archeion_CXX.pdf.

Bibliography

Archiwa Państwowe. "Dzień Archiwisty 2020 i warsztaty 'Zostań rodzinnym archiwistą." Accessed February 20, 2021. https://www.archiwa.gov.pl/pl/aktualnosci/5256-dzie%C5%84-archiwisty-2020-i-warsztaty-%E2%80%9Ezosta%C5%84-rodzinnym-archiwist%C4%85%E2%80%9D.

Archiwa Państwowe. "Struktura organizacyjna." Accessed February 20, 2021. https://www.archiwa.gov.pl/pl/o-nas/archiwa-pa%C5%84stwowe/struktura-organizacyjna

Archiwa Państwowe. "Szukaj w Archiwach." Accessed February 20, 2021. https://www.szukajwarchiwach.gov.pl/.

Archiwa Państwowe. "Warsztaty i lekcje archiwalne w archiwach państwowych." Accessed February 20, 2021, https://www.archiwa.gov.pl/pl/aktualnosci/4957-warsztaty-i-lekcje-archiwalne-w-archiwach-pa%C5%84stwowych.

Archiwa Państwowe. "Wspieranie działań archiwalnych 2020 – wyniki konkursu." Accessed February 20, 2021. https://www.archiwa.gov.pl/pl/aktualnosci/5213-%E2%80%9Ewspieranie-dzia%C5%82a%C5%84-archiwalnych-2020%E2%80%909D-wyniki-konkursu.

Archiwa Rodzinne Niepodległej. "Ogólnopolska wystawa 'Archiwa Rodzinne Niepodległej. Zbiorowy portret rodzin II Rzeczypospolitej." Accessed February 20, 2021. https://archiwarodzinne.gov.pl/o-projekcie/ogolnopolska-wystawa-archiwa-rodzinne-niepodleglej-zbiorowy-portret-rodzin-ii.

Archiwa społeczne. "Działalność." Accessed February 20, 2021. https://archiwa.org/content/dzia%C5%82alno%C5%9B%C4%87.

Bednarek, Jerzy, and Rafał Leśkiewicz, eds. *Informator o zasobie archiwalnym Instytutu Pamięci Narodowej (stan na dzień 31 grudnia 2008 roku)*. Warszawa: IPN, 2009. https://inwentarz.ipn.gov.pl/doc/informator.pdf.

Chorążyczewski, Waldemar. "Zarys dziejów i charakterystyka archiwów państwowych." In *Archiwa polskie wczoraj i dziś*, edited by Kazimierz Kozłowski and Władysław Stępniak, 177–185. Warszawa: NDAP, 2012.

Dębowska, Maria. *Archiwa Kościoła katolickiego w Polsce. Informator*. Kielce: Wydawnictwo Jedność, 2002.

Eisler, Jerzy. "Dzieje Archiwum Instytutu Pamięci Narodowej." In *Archiwa polskie wczoraj i dziś*, edited by Kazimierz Kozłowski and Władysław Stępniak, 171–174. Warszawa: NDAP, 2012.

Forum Edukatorów Archiwalnych. Accessed February 20, 2021, http://edukacjaarchiwalna.pl/.

Gluza, Zbigniew. "Archiwa Ośrodka KARTA." In *Archiwistyka społeczna*, edited by Katarzyna Ziętal, 27–35. Warszawa: Ośrodek KARTA, 2014.

Górski, Robert, et al., eds. *Archiwa rodzinne. Prace laureatów konkursu „Zostań rodzinnym archiwistą."* Warszawa: NDAP, 2013. https://www.archiwa.gov.pl/images/docs/ARCHIWA_RODZINNE.pdf.

Harc, Lucyna. "Współczesna archiwistyka." In *Historia w przestrzeni publicznej*, edited by Joanna Wojdon, 227–238. Warszawa: PWN, 2018.

Instytut Pamięci Narodowej. "O IPN." Accessed February 20, 2021. https://ipn.gov.pl/pl/o-ipn/24154,O-IPN.html.

Instytut Pamięci Narodowej. "Z archiwum IPN lekcje i warsztaty." Accessed February 20, 2021, https://edukacja.ipn.gov.pl/edu/lekcje-i-warsztaty/z-archiuwm-ipn-lekcje-i.

Kośka, Małgorzata, ed. *Porady praktyczne dla osób planujących poszukiwania genealogiczne w Archiwum Głównym Akt Dawnych*. Warszawa: AGAD, 2020.

Krochmal, Anna, ed. *Zbiorowy portret rodzin II Rzeczypospolitej*. Warszawa: NDAP, 2020.

Kufel, Robert. "Powstanie archiwów kościelnych w Polsce. Zarys problematyki." *Adhibenda. Rocznik Archiwum Diecezjalnego w Zielonej Górze*, no. 1 (2017): 71–88.

Mazur, Hubert, and Agnieszka Rosa. "Archiwa a publiczność." In *Historia w przestrzeni publicznej*, edited by Joanna Wojdon, 263–271. Warszawa: PWN, 2018.

Mendykowski, Grzegorz. "Archiwa państwowe w czasach pandemii." *Rocznik Kultury Polskiej*, (2020): 44–49.

Ośrodek KARTA. "O nas." Accessed February 20, 2021. https://karta.org.pl/nas

Polskie Radio. "Moje Archiwum 2020." Accessed February 20, 2021. https://www.polskieradio.pl/447/8794/.

Poraziński, Jarosław, and Zbigniew Pustuła, eds. *Archiwa samorządowe w służbie mieszkańców i administracji publicznej. Referaty II Krajowego Sympozjum Archiwalnego 28–29 września 1999 r.* Warszawa: Stowarzyszenie Archiwistów Polskich, 1999.

Prejs, Roland. "Organizacja i funkcjonowanie archiwów w domach zakonnych." *Archiwa, Biblioteki i Muzea Kościelne* 75 (2001): 139–151.

Rosa, Agnieszka. "O społecznych rolach archiwów we współczesnym dyskursie archiwalnym w Polsce na marginesie dyskusji panelowej 'Archiwa w przestrzeni publicznej.'" *Archeion* 120 (2019): 149–167.

Stowarzyszenie Archiwistów Kościelnych. "Archiwa kościelne." Accessed February 20, 2021, http://stowarzyszenie-archiwistow-koscielnych.pl/index.php/archiwa-koscielne/

Wancerz-Gluza, Alicja, ed. *Ruch archiwów społecznych*. Warszawa: Ośrodek KARTA, 2014.

Ziętal, Katarzyna. "Wstęp." In *Archiwistyka społeczna*, edited by Katarzyna Ziętal, 7–13. Warszawa: Ośrodek KARTA, 2014.

9 Book Publishers as Public Historians

The Polish Case

Ewa Jabłońska-Stefanowicz

The words "to publish" and "public" have common roots: they originate from the Latin words *publicare* and *publicus*. *Publicare* means "to make public," while "the public" is people in general. This reminder will inform our reflection on the relationships between the activities of the representatives of two professions: historical book publishers and public historians. The shared linguistic origins of these professions are meaningful and indicate similarities with respect to the scope, methods and objectives of their activities in the publishing market. While we focus on the publishing market of Poland, the observed phenomena and trends are consistent with global tendencies, including the chief trend: digitization. Digitization is clearly not only a format change – from printed to electronic – but also a force causing significant disruptions in the entire publishing process.

Book Publisher and Public Historian in the Digital World

Until recently, the publishing process did not differ significantly in its principles from the process described by Sir Stanley Unwin in the 1920s. This outstanding publisher begins his professional testament, republished many times, with this warning: "It is easy to become a publisher, but difficult to remain one; the mortality in infancy is higher than in any other trade or profession."[1] A publisher was required to combine fire and water – that is an art, a craft and a business – and use them to publish books which could be sold for profit. In selecting among proposals submitted by authors or evaluating commissioned materials, the publisher was taking a risk. In order to reduce the risk, he relied on the assistance of external reviewers and consultants, adding their opinions to his knowledge of the market, experience and aesthetic taste. Whether his decisions were correct would be revealed only after a book was completed and launched on the market.

After accepting a piece, the publisher prepared a cost estimate for its publication. Agreement regarding the budget was required before the work could be acquired from its author and the contract signed. When the text was complete, the product development stage began, supervised by editors. They were tasked with adding sufficient value to ensure that the final

DOI: 10.4324/9781003165767-12

product could be sold at a profit. Copyeditors worked on content-related and linguistic aspects of the text, closely collaborating with the author and book designer. The digital file containing the book thus developed and, when approved by the author, was then passed on to the typesetter who, using appropriate software, arranged the pages of the book. Those were checked in the proofreading process by the author and editor. The finished files reached the printing house, and the printed books – via the wholesaler – arrived in bookstores.

All decisions made during the publishing work – from acceptance of the text, through the stages of editing and design, to agreement on the final title of the book, the price and the print run – were dependent on the needs, expectations and capabilities of its target readers. Publication made a book publicly available. Potential success, announced after the sale of a significant number of copies, was evidence that the publisher had performed his work properly.

At the turn of the twentieth century the "hidden revolution" transformed the book market. Reports predicted that revenues from publishing e-books would soon reach 12% of total revenues in the book market.[2] Some publishers treated the forecast seriously and began preparing to modify their procedures. Most of them waited, still believing in the unshakable position of the printed book, with its unique features valued by readers, such as an attractive cover, aesthetically pleasing layout, convenience of use, a potential for lending and placement on a shelf. Starting in 2007, with the appearance of the Kindle reader and then the iPad (2010), the direction of the book market's evolution became obvious. It became clear that the production of e-books would become both necessary and unavoidable for anyone intent on remaining in the publishing business.

Since that time, sales of e-books have had different dynamics in individual countries. However, even in the places where – as in Poland – they generate revenue at the level of only 3% of the entire publishing market, it is difficult not to notice the effects of the technological revolution that began with the appearance of computers in publishing houses. Contrary to expectations, the "hidden revolution" concerns not so much the product as the process, with its influence observable at several levels. At the beginning, the changes occurred at the level of computerization in publishing houses themselves, which resulted, among other things, in moving book-related communication to the Internet. More importantly, the book's form also changed. Thompson writes: "The reconstitution of the book as a digital file is a crucial part of the hidden revolution."[3] From the very beginning, i.e., from receipt of the text from the author, through the editorial stage, typesetting and printing, the content is a digital file from which the book can be printed quickly. Digital printing abolishes restrictions concerning print runs, as it is possible to print as few as several dozen copies, which changes the previous paradigm: "It used to be print book, sell book. We say no, no. Sell book, print book."[4] The digital revolution basically reshapes marketing and sales, too. Moving them to the Internet allows us, for instance, to acquire more knowledge about sales results, and thus to react to them faster. It also allows getting in touch and maintaining contact with book readers. And finally, the digital content exists independently of its material form, so it can be sent instantly to any interested recipient. This has marked practical consequences, leading to changes in the existing relations between the main players in the book market and even to the elimination of some of them.

For some, enforcing changes in the existing, well-known practices causes problems. For others, it creates an opportunity to enter the game. Amazon is not only a global platform for selling books in various forms and formats, but also a service for authors, whereby they can publish and disseminate their work on their own, bypassing the publisher, in an "easy, clear and free way."[5] This and many other local digital platforms rely on authors who wish to take matters into their own hands. "Luckily, many of the tools for publishing and distribution are freely available to authors, and this book is one such"[6] – in these words Mark Coker, founder of Smashwords, recommends a particular guide for self-publishers. And although the self-publishing phenomenon is not new, thanks to digital technologies and innovative companies it has ceased to be a niche phenomenon of dubious reputation. It even "acquires a new respectability,"[7] as for authors it has become a conscious choice rather than a necessity. The communication circuit reflecting this situation is very simple: literary agents and publishers disappear, and authors remain, who send their e-books directly to the distributors, who send them to the public.[8]

Thus, the change of the book's format to an electronic one, has ruptured the accustomed system – now everyone who has, or is able to acquire, content may become a publisher of this new type. Apart from the authors themselves, entities such as scholarly institutions, associations, libraries and magazines have joined this group. Consequently, competition from their quarter has caused the traditional publishers to enter the self-publishing market, and to sell such books on their own websites. That is why in the digital publishing communication circuit the boxes overlap: the tasks once assigned to one player are now performed by others.[9]

Therefore, alongside technology companies, also the readers of the content become beneficiaries of the ongoing revolution. They had a lot of influence even as traditional readers/clients of bookstores or users of libraries. It was through their collective decisions that the author's writing career and the success of the publisher were determined. Now they are even more influential: by belonging to internet reading communities and maintaining book blogs or profiles on social media, they share their reviews and ratings with others. Some people engaging in literary criticism on an amateur basis cooperate with commercial publishers, giving word-of-mouth recommendations of selected titles. The power of readers is revealed particularly clearly on crowdfunding platforms.[10] Readers can appear there in the role of the author's patrons; it is on their preferences (and money) that publication depends.

Digital revolution has also changed the world of history. The idea that ordinary people help make history is not new. However, the development of technology has opened completely new opportunities for them. Easy access to many diverse sources of digitized information and competency in using computer tools allow anyone to conduct research and share their ideas with an enormous audience. The internet has made it easier also for academic historians to perform research, publish results and contact other research-ers. It seems, however, that public historians are the specialists who could utilize the capabilities of the internet to an even greater extent. Their task is to reach a broad range of persons with an interesting, attractively packaged message, in order to get them involved and encourage them to take action.

Jorma Kalela argues that the role of public historians has changed, from mainly providing history-related content to encouraging people to become interested in the past, supporting such interest and providing expert advice when necessary.[11] Thanks to the ease of using technology and its omnipres-ence, finding content producers and consumers is easiest on the Internet. Therefore, the public historian's task is to choose those communication channels which allow a dialogue with the public, followed by offers of help.

The Historical Book in the Polish Publishing Market

Publishing Production

Information concerning the total number of titles published in Poland in a given year can be found in the National Library's annual statistics volume titled *Polish Publishing in Figures*. The statistics are based on the books sent to the National Library by publishers as "legal deposit."

At the beginning of the second decade of the twenty-first century, the number of titles published in Poland annually exceeded 30,000 and still shows a small growth tendency (Table 9.1).

The market growth rate is most evident when we compare the current number of annually-published titles to their number in the early 1990s, when the number was more than three times lower.

Book printing is becoming progressively easier and cheaper. The im-provement of publishing and printing technologies benefits both conven-tional publishing firms which, by expanding their offerings, strive to meet the needs of a greater number of smaller groups of readers, and by persons and organizations publishing their texts on their own. This is reflected in the percentage of new items in the outputs of publishing houses. In recent

Table 9.1 Number of titles published in the years 2010–2019

Years	2010	2011	2012	2013	2014	2015	2016	2017	2018	2019
Number of titles	29,539	31,515	34,147	32,863	32,716	33,454	34,235	36,260	33,919	36,138

Data collected by Ewa Jabłońska-Stefanowicz, based on *Polish Publishing in Figures*, yearbooks 2010–2019.

years, the percentage of first editions increased steadily by several percentage points each year, in 2016 reaching more than 60% of the number of all published titles.[12] One effect of this is a drop in the average print run: in 2016 it was the lowest in many years, at 2,435 copies.[13] Notably, the growth of publishing output does not necessarily mean increase in revenue.

A similar situation exists in other countries, but Poland-specific indices differ considerably from average European figures. For example, in the years 2007–2017, the number of titles published in Poland increased by 44% (while in Europe by 24%), but the revenue from book sales decreased by 23% (while in Europe by 6%).[14] The Polish market was significantly impacted by the introduction of the 5% VAT rate for books in 2011 (previously the zero rate applied) and by changes in the laws and rules governing the educational sector (since 2014, textbooks are funded by the state budget and ordered directly by schools). However, the major factor reducing the profitability of Polish publishing is low readership, as less than 40% of respondents reported reading at least one book per year.[15]

The Historical Book and Its Types

The National Library places historical books in its history and biography categories. In the years 1991–1995, approximately 850 titles in this subject area were published per year, but in the first years of the twenty-first century nearly twice as many were published, on average 1,458 per year. This growth lasted until 2011, when the number stabilized at a level of 2,400–2,800 per year.[16] In 2018, historical books constituted 8% of all published titles. Among subject-based categories, history holds the second position, alongside the religion and theology categories. Similarly to preceding years, literary works remain the dominant category (27%).[17]

Apart from subject matter, available statistics also reflect the formal and functional types of books serving the various purposes and needs of their readers. Table 9.2 summarizes the most popular types of historical books.

Table 9.2 Types of books in the history and biography categories

Book type	Percentage of books in the history and biography topic categories (%)				
	2015	2016	2017	2018	2019
Scholarly	44	43	44	41	35
Popular	21	24	27	23	26
Documentary	26	26	24	28	28
Photography/reproduction and art books	2	2	0	2	1
Encyclopedias and dictionaries	1	2	2	1	2
Handbooks, textbooks and teaching aids	3	2	1	2	2

Data collected by Ewa Jabłońska-Stefanowicz, based on *Polish Publishing in Figures*, yearbooks 2016–2020, tables *Książki według treści. Nowa typologia*.

As this data shows, historical content appears most often in scholarly, popular interest and documentary books (this last category includes the recently-trendy biographical and autobiographical texts, and works presenting an author's interpretation of events). Only 8% of all published scholarly books concern history[18] One in ten historical books is translated from a foreign language, mainly English.[19]

The situation is different in the case of popular and documentary books, where historical topics appear in one out of three titles. For years, the most popular subject matter has remained the Second World War with, for example, as many as 124 titles dedicated to it in 2019. The 100th anniversary of Poland's regaining independence (after more than 120 years of foreign partitions) occasioned the development of many publications concerning the First World War and the formation of the new Polish state – 81 such publications in 2018, and 115 in 2019.[20]

Publishers

One of the tasks of the National Library is to assign ISBN identification numbers to Polish book publishers. On this basis, the Library indicated in its Report that the database of Polish publishers at the end of 2018 included 40,540 records. During that year, 3,484 entities were assigned numbers (2,538 of those had applied for the first time).[21] It is estimated that, in Poland, several thousand registered entities publish at least two books per year, and approximately 800 publish more than ten books per year. The remainder are institutions and private persons who publish books only occasionally and in very small print runs.[22]

It is difficult to identify the largest publishers of historical books when "history" is not the sole subject-matter of their offerings and when "historical books" are found in various functional categories. Therefore, it is difficult to determine the share of revenue from historical book sales in a given

Table 9.3 Leaders in the historical book publishing market (2012)

No.	Publisher	Market share (%)
1	Bellona	15.15
2	Znak	9.20
3	Dom Wydawniczy Rebis	7.97
4	Zysk i S-ka	5.22
5	Grupa PWN	4.60
6	Wydawnictwo Literackie	3.64
7	Weltbild Polska[23]	3.61
8	Publikat	3.39
9	Iskry	3.15
10	L & L Firma Dystrybucyjno-Wydawnicza	2.66

publisher's total turnover or to rank publishers on such basis. Assistance comes from the study *Rynek książki historycznej* (*Historical book market*) by Zbigniew Czerwiński,[24] who has been for years associated with the Bellona publishing house. Based on an analysis of purchases made in 140 bookstores all over Poland between September 2011 and July 2012, Czerwiński assembled a list of 40 Polish publishers of historical books. In his opinion, "The extensive research sample [...] supports the conclusion that similar percentages are found in the entire historical book market."[25] Table 9.3 presents the ten largest publishers.

The numerical data reflecting the structure of the offerings of the several publishing houses in this list can be found in the reports of the National Library. Apart from these, two other publishers are included in Table 9.4: Edipresse and Napoleon V. Broadly-understood history occupies an important place in their offerings. Data reflecting market changes was registered at two points in time.

The analysis of data based on the National Library's statistics leads to the following conclusions:

- Based on what type of books predominate among their offerings, publishing houses can be divided into three groups. For Edipresse and Prószyński, the main category is fiction: fiction's share in the total number of their titles has increased to 66% and 73% respectively. An example of a publishing house in which popular books constitute the vast majority (approximately 70%) is Bellona; while in two publishing houses, Napoleon V and PWN, scholarly books predominate.
- Scholarly books appear in the offerings of almost all publishers analyzed. Their total number in recent years has dropped significantly: from 320 in 2015 to 196 in 2019.
- The trend for popular books is the opposite, as the growth of such offerings is observed in five publishing houses (Rebis, Napoleon V, Publicat, Wydawnictwo Literackie and Znak) and is reflected in their higher total outputs: in 2015 they published 678 titles, and in 2019 they published 810.
- The youngest publishing house in the list is Napoleon V, which has a distinctive breakdown of offerings. In 2015, more than 80% of its titles were scholarly books. In 2019, the number of both types of books almost levelled out. In order to establish whether this is random, the intermediate years were analyzed (Table 9.5).

The data confirms a trend change, namely: clear growth in the importance of popular publications at the expense of scholarly publications. Scholarly books are issued by PWN, as well as academic publishing houses and two others: Adam Marszałek (https://marszalek.com.pl/) and Universitas (https://universitas.com.pl/).[26] Only two publishing houses, Napoleon V and

Table 9.4 Publishers of historical books and the structure of their offerings

Publisher	2015				2019			
	Titles total	Scholarly books	Popular books	Fiction	Titles total	Scholarly books	Popular books	Fiction
Bellona https://www.bellona.pl/	223	49	157	13	94	6	70	17
Edipresse https://hitsalonik.pl/ksiazki	278	–	125	153	481	–	162	319
Rebis https://www.rebis.com.pl/	328	24	128	171	326	11	171	134
Napoleon V https://napoleonv.pl/	149	126	20	–	129	50	59	6
Prószyński i S-ka https://www.proszynski.pl/	194	13	61	120	231	2	60	169
Publicat https://publicat.pl/	160	–	26	133	101	–	33	68
Replika https://replika.eu/	Nd	nd	nd	nd	95	1	24	70
Wydawnictwo Literackie https://www.wydawnictwoliterackie.pl/	158	5	38	94	115	8	47	60
Wydawnictwo Naukowe PWN https://wydawnictwo.pwn.pl/	215	91	51	16	231	106	42	9
Znak https://www.znak.com.pl/	171	12	72	87	272	12	142	118

Data collected by Ewa Jabłońska-Stefanowicz, based on: *Polish Publishing in Figures*, yearbooks 2015 and 2019, tables *Książki według wydawców*. "Nd" indicates no data.

Table 9.5 Structure of the offerings of Napoleon V publishing house

Year	Total number of books	Scholarly books	Popular books	Share of scholarly books in the offerings (%)	Share of popular books in the offerings (%)
2015	149	126	20	85	13
2016	180	106	66	59	37
2017	136	61	72	45	53
2018	166	94	70	57	42
2019	129	50	59	39	46

Data collected by Ewa Jabłońska-Stefanowicz, based on *Polish Publishing in Figures*, yearbooks 2015–2019, tables *Książki według wydawców*.

Bellona, specialize in historical books. Two other publishing firms serving historians, LTW (https://ltw.com.pl/) and Czarne (https://czarne.com.pl/), have a different model, in that their historical books are published among popular productions for a broader circle of readers.

The publishing business model of the Institute of National Remembrance stands apart.[27] The Institute began its activities in 2000 and deals with transitional justice.[28] At the same time, it engages in actions in the legal, research, archival and educational areas, becoming one of the largest public history institutions, even outside of Poland. Interesting details concerning the functioning of this publishing house are given by its director Izabela Matuszewska.[29] Its publishing, like all other activities of the Institute, is fully funded by the state budget and the revenue from sales of books must be immediately returned to that budget. Consistent with the mission of disseminating education and science, approximately 60% of its published titles are handed over free of charge to libraries, schools, associations and Polish institutes abroad. All its publications are available in several dedicated bricks-and-mortar bookstores, as well as in internet bookstores. Currently, the Institute has about one thousand titles available for sale and almost all of them are dedicated to history. They include "scholarly and popularizing studies, monographs and source editions, biographies and memoirs, photo collections but also comics, teaching aids and games, even puzzles."[30] Specialist books are published in print runs of approximately 800 copies, while printed collections of photographs, illustrations, or reproductions reach as many as 2,000 copies. In recent years, the comic series *Wojenna Odyseja Antka Srebrnego 1939–1946* (The *War Odyssey of Antek Srebrny*) has turned out to be a bestseller. The initial print runs of individual volumes were 5,000 copies, and reprints reached as many as 8,000 copies. The game *Kolejka* (*Queue*), which has thus far sold in a print run of more than 100,000 copies, also enjoys great popularity.[31]

Intensive publishing activities are also performed by another important public history institution, the Foundation of KARTA Center. The story of this independent non-governmental organization goes back to the beginning of the 1980s, when the publishing of *Karta*, an underground opposition bulletin, began. Currently, the objective of the Foundation is to document the recent history of Poland and East-Central Europe. The Foundation keeps the largest twentieth-century social archive in Poland because it is interested in "history perceived from the perspective of the individual."[32] This has a direct influence on the types of books they publish, which include the greatest number of diaries, memoirs, letters, testimonies and printed photo/reproduction collections.[33]

Publishing units also exist at other public history facilities such as museums[34] and science popularizing centers.[35] They have their own source materials and specialists. Access to publishing technologies allows them to prepare publications independently, which are then distributed mainly among the visitors.

Publisher as a Public Historian

At the beginning of each project, public historians ask themselves the following questions: What? Why? With or for whom? How?[36] In order to start work on publishing projects, similar questions must be answered by publishers, including those of historical books. Professional historians, both individual authors and teams of reviewers, are a publisher's substantive resource. Reading historical books is among the most popular forms of public engagement with the past, thus demonstrating the considerable power inherent in teamwork coordinated by the publisher, and the great responsibility of all team members involved.

The result of work performed by both – the publishers and the public historians – is content, that is, a broadly understood publication aiming to generate interest, involvement, education, development and enjoyment by a certain group of readers. The concept of such publication is created by considering the knowledge, taste, desires and capabilities of the intended readers. New technologies provide greater access to information about the readers than was previously available. The publisher analyzes sale reports, gets in touch with the clients of internet bookstores by suggesting subsequent titles to them and interacts with readership on social media. Most recently, the developments in the area of self-published books are also taken into consideration, with authors who have achieved market success often receiving proposals to publish subsequent work through conventional publishing houses. Many accept such offers.[37] Similarly, public historians, thanks to their presence on the Internet, may follow initiatives and events organized by others, both professionals and amateurs. These are sources of priceless information about the popularity of certain topics and working methods, about the institutions and people involved in them, as well as about the responses of participants. This is a form of bartering, in that "doing history in public means exposing one's craft, opening up the historian's workshop

(...). Finally, doing history in public also means being a co-producer of history with those outside the academy," as Pedro Ramos Pinto and Bertrand Taithe have written.[38]

In an increasingly competitive market, publishers of historical books shift focus and resources to the reader. While promoting their titles, historical publishers utilize the tools used by public historians: organizing topical meetings, preparing and disseminating educational materials, initiating dialogue with readers on social media, and organizing fairs, field games and contests.

Fairs

For nearly 30 years, the Historical Book Fair has been held in Warsaw every autumn. In an interview prior to its 24th edition (November 2016), the organizers admitted that the Fair had been initially organized in an attempt to "rescue the position of the historical book,"[39] which was being overshadowed by the flood of commercial fiction produced in the early 1990s. The first initiative, dating back to 1992, was the Agreement of Historical Book Publishers, between eight companies which committed to "act together for the purpose of popularization, advertisement, and promotion of book publications, periodicals, audio-visual publications, computer programs, and games with historical topics."[40] Currently, approximately 60 publishers work within the Agreement, and the organization of the Fair is entrusted to the History & Culture Foundation.[41]

During meetings accompanying the Fair, views are exchanged and the opinions of historians regarding current political, educational and social challenges are shaped. For example, in 1995 the discussions focused on textbooks and teaching aids for teachers, while four years later the session was entitled 'Common Heritage: Europe in Poland, Poland in Europe,' and in 2003 panel deliberations were titled 'Polish Historians on the Expulsions, Displacements, Escape and Relocations of the Polish Population in the Years 1939–1947.' In 2006, under the patronage of the Book Institute, the conference focused on the topic of fundraising, and in 2007 the seminar 'History on the Internet' was organized. In 2010, the Book Fair offerings were first organized into "salons:" the Salon of Museums (with museum lessons), the Salon of Libraries, the Salon of the Byelorussian Book and the Salon of the Russian Book.

The success of the Fair can be measured by the number of exhibitors and visitors, and is indisputably impressive. During recent years in the Kubicki Arcades in the Royal Castle in Warsaw, a total of 3,500–4,000 titles, that is nearly 90% of the entire Polish publishing market in this area, have been presented by approximately 200 publishers. In the course of its four days, the Fair was visited by 20,000–25,000 history lovers, for whom the *Catalogue of Historical Publications* is prepared,[42] a guide to the new titles and their publishers. For instance, in the 2019 catalogue, 110 organizations presented the

covers of their books. They included commercial publishing houses specializing in history, as well as publishing firms also publishing on non-historical
topics. University publishing houses, publishing departments of museums
and libraries, and institutes of the Polish Academy of Sciences were well
represented. The historical book publishing market includes a great many
small private companies publishing books which are unlikely to appear in
bookstores, either because the publisher does not pursue nationwide distribution or because of niche topics, low print runs, or controversial content.
As long as laws are complied with, "[t]he only censorship applicable in the
fair is… the ISBN," declare the organizers.[43]

Even in 2020, when the Fair could not be held because of the COVID
pandemic, the Polish publishers still strove to reach out to the readers. The
traditional on-site, in-person format of the Fair was replaced with the Program of Internet Authors' Meetings taking place in three subject areas: the
Salon of Authors from the Institute of National Remembrance, the Salon
of Museum Book Authors and the Salon of the Historical Book. Over the
course of four days, more than 50 discussions took place in total, and most
recordings are still available.[44] At the same time, the commercial purpose –
the sale of books at attractive fair prices – was also still achieved. After
scanning, QR codes presented during the meetings redirected the participants to places where they could purchase the books.[45]

Contests

"Best book" contests attract media attention, and in its early days the
Historical Book Fair greatly needed media exposure.[46] Thus, in 1995 the
KLIO Award was established, awarded to books popularizing history and
historically-themed literature. In the Authors category, the individual contribution of a given author is recognized. In the Monograph category, the
quality of historical research is recognized, while in the Editor category
interesting publishing initiatives are rewarded. The Varsaviana category
concerns books popularizing the history of Warsaw. An independent jury
consisting of prominent historians and journalists selects the winners from
among the submitted titles, announces the results and grants the awards.
The complete list of winners for the years 2015–2020 can be found on the
website of the History and Culture Foundation.[47] In the opinion of one
of the Fair's organizers, the KLIO Award has gained the rank of Poland's
"historical Nobel Prize,"[48] that is the most important award for a book in
the field of history, even though other similar contests exist.

Among the remaining competitions, the oldest is the Historical Awards
competition of the Polish weekly *Polityka*,[49] initiated in 1959, two years after the weekly journal was founded. Since that time, the competition was
held 59 times, with 1965 and 1981 being the only years in which no awards
were granted. In total, 395 authors have been recognized.[50] For the pandemic edition of 2020, approximately 180 proposals were submitted, slightly

more than the previous year. The jury granted awards in four categories: Monographs and scholarly works; Popular books and journalism; Diaries, reports, memoirs; and Sources. In addition, it decided to grant a special award for "a world-scale event:" to the book *Chasydyzm. Atlas historyczny (Hasidism. Historical atlas)* by Marcin Wodziński and Waldemar Spallek.

Another contest of national scope is the Historical Book of the Year contest, organized and founded by the Polish Radio, the Polish Television, the Institute of National Remembrance and the National Cultural Centre. The year 2019 turned out to be exceptional, due to the scandal of withdrawing two titles previously accepted by the jury: *Wobec nadchodzącej drugiej wojny światowej (In the Face of the Approaching Second World War)* by Władysław Studnicki, and *Wołyń zdradzony, czyli jak dowództwo AK porzuciło Polaków na pastwę UPA (Volhynia Betrayed, or How the AK Command Abandoned the Poles to the UPA)* by Piotr Zychowicz. Zychowicz's book, which restated positions repudiated by many Polish historians, was a favorite among internet users who voted online. However, without informing the jury, the organizers elected to withdraw it from the contest, because they deemed the book to be "anti-Polish and pro-German,"[51] and thus contrary to the Polish national interests. Finally, "taking into account controversies connected with the contest,"[52] the decision was made to cancel the 2019 competition entirely.

Less known to the general public are competitions for prominent scholarly publications held under the auspices of important historians, activists and writers. Every three years, the Joachim Lelewel Award is granted by Department I of the Humanities and Social Sciences of the Polish Academy of Sciences.[53] The Karol Modzelewski "Historical Book of the Year" competition is coordinated by the Historical Institute of the University of Wrocław, although decisions about the awards are made by the directors of all historical university institutes in Poland.[54] Authors of books discussing the recent history of Poland can compete in the contest for the Kazimierz Moczarski Historical Award of the city of Warsaw,[55] and the Kraków branch of the Polish Historical Society also gives out awards. Since 2001, the Wacław Felczak and Henryk Wereszycki Award is granted to a Polish or foreign author dealing with the history of East-Central Europe in the nineteenth and twentieth centuries.[56] The Professor Stanisław Herbst contest for the best master's thesis in history, organized by the Polish Historical Society and the Society of Lovers of History in Warsaw,[57] is also worthy of note.

Conclusion: A Shared Future

In a 2007 book meaningfully titled of *The Cult of the Amateur*,[58] Andrew Keen outlines a pessimistic vision of the world, in which Web 2.0 plays the leading role. In that world, the democratization of access to the production and dissemination of content leads to a reduction of its quality and reliability. It becomes difficult to distinguish readers from writers and amateurs from experts. The voice of a fool becomes equal in importance to the voice of a wise man. In the hour of the amateur, the audience becomes the star.

Indeed, during the last two decades the number of new publishers and new historians has drastically increased. They reap the benefits of the technological revolution. Conventional publishers and professional historians are left fighting for their lives: they must carefully observe the growing competition, learn from it, respond to the changing expectations of readers, and invent new ways to hold their attention. However, the real challenge facing both groups is simply abundance. As a result of digital technologies, information, once available to few, is now everywhere. The methods for its discovery, storage and dissemination have become easy, fast and cheap. Information overload is one of the examples of abundance that contemporary humanity has to cope with and will continue to contend with.

With approximately 2,500 new history-related titles appearing in the Polish book market annually, from more than 200 publishers, the Historical Book Fair, as well as various types of "best book" contests, become a useful screening and selection tool for history aficionados, both professional and amateur. These endeavors may be interpreted as part of the global strategy for coping with the abundance of information proposed by the writer, researcher and digital publisher Michael Bhaskar.[59] The umbrella term is "curation" which derives from museum-based activity, but currently its meaning is broader. Curation is "a kind of membrane or purposeful filter that balances our needs and wants against great accumulations of stuff."[60] Everywhere we have to deal with "too much," and thus we need help in making selections. This is the role of curators, new cultural and business intermediaries, who are right now more important than content creators. Moving the focus from producing more and more to a "user-centric Consumer-curated Model,"[61] concentrating on "better instead of more," is the task facing both the contemporary publisher and the public historian because, as professionals, they both are able to facilitate wise choices for the audience, by indicating what is important and interesting.

Translation of this chapter was financially supported by the Excellence Initiative – Research University (IDUB) programme for the University of Wrocław. The Editor is deeply indebted to Urszula Tempska for proofreading this chapter.

Notes

1 Stanley Unwin, *The Truth about Publishing* (New York: Lyons & Burford, 1995), 9. The first edition of the book was published in 1926.
2 John B. Thompson, *Merchants of Culture. The Publishing Business in the Twenty-first Century* (New York: A Plume Book, 2012), 326.
3 *Ibid.*, 328.
4 *Ibid.*, 331.

5 Amazon, Kindle Direct Publishing, accessed May 15, 2021, https://kdp.amazon.com/en_US/.
6 Alison Baverstock, *The Naked Author. A Guide to Self-Publishing* (London: Bloomsbury, 2011), IX.
7 *Ibid.*, XV.
8 Claire Squires and Padmini Ray Murray, "The Digital Communication Circuit," *Book 2.0* 3, no. 1 (2013): 6.
9 Squires and Murray, "The Digital," 8.
10 Fund raising for book publication is carried out on several Polish platforms, however Wspieramkulture.pl platform is dedicated mainly to supporting cultural projects.
11 Meg Foster, "Online and Plugged In? Public History and Historians in the Digital Age," *Public History Review* 21 (2014): 12.
12 Paweł Waszczyk, ed., *Rynek książki w Polsce 2017. Wydawnictwa* (Warszawa: Biblioteka Analiz, 2017), 57, accessed May 15, 2021, https://rynek-ksiazki.pl/wp-content/uploads/2018/06/RPK_T1_2017_elektr.pdf. Data included in subsequent yearbooks is developed on the basis of questionnaires completed by approximately 300 publishers, as well as information generally available in reporting and financial documentation.
13 Waszczyk, *Rynek*, 37–38.
14 *Polish Publishing in Figures*, 69 (2019): 6, accessed May 15, 2021, https://www.bn.org.pl/download/document/1592997703.pdf.
15 Biblioteka Narodowa, *39% Lekki wzrost czytelnictwa w Polsce*, accessed May 15, 2021, https://www.bn.org.pl/w-bibliotece/3966-39%25---lekki-wzrost-czytelnictwa-w-polsce.html.
16 *Polish Publishing*, 91–92.
17 *Ibid.*, 11.
18 *Ibid.*, 15.
19 *Ibid.*, 16.
20 *Ibid.*, 17.
21 *Sprawozdanie Biblioteki Narodowej za rok 2018* (Warszawa: Biblioteka Narodowa, 2019), 43, accessed May 15, 2021, https://www.bn.org.pl/download/document/1557405915.pdf.
22 Waszczyk, *Rynek*, 125–126.
23 Weltbildt publishing house ceased business in Poland in 2013. Its successor is Świat Książki sp. z O.O.
24 Zbigniew Czerwiński, "Rynek książki historycznej. Analiza porównawcza" (Warszawa, 2012, unpublished text).
25 Czerwiński, "Rynek," 12.
26 *Polish Publishing*, 52–60.
27 "Institute of National Remembrance," accessed May 15, 2021, https://ipn.gov.pl/en/.
28 Łukasz Kamiński, "Instytut Pamięci Narodowej," in *Historia w przestrzeni publicznej*, ed. Joanna Wojdon (Warszawa: PWN, 2018), 92.
29 *Rozmowy o rynku książki* (Warszawa: Biblioteka Analiz, 2020), 300–308.
30 *Katalog wydawnictw IPN. Jesień-zima 2020/2021*, ed. Natalia Cichocka, accessed May 15, 2021, https://ipn.gov.pl/pl/publikacje/katalog-publikacji/121895,Katalog-wydawnictw-IPN-Jesien-zima-20202021.html, p. 6
31 *Rozmowy o rynku książki* (2020), 303–304, 307. For more details about board games, see the chapter by Joanna Wojdon in this volume.
32 Ośrodek KARTA, "O nas," accessed May 15, 2021, https://karta.org.pl/nas. For more details about KARTA and social archives in Poland, see the chapter by Marta Kurkowska-Budzan in this volume.

33 Ośrodek KARTA, "Księgarnia," accessed May 15, 2021, https://ksiegarnia.karta.org.pl/.
34 See e.g. Muzeum II Wojny Światowej, "Wydawnictwo," accessed May 15, 2021, https://muzeum1939.pl/wydawnictwo.
35 See e.g. Kolegium Europy Wschodniej, "Księgarnia," accessed May 15, 2021, http://www.kew.org.pl/ksiegarnia/.
36 Fien Danniau, "Public History in a Digital Context. Back to the Future or Back to Basics?," *BMGN-Low Countries Historical Review* 128, no. 4 (2013): 143.
37 One spectacular example of such an author is Amanda Hocking who, after the great success of her self-published books, has been connected with a conventional publisher, http://hockingbooks.com/, accessed May 15, 2021.
38 Pedro Ramos Pinto, and Bertrand Taithe, "Doing History in Public? Historians in the Age of Impact," in *The Impact of History? Histories at the Beginning of the 21st Century*, ed. Pedro Ramos Pinto, Bertrand Taithe, (New York: Routledge, 2015), 18.
39 *Rozmowy o rynku książki* (2016), 168.
40 Fundacja Historia i Kultura, "Porozumienie Wydawców Książki Historycznej," accessed May 15, 2021, http://historiaikultura.pl/porozumienie-wydawcow-ksiazki-historycznej/.
41 Fundacja Historia i Kultura, "Targi Książki Historycznej," accessed May 15, 2021, http://historiaikultura.pl/targi-ksiazki-historycznej/.
42 Fundacja Historia i Kultura, "Targi Książki Historycznej 2014–2019," accessed May 15, 2021, http://historiaikultura.pl/targi-ksiazki-historycznej-2014-2019/.
43 *Rozmowy o rynku książki* (2016), 171.
44 See YouTube channel of Fundacja Historia i Kultura, accessed May 15, 2021, https://www.youtube.com/channel/UCw3wsFk8IW0RsnVmhFAEbmQ.
45 Fundacja Historia i Kultura, "Internetowe Spotkania Autorskie Targów Książki Historycznej," accessed May 15, 2021, http://historiaikultura.pl/internetowe-spotkania-autorskie-targow-ksiazki-historycznej/.
46 *Rozmowy o rynku książki* (2016), 169.
47 Fundacja Historia i kultura, "Konkurs," accessed May 15, 2021, http://historiaikultura.pl/nagroda-klio/.
48 *Rozmowy o rynku książki* (2016).
49 *Polityka* (Politics) is a weekly magazine established in 1957 as the press organ of the Polish United Workers' Party. It quickly became one of the major magazines in the Polish market. Since 1990, it has been published by its own cooperative. In the years 2004–2010, *Polityka* had the largest sales among Polish opinion-forming magazines and is currently in second position.
50 Mariusz Kowalczyk, "Przyznano Nagrody Historyczne 'Polityki'," *Press*, May 13, 2020, accessed May 15, 2021, https://www.press.pl/tresc/61656,przyznano-nagrody-historyczne----polityki---.
51 "Książka Piotra Zychowicza usunięta z konkursu przez TVP, NCK i Polskie Radio. Cenckiewicz odchodzi z jury, Warzecha chce bojkotu," *Wirtualne Media*, accessed May 15, 2021, https://www.wirtualnemedia.pl/artykul/ksiazka-piotra-zychowicza-wolyn-zdradzony-wykluczony-z-ksiazka-historyczna-roku-gorzej-niz-za-tuska.
52 Książka Historyczna Roku, Oświadczenie organizatorów Konkursu "Książka Historyczna Roku," accessed May 15, 2021, http://ksiazkahistorycznaroku.pl/45012892/oswiadczenie-organizatorow-konkursu-ksiazka-historyczna-roku.
53 PAN, "Nagrody naukowe Wydziału I Nauk Humanistycznych i Społecznych PAN," accessed May 15, 2021, https://instytucja.pan.pl/index.php/nagr-nauk-wl.
54 Polskie Towarzystwo Historyczne, "Konkurs Historyczna Książka Roku im. Karola Modzelewskiego," accessed May 15, 2021, http://pth.net.pl/konkursy/konkursu-historyczna-ksiazka-roku-im-karola-modzelewskiego.

55 "The Kazimierz Moczarski History Prize," accessed May 15, 2021, http://nagrodamoczarskiego.pl/index.php/front/englishtexts#prize.
56 Polskie Towarzystwo Historyczne, "Konkurs im. Wacława Felczaka i Henryka Wereszyckiego," accessed May 15, 2021, http://pth.net.pl/konkursy/konkurs-im-waclawa-felczaka-i-henryka-wereszyckiego.
57 Polskie Towarzystwo Historyczne, "Konkurs im. Profesora Stanisława Herbsta," accessed May 15, 2021, http://pth.net.pl/konkursy/konkurs-im-profesora-stanislawa-herbsta.
58 Andrew Keen, *The Cult of the Amateur: How Blogs, MySpace, YouTube and the Rest of Today's User-generated Media Are Killing Our Culture and Economy* (London: John Murray Press, 2008).
59 Michael Bhaskar, *Curation. The Power of Selection in a World of Excess* (London: Piatkus, 2017).
60 *Ibid.*, 85.
61 *Ibid.*, 208.

Bibliography

Baverstock, Alison. *The Naked Author. A Guide to Self-Publishing.* London: Bloomsbury, 2011.
Bhaskar, Michael. *Curation. The Power of Selection in a World of Excess.* London: Piatkus, 2017.
Biblioteka Narodowa. "39% Lekki wzrost czytelnictwa w Polsce," last modified April 23, 2020. Accessed May 10, 2020. https://www.bn.org.pl/w-bibliotece/3966-39%25---lekki-wzrost-czytelnictwa-w-polsce.html.
Cichocka, Natalia, ed. *Katalog wydawnictw IPN.* Jesień–zima 2020/2021. Warszawa: IPN, 2021. Accessed May 15, 2021. https://ipn.gov.pl/download/1/538397/ katalog-publikacjijesien-zima2020–2021internet1.pdf
Czerwiński, Zbigniew. "Rynek książki historycznej. Analiza porównawcza," unpublished manuscript. Warszawa, 2012.
Danniau, Fien. "Public History in a Digital Context. Back to the Future or Back to Basics?" *BMGN-Low Countries Historical Review* 128, no. 4 (2013): 118–144.
Foster, Meg. "Online and Plugged In? Public History and Historians in the Digital Age." *Public History Review* 21 (2014): 1–19.
Kamiński, Łukasz. "Instytut Pamięci Narodowej." In *Historia w przestrzeni publicznej,* edited by Joanna Wojdon, 92–96. Warszawa: PWN, 2018.
Keen, Andrew. *The Cult of the Amateur: How Blogs, MySpace, YouTube and the Rest of Today's User-generated Media Are Killing Our Culture and Economy.* London: John Murray Press, 2008.
Korte, Barbara and Paletschek, Sylvia. "Historical Edutainment: New Forms and Practices of Popular History." In *Palgrave Handbook of Research in Historical Culture and Education,* edited by Mario Carretero, Stefan Berger, Maria Grever, 191–205. Cham: Palgrave Macmillan, 2017.
Kowalczyk, Mariusz. "Przyznano Nagrody Historyczne 'Polityki.'" *Press,* last modified May 13, 2020. Accessed May 15, 2021. https://www.press.pl/tresc/61656,przyznano-nagrody-historyczne----polityki---.
"Książka Historyczna Roku. Oświadczenie organizatorów Konkursu 'Książka Historyczna Roku,' " last modified October 25, 2019. Accessed May 15, 2021. http://ksiazkahistorycznaroku.pl/45012892/oswiadczenie-organizatorowkonkursu-ksiazka-historyczna-roku.

"*Polish Publishing in Figures.*" Accessed May 15, 2021. https://www.bn.org.pl/raporty-bn/ruch-wydawniczy-w-liczbach.

Ramos Pinto, Pedro and Bertrand Taithe. "Doing History in Public? Historians in the Age of Impact." In *The Impact of History? Histories at the Beginning of the 21st Century*, edited by Pedro Ramos Pinto and Bertrand Taithe, 1–20. New York: Routledge, 2015.

Rozmowy o rynku książki. Warszawa: Biblioteka Analiz, 2016.

Rozmowy o rynku książki. Warszawa: Biblioteka Analiz, 2020.

Squires, Claire, and Padmini Ray Murray. "The Digital Communication Circuit." *Book 2.0* 3, no. 1 (2013): 6.

Thompson, John B. *Merchants of Culture. The Publishing Business in the Twenty-first Century.* New York: A Plume Book, 2012.

tw. "Książka Piotra Zychowicza usunięta z konkursu przez TVP, NCK i Polskie Radio. Cenckiewicz odchodzi z jury, Warzecha chce bojkotu." *Wirtualne Media*, last modified October 25, 2019. Accessed May 15, 2021. https://www.wirtualnemedia.pl/artykul/ksiazka-piotra-zychowicza-wolyn-zdradzonywykluczony-z-ksiazka-historyczna-roku-gorzej-niz-za-tuska.

Unwin, Stanley. *The Truth about Publishing.* New York: Lyons & Burford, 1995.

Waszczyk, Paweł, ed. *Rynek książki w Polsce 2017. Wydawnictwa.* Warszawa: Biblioteka Analiz, 2017. Accessed May 15, 2021. https://rynek-ksiazki.pl/wp-content/uploads/2018/06/RPK_T1_2017_elektr.pdf.

Websites

Amazon, Kindle Direct Publishing. Accessed May 15, 2021. https://kdp.amazon.com/en_US/.

Fundacja Historia i Kultura. Accessed May 15, 2021. http://historiaikultura.pl/ and http://hockingbooks.com/

"The Kazimierz Moczarski History Prize." Accessed May 15, 2021. http://nagroda-moczarskiego.pl/index.php/front/englishtexts#prize.

Kolegium Europy Wschodniej. Accessed May 15, 2021. http://www.kew.org.pl/.

Muzeum II Wojny Światowej. Accessed May 15, 2021. https://muzeum1939.pl/.

Ośrodek Karta. Accessed May 15, 2021. https://karta.org.pl/.

Polska Akademia Nauk. Accessed May 15, 2021. https://instytucja.pan.pl/index.php/nagr-nauk-wl.

Polskie Towarzystwo Historyczne. Accessed May 15, 2021. http://pth.net.pl/

10 Pro-Social and Socialized Archaeology (Public Archaeology) in Polish Style

Anna Izabella Zalewska

Introduction

Activities and conceptualizations taking place on a global scale under the metaphorical umbrella of "public archaeology" engage with material elements and remains of the past at various levels. The gradual and clear involvement of archaeologists in social interactions results from a growing acceptance, at least in some archaeological circles, of the belief that the emphasis should be shifted from archaeology as a way of interpreting and learning about the past to archaeology understood also as a system of relations in the present.[1]

The defining factors of public archaeology are the relations of archaeologists with the public and references to problems that are not related to the strictest cognitive and academic practice, but are the result of the transmission of the effects of archaeologists' activities. So far, a broad understanding of public archaeology has been proposed which considered it as referring to: ways of presenting the achievements of archaeology to the public; activities aimed at public understanding of the specificity and value of archaeological heritage; and stimulating public involvement in archaeology, from spectator through stakeholder to witness.[2]

Being at the same time both a method of practical material and discursive activities and a theoretical concept functioning in a wide range of social and academic contexts, pro-social and socialized archaeology (public archaeology) in the Polish style can be considered as a form of engaged humanities.[3] It expresses itself through varied activities, especially those resulting in both micro- and large-scale "interventions" in the social and mental environment, as well as in its attitude to changing the status quo (see the case study below), but also in the need to recognize the relationships between different ways of thinking, methods, fields of knowledge, experiences and imaginations of various participants in culture-creating situations and recipients (see the concept of reactivated matter below).

The introduction of the concept and term "public archaeology" is attributed to Charles McGimsey.[4] The term appeared in Polish literature with a significant delay and has not since been intensively used in the Polish milieu.[5]

DOI: 10.4324/9781003165767-13

The following chapter does not pretend to be a comprehensive presentation of public archaeology as a whole from a local (Polish) perspective. Rather, it is an indication of the considerable diversity and potential of pro-social and socialized archaeologies.

The Prehistory of Pro-Social Archaeology in Poland

The dissemination of archaeological knowledge in Poland has a relatively distant tradition, which was formed both in the context of the creation and development of regional and national museums, as well as in the process of constituting academic archaeology.[6] The public presentation of research results by archaeologists, even during the course of excavations, has been positively valued in Poland, especially at the beginning of the path of constituting an academic model of archaeology in Polish society.[7] The interaction with the public has been colored by the model of educational orientation, driven to a significant extent by the ideological and patriotic mission. A great advocate of propagating and encouraging archaeological knowledge was Józef Kostrzewski (1885–1969). One of his students and later an associate, Zdzisław Rajewski (1907–1954), was particularly active in the domain of popularizing archaeological knowledge and educating about the value and need for protection of monuments. He tried to convey to the public the achievements of painstaking archaeological research through presenting "in constant progress" exhibitions, lectures and interviews, and using all mass media, ranging from posters, postcards and leaflets, to the design of postage stamps. Rajewski also founded the "archaeological emergency squad" that was available on call to deal with archaeological finds made by members of the public, and introduced the obligation on archaeologists to organize field exhibitions at each excavation site.

Unfortunately, in the following decades this idea gradually faded and with time began to be a rarity rather than a custom. Moreover, since the 1990s in the course of the commercialization of the activities of archaeologists, and especially because of the pace of large-scale pre-investment works and so-called rescue research, archaeologists have quite commonly focused on goals quite different from pro-social ones. Although this has not become the norm, it has seriously shaken the rather positive image of the archaeologist in Poland.

It is justified to emphasize that in the long-term functioning of Polish archaeology, there were many archaeologists for whom it was an obvious element of their research to make research results public and socially valuable. Among them were the precursors of medieval archaeology Eleonora (1931–2015) and Stanisław Tabaczyński (1930–2020). Eleonora Tabaczyńska emphasized that key features of interaction with the public were the motifs of meeting, joint work and shared joy in discovering the secrets of the past. This type of approach, recognized today as an important aspect of socialized archaeology, is manifested (among other things) in involving a wide range of people, including local children and young people in the archaeological research process and in dialogue on the values and uniqueness of elements of the past around us and our shared responsibility for cultural heritage.

So far, however, archaeology in Poland has seldom been perceived as an inalienable element of culture-creating practices by a wide range of society. As a result, the reception of knowledge created by archaeologists and museologists in Poland rarely arouses a response that can be classed as widespread and enthusiastic. Polish archaeology first achieved spectacular success in public reception with the investigations of the remains of the Bronze Age fortified center in Biskupin, being identified as related to the "cradle of the Slavs" and therefore important for ideological and identity-creating reasons, especially in the 1930s and 1940s.[8]

Another peculiar peak, also highly ideological and, in the mind of the government paymasters, intended as an identity-creating interaction of archaeology with society were the investigations carried out from the end of the 1940s until the 1960s involved in Poland's so-called Millennium.[9] Extensive excavations were accompanied by a desire to celebrate the 1000th anniversary of the beginning of the Polish state and its conversion to Christianity. As a result, archaeology found itself in a metaphorical ideological clinch between the sacred and the profane.[10]

The next and most recent example in which the research process itself (including excavations) and the results of it were on the front pages of newspapers was the search for the remains of the members of the anti-communist partisans murdered after the Second World War (called the "Cursed" or "Steadfast" (Unbroken) soldiers).[11] The research (rightly debated as a very complex and controversial socio-ideological problem) was initiated at the beginning of the second decade of the twenty-first century within the complex socio-political context.[12] The involvement of a very small team of archaeologists and large groups of volunteers in this process is without precedent in Poland.

The intensification of socialization of archaeology is often, as in the cases mentioned above, associated with its hyper-politicization. It is clearly seen in the Polish examples of archaeological involvements in identity-shaping processes as well as in exhumation works, where archaeologists, like the descendants of some of the murdered, often regardless of their own desire or views, were drawn into the machine of political tensions and clashes. The introduction of values to the evidence, as postulated by the proponents of inclusive formulas for practicing archaeology, is not axiologically neutral, and therefore should be constantly subject to critical reflection.

Favorable Circumstances and Obstacles

The complexity as well as potential benefits of community/public archaeology activities have not yet been systematically and critically analyzed in

Poland. Meanwhile, the implementation of various types of activities[13] as well as research on the public's understanding, significance and attitude towards cultural heritage by national and local communities has become the subject of research and critical reflection by the National Heritage Institute.[14] Data for this type of diagnosis is also provided by increasingly systematic comparative studies, on both a European and national scale.[15] The results of research on the attitudes of diverse communities towards archaeology, archaeologists and the archaeological heritage are very helpful, including in breaking down our suppositions and delusions. They show for example that – next to the uplifting diagnosis that as many as 92% of Poles perceive archaeology as useful, despite the assumption commonly accepted by archaeologists that by their very nature, all forms of cognitive activity of archaeologists are both "educational" and "public" – only 44% Poles (and an average of 40% of Europeans) surveyed between 2013 and 2018 believe that the role of archaeology is to pass on knowledge about the past to younger generations. Even fewer in this group (40% Poles and an average of 46% of Europeans) believe that archaeology allows them to understand the past to be better prepared for the future.[16]

In theory, this should motivate and oblige archaeologists to care for closer, comprehensive and thoughtful relations with society. In reality, however, both in the past and today, in the course of many archaeological initiatives, there has been little reflection on the need to relate them to social expectations. Also difficult to overlook is the lack of public debate on heritage perceived as a non-renewable, common good and on the needs of in situ protection. Such a situation may come as a surprise because of the formal conditions and doctrinal assumptions (that promote archaeology as a community asset, in the spirit of the Valetta convention and the Faro convention) for such a debate and a positive valorization of the value of heritage are theoretically favorable.

However, even within academia, the activities in the field of pro-social and socialized archaeology are often perceived as "unnecessary," "too time-consuming" or too "banal." Another perception is that they not only consume part of the already very limited financial resources that the state assigns from public funds to archaeology, but also squander some of the valuable intellectual energy of the research community. Such views are accompanied by resistance to "excessive" involvement in contacts with the local population. Although positive changes can be observed, reflected by a number of research projects in which pro-social activities are an important element that have been completed as well as those currently in the course of implementation. This concerns both archaeological projects related to the discovery and dissemination of knowledge on the subject of the prehistory of the Polish lands as well as pro-social and participatory activities in relation to the elements and material remains of the recent past.[17]

Another obstacle on the route to the development of public archaeology in Poland is the current prevailing low value placed in academia on popularization, thus depreciating the work of some scholars who are subject to constant evaluation according to rigid state-imposed criteria that poorly reflect the needs of development of both research and civil society. In spite of these tendencies, there seem to be very few popular academic magazines, such as the quarterly *Archaeologia Żywa* (Living Archaeology), the value of which cannot be overestimated due to its uniqueness on a national scale, but whose links with the detectorist lobby are very obvious (e.g. in the form of numerous advertisements for detectors in its pages). It is regrettable to note the gradual disappearance of the popular periodical *Z Otchłani Wieków* (*From the Abyss of Time*), that has appeared since 1926 and was very solid in content, with great attention paid to the readability of the message, developed with a view to broad public reception. In the era of progressive digitization of the media, there are some noteworthy examples of internet resources such as online magazines that have been established to perform an important function in the domain of pro-social archaeology, for example, the journal *Biografia Archeologii* (*Biography of Archaeology*) which operates in line with the motto "The past already begins today."[18]

On the other hand, among inhibitory factors there are also, especially in the domain of the archaeology of the recent past, fears (often, unfortunately, fully justified) of the ("excessive") openness to the participation of entities without archaeological education in the process of searching for and discovering material remnants of the past, improper consumption of such material (sic!) and the commodification of knowledge obtained with the use of archaeological methods. This refers to the very intense activity of people involved in the collection-driven exploitation of the archaeological record (so-called detectorists) who pursue their own goals, often using the results of research by archaeologists and the research methods they describe. At the same time, it may be observed that it is precisely this milieu that strives to diminish the importance of the professional competences of archaeologists, which affects the image of archaeologists and archaeology in some social circles. Detectorists, in particular, use very brutal black PR tools in order to justify their demands that their artefact hunting should be exempt from the regulations resulting from the amendment of the legislation concerning the archaeological heritage and their desire to establish for themselves the freedom to extract valuable finds from the ground (not always for a substantive reason) as they see fit.

There is a significant risk in cooperation (especially with excessive fraternization) with amateurs engaged in illegal searches with metal detectors, the so-called "black archaeology" defined as the single or group-based activities which are related to the illegal non-scientific excavation, removal and selling of archaeological heritage originating from illicit or official excavations, including but not limited to the preliminary research and communication activities, search, and excavation works, removal and cleansing of finds, any support activities, networking and contracting, and the offering for sale and selling of finds to the previously identified or non-identified buyers in the country of origin and abroad.[19] The artifact hunters act contrary to Polish law and ignore the threat of legal penalties and their activities result in the destruction of the archaeological record and appropriation of material elements of the heritage.[20] A few archaeologists have attempted to engage them in cooperation, but this has had varying results, sometimes spectacular, sometimes overwhelmingly bad. In general, the involvement of metal detectorists in the process of socialization of archaeology has so far unfortunately not been conducive to the development of Public Archaeology. It is in this context that the problem of the excessive risk (especially for archaeological finds and sites) accompanying activities in the PA domain is emphasized by Polish scholars intent on refusing to accept the legitimacy of the deepening of the process of socialization of archaeology.

Further to the detriment of serious treatment of public archaeology, in some segments of Polish society there is the connotation of public property as something that belongs to all. This is a distorted shadow of warped thinking engendered in the period of communist rule that then later underwent escalation in the culture of consumerism. This perception has positive effects when it is accompanied by the vision of a "responsible events" or "responsible community"[21] (such as a community that takes on community obligations, as in concern for the common good, including the common cultural heritage and therefore the protection and care of archaeological monuments).

However, it becomes dangerous if it is accompanied by the assumption: "common property, therefore mine too, so I can do what I want with it."[22] The latter issue, unfortunately, has a real impact on the problem of acknowledgement by some individuals and groups that archaeological finds belonging to the State Treasury on behalf of all citizens. This in theory should ensure their inviolability (e.g. in situ – as traces of past processes and events at the place of their occurrence), but in practice it causes demands for remuneration of the finder for the effort of "accidentally" discovering an ancient artifact and informing the relevant monument protection services about it.

Due in part to the unfortunate associations of the literal translation of the term "public archaeology" (*archeologia publiczna*) with the Polish term for brothel, or public house (*dom publiczny*), in the linguistic (discursive) context of Polish archaeology, other terms have been used instead of, or in addition to, the literal translation of the term "public archaeology." The terms "socialized archaeology" (in Polish: *archeologia uspołecznianal uspołeczniona*), "pro-social archaeology" (*archeologia prospołeczna*) and "participatory archaeology" (*archeologia partycypacyjna*), or more simply "archaeology in society" or "archaeology for society"[23] have been considered more accurate.[24]

In the Polish context, in the field referred to in the English language as "public archaeology," there also appear[25] the terms "community archaeology" (*archeologia społeczności*), defined as archaeology created by the people and for the people, and social archaeology (*archeologia społeczna*), although the promotion of the latter term carries the risk of some semantic surplus that needs to be taken into account and neutralized. The last of the above-mentioned terms is used to describe (so far individually)[26] those types of activities of researchers that are included in the concept of community archaeology to which the Polish terms *archeologia wspólnotowa* (archaeology of communities)[27] and *archeologia wspólnot lokalnych* (archaeology of local communities) are applicable. In itself, this polyphony of terms gives an insight into the Polish style of constituting and describing cognitive issues.

In Poland, as in many other corners of the world, despite the current obstacles, archaeology is gradually developing solutions favoring the possibility of direct and indirect involvement of communities and individuals in the cognitive processes. Especially since the first decades of the twenty-first century, activities that result directly from situational rather than institutional conditions are being carried out increasingly often.

With the Public and for the Public: Conditions and Manifestations of Pro-Social Activities in Poland – a Case Study

From the Polish perspective presented here, the most needed orientations and strategies for the pro-social and socialized activities and reflections are seen as the ones that emphasize the importance of what makes archaeology inclusive, conciliatory (but not submissive to symbolic violence), applied and responsible. To meet these values, competences are necessary, which, unfortunately, are usually not acquired during the course of studies, as many can only be achieved through practice.

Examples of such acquisition of social competences through practice and methodological reflection may be indicated by the activities carried out in the field perceived as the cognitive, social and curatorial challenge of archaeology of the Eastern Front of the Great War and of the legacy of armed conflicts. These activities were carried out in several stages. The first of them implemented right at the beginning of the second decade of the twenty-first century was the project titled "Archaeology as an antidote to oblivion and vandalism," introducing archaeology and the value of in situ monuments, to the chosen local community in central Poland. It resulted in the creation of a community of interest in the local recent past and of two educational paths with information boards located in consultation and in cooperation with landowners and/or administrators entitled "Life and Death in the Trenches" and "Life at the Back of the Front." The next step "Archaeology of Reconciliation: Roadside History Lessons on the Great War on the Rawka as Reconciliation Lessons (1915–2015)" was to look for answers to the following questions: what does the local community expect from us, why deal with the archaeology of conflict and exhibit material traces of wars, what values are being sought; why is it worth treating with seriousness and thought (and concern for their duration towards the future) the roadside history lessons that mark the landscape around us; and what precise purpose should be served by both cognitive and educational activities relating to the history of past conflicts, etc.?

The conclusions drawn from pro-social activities and the challenges posed by the questions that were multiplying in their course, prompted us to publish locally well-received popularizing publications entitled "The Great War on the Rawka 1914–1915 and its Material Remains" and "Traces and Testimonies of the Great War on Rawka and Bzura"[28] and to implement a project oriented equally pro-socially and cognitively. The main goal of the project entitled "Archaeological Revival of the Memory of the Great War: Material remains of life and death in the trenches of the Great War in the area of the Rawka and Bzura" (acronym: ARM)[29] was to restore the memory of the Eastern Front of the First World War by enriching the knowledge about the everyday life of the soldiers and by updating the ideas about the specificity, meaning and short- and long-term consequences of the military operations driven by principles of the industrial war of plunder with the use of weapons of mass destruction on a massive scale in combat situations that caused long-term traumas and social challenges.[30] Activities carried out under the ARM project were both cognitive and culture-creating. They included field workshops, lectures and on-site talks, archaeological exhibitions, knowledge contests about the events of 1914–1915 for schoolchildren, etc. These contributed to the visible in individual and collective activities which deepened historical sensitivity and awareness among local people and the growing interest in the events of 1914–1915 and their material remains, which gradually begin to be treated as socially and cognitively valuable cautions worthy of commemorating and protection.

There has been special interest aroused concerning until recently neglected and forgotten war cemeteries, those rediscovered in cooperation with local history enthusiasts and those presented as the results of archaeological research.[31] An expression of this are some already legible and ordered war resting places, including delimitations of zones of sensitive places; the locations of memorial stones and bricolage-like monuments in some cemeteries; and the creation of the (first in Poland) Ossuary of the Fallen of the Great War in Joachimów Mogiły.

Another result of the ARM project worth noting is based on the outcomes of the archaeological research, community initiatives and decisions of the Bolimów commune council towards establishing museums of the First World War and the establishment of part of the post-battle landscape as a cultural park – a form of legal protection of the remains in an area delimited as a result of the archaeological and historical research.[32] A further important result for outreach and education via pro-social and socialized archaeology within the archaeology of the Eastern Front of the First World War has been the numerous representations of the issues that were the subject of research with inclusion of the results of the archaeological projects, ranging from a commemorative display in Bolimów and a memorial depository in Nowa Sucha, where archaeological finds from the First World War and board exhibitions based on the results of the ARM research are represented; through in situ marking of relics on tourist maps, publications and updated information boards; to the production of four films on the recognized heritage of the Great War on a national scale[33] and internationally.[34] As well, the number of tourists visiting the relic landscape of the Great War during and after the field work has increased.

Final Remarks

The activities that could be described as engaged pro-social or socialized humanistic archaeology and may be perceived as those that have resulted in sensitive and significant interactions between (a) material elements and remnants of the past, (b) individuals or social groups and (c) archaeologist or archaeologists, should not be done solely intuitively and spontaneously. Such a conditioning triangle should itself be the immediate subject of archaeological and/or transdisciplinary research.[35] One may consider it helpful in analyzing, and in a way in practicing and describing, public archaeology, the approach of the archaeology of reactivated matter[36] and/or second-degree archaeology.[37] The proposed concept focuses on the instances of secondary exploitation of archaeological knowledge, material elements and traces of the past, as well as how the "memory of matter" and its "agency" might help in investigating temporary and transitory attempts to come in contact with each other, with the material elements of the past, and with our historicity and materiality. In other words, it is to penetrate processes that allow for the observation of the modes of communications and interactions, manners and consequences of re-exploiting (reactivating) material traces of the past, archaeological knowledge and what has been or can be valued as "memory matter" or circumferential memory, i.e., as a potentially efficient medium or stimulator of reflection, memory, emotions, empathy, solidarity, responsibility, visions, etc.

I see such observations as inalienable because as archaeologists, when deciding to implement pro-social or socialized archaeology projects, we have to face reasonably various types of challenges, including those connected with exposing material remnants from the past to politicization and manipulation of their interpretation, as well as illegal searches for archaeological remains and plunder,[38] acts of vandalism,[39] encouraging shallow commodifications, commerce in artifacts, or tensions resulting from violating the issue of privacy and property associated with the finds, and many others.

Despite the threats and doubts, the belief in the multiplicity and diversity of social benefits of public or community archaeology (pro-social or socialized archaeology) should not be rejected.[40] The outcomes of such an assumption generate the radical shift in attention from the pursuit of knowing or understanding the past to the pursuit of knowing or understanding the present.

The selected examples and results of specific activities from the field of archaeology of the recent past and painful heritage are mentioned above as an example of the outcomes of such a shift. Activities driven by the assumptions important within public archaeology can truly contribute to the development of new, non-patronizing forms of communication and even cooperation with the inhabitants of the areas containing these remains. As in the case study presented above, pro-social archaeology has positioned those living in the shadow of the Great War's heritage beyond the concept of passive "informants" and transcended the limitations of the "educational model" and "deficit model" in social interactions, understood here after Nick Merriman.[41]

The social impact of the archaeology of the Eastern Front of the Great War, aimed at restoring the memories and memorabilia including the use of weapons of mass destruction in 1915 and those (un)buried (repressed from cultural memory, but trapped in many biographical and material memories), can be considered as very significant. This took place both at the local and international levels (thanks to cooperation with the Ministry of Foreign Affairs and the permanent representative of Poland at the Organization for the Prohibition of Chemical Weapons in The Hague, where the exhibition and lectures constituting the results of the archaeological research were presented).

From the Polish perspective, the principles appreciated in the domain of public archaeology turn out to be perfectly consistent with the assumptions, goals and practice promoted especially in the domain of the field of archaeologies of the recent past (archaeology of modern times, including the archaeology of contemporary armed conflicts, terror, crime, etc.). The completed pro-social projects contributed not only to the broadening of suppressed knowledge (on the forgotten people, "episodes," processes, etc.), but also to strengthening the local sensitivity, historical awareness and effectiveness of the communication of the present around us with elements of the past (as in the given case, anchored in the Great War).

In general, the pursuit of escapes from the limitations of "deficit models" comes with a drive to abandon the rigid *doxa*, including activities conducted under the banner of "science for science's sake." However, moving towards science for the public, done together with the public, is sometimes risky. These principles no longer comply fully with what were previously considered as the canonical criteria of science. The significance of this should not be underestimated, as abandoning the application of criteria from the spectrum of the scientific regime to such activities would expose them to the danger of dropping out of the field of scientific awareness (including that of traditional archaeology) into other domains of activities spread on the axis from shallow entertainment and the entertainment industry to sharp political games that do not require conclusions from scientific knowledge but rhetorical figures to be used for egotistic party purposes. The conclusions from the observations of the long-term pro-social and socialized archaeological activities as well as from my own experiences gained from the praxis, allow us to confirm that from the Polish perspective public archaeology also deserves the highest recognition and is worthy of efforts in its practices and conceptualizations.

Acknowledgments

I would like to thank Paul Barford for the linguistic proofreading and valuable comments, as well as the editor of this volume for invaluable help in dealing with the excess of words.

Mostly, however, I would like to thank all those whose support and understanding has been so important, especially when in one endeavor it is so difficult to reconcile two equally important (though not always coherently harmonized) goals: the scientific and pro-social ones.

Thank you Dorota, Jacek and Janek.

Conclusions presented here are part of the project (No. 4445/20/FPK/NID) co-financed by the Minister of Culture and National Heritage from the Culture Promotion Fund.

Notes

1 Cf. Gabriel Moshenska, ed. *Key Concepts in Public Archaeology* (London: UCL Press, 2017); Cornelius Holtorf, *From Stonehenge to Las Vegas* (Altamira: Walnut Creek, 2005), 12; Angelo Dante, "Public Archaeology. The Move Towards," in *Encyclopedia of Global Archaeology*, ed. Claire Smith (Cham: Springer, 2014), 6182–6188; there other literature.
2 Cf. discussion in Anna I. Zalewska, "Relevant and Applicable Archaeology. The Material Remains of the First World War: Between 'Foundational' and 'Biographical' Memory, Between 'Black Archaeology' and 'Conflict Archaeology'," *Sprawozdania Archeologiczne* 65 (2013): 9–49; Xurxo Aya´n-Vila and Alfredo González-Ruibal, "'Public' and Archaeology," in *Encyclopedia of Global Archaeology*, ed. Claire Smith (Cham: Springer, 2014), 6198; there other literature.
3 Ryszard Nycz, *Kultura jako czasownik. Sondowanie nowej humanistyki. Seria: Nowa Humanistyka* (Warszawa: IBL PAN, 2020), 46–47.
4 Charles McGimsey, *Public Archaeology* (New York and London: SPCK Publishing, 1972).
5 Krzysztof Deskur "Idea public archaeology – edukacja archeologiczna i popularyzacja archeologii," *Fontes Archaeologici Posnanienses* 45 (2009): 283–292. This concept was presented together with the definition and its understanding proposed by Tim Schadla-Hall "Public Archaeology in the Twenty-First Century," in *A Future for Archaeology: The Past in the Present*, ed. Robert Layton, Stephen Shennan, and Peter G. Stone (London: Routledge, 2006), 75–82.
6 It is recognized in Polish literature that the oldest museum, the collections of which were gathered to make them available to a wide audience, and in which were exhibited so-called antiquities, was the museum in the Temple of the Sybils founded in Puławy by Izabella Czartoryska in 1801. The oldest university archaeological institution in Poland is the Institute of Archaeology of the Jagiellonian University, which has been continuously conducting research, teaching and popularizing activities since 1863.
7 Jacek Wrzesiński, "150 lat popularyzacji archeologii w Poznaniu," in *Archeologia polska i jej czasy*, ed. Michał Brzostowicz (Poznań: Seria Prace Komisji Archeologicznej, 2009), 71–102.
8 Cf. Danuta Piotrowska, "Biskupin – ideologie – kultura," in *Archeologia. Kultura. Ideologie,* ed. Bogusław Gediga and Wojciech Piotrowski (Biskupin – Wrocław: MA – PAN), 91–155, see also Anna I. Zalewska "Archaeology (of Second Degree) as the Element of the World of Cultural Representations," *Analecta Archaeologica Ressoviensia* 4 (2009): 150–152.

9 The research was initially conducted by the Directorate of Research into the Origins of the Polish State. Cf. Adrianna Szczerba, "Z historii polskiej archeologii. Badania nad początkami Państwa Polskiego 1948–1966 (Program 'Millenium')." *Acta Universitatis Lodziensis. Folia Archaeologica* 33 (April 2019): 247–254.

10 Cf. widely commented Bartłomiej Noszczak, *"Sacrum" czy „profanum"? Spór o istotę obchodów Milenium polskiego (1949–1966)* (Warszawa: IPN, 2002).

11 Krzysztof Szwagrzyk, "From the 'Coursed Soldiers' to the 'Steadfast (Unbroken) Soldiers' in Poland. Towards Restoring Individual Identity of the Stalinism Victims," in *The Materiality of Troubled Pasts. Archaeologies of Conflicts and Wars*, ed. Anna I. Zalewska, John M. Scott, and Grzegorz Kiarszys (Warszawa–Szczecin: Fundacja Przydrożne Lekcje Historii, USz, 2017), 85–98.

12 Kornelia Kończal, "The Invention of the 'Cursed Soldiers' and Its Opponents: Post-war Partisan Struggle in Contemporary Poland," *East European Politics and Societies* 34, no. 1 (2020): 67–95.

13 Cf. Roksana Kończa and Wiesław Więckowski, eds, *Archaeological Heritage: Methods of Education and Popularization* (Oxford: BAR International Series, 2012).

14 Cf. *Dziedzictwo kulturowe w badaniach. Tom 1: Polacy wobec dziedzictwa. Raport z badań społecznych* created by editorial team Aleksandra Chabiera, Adam Dąbrowski, Anna Fortuna-Marek, Anna Kozioł, Piotr Nowak, Bartosz Skaldawski and Konrad Stępnik (Warszawa – Kraków: Narodowy Instytut Dziedzictwa, Uniwersytet Jagielloński, 2017).

15 Cf. the outcomes of the *NEARCH: New Scenarios For a Community-Involved Archaeology*, accessed May 10, 2021, http://www.nearch.eu/ that also took the Polish case into consideration.

16 Cf. research coordinated by Inrap. There among others: *Europeans and Archeology* (also in Polish *Europejczycy i Archeologia*, translated by Kornelia Kajda), 8–17, NEARCH, accessed December 17, 2020, http://nearch.eu/IMG/pdf/nearch_europeans_and_archaeology_pl.pdf.

17 Cf. current examples of pro-socially driven activities such as those coordinated by Olgierd Ławrynowicz, "The Places of Remembrance and Oblivion project. Interdisciplinary studies of the northern territories of the Kraków-Częstochowa Jura" that assume research in places that may constitute an impulse for multifaceted learning about history, cultural reality, social climate, local memory, cultural heritage and the present-day identity of the inhabitants of the northern areas of the Kraków-Częstochowa Jura (http://najurze.uni.lodz.pl/projekt/, accessed May 10, 2021), or those coordinated by Dawid Kobiałka, "Archaeology of The Death Valley," focused on the area where, during the first months of the Second World War, the local fields were used by the Germans as execution sites for the inhabitants of Chojnice and the region of the Pomeranian Voivodeship (http://archeologiadolinysmierci.pl/, accessed May 10, 2021).

18 Cf. Biografia Archeologii. "Przeszłość zaczyna się już dzisiaj," accessed December 17, 2020, https://www.facebook.com/biografia.archeologii.

19 Cf. Ingrid Ulst, "The Problems of 'Black Archaeology' in Estonia, *Estonian Journal of Archaeology* 14, no. 2 (2010): 154. Cf. Zalewska "Relevant and Applicable Archaeology," 19–22.

20 See valuable comments in Paul Barford "Artefact Collecting: Creating or Destroying the Archaeological Record?," *Folia Praehistorica Posnaniensia* 25 (2020): 39–91.

21 Marek Ziółkowski, "Zmiany systemu wartości, in *Współczesne społeczeństwo polskie. Dynamika zmian*, ed. Jacek Wasilewski (Warszawa: Scholar, 2006), 153.

22 This phenomenon can be interpreted as a delayed echo of the tendency to develop and continue the so-called "second society" (i.e., one that operates alongside

official structures, bypasses it, uses informal acquaintances and connections, and looks for loopholes in the applicable law), which since the beginning of the 1970s in countries experiencing "real socialism" (especially in Poland and Hungary) has digested the healthy tissue of community responsibility for the common good, after Ziółkowski, "Zmiany systemu."

23 The last two terms have been proposed as a "working translation" of the term public archaeology, cf. Michał Pawleta, *Przeszłość we współczesności. Studium metodologiczne archeologicznie kreowanej przeszłości w przestrzeni społecznej* (Poznań: UAM, 2016), 121, 374.

24 Anna I. Zalewska "Roadside Lessons of Historicity. The Roles and the Meanings of the Material Points of References to The Great War and in Shaping Historical Sensitivity and Awareness," *Sensus Historiae* 13, no. 4 (2013): 82.

25 These and similar concepts are literal translations from English, often mechanical and by automated means.

26 Anna I. Zalewska, "Archeology (of Second Degree) as the Element of the World of Cultural Representations," *Analecta Archaeologica Ressoviensia* 4 (2009/2011): 119–154.

27 Anna I. Zalewska, "Prospołeczna, partycypacyjna i 'wspólnotowa' archeologia bliskiej przeszłości jako sposób na nadawanie sensu trwaniu (ludzi i rzeczy) oraz jako antidotum na niedostatki wiedzy i trywializację przeszłości." *Studia Humanistyczne AGH* 13, no. 2 (2014): 19–39.

28 Anna I. Zalewska, Jacek Czarnecki, and Stanisław Kaliński, *Wielka Wojna nad Rawką i materialne po niej pozostałości* (Warszawa: IAE PAN, Fundacja Przydrożne Lekcje Historii, 2014); Anna I. Zalewska and Jacek Czarnecki, *Ślady i świadectwa Wielkiej Wojny nad Rawką i Bzurą* (Warszawa: Przydrożne Lekcje Historii, 2016).

29 This project was carried out in 2014–2019 and was financed as the first of such a kind in Poland with a grant from the National Science Centre (DEC–2013/10/E/HS3/00406).

30 See details at Anna I. Zalewska, "The 'Gas-scape' on the Eastern Front, Poland (1914–2014): Exploring the Material and Digital Landscapes and Remembering Those 'Twice-Killed'" in *Conflict Landscapes and Archaeology from Above*, ed. Birger Stichelbaut and Dave Cowley (London: Routledge, 2016), 147–165.

31 Anna I. Zalewska and Grzegorz Kiarszys, "Absent Presence of Great War Cemeteries in the Municipality of Bolimow, Central Poland" in *The Materiality of Troubled Pasts. Archaeologies of Conflicts and Wars*, ed. Anna I. Zalewska, John M. Scott, and Grzegorz Kiarszys (Warszawa – Szczecin: Fundacja Przydrożne Lekcje Historii – USZ, 2017), 55–82.

32 Cf. Anna I. Zalewska, Jacek Czarnecki, and Michał Jakubczak, "Archaeological Revival of Memory of the Great War. The role of LiDAR in Tracing of the Boundaries of the Planned Cultural Park, The Rawka Battlefield (1914–1915) – In Memory of War Victims," *Archaeologia Polona* 53 (2015): 407–412.

33 (1) "Bolimów 1915" directed by Tomasz Świątkowski, for TVP Historia, (2) "Clouds of Death" by Ireneusz Skruczaj (http://oblokismierci.pl/).

34 (3) "Buried Memories" by Eric Vander Borght, for OPCW 2015 (https://www.opcw.org/fires) in six Congress Languages and (4) "At the Site of the First German Gas Attack" The Great War Special by: Indiana Neidell, directed by Toni Steller & Florian Wittig (https://www.youtube.com/watch?v=-3oSd8DC8Kc).

35 In deepening our understanding of different types, always complex and dynamic, interdependencies that shape that conditioning triangle and bind it with multi-temporal entities (human and other than human), it can be helpful to track down very specific pro-social practices, helpful in demonstrating the value of research targeted into the actuality, rather than into the factuality of the past. Such approach has been applied to the discursive and material remains,

burdened with the experiences of chemical weapon – lasting in time, undergoing continuous changes (both physically and semantically) and gaining and / or losing their power, agency and values, see details: Anna I. Zalewska, "The Use of Chemical Weapons on the Eastern Front of World War One (1915) and its Material and Discursive Remains – the Challenge and Stimuli for Attentive Travel, Systematizing, Storage, Connecting, in situ Preservation and Making Public Real Virtual and Digital Heritage of Weapons of Mass Destruction." *Acta Universitatis Lodziensis. Folia Archaeologica* 35 (2020): 243–273.

36 Cf. Anna I. Zalewska, "Social Production of the Past. Archaeology of Reactivated Matter," *Sensus Historiae* 2, no. 1 (2011): 66–70, accessed May 10, 2021, http://www.sensushistoriae.epigram.eu/english/index.php/sensus/article/view/64/63.

37 Zalewska, "Archaeology (of Second Degree)."

38 The practice of plunder, hunting for and collecting of archaeological artefacts is in Poland as in many other countries condemned and restricted because it is destructive to the archaeological remains, cf. Barford, "Artefact Collecting"; Zalewska "Relevant and Applicable Archaeology," 19–22.

39 Zalewska "Roadside Lessons."

40 For further important arguments cf. Barbara Little, ed. *Public Benefits of Archaeology* (Gainesville: University Press of Florida, 2002); Faye Simpson, "Community Archaeology Under Scrutiny," *Conservation & Management of Archaeological Sites* 10, no. 1 (2008): 3–16.

41 Nick Merriman, *Public Archaeology* (New York: Routledge, 2004).

Bibliography

Barford, Paul. "Artefact Collecting: Creating or Destroying the Archaeological Record?" *Folia Praehistorica Posnaniensia* 25 (2020): 30–91.

Chowaniec, Roksana, and Wiesław Więckowski, eds. *Archaeological Heritage: Methods of Education and Popularization*. Oxford: BAR International Series, 2012.

Dante, Angelo, "Public Archaeology. The Move Towards." In *Encyclopedia of Global Archaeology*, edited by Claire Smith, 6182–6188. Cham: Springer, 2014.

Deskur, Krzysztof. "Idea public archaeology – edukacja archeologiczna i popularyzacja archeologii." *Fontes Archaeologici Posnanienses* 45 (2009): 283–292.

Dziedzictwo kulturowe w badaniach. Tom 1: Polacy wobec dziedzictwa. Raport z badań społecznych, created by editorial team Aleksandra Chabiera, Adam Dąbrowski, Anna Fortuna-Marek, Anna Kozioł, Piotr Nowak, Bartosz Skaldawski and Konrad Stępnik. Warszawa – Kraków: Narodowy Instytut Dziedzictwa, Uniwersytet Jagielloński, 2017.

"Europeans and Archeology." NEARCH. Accessed December 17, 2020. http://nearch.eu/IMG/pdf/nearch_europeans_and_archaeology_pl.pdf.

González-Ruibal, Alfredo, ed. *Reclaiming Archaeology: Beyond the Tropes of Modernity*. London: Routledge, 2013.

Holtorf, Cornelius. *From Stonehenge to Las Vegas*. Altamira: Walnut Creek, 2005.

Kończal, Kornelia. "The Invention of the 'Cursed Soldiers' and Its Opponents: Post-war Partisan Struggle in Contemporary Poland." *East European Politics and Societies* 34, no. 1 (2020): 67–95.

Little, Barbara, ed. *Public Benefits of Archaeology*. Gainesville: University Press of Florida, 2002.

McGimsey, Charles. *Public Archaeology*. New York – London: SPCK Publishing, 1972.

Merriman, Nick. *Public Archaeology*. New York: Routledge, 2004.

Moshenska, Gabriel, ed. *Key Concepts in Public Archaeology*. London: UCL Press, 2017.

Noszczak, Bartłomiej. *"Sacrum" czy „profanum"? Spór o istotę obchodów Milenium polskiego (1949–1966)*. Warszawa: IPN, 2002.

Nycz, Ryszard. *Kultura jako czasownik. Sondowanie nowej humanistyki*. Warszawa: IBL PAN, 2020.

Pawleta, Michał. *Przeszłość we współczesności. Studium metodologiczne archeologicznie kreowanej przeszłości w przestrzeni społecznej*. Poznań: UAM, 2016.

Piotrowska, Danuta, "Biskupin – ideologie – kultura." In *Archeologia. Kultura. Ideologie*, edited by Bogusław Gediga and Wojciech Piotrowski, 91–155. Biskupin–Wrocław: Muzeum Archeologiczne w Biskupinie – PAN, 2004.

Schadla-Hall, Tim. "Public Archaeology in the Twenty-First Century." In *A Future for Archaeology: The Past in the Present*, edited by Robert Layton, Stephen Shennan, and Peter G. Stone, 75–82. London: Routledge, 2006.

Simpson, Faye. "Community Archaeology under Scrutiny." *Conservation & Management of Archaeological Sites* 10, no. 1 (2008): 3–16.

Szczerba, Adrianna. "Z historii polskiej archeologii. Badania nad początkami państwa polskiego 1948–1966 (Program 'Millenium')." *Acta Universitatis Lodziensis. Folia Archaeologica* 33 (April 2019): 247–254.

Szwagrzyk, Krzysztof. "From the 'Coursed Soldiers' to the 'Steadfast (Unbroken) Soldiers' in Poland. Towards Restoring Individual Identity of the Stalinism Victims." In *The Materiality of Troubled Pasts. Archaeologies of Conflicts and Wars*, edited by Anna I. Zalewska, John M. Scott, and Grzegorz Kiarszys, 85–98. Warszawa–Szczecin: Fundacja Przydrożne Lekcje Historii, USz, 2017.

Ulst, Ingrid. "The Problems of 'Black Archaeology' in Estonia." *Estonian Journal of Archaeology* 14, no. 2 (2010): 153–159.

Wrzesiński, Jacek. "150 lat popularyzacji archeologii w Poznaniu." In *Archeologia polska i jej czasy*, edited by Michał Brzostowicz, 71–102. Poznań: Seria Prace Komisji Archeologicznej 2009.

Zalewska, Anna I. "Archaeology (of Second Degree) as the Element of the World of Cultural Representations." *Analecta Archaeologica Ressoviensia* 4 (2009): 119–154.

Zalewska, Anna I. "Relevant and Applicable Archaeology. The Material remains of the First World War: Between 'Foundational' and 'Biographical' Memory, Between 'Black Archaeology' and 'Conflict Archaeology.' *Sprawozdania Archeologiczne* 65 (2013): 9–49.

Zalewska, Anna I. "Roadside Lessons of Historicity. The Roles and the Meanings of the Material Points of References to The Great War and in Shaping Historical Sensitivity and Awareness." *Sensus Historiae* 13 (2013/2014): 69–85.

Zalewska, Anna I. "The Use of Chemical Weapons on the Eastern Front of World War One (1915) and its Material and Discursive Remains – the Challenge and Stimuli for Attentive Travel, Systematizing, Storage, Connecting, in situ Preservation and Making Public Real Virtual and Digital Heritage of Weapons of Mass Destruction." *Acta Universitatis Lodziensis. Folia Archaeologica* 35 (2020): 243–273.

Zalewska, Anna I., and Jacek Czarnecki. *Ślady i świadectwa Wielkiej Wojny nad Rawką i Bzurą.* Warszawa: Przydrożne Lekcje Historii, 2016.

Zalewska, Anna I., Jacek Czarnecki, and Michał Jakubczak. "Archaeological Revival of Memory of the Great War. The role of LiDAR in Tracing of the Boundaries of the planned Cultural Park, The Rawka Battlefield (1914–1915) – In Memory of War Victims." *Archaeologia Polona* 53 (2015): 407–412.

Zalewska, Anna I., Jacek Czarnecki, and Stanisław Kaliński. *Wielka Wojna nad Rawką i materialne po niej pozostałości.* Warszawa: IAE PAN, Fundacja Przydrożne Lekcje Historii, 2014.

Ziółkowski, Marek. "Zmiany systemu wartości." In W*spółczesne społeczeństwo polskie. Dynamika zmian*, edited by Jacek Wasilewski, 145–174. Warszawa: Scholar, 2006.

Part III
Public History and Leisure

11 Polish Feature Films as Public History

Piotr Zwierzchowski

I. Introduction

Andrzej Wajda, one of the most important Polish directors, author of many historical films, honored with an Academy Honorary Award, had no doubt that

> We know who Caesar and Brutus were more from Shakespeare than from Mommsen or Edward Gibbon. We know what the French Revolution was not so much from the historian Michelet, but from David, who painted a poignant vision of the events and people of the Revolution.[1]

He recalled Tolstoy, who drew the image of Napoleon's Russian campaign, and Dickens, thanks to whom we still get to know Victorian England. Finally, he added, "The American conquest of the West, that amazing process of creating civilization on new territories is known by the world primarily from the American western movies."[2]

One has to agree with Wajda's opinion. Although he did not consider himself a historian, he has proved it more than once with his own works. It was his films, among others, that shaped the awareness of their own history among Poles. Traversing his own words, one could say that the image which many Poles had about the Warsaw Uprising of 1944 was for many years influenced primarily by *Kanał* directed by Wajda (1957), and the image of the beginning of the Second World War by *Lotna* (1959). *Popioły*, (Ashes, 1966) formed the vision of the fate of Poles in the Napoleonic era, and *Katyń* (2007) depicted the Stalinist crime committed on Polish soldiers.

Piotr Witek presents Andrzej Wajda not as a filmmaker shooting a historical film but rather as a historian reflecting on the past, who during his work takes an active part in the discussion on the complicated history of Poland and the tragic fate of Poles. He consciously gets involved in shaping social perceptions of the past of contemporary generations.[3] The director can also be considered a public historian who not only conducts research, but above all tries to reach the audience. Historical themes have always been of fundamental importance to Polish cinema. This is proven not only by several

DOI: 10.4324/9781003165767-15

hundred films about history, but also by their being among the most frequently watched, as clearly evidenced by box-office results. For several decades now, *Teutonic Knights* (*Krzyżacy*, 1960) by Aleksander Ford has topped the list. It is a screen adaptation of the novel by the 1905 Nobel Prize laureate Henryk Sienkiewicz about the war with the Order of Brothers of the German House of Saint Mary in Jerusalem, i.e., the Teutonic Order, which culminated in the Battle of Grunwald, a victory for the Polish-Lithuanian army (1410). The image of the Swedish invasion of Poland in the middle of the seventeenth century was created by Jerzy Hoffman's *The Deluge* (*Potop*, 1974), also based on a Sienkiewicz's novel (this connection with literature is one of the characteristic features of Polish historical cinema), while the perception of the Second World War was largely shaped by the popular TV series *Four Tankmen and a Dog* (*Czterej pancerni i pies*, 1966–1970) by Konrad Nałęcki and Andrzej Czekalski and *More than Life at Stake* (*Stawka większa niż życie*, 1967–1968) by Janusz Morgenstern and Andrzej Konic.

These are just a few of the most prominent examples. The images of the past in Polish films have often had a significant impact on the social perception of history, creating its meaning and understanding, while also relating them to contemporary problems. The cinema has been educational, has shaped historical consciousness and created visual images of the past. Sometimes it reads history differently than the canonical academic or cultural versions, while at other times it has supported it. The authors' intention has not always been to provide the audience with historical knowledge in accordance with its current state. The image of the past was also the result of the artists' assumptions – it served as a particular piece of propaganda or was a means of entertainment and could be used to build or deconstruct national identity. According to public history, the most crucial aspect is to reach the audiences, to consider their expectations and needs, cultural competences, aesthetic habits, perceptual abilities, value systems, collective memory and finally, the socially established vision of the past. Not without significance are the methods of film distribution, forms of circulation (cinemas, television, internet, video, school film libraries), presence in the public discourse and various (para)texts. All these factors determine whether or not audiences will be convinced by both the reconstruction of the past and its interpretation. By referring to arbitrarily selected Polish historical films, I want to look at a few issues precisely related to their treatment as public history.

II. Historical Outline

The first Polish historical films began to appear at the beginning of the second decade of the twentieth century. It may seem quite late when compared to world cinematography, but it must be considered that at that time Poland was partitioned by three powers: Russia, Germany and the Austro-Hungarian Empire. Historical topics were often connected with the problem of national identity, later repeatedly addressed. Polish historical film has had, until today, "a specific character, based on highlighting national distinctiveness, national drama, presented in the form of a historical spectacle."[4] It is not without reason that the vast majority of these productions refer to Polish history.

After Poland regained independence, history was to become both a unifying factor for Polish society after years of statelessness, and a political vehicle. Over time, a popular vision of history was more readily created, combining patriotic and identity themes with genre conventions, especially melodrama. Such productions catered to the needs and competences of the audience. In the 1930s, after the introduction of sound film, patriotic functions began to play a lesser role, although historical film was still used to shape official politics of memory.

In the historical cinema of 1944–1989, the possibility of discourse was limited by the politics and ideology of the ruling Polish United Workers' Party, the specifics of the media market in a centrally controlled economy and the technological conditions relating to the reach and freedom of social communication. In the cinema of the People's Republic of Poland it was impossible to present historical events totally at variance with the official interpretation. Each film was carefully supervised. The screenplay had to be approved by the Screenplay Evaluation Committee or, at other times, by the Policy Councils of the Film Groups. A finished film was evaluated by the inspection committee, and still later had to be accepted by the censors. The Department of Culture of the Polish United Workers' Party, the army, veterans' organizations and other institutions also presented their opinions, which sometimes had a great influence on the film's fate.[5]

Cinematic representations of the past were not much different from the messages conveyed in textbooks, journalism or fiction and created a kind of intertext.[6] Using the properties of the message, cinema reinforced Marxist historiography, also indicating official interpretations of particular phenomena, e.g., the negative evaluation of the Second Polish Republic or the strength of friendship with the Soviet Union in films about the Second World War. There were also subjects that were not discussed at all, especially the Polish-Soviet War of 1920, the Soviet aggression against Poland in September 1939, or the murder of Polish soldiers in Katyń and other places in 1940.

Sometimes films that disturbed the dominant images appeared, an example being Stanisław Różewicz's excellent half-hour film *On the Hideout* (*Na melinę*, 1965), which offered an image of Polish partisans that was far from heroic. Portraits of soldiers increasingly addicted to killing did not fit the officially promoted image of the Polish mindset during the Second World War. However, the film could not impact the audience as it was not released.[7]

The development of technology and new inventions encouraged the democratization of historical knowledge. One of the most significant phenomena of the 1980s was the video revolution. Thanks to VCRs and VHS cassettes, at least some films about the past were able to bypass the supervision by political powers over the distribution system. The most interesting example is Ryszard Bugajski's *Interrogation* (*Przesłuchanie*), at the time the strongest indictment of Polish Stalinism, which tells the story of a singer who was wrongly arrested, only to become a witness against someone else. Subjected to constant psychological and physical torture in prison and treated inhumanely, she finds her strength and dignity. The production ended in 1982, already after the introduction of martial law. The film was not allowed to be distributed and its copies were ordered to be destroyed. The director, however, managed to copy the film onto a magnetic tape.[8] In the 1980s, *Interrogation*, despite the often very poor quality of the copies, was screened at dozens of unofficial and illegal screenings organized by, for example, the Catholic Church. This way it became an element of the political and historical education of Poles, giving access, provided by technological achievements and new circulations of cultural texts, to a historical message that was an alternative to the official one.

After 1989, themes connected to recent history which had not previously been possible emerged in Polish cinema. Memory was restored. After a break of over 20 years, caused by the anti-Semitic policy of the government in the late 1960s, there was a return to the subject of Polish-Jewish relations, especially in the context of the Second World War. Issues concerning relations with the Soviet Union, previously absent from the screen, could finally be taken up. The history of the People's Republic of Poland became one of the major themes of Polish historical cinema.

However, the situation of the cinema itself has changed, as well as that of the viewer, who has gained access to cultural texts that offer historical knowledge in an (almost) unregulated way. Movie visions of the past became but one of the plethora of possibilities. The viewer can obtain knowledge from a variety of sources and can choose different media, narratives, canons, etc. Therefore, a cultural text has to garner attention, e.g., by its spectacular form or by violating the status quo related to collective and individual memory.

Reflection on Polish films in the context of public history must address the conclusions of a 2012 study by Maciej Białous, unfortunately conducted on only a small group of respondents. It shows that Polish viewers are more familiar with and appreciative of foreign historical films. They believe that Polish cinema lacks adequate production competence and financing to tell stories attractively. As a result, films

> lose their chance to inspire viewers to take an interest in the history of their country. Viewers' interests are shifting towards the history of other countries and nations. Foreign productions are enjoyable to watch, because they are produced in an accessible way, which does not require the viewer to have any prior preparation or extensive knowledge [...].[9]

However, there is no doubt that cinema is an important source of Poles' knowledge about the past. According to a Gfk Polonia survey, "Poles mainly learn about Poland's recent history from TV programs (66%). They are followed by books (28%), the internet (25%), films and TV series (24%), and talks with family and friends (18%)." As indicated by research conducted in the same year on the presence of the Second World War in the collective memory of Poles, films are also one of the most important sources of knowledge about the Second World War (61%). The respondents indicated more frequently only television, newspapers and radio (66.7%). Subsequent places, with much poorer results, were taken by general interest publications (34.8%) and scholarly publications (25.7%), stories of family members who were direct witnesses of the events (32.2) and unrelated witnesses (27.3%), museums and exhibitions (24.9%), textbooks (24.1%), etc. Relatively few people chose the internet (24%) and videogames (6.1%), although these results would most likely look different today.

III. Reception by the Public

Producers and authors of historical films and series need to keep audiences interested and therefore do not necessarily focus on what seems most important from the point of view of academic history.[10] Fundamental for the approval or disapproval of film visions of the past are the viewers' competences and habits. Each new historical film is confronted not only with historical knowledge, but also with dozens of other cultural texts, social perceptions, individual and collective experience, and memory. It is worth remembering, however, that from the perspective of the viewer "It doesn't matter if the historical details of the films are genuine; they just have to look authentic to the audience."[11]

Historical films can have a problem with viewers' acceptance not because their writers reconstructed the past inadequately, but because their interpretation was not in line with the beliefs and expectations of viewers, for whom clichés and genre patterns, as well as stereotypes related to the characters and events are the most frequent point of reference. This is not only due to the attitude towards history, but also due to the viewer's aesthetic habits and expectations. One of the most significant examples is *Barbara Radziwiłłówna* (1936) by Józef Lejtes, with screenplay by Anatol Stern. Initially, the authors wished to show the heroine in keeping with the historical records of the day, which increasingly debunked her.

Stern studied numerous historical sources and related texts, and the authors consulted historians, initially wanting to show an ambitious woman caught up in political scheming. "However, the image of Barbara as simpleminded, stupid and spiteful, dry, lazy and preoccupied only with herself clashed with the interests of the scandal-fearing cinema owners and moreover failed to appeal to the imagination of the intelligentsia."[12] Eventually, the filmmakers decided on a melodramatic version, in line with one of the best-known national myths and audience expectations. The historical realities were also adjusted to this version. The film, which was supposed to undermine the prevalent image of the wife of King Sigismund Augustus, Barbara Radziwiłłówna, who came from a Lithuanian magnate family and married against the will of the Sejm, contributed to an even stronger consolidation of her image in Polish historical consciousness. This is indirectly confirmed by the fact that viewers acclaimed *Barbara Radziwiłłówna* as the film of the year.[13]

Certain images are so firmly encoded in the minds of the audiences that showing them in accordance with historical reality would be seen as a dissonance in a coherent vision of the past. This applies, for example, to the image of the characters, the set design, the costumes, etc. Jerzy Hoffman was faced with such a dilemma during the production of *The Deluge*. Since Poles are aware of the image of Jasna Góra with its characteristic monastery tower from the nineteenth century, showing it on screen in a film about the seventeenth century is ahistorical. However, this image is so strongly ingrained that abandoning it could distort the impression of iconographic credibility.

Without a doubt the greatest success of Polish historical cinema has been the *Teutonic Knights*, watched in cinemas across Poland by over 33 million viewers by the end of the twentieth century.[14] The figure does not take into account TV screenings and the use of media such as VHS cassettes or DVDs. This Aleksander Ford's movie was fully in line with the underpinnings and requirements of the ideology and politics of the time as well as with the historical knowledge and its official interpretation. However, these were not the features that ultimately contributed to its success and effective impact on historical knowledge and consciousness.[15] The war with the Teutonic Order and the Battle of Grunwald not only belongs to Polish history but also to the collective memory, the cultural canon and the national imaginary, shaped, among others, by the writings of Henryk Sienkiewicz and the paintings of Jan Matejko. The spectator watched not only a skillful reconstruction of the events in line with these works of art, but also a story of great love and great victory over eternal enemies. It was to this combination that the *Teutonic Knights* owed its great success, and this, in turn, reinforced the film's vision of history.

In 1960, the spectacular character of the *Teutonic Knights* movie was beyond doubt. Decades later, the film has aged somewhat as a spectacle. However, it is still in circulation; it was screened in the Museum of the Battle of Grunwald, copies were released on VHS cassettes, later on DVD (also the digitally restored edition) and Blu-ray, and is quite often broadcast by various TV stations. It is also a very evocative and credible image of the past, because regardless of changes in professional academic knowledge of the Polish-Teutonic war, including the course of the battle itself, its message is still consistent with the popular perception of the past.

Cinema takes up themes that, even if they appear in academic history, do not make it into public discourse. In the late 1960s and early 1970s, the introduction of regional stories became such an unobvious approach. This was done by Kazimierz Kutz in his story about the Second Silesian Uprising (1920) – *Salt of the Black Earth* (*Sól ziemi czarnej*, 1969), and one devoted to the strike of Polish miners in a German mine in 1934 – *The Pearl in the Crown* (*Perła w koronie*, 1971). The director showed the history of Silesia in his later films, too: *I will Stand on Guard* (*Na straży swej stać będę*, 1983) about the Second World War, *The Turned Back* (*Zawrócony*) and *Death as a Slice of Bread* (*Śmierć jak kromka chleba*, both 1994) about the early 1980s and martial law. Even if strict historical reconstruction played a secondary role, giving way, for example, to myth, all these films can be considered as a coherent picture of the past. Moreover, "Kutz's Silesian films are known throughout the country and his vision of Upper Silesia and its history is so attractive that the director was able to impose it on Poland."[16]

Cinema can also choose an unobvious way of looking at events or figures that are well known from academic or journalistic studies. Filip Bajon in *Poznań '56* (1996) showed a bloody suppression of workers' protests from the perspective of a child. In *General Nil* (*Generał Nil*, 2009) by Ryszard Bugajski, dedicated to General August Emil Fieldorf, Deputy Commander in Chief of the Home Army during the Second World War, organizer and commander of the Home Army Diversion Directorate, murdered by the communist regime, the director exposed the protagonist's:

> willingness to stop his military activity and his doubts about its effectiveness. As a result, out of the biography of a soldier of the legions, a participant in the Kiev expedition and the September campaign, an officer from the borderlands between the wars and a wartime fugitive from an internment camp, a secret emissary trained in France, and then the chief of armed operations of the underground state, one whose subordinate said that "the Germans were afraid of him like a fire," we get only the image of a sick, lost man in a "dirty jumper."[17]

Cinema can reconstruct or deconstruct academic visions of history. In recent years, one of the most interesting examples has been the *General: Assassination in Gibraltar* (*Generał. Zamach na Gibraltarze*, 2009) by Anna Jadowska, addressing the death of General Władysław Sikorski in 1943. The death of Poland's Prime Minister and Commander-in-Chief gave rise to numerous conspiracy theories according to which he had been murdered earlier and the plane crash was nothing but a hoax. Since 2002, this vision has also been argued in the press and television programs by Dariusz Baliszewski, a publicist and historian (also by education), who is not, however, active in academic circles. Based on his publications, Anna Jadowska wrote the script for her film and that very year, in collaboration with Baliszewski, prepared a four-part documentary series with fictionalized scenes titled, *General* (*Generał*).

Despite the sensational version of the life story of one of the best-known wartime heroes, viewers' interest proved negligible. *General: Assassination in Gibraltar* can be considered one of the most interesting Polish films in formal terms, one proposing "a kind of interplay of fictional and factual discourses," focusing on "processes that determine our understanding of the past." In this context, the movie would aim not at "reconstructing the real causes of the catastrophe, but rather at constructing a plausible and acceptable (socially agreed) narrative."[18] For viewers expecting a more traditional formula of the genre, however, Jadowska's film, overloaded with visual attractions, was difficult to accept. This may have been due to the film's poetics, but there was also the issue of historical probability. The context of the production imposed on the viewer a perception of the film as a reconstruction of historical facts and the circumstances of its premiere undermined this interpretation. Work on the film took place at a time when the investigation conducted by the Institute of National Remembrance implied a discovery of the true course of events and the uncovering of the motives for the crime. This led, among other things, to the exhumation and examination of the General's remains. According to the official report published before the premiere of the film, Sikorski died as a result of multiple organ injuries, typical of accident victims. Thus, the official version of his death was confirmed. This is one of the reasons why the interest of viewers turned out to be negligible.

Controversies connected with the unique nature of the events described and with the message of the film, help publicize specific titles and thus influence increased interest in them and, consequently, foster a wider dissemination of the visions of history they offer. Of fundamental importance for the popularity of the message, however, is also the poetics. Original artistic expression does not necessarily have a positive impact on the success of a film among viewers. Films that are narratively complex or subordinated to expressive aesthetic means are appreciated by critics, yet undoubtedly it is classic historical dramas that have the greatest impact on the historical awareness of viewers. Such dramas

> have no clear-cult style, employ transparent visual means on the screen (from the perspective of contemporary reception practice), have an unambiguous, comprehensible, generally chronological and objectively told storyline, with dramatic progression, with a closed ending, and present a story with the semblance of realism. Classical historical drama offers a clear opportunity to open up to the "voice of history" on screen, because it does not expose stylistic solutions; a narratively unambiguous story can evoke in the viewer a sense of participation in a reliable exploration of the past.[19]

It is not without reason that classic historical dramas as well as films that fit the historical story into genre conventions are most popular with audiences. This was the way history was told in the *Teutonic Knights* and *The Deluge*.

According to the aforementioned 2009 study, the best-known Polish films about the Second World War were the television series *Four Tankmen and a Dog* (50.1%) and *More than Life at Stake* (37.4%).[20] For many years, they were the films that most strongly influenced the image of the Second World War in the public consciousness. To this day, they occupy an important place in Polish popular culture, being released on VHS cassettes and DVDs and shown by many television stations; references to them appear in various cultural texts. Despite the fact that their storyline was subordinated to propaganda, most viewers find it of little significance. As in the case of the *Teutonic Knights* and *The Deluge*, this was due to the clear and attractively presented vision of history that corresponded with the Poles' self-perception and the expert use of the adventure film convention.

IV. Debates

The presence of a film in public sphere is marked by its box-office results, reception in the media[21] and online posts.[22] Films are often the subject of public debates involving film critics, historians, politicians, socio-political journalists and historians. The specific nature of electronic media makes viewers' comments increasingly visible. In these discussions, artistic value or efficiency of production is also assessed, but usually films are a pretext for, a catalyst of, or one of the arguments in a historical or political debate.

In the cinema of the People's Republic of Poland, the most turbulent disputes accompanied Andrzej Wajda's *Ashes*. This film, set in Napoleonic times, depicted the situation of Poles who, wishing to regain their independence, were often used by foreign powers for their own ends, and whose freedom aspirations led them to participate in terror. Above all, emotions were aroused by reading the film in the context of the ideological disputes of the mid-1960s as a picture of the nation's wasted chances for independence and an assault on "national values."

The major public debates were also aligned to other historical movies.[23] These are, for instance, *Katyń* (2007) and *Wałęsa: Man of Hope* (*Wałęsa. Człowiek z nadziei*, 2013) by Andrzej Wajda, *Hatred* (*Wołyń*, 2016) by Wojciech Smarzowski, *Ida* (2013) by Paweł Pawlikowski, *The Secret of Westerplatte* (*Tajemnica Westerplatte*, 2013) by Paweł Chochlew and *Aftermath* (*Pokłosie*, 2012) by Władysław Pasikowski (a film set in contemporary times but devoted to history). These films dealt with the Second World War, Polish-Jewish relations, or particularly controversial heroes of most recent history, such as Lech Wałęsa, i.e., they address subjects that strongly engaged public opinion.

Public reactions to films never take place in a social vacuum. The social life of a historical film is determined not only by the viewers' competences, worldview or nationality, but also by the context of reception: where, when and in what circumstances the film was viewed,[24] etc.

Ida, criticized in Poland from all political sides, albeit with the use of different arguments, garnered enthusiastic opinions of the foreign press; *Katyń*, having evoked a rather positive (if politicized) response in Poland, met with a complete lack of understanding in other countries. The reception was also influenced by the time the films were viewed, which can best be seen in the case of *Ida*: right-wing commentators became interested in the film only on the occasion of the Oscar nomination which coincided with the presidential campaign in Poland.[25]

The significant presence of *Katyń* in public debate is proven by the publication in each of the major Polish dailies of *Gazeta Wyborcza*, *Rzeczpospolita* and *Dziennik. Polska. Europa. Świat* of around 40 texts about the movie in the years 2007–2010. Importantly, the film itself was rarely analyzed, *Katyń* was most often written about in the context of historical, political and ideological disputes. The most significant contexts for its reception were, for example, the 2007 parliamentary elections, the Oscar nomination for the best foreign language film, and the Smolensk plane crash in 2010, which killed Polish President Lech Kaczyński and 95 other people flying to the ceremony commemorating Polish soldiers massacred in Katyń.[26]

After 2000, one of the most important reference points for those taking up the subject of Polish-Jewish relations during the Second World War was Jan Gross's book *Neighbors: The Destruction of the Jewish Community in Jedwabne*,[27] which sparked a huge and very emotional debate about Poles' attitudes towards Jews. The author wrote about the town of Jedwabne, where in 1941 Polish inhabitants, inspired by the Germans, murdered their Jewish neighbors. Of special importance in the debate sparked by the book were such films as *Joanna* (2010) by Feliks Falk, *In Darkness* (*W ciemności*, 2011) by Agnieszka Holland, *Ida*, awarded with the Oscar Academy Award for the best foreign language film and *Demon* (2015) by Marcin Wrona. *Aftermath*, a most acute reference to *Neighbors* and its image of Poles, stirred the most heated debates.[28] The protagonist estranges himself from his neighbors as he tries to uncover a past that the whole community wants to forget. The truth is inconvenient for everyone: during the war Poles murdered Jews in the town, and his father was one of the accomplices. *Aftermath* presented a very simplified picture of reality, was unreliable in terms of narrative, but played a large role in the discussion on the attitudes of Poles during the Holocaust and the memory of them. Its importance for the public debate is evidenced by the unflagging and ongoing emotions and disputes, for example, on internet forums.[29]

V. Educational Aspects

It is not easy to shoot a film to make a statement about history. Production requires a lot of effort, a large team and above all, a lot of money. For most historical and film educators this is a task beyond their capabilities and competences. In fact, this is not their goal. They use existing films to talk about history. They hold screenings, reviews,[30] meetings, training sessions, debates, lectures and set up educational portals. They often cooperate with schools, although their activities are usually aimed at a wider audience.

Feature films are one of the most important sources of knowledge about the past, but they are used relatively rarely in the school context. The core curriculum for classes 4–8 mentions film as one of the teaching aids yet offers no details. Interestingly, the core curriculum for secondary schools mentions films about the past, but in the context of the Polish Language, not History classes. Another thing is that in educational practice, historical films serve primarily as an illustration of given events. Much less frequent is an attempt to reflect on the credibility of a film image of history or ways of constructing it.

Increasingly, historical films are becoming the subject of interest of organizations not directly connected with institutional education, although they also address their offer to schools, teachers and students. Poland's National Film Archive (*Filmoteka Narodowa – Instytut Audiowizualny*, FINA) runs an educational program called Polish Film Academy (*Akademia Filmu Polskiego*), dedicated to the history of Polish cinematography. During screenings combined with lectures and talks, participants learn both the nuances of Polish history and the history of cinema. The program allows students from a wide variety of fields to gain ECTS credits, but is entirely voluntary and addressed to all interested parties, regardless of age or status.

Another program run by FINA, School Film Archive (*Filmoteka Szkolna*), enables teachers to use, at their own discretion, Polish films as part of their lessons. This also applies to history. In addition, in 2021 FINA offered a webinar called "Film and Historical Studies." Schools can also benefit from workshops organized by the Itinerant Film Scholars program.

The offer for secondary school students includes the series "Film History of Poland," run by the New Horizons of Film Education (*Nowe Horyzonty Edukacji Filmowej*). Films produced in the last dozen or so years, depicting various phenomena, events and characters from the twentieth century, contribute to the discussion not only about themselves, but also about history.[31] Moreover, FINA and Venae Artis Education and Culture Association and the Central Office of Film Education of the Julian Tuwin Palace of Youth in Łódź (*Centralny Gabinet Edukacji Filmowej Pałacu Młodzieży im. Juliana Tuwima w Łodzi*) run a portal called EdukacjaFilmowa.pl, where one can find, for example, *Suggestions for using film in the implementation of the History core curriculum for grades 4–8 of primary school*. For activities related to public history, the series *Film Waves of History*, organized by the above institutions in cooperation with the Network of Art House Cinemas, is of particular importance. As part of the series, books are being written and the whole project is also available on the portal. The film studies and historical analyses they contain, concerning selected films or issues, can be useful for teachers, students and anyone interested in the interfaces of cinema and history. Teachers and educators may moreover use scripts for classes appended to each topic, not necessarily in the school context. As a result, based on the *Stones for the Rampart* (*Kamienie na szaniec*, 2014) by Robert Gliński, they will be able to discuss *Poles' social attitude during the German occupation of the Second World War*, and while referring to the *Short Working Day* (*Krótki dzień pracy*, 1981/1996) by Krzysztof Kieślowski they will demonstrate the *power of strikes in the Poland of Edward Gierek.*[32]

Although the aforementioned projects are mainly used by pupils, students and teachers, those interested may also participate in them outside the school context. Most of these proposals are addressed to cinema and history aficionados.

VI. Conclusions

The past invariably remains one of the most important elements of Polish identity. As such, it is a vital element of education, appears constantly in public discourse and is also the focus of cultural texts, including film. Its authors engage in historical discourse, propose various images of the past, thus supplementing rather than replacing academic history, often agreeing with it, at other times offering solutions contradictory to it. They attempt to record emotions, visualize the past, and offer the specificity of a spectacle, they concentrate on individual events, show the actions of individual characters, choose them freely, and use the properties of the film message to convince the viewer of the proposed image of history and its interpretation. In this way, thanks to its authors, educators and promoters, cinema becomes a part of public history. After all, our knowledge about the Warsaw Uprising owes a lot to Andrzej Wajda and other filmmakers dealing with this topic.

Notes

1 Andrzej Wajda, "Moje spotkania z historią," *Film na Świecie* no. 383 (1991): 70.
2 *Ibid.*
3 Piotr Witek, *Andrzej Wajda jako historyk. Metodologiczne studium z historii wizualnej* (Lublin: UMCS, 2016), 32.
4 Małgorzata Pośpiech, "Mit a historia. *Potop* J. Hoffmana," in *Kino – film: poezja optyczna?*, ed. Jan Trzynadlowski (Wrocław: Wydawnictwo Uniwersytetu Wrocławskiego, 1995), 227.
5 Cf. Paul Coates, *The Red and The White. The Cinema of People's Poland* (London: Wallflower Press, 2005), 78–79.
6 Joanna Wojdon, "The Impact of Communist Rule on History Education in Poland," *Journal of Educational Media, Memory and Society* 4, no. 1 (2012): 61–77; Joanna Wojdon, *Textbooks as Propaganda. Poland under Communist Rule, 1944–1989* (New York: Routledge, 2018).
7 Jarosław Grzechowiak, "*Na melinę* – zapomniane dzieło Stanisława Różewicza," *Panoptikum* no. 20 (2018): 193–208.

8 The story of his film is described in detail by Ryszard Bugajski, *Jak powstało "Przesłuchanie"* (Warszawa: Świat Książki, 2010).

9 Maciej Białous, *Społeczna konstrukcja filmów historycznych. Pamięć zbiorowa i polityka pamięci w kinematografii polskiej* (Gdańsk: Wydawnictwo Naukowe Katedra, 2017), 439.

10 References to it may be an important criterion for various types of institutions. The Polish Film Institute requires from an applicant seeking funding for a historical film "an obligatory opinion of an expert historian as to whether the events presented in the screenplay are basically consistent with the historical facts or else are probable in the presented context in the case of a historical film and others, if the project contains historical plots. This expert opinion should be accompanied by information on the academic record of its author." https://pisf.pl/wp-content/uploads/2020/04/Programy-Operacyjne-2020-zmienione-16.04.2020.pdf, last modified April 16, 2020, accessed February 23, 2021.

11 Martha W. Driver, "What's Accuracy Got to Do with It? Historicity and Authenticity in Medieval Film," in *The Medieval Hero on Screen. Representations from Beowulf to Buffy*, ed. Martha W. Driver and Sid Ray (Jefferson: McFarland, 2004), 20. Martha Driver refers to her conversation with Jonathan Rosenbaum.

12 Alina Madej, *Mitologie i konwencje. O polskim kinie fabularnym dwudziestolecia międzywojennego* (Kraków: Universitas, 1994), 104.

13 *Ibid.*, 105.

14 Krzysztof Kucharski, *KINO PLUS. Film i dystrybucja kinowa w Polsce 1990–2000* (Toruń: Oficyna Wydawnicza Kucharski, 2002), 388.

15 Cf. Janusz Rulka, *Wpływ filmu na rozwój myślenia historycznego uczniów* (Bydgoszcz: Bydgoskie Towarzystwo Naukowe, 1969), 53–67.

16 Jan F. Lewandowski, *Historia Śląska według Kutza* (Katowice – Warszawa: Wydawnictwo Naukowe Śląsk, 2004), 7.

17 Marcin Adamczak, "Czy II wojna światowa już się skończyła? Kino, polityka historyczna i stosunki międzynarodowe jako „bitwa na opowieści," in *Kino polskie wobec drugiej wojny światowej*, ed. Piotr Zwierzchowski, Daria Mazur, and Mariusz Guzek (Bydgoszcz: Wydawnictwo Uniwersytetu Kazimierza Wielkiego, 2011), 18. Interestingly, fearing the reactions of the viewers, Bugajski censored the theme of General Fieldorf's lover from his story. The person appears on the screen only as his secretary.

18 Cf. Natasza Korczarowska-Różycka, *Inne spojrzenie. Wyobrażenia historii w filmach Wojciecha Jerzego Hasa, Jana Jakuba Kolskiego, Filipa Bajona i Anny Jadowskiej – studium przypadków* (Łódź: Wydawnictwo Biblioteki Państwowej Wyższej Szkoły Filmowej, Telewizyjnej i Teatralnej, Wydawnictwo Uniwersytetu Łódzkiego, 2013), 320.

19 Krzysztof Kornacki and Piotr Kurpiewski, "Kino jako nauczyciel. Klasyfikacja działań autorskich współczesnego polskiego kina historycznego (propozycje)," in *Historia wizualna w działaniu. Studia i szkice z badań nad filmem historycznym*, ed. Dorota Skotarczak, Joanna Szczutkowska, and Piotr Kurpiewski (Poznań: Wydział Historii UAM, 2020), 72.

20 Piotr T. Kwiatkowski, Lech M. Nijakowski, Barbara Szacka, Andrzej Szpociński, *Między codziennością a wielką historią. Druga wojna światowa w pamięci zbiorowej społeczeństwa polskiego* (Gdańsk and Warszawa: Muzeum II Wojny Światowej and Scholar, 2010), 79.

21 Magdalena Saryusz-Wolska, "The Framework of Reception: Public Responses to Historical Fiction Films," *Res Historica* no. 50 (2020): 551–571.

22 Cf. Maciej Białous, "Dyskurs użytkowników filmowych portali internetowych wobec konfliktów pamięci zbiorowych we współczesnej Polsce," in *Historia*

204	*Piotr Zwierzchowski*

wizualna w działaniu. Studia i szkice z badań nad filmem historycznym, ed. Dorota Skotarczak, Joanna Szczutkowska, and Piotr Kurpiewski (Poznań: Wydział Historii UAM, 2020), 9–23.
23 Krzysztof Kornacki, "Współczesne polskie kino historyczne. Rekonesans," *Script*, no. 3 (2019): 13.
24 Saryusz-Wolska, "The Framework," 562–568.
25 *Ibid.*, 564.
26 *Ibid.*, 554–557. More on this: Magdalena Saryusz-Wolska, "Prasa o *Katyniu* Andrzeja Wajdy," in *Polskie piśmiennictwo filmowe*, ed. Piotr Zwierzchowski and Barbara Giza (Bydgoszcz: Wydawnictwo Uniwersytetu Kazimierza Wielkiego, 2013), 203–216.
27 Jan T. Gross, *Neighbors: The Destruction of the Jewish Community in Jedwabne* (Princeton: Princeton University Press, 2001). The Polish edition came out a year earlier.
28 Marek Haltof, *Polish Cinema. A History*, second, updated edition (New York – Oxford: Berghahn Books, 2019), 379–387.
29 Białous, "Dyskurs użytkowników."
30 The best known are festivals of documentaries, such as Zamość Film Festival (*Spotkania z historią*) Encounters with History and *Niepokorni Niezłomni Wyklęci*. (The Insubordinate. The Steadfast. The Cursed)
31 https://nhef.pl/program/cykle/filmowa-historia-polski, accessed February 23, 2021.
32 Anna Kołodziejczak, Dorota Gołębiowska, Ewa Kanownik, and Maciej Dowgiel, eds., *Filmowe fale historii* (Łódź: Stowarzyszenie Edukacyjno-Kulturalne Venae Artis, 2016).

Bibliography

Adamczak, Marcin. "Czy II wojna światowa już się skończyła? Kino, polityka historyczna i stosunki międzynarodowe jako 'bitwa na opowieści.'" In *Kino polskie wobec drugiej wojny światowej*, edited by Piotr Zwierzchowski, Daria Mazur, and Mariusz Guzek, 9–23. Bydgoszcz: Wydawnictwo Uniwersytetu Kazimierza Wielkiego, 2011.
Białous, Maciej. "Dyskurs użytkowników filmowych portali internetowych wobec konfliktów pamięci zbiorowych we współczesnej Polsce." In *Historia wizualna w działaniu. Studia i szkice z badań nad filmem historycznym*, edited by Dorota Skotarczak, Joanna Szczutkowska, and Piotr Kurpiewski, 9–23. Poznań: Wydział Historii UAM, 2020.
Białous, Maciej. *Społeczna konstrukcja filmów historycznych. Pamięć zbiorowa i polityka pamięci w kinematografii polskiej.* Gdańsk: Wydawnictwo Naukowe Katedra, 2017.
Bugajski Ryszard. *Jak powstało „Przesłuchanie."* Warszawa: Świat Książki, 2010.
Coates, Paul. *The Red and the White. The Cinema of People's Poland.* London: Wallflower Press, 2005.
Driver, Martha W. "What's Accuracy Got to Do with It? Historicity and Authenticity in Medieval Film." In *The Medieval Hero on Screen. Representations from Beowulf to Buffy*, edited by Martha W. Driver and Sid Ray, 19–22. Jefferson: McFarland, 2004.
Gross, Jan T. *Neighbors: The Destruction of the Jewish Community in Jedwabne.* Princeton: Princeton University Press, 2001.
Grzechowiak, Jarosław. *"Na melinę* – zapomniane dzieło Stanisława Różewicza." *Panoptikum* no. 20 (2018): 193–208.

Haltof, Marek. *Polish Cinema. A History*, second, updated edition. New York – Oxford: Berghahn Books, 2019. https://nhef.pl/program/cykle/filmowa-historia-polski https://pisf.pl/wp-content/uploads/2020/04/Programy-Operacyjne-2020-zmienione-16.04.2020.pdf.

Kołodziejczak, Anna, Dorota Gołębiowska, Ewa Kanownik, and Maciej Dowgiel, eds. *Filmowe fale historii.* Łódź: Stowarzyszenie Edukacyjno-Kulturalne Venae Artis, 2016.

Korczarowska-Różycka, Natasza. *Inne spojrzenie. Wyobrażenia historii w filmach Wojciecha Jerzego Hasa, Jana Jakuba Kolskiego, Filipa Bajona i Anny Jadowskiej – studium przypadków.* Łódź: Wydawnictwo Biblioteki Państwowej Wyższej Szkoły Filmowej, Telewizyjnej i Teatralnej, Wydawnictwo Uniwersytetu Łódzkiego, 2013.

Kornacki, Krzysztof. "Współczesne polskie kino historyczne. Rekonesans," *Script* no. 3 (2019): 12–40, edited by Krzysztof Kornacki, Paweł Biliński, Adam Kamiński.

Kornacki, Krzysztof, and Piotr Kurpiewski, „Kino jako nauczyciel. Klasyfikacja działań autorskich współczesnego polskiego kina historycznego (propozycje)." In *Historia wizualna w działaniu. Studia i szkice z badań nad filmem historycznym*, edited by Dorota Skotarczak, Joanna Szczutkowska, and Piotr Kurpiewski, 59–90. Poznań: Wydział Historii UAM, 2020.

Kucharski, Krzysztof. *KINO PLUS. Film i dystrybucja kinowa w Polsce 1990–2000.* Toruń: Oficyna Wydawnicza Kucharski, 2002.

Kwiatkowski, Piotr T., Lech M. Nijakowski, Barbara Szacka, and Andrzej Szpociński. *Między codziennością a wielką historią. Druga wojna światowa w pamięci zbiorowej społeczeństwa polskiego.* Gdańsk and Warszawa: Muzeum II Wojny Światowej and Scholar, 2010.

Lewandowski, Jan F. *Historia Śląska według Kutza.* Katowice – Warszawa: Wydawnictwo Naukowe Śląsk, 2004.

Madej, Alina. *Mitologie i konwencje. O polskim kinie fabularnym dwudziestolecia międzywojennego.* Kraków: Universitas, 1994.

Pośpiech, Małgorzata. "Mit a historia. *Potop* J. Hoffmana." In *Kino – film: poezja optyczna?*, edited by Jan Trzynadlowski, 227–239. Wrocław: Wydawnictwo Uniwersytetu Wrocławskiego, 1995.

Rulka, Janusz. *Wpływ filmu na rozwój myślenia historycznego uczniów.* Bydgoszcz: Bydgoskie Towarzystwo Naukowe, 1969.

Saryusz-Wolska, Magdalena. "The Framework of Reception: Public Responses to Historical Fiction Films," *Res Historica* 50 (2020): 551–571.

Saryusz-Wolska, Magdalena. "Prasa o *Katyniu* Andrzeja Wajdy." In *Polskie piśmiennictwo filmowe*, edited by Piotr Zwierzchowski and Barbara Giza, 203–216. Bydgoszcz: Wydawnictwo Uniwersytetu Kazimierza Wielkiego, 2013.

Stróżyk, Jarosław. "Polacy chcą filmów o najnowszej historii." *Rzeczpospolita*, March 19, 2009: A3.

Wajda, Andrzej. "Moje spotkania z historią." *Film na Świecie* no. 383 (1991): 70.

Witek, Piotr. *Andrzej Wajda jako historyk. Metodologiczne studium z historii wizualnej.* Lublin: UMCS, 2016.

Wojdon, Joanna. "The Impact of Communist Rule on History Education in Poland." *Journal of Educational Media, Memory and Society* 4, no. 1 (2012): 61–77.

Wojdon, Joanna. *Textbooks as Propaganda. Poland under Communist Rule, 1944–1989.* New York: Routledge, 2018.

12 *Polandball*

Memes and Graphic Novels as Public History

Anna Borkiewicz

The Concept of the Internet Meme

The word "meme" was introduced by Richard Dawkins, a British ethologist, evolutionary biologist and author, in his 1976 book *The Selfish Gene*. According to Dawkins, a meme is the smallest unit for carrying cultural information – analogical to a gene, which is a unit for carrying biological information.

> Examples of memes are tunes, ideas, catch-phrases, clothes fashions, a way of making pots or of building arches. Just as genes propagate themselves in the gene pool by leaping from body to body via sperms or eggs, so memes propagate themselves in the meme pool by leaping from brain to brain via a process which, in the broad sense, can be called imitation. If a scientist hears or reads about a good idea, he passes it on to his colleagues and students. He mentions it in his articles and his lectures. If the idea catches on, it can be said to propagate itself, spreading from brain to brain.[1]

Memes themselves are thus older than the concept of "meme" itself. Dawkins' work was expanded upon by Richard Brodie[2] and Susan Blackmore,[3] which started a new discipline: memetics, the study of information and culture based on an analogy with Darwinian evolution. Notwithstanding its origins, nowadays the word "meme" has been almost completely appropriated by internet users and in "its current meaning describes a genre of communication, not a unit of cultural transmission."[4] Dawkins himself acknowledges "the hijacking."[5]

There are many definitions of internet memes. According to Linda Börzsei: "The internet meme is a form of visual entertainment, which can manifest in many different formats, such as a still image (for example an image macro[6]), an animated GIF, or even a video."[7] In addition, she also notes that defining internet memes is very difficult, because they are a very subjective concept.[8] Jakub Sroka defines internet memes, as

> a representation of a concept or of an idea, which can take any form from a picture to an e-mail or video, which spreads in a viral way through the

DOI: 10.4324/9781003165767-16

internet. The most popular form of a meme is a picture of a person or an animal with a funny or sarcastic caption. Most of the memes use humor and they are targeted towards teenagers and young adults, who have the highest probability of finding memes, understanding them and sharing them with friends.[9]

The newest definition comes from Bradley E. Wiggins, Associate Professor and Head of Media Department at Webster University Vienna. He defines an internet meme as a

> remixed, iterated message that can be rapidly diffused by members of participatory digital culture for the purpose of satire, parody, critique, or other discursive activity. An internet meme is a more specific term for the various iterations it represents, such as image macro memes, GIFs, hashtags, video memes, and more. Its function is to posit an argument, visually, in order to commence, extend, counter, or influence a discourse.[10]

Each definition emphasizes different aspects of the internet memes, but in this chapter the last one will be used, as in the author's opinion it is the fullest.

With this in mind, memes are one form of communication inside the internet; they are carriers of certain information as well as records of interpretations of the culture they come from. An important characteristic of internet memes is their ability to replicate. This allows them to be easily shared, spreading those cultural interpretations. If presented in an attractive or exploitable form, the internet memes can reach a vast audience around the world. Sufficiently popular memes will be remixed by subsequent users and mutate into new forms and meanings. This remix culture is significant for modern virtual communication.

Although, in the anonymity of the internet it is very difficult to identify arbitrarily the nationality of the original author/poster of a meme (especially because memes are often translated and reposted, and the authorship is not marked), Polish history turns out to be known well enough to get satirized. That is how *Polandball* started and that is what will be analyzed in this chapter.

Methodology

Historians often lack proper training in analyzing visual materials, so we have to use techniques found in other disciplines to conduct a proper analysis. As Ludmilla Jordanova[11] suggests, rather than developing a specific methodology we should seek open-ended approaches to interpret memes. She gives some guidelines, such as always asking basic questions of sources or emphasizing the importance of describing the visual materials being studied. But other than that, depending on the research questions and type of visual material, historians should work out their own methods.

As *Polandball* is a mix of an internet meme and a comic strip, I suggest an interdisciplinary research method of semiotics (looking at both text and visuals), accompanied with discourse analysis, as there is a long history in linguistics studies with such a framework being used for comics.[12] For both, the frameworks described by Gillian Rose are useful.[13] She has distinguished seven methodologies for analyzing visual materials, two of which are particularly relevant to our task: semiology and discourse analysis.

All memes in this chapter come from the vanity sites, i.e., websites whose main purpose is to provide amusement.[14] Most commonly used was *9gag* (http://9gag.com). Others come from *Reddit* (https://www.reddit.com) – a community forum where some companies also have their official pages because it has become a place for communication and discourse.

While *9gag* is a fairly international community,[15] Reddit seems to be more US-centric.[16] Neither site is strictly oriented towards historical content (although Reddit has history-related subpages), but the content of both is created, remixed, submitted and rated by its users. For better understanding the context of some memes, a website *Know Your Meme* (http://knowyourmeme.com/) was used. It is an internet encyclopedia of memes and web phenomena run by volunteer contributors. As Linda Börzsei remarks in her concise history of internet memes, it is the largest site of this type and we lack other, more complete databases.[17]

The internet memes presented in this chapter are a tiny fraction of all memes. New memes are produced every day, the sheer number of which renders it impossible to conduct proper quantitative analysis. Case studies, although flawed, are in the author's opinion a better way of writing about memes.

Memes analyzed in this chapter come from the so-called "pre-war" era of the internet. "The Great Meme War" is one of the colloquial names given to a conflict which arose between supporters of Donald Trump and Hillary Clinton around the 2016 United States Presidential Election. During the years of 2015 and 2016, the sites of Reddit and *4chan* (www.4chan.org) particularly saw a significant polarization between these opposing factions and a tremendous burst of activity which was principally reflected in a myriad of politically charged memes which saw widespread diffusion. Even though this started as a clearly American issue, it greatly affected the broader internet. Thus, post–Presidential Election 2016 memes would require separate analysis, through the lenses of memetic warfare and propaganda studies.

Polandball Memes between Comics and Caricatures

Polandball (a combination of "Poland" and "ball") is a series of memes and comic strips whose titular hero is an anthropomorphized ball decked in the colors of the Polish flag (reversed, however, with Polandball being red on top and white on the bottom as opposed to the actual orientation of the flag), which commonly speaks in broken English with a sprinkling of some of the most popular Polish swear words. According to the "Official Polandball Tutorial" from Polandball subreddit: "everything in Poland is upside down. The people, cars, trucks, even entire towns! That's why Poland is drawn upside down."[18] As the more metaphorical meaning of "upside down" may suggest, Poland is in great disorder in general, and that is how it is seen abroad.

Polandball was created in September of 2009 in Krautchan, a German imageboard, to mock the poor English language skills of a Polish user,[19] but soon afterwards it spread around the Web, and other countries were also added into the cast (as a whole called *countryballs*). The *Polandball* series is used to make fun of national stereotypes, international relationships and of course, history. The main hub of English language Polandball memes is a subpage of reddit, called "subreddit" (https://www.reddit.com/r/polandball/), the content of which is created by users from around the world. There are also smaller regional hubs throughout the web, for example the Costa Ricaball Facebook page (https://www.facebook.com/CostaRicaball506/) which concentrates on Costa Rican and Central American memes in Spanish.

Most *Polandball* memes can be analyzed both as comics and caricatures. As a general rule, *Polandball* memes follow the standard conventions seen in sequential art, i.e., comics: images laid out in panels to be read in a certain order, speech balloons to convey dialogue, etc. All memes mentioned above use panel sequencing to indicate the flow of the story, some use speech bubbles (although without "bubble" itself – the text is often written on the image itself; the only indication of who is speaking being the closeness of a dialogue to the speaker or a line connecting them). Captions indicate a year or a date that the whole comic or just one panel wants to be associated with, and onomatopoeia implies sounds (such as "Pang!" to imitate the sound of a gun).

For example, one strip starts in the year 1795, as indicated by the text in the upper left corner. We can see the Polish ball looking happy, accompanied by ominous Prussian, Habsburgian and Russian balls. Poland greats them "Hey guys!" to which Prussia responds "Hallo Polen." Both Prussian and Habsburgian balls are holding pencils. On the next panel Polandball is ripped apart by those other balls, according to sketched lines (partitions of Poland).

In a later panel, taking place already in 1918: Germanyball is exhausted by the First World War (looks beaten, is bleeding, has a black eye and a band-aid), while Russiaball is changing into the USSR (it looks as if it is struggling with a split personality). It makes contradictory statements, such as "Fuck the bourgeois!", "Red pigs!", "Tsardom!" and "Equality!" (referring to the Russian Civil War).

The post-war situation allows Polandball to be complete again and despite scars it happily expresses "Yay! Is such pretty today. I am love to live [sic]" (establishment of the Second Republic of Poland). However, this does not last for long as a dark shadow looms over Polandball and, in the panel described as 1939, Nazi Germany ball with a saw and USSRball with a pencil approach to divide Poland again. Its only response is *"kurwa"* (which can be literally translated as "whore" but can also be considered the Polish equivalent of the English expletive "fuck" when used as a noun) – a representation of the Molotov-Ribbentrop Pact and the beginning of the Second World War. But it is not the end for Polandball.

In the panel with the year 1945, Poland has a new scar and is missing an eye. At the same time USSRball now apologizes for trying to kill Poland ("Hello Poland! Sorry I am bring kill to yuo...[sic]") and explains that they are now comrades as it marks Poland with a hot iron in the shape of a hammer and sickle. This represents Poland being part of the Eastern bloc during the Cold War.

In 1989, some voice from outside the panel shouts "Solidarity! You're free!" This is a reference to the end of communism in Poland and the key role in this event of trade union Solidarity (Polish: *Solidarność*), but Polandball does not look happy. In the end, Polandball goes to the UK in search of work. UKball responds "You need a job? You can clean my shitter. Fitting. How does that make you feel?" In the last panel we can see Polandball mopping its own tears of the floor and a voice from outside the frame which says "Good little Pole, mop that floor until it shines! If you can still see your reflection then you haven't done a proper job, I don't want to see Slav!", to which Poland responds "Polan not feel anymore [sic]." Poles have become wage-slaves to the richer Western Europeans (referring to the opening of work markets in Western Europe for economic migrants from Poland after joining the EU, in this meme represented by UKball).

The fact that a meme like this surfaced on an international site like *9gag*,[20] shows us which events in Polish history are known to the international audience, and how the Polish past is present in world history context. They also provide us with some insights on the public's interpretation of the Polish past (and present): Polandball is presented as a passive object of history, rather than an active subject. Polandball's agency is limited to reacting to the realities imposed from outside.

Some historical knowledge and knowledge of this and other countries' stereotypes is required to understand *Polandball* memes. Nevertheless, the brevity of the format does not lend itself to providing detailed historical accounts, and often we see historical accuracy sacrificed in favor of unnuanced simplifications – from which a measure of humor may be derived.

In one comic Germanyball tries to produce victorious warriors in different periods of time but fails twice at first. And although the two of those three dates in this comic make sense (1939 and Nazi soldiers; 2014 with soccer players and winning the World Cup – the only victory in this comic), the first date, 1054, at least to the author's knowledge, has no particular significance in German history that could be tied to the comic. If we had to speculate, the creator of the meme just chose a random date to imply a long history of those German efforts. Historians may protest at the groundlessness of this particular date, but to the average person this is perhaps an unimportant detail parsed simply as "a long time ago," which would not impede the enjoyment of a simple comic about the 2014 soccer World Cup with a historical backdrop.

A caricature is a "comically distorted drawing or likeness, done with the purpose of satirizing or ridiculing its subject."[21] They are used primarily for conveying political commentary and for social comedy.[22] The *Polandball* memes can also be regarded as political cartoons which "in general need not represent any known political figure."[23] So a circle with a national flag on it can become a stand-in for an entire country. As caricatures, memes use exaggeration to satirize some events or characteristics (such as the above-mentioned Polish failures and defeats). Like caricatures, memes can also be regarded as a litmus test of the social climate regarding current events. For example, the comic about Germanyball was probably created around the time of the 2014 FIFA World Cup and, like a caricature, it commented on a current event with some historical humor by way of exaggerating Germany's past bellicosity, suggesting it had been sublimated into sports.

Similar in message to the strip starting in 1795 is another meme which comments on the present by contrasting it with the past. No dialogue is spoken. Polandball is chained to three other balls: Prussian, Habsburgian and Russian. Then it is chained to the German Empire, the Austro-Hungarian Empire and the Russian Empire. In the next panel, it is Nazi Germany and the USSR. In the last scene, Polandball looks like it is free of any chains. It starts to look happy, but then it notices a new set of chains: to Germany, the EU and NATO.

As mentioned above with the Costa Ricaball Facebook page, *Polandball* memes can be made about any country in any time period. Topics are limited only by a creator's creativity. Another comic takes us to an earlier period. Polandball is the Polish-Lithuanian Commonwealth ball and is wearing winged hussars' armor. In the first two panels the ball is exclaiming "Poland stronk! Poland into relevancy! Poland also king of Lithuania! So very relevancy! many of knights! King of everything! [sic]." Swedenball only looks at it with contempt. When Polandball notices Sweden it asks "Poland... king of... Sweden..? [sic]." The other ball responses "Oh no you of not [sic]" and shoots Polandball with a gun. This meme is referring to the brief personal union of the Commonwealth and the Kingdom of Sweden, until Sigismund III Vasa was removed from the throne of Sweden which started a war between these nations.

These are some of the many examples which can be collected online. They fit into a broader narrative that Polish national history is a constant string of defeats and tragedies. Starting as early as many of the Polish wars in the seventeenth century, through partition, loss of independence, the Second World War and another partition by Nazi Germany and the USSR, to forceful incorporation into the Eastern bloc and the loss of sovereignty. Those events are part of political/military history – not cultural or social.

Despite the vast cast and lack of just one protagonist, Polandball as the titular character, stars in many strips. Because of that we can easily notice how Poland is seen in the English-speaking part of the internet. Those interpretations are in the author's opinion dominant codes of Polish history abroad. A code, in semiotic meaning, "is a set of conventionalized ways of making meaning that are specific to particular groups of people."[24] A dominant code is part of the ideology and the ideology is "knowledge that is constructed in such a way as to legitimate unequal social power relations; ... Ideology is those representations that reflect the interests of power."[25] In semiology, the ideology is what we find "obvious" when interpreting. Those obviousnesses are dominant codes. In *Polandball* the dominant code is Polandball (and by proxy Poland itself) as a passive victim of history, perhaps powerful once, but now just pitiful; Poland is full of complexes (resulting from its difficult history) and longs for its past glory.[26]

Memes as Public History

Public history is often defined as history *for* the public, *by* the public, *with* the public and *about* the public,[27] and memes meet every criterion of this definition.

For the public. Memes' principal medium is the internet, they are posted on sites visited by a broad audience, mostly for amusement, even though they can also have educational value (just like other public history endeavors, i.e., historical movies, concerts or exhibitions). As mentioned earlier, they can be a political tool (e.g. the Great Meme War), so they also have the potential to become a tool for the politics of history, although this does not seem to be the case thus far, at least not with the *Polandball* memes. They are mostly satirical and self-deprecating in nature – none of the countryballs seems to be favored and all are made fun of. And it may be that this lack of didactic message makes them attractive to the audience.

Although most of the Polandball memes are made in English (which facilitates their spread all over the internet), it cannot be dismissed that some of those memes are created by Poles themself as a manifestation of self-deprecating humor, also exhibited in the memes unrelated to history, i.e., memes about a certain species of long-nosed monkey (*nasalis larvatus*) which is said to resemble the stereotypical, middle-aged male Pole.[28]

The use of humor is the memes' main advantage in comparison to traditional historical comic books. The Polish historical comic book market, in particular, is not very attractive to a typical reader. Polish historical comics are usually didactical, serious in tone and drawn realistically. Justyna Czaja, Professor of Film at Adam Mickiewicz University in media and audio-visual studies, divides them into two categories: "reporting comics" and "creational comics."[29] Reporting comics are an attempt to make "a picture textbook," showing national history but constraining the artist to realistic convention. These comics recreate facts, instead of showing them in a creative way. They often offer a simplified version of history and present the past in a straightforward, illustrative way: they do not pretend to inspire questions for readers that they may seek answers to independently. One example is *Epizody z Auschwitz* (Episodes from Auschwitz), the main purpose of which is to be didactic material. One of the reasons behind this trend may be the fact that most Polish historical comics are published by state institutions, for example, the Institute of National Remembrance (*Wrzesień pułkownika Maczka* (The September of Colonel Maczek) or the series *W imieniu Polski Walczącej* (In the Name of the Fighting Poland) and *Wilcze tropy* (Wolves' Tracks)), Ossolineum (*Kurier z Warszawy*) or Remembrance and Future Center in Wrocław (*Tajemnica Madonny z Wrocławia* (The Mystery of a Wrocław Madonna)). This type of publication imposes limitations on the artists. "Creational" comics use history to tell an interesting story: history may be just a background or a very important element of the plot, but the story itself is the focus. This type of comics is non-existent in Poland. Instead, *Polandball* fills this niche.

By the public – because, most of the time, memes are created by amateurs and laymen. Meme "templates," i.e., stripped-down versions of memes which can be filled with one's own text, are readily available online and contribute to meme proliferation by significantly lowering the bar for creation. To produce a *Polandball* meme, a high level of skill is not required. All characters are balls in the colors of a given country's national flag and the only expressive features are their eyes; countryballs do not have any other facial features and no limbs. These characteristics make them extremely easy to draw or just copy-paste. Almost anyone can contribute to this meme even using the simplest of free graphic editors. This has very likely helped *Polandball* achieve its current broad success. By way of contrast, *Polandball* was created around the same time (2009) as other webcomics about personifications of countries like the Japanese *Hetalia: Axis Powers* or the Danish *Scandinavia and the World*. Both *Hetalia*'s and *Scandinavia*'s character design is more "traditionally comic-like," making them much harder to replicate for an amateur. While both are successful in their own rights, neither is as widespread as *Polandball*.

With the public – the public is simultaneously the audience – when they browse "vanity sites" in search of the memes, and the creator – when they modify or remix existing memes. Like many other aspects of the internet, the reach and the audience reaction (shares, likes, retweets, etc.) are determinants of the success of a meme. *Polandball* definitely has "caught on" with the internet worldwide and engaged audience to participation. It is hard to tell what exactly make memes go viral: some research points out the collaborative aspect,[30] other the emotional impact.[31] *Polandball* meets both criteria as it is created by many different authors and often references emotional events (in the past and in the present).

About the public – in theory, history-related *Polandball* memes are about the past, and the subjects are the countries portrayed in them. However, they can also tell us how the past is seen by their creators (and audiences), what their ideas of the past are and what their insecurities are regarding the past and the present. Memes let us see how the past is perceived by the public, how it is understood and interpreted: as simple, unambiguous, sometimes cruel or sarcastic, often emotional and connected with the great events and dates (an effect of school education, perhaps); politically incorrect, often devoid of nuance, but also fresh and unconventional.

Conclusion

Wiggins notes

> the paradox of internet memes is that, on the one hand, they are re-markably robust units of digital culture whose utility resides in their communicative function. However, on the other hand, this function also constrains, delimits, and frames how individuals view and think about real-world events and issues.[32]

Memes will always be limited by their creators.

Both the phenomenon of internet memes and their contents can be analyzed through modern audio-visual culture. Adam Regiewicz, a researcher of medievalism in popular culture, notes that the

> contemporary user of culture – similarly to a medieval human – expresses their thought through pictures, which, in an allegorical way, render (emotionally and psychologically) hidden and inexpressible meanings. At the same time, just as their predecessors, [modern humans] avoid abstract thinking in favor of conventional forms, typological portraits, codified allegories and symbols that refer to reality, here understood as media or virtual reality.[33]

The content of history-related internet memes is trivialized and often lacks context. It is not decided by a drive to understand historical facts objectively, but rather by the author's subjective interpretation, which is then tailored for brevity and attractiveness to other users. For professional historians, the relationship between history-related internet memes and academic history can be surprising, as the success of a meme is determined by its popularity among internet users with different levels of knowledge and academic backgrounds – this popularity is often a result of an outstanding joke or of the simplification of content.

The substantially humorous manner of internet memes is a trivialization and modernization of the past. Memes remix history with contemporary popular culture, e.g., by using modern colloquial language. *Polandball* requires that a viewer have some amount of historical knowledge – without it, a joke may be difficult to comprehend. The Internet users comment on history and historical discourse using mockery and black humor. Just like newspaper caricatures in earlier eras, memes are a litmus test of social moods, mentality and memory.

It is difficult to interpret internet memes that comment on current events in isolation from the social climate and emotions at the moment of their conception. Subjectivity, sensibility and abstraction from textbook interpretation make memes a part of unconventional history[34] – existing in the realm of popular culture, next to the academic one. Interpreting history through the lens of the current moment is a crucial feature of internet memes.

Acknowledgment

The author wishes to thank Esteban E. Hernández Garay for his feedback on the entire chapter and for first-hand information on the Great Meme War.

Notes

1 Richard Dawkins, *The Selfish Gene* (Oxford: Oxford University Press, 1989), 192.
2 Richard Brodie, *Virus of the Mind: the New Science of the Meme* (Carlsbad: Hay House, 2011).
3 Susan Blackmore, *The Meme Machine* (Oxford: Oxford University Press, 2000).
4 Bradley E. Wiggins, *The Discursive Power of Memes in Digital Culture: Ideology, Semiotics, and Intertextuality* (New York: Routledge, 2019), 3.
5 Wiggins, *The Discursive Power*, 8.
6 "An image with text (generally white letters with black borders, and in Impact font) superimposed. Most widely used format for e.g. LOL-Cats." (Linda Börzsei, "Makes a Meme Instead: A Concise History of Internet Memes," *New Media Studies Magazine*, Utrecht University (2013): 5, accessed March 15, 2021, https://www.academia.edu/3649116/Makes_a_Meme_Instead_A_Concise_History_of_Internet_Memes.
7 Börzsei, "Makes a Meme," 5.
8 Börzsei, "Makes a Meme," 4.
9 Jakub Sroka, *#OBRAZKOWE #MEMY #INTERNETOWE* (Warsaw: CeDeWu, 2014), 33-34. Author's translation. In Polish: "Mem internetowy to, przybierająca formę począwszy od obrazka, skończywszy na wiadomości e-mail lub pliku wideo, reprezentacja pojęcia lub idei, która w sposób wirusowy rozprzestrzenia się pomiędzy osobami za pośrednictwem Internetu. Najpopularniejszą formą memu jest obraz osoby lub zwierzęcia opatrzony zabawnym lub uszczypliwym podpisem. Większość posługuje się humorem i apeluje głównie do nastolatków i młodych dorosłych, którzy wykazują największe prawdopodobieństwo ich odkrycia, zrozumienia humoru, a także przekazania dalej swoim znajomym."
10 Wiggins, *The Discursive Power*, 11.
11 Ludmilla Jordanova, "Approaching Visual Materials," in *Research Methods for History*, ed. Simon Gunn and Lucy Faire (Edinburgh: Edinburgh University Press, 2012), 31–51, 47.
12 Hannah Miodrag, *Comics and Language: Reimagining Critical Discourse on the Form* (Jackson: University Press of Mississippi, 2013), 11.

13 Gillian Rose, *Visual Methodologies: An Introduction to Researching with Visual Materials* (Los Angeles: Sage, 2016).

14 Magdalena Kamińska, *Niecne memy: Dwanaście wykładów o kulturze Internetu* (Poznań: Galeria Miejska Arsenał, 2011), 65.

15 "9gag," SimilarWeb. Website Traffic – Check and Analyze any Website, accessed February 22, 2021, https://www.similarweb.com/website/9gag.com/#overview.

16 "Reddit.com," SimilarWeb. Website Traffic – Check and Analyze any Website, accessed February 22, 2021, https://www.similarweb.com/website/reddit.com/.

17 Börzsei, "Makes a Meme" 4.

18 "Official Polandball Tutorial," accessed February 23, 2021, https://imgur.com/dcW9rpR.

19 "Polandball" Know Your Meme, accessed February 23, 2021, https://knowyourmeme.com/memes/polandball.

20 "Poor Poland." 9GAG, 11 April 2015, accessed March 9, 2021, https://9gag.com/gag/aD3VPOK.

21 Winslow Ames, "Caricature and Cartoon," in *Encyclopædia Britannica*, accessed March 9, 2021, https://www.britannica.com/art/caricature-and-cartoon.

22 Ames, "Caricature."

23 Perkins, David. "A Definition of Caricature and Caricature and Recognition," *Studies in Visual Communication* 2, no. 1 (1975): 1.

24 Rose, *Visual Methodologies*, 88.

25 Rose, *Visual Methodologies*, 70.

26 Wojciech Oleksiak, "Polandball – A Case Study," *Culture.pl*, accessed February 23, 2021, https://culture.pl/en/article/polandball-a-case-study.

27 Barbara Franco, "Public History and Memory: A Museum Perspective," *The Public Historian* 19, no. 2 (1997): 65.

28 Bartosz Godziński, "Nosacz a sprawa polska. Dlaczego małpy stały się tłem do popularnych memów o Polakach?," *naTemat.pl*, accessed February 23, 2021, https://natemat.pl/210833,co-ma-nosacz-do-polaka-malpa-z-borneo-bohaterem-przesmiewczej-serii-memow.

29 Justyna Czaja, *Historia Polski w komiksowych kadrach* (Poznań: Wydawnictwo Poznańskiego Towarzystwa Przyjaciół Nauk, 2010), 253.

30 Michele Coscia, "Competition and Success in the Meme Pool: A Case Study on Quickmeme.com," accessed March 9, 2021, http://www.michelecoscia.com/wp-content/uploads/2013/03/icwsm13.pdf.

31 Jonah A. Berger and Katherine L. Milkman, "What Makes Online Content Viral?" *Journal of Marketing Research* 49, no. 2 (2012), 192.

32 Wiggins, *The Discursive Power*, 157.

33 Adam Regiewicz, *Mediewializm wobec zjawisk audiowizualnych i nowych mediów* (Warszawa: DiG, 2014), 67. Author's translation. In Polish: "współczesny użytkownik kultury – podobnie jak człowiek średniowiecza – wyraża swoje myśli za pomocą obrazów, które w sposób alegoryczny oddają istotę i sens ukrytych, niewyrażalnych (szczególnie na płaszczyźnie emocjonalnej i psychologicznej) znaczeń. Jednocześnie, tak samo jak jego poprzednik, ucieka od myślenia abstrakcyjnego w konwencjonalne formy, typologiczne przedstawienia, skodyfikowane alegorie i symbole, mające swoje odniesienie do rzeczywistości rozumianej tu także jako rzeczywistość medialna czy Wirtualna."

34 Ewa Domańska, *Historie niekonwencjonalne. Refleksja o przeszłości w nowej humanistyce* (Poznań: Wydawnictwo Poznańskie, 2006), 61–66.

Bibliography

"9gag." SimilarWeb. Website Traffic – Check and Analyze any Website. Accessed February 22, 2021. https://www.similarweb.com/website/9gag.com/#overview.

Ames, Winslow. "Caricature and Cartoon." Encyclopædia Britannica. Accessed March 9, 2021. https://www.britannica.com/art/caricature-and-cartoon.

Berger, Jonah A., and Katherine L. Milkman. "What Makes Online Content Viral?" *Journal of Marketing Research* 49, no. 2 (2012): 192–205.

Blackmore, Susan. *The Meme Machine.* Oxford: Oxford University Press, 2000.

Brodie, Richard. *Virus of the Mind: The New Science of the Meme.* Carlsbad: Hay House, 2011.

Börzsei, Linda. "Makes a Meme Instead: A Concise History of Internet Memes." *New Media Studies Magazine,* Utrecht University, 2013. https://www.academia.edu/3649116/Makes_a_Meme_Instead_A_Concise_History_of_Internet_Memes.

Coscia, Michele. "Competition and Success in the Meme Pool: A Case Study on Quickmeme.com," 2013. Accessed March 9, 2021 http://www.michelecoscia.com/wp-content/uploads/2013/03/icwsm13.pdf.

Czaja, Justyna. *Historia Polski w komiksowych kadrach.* Poznań: Wydawnictwo Poznańskiego Towarzystwa Przyjaciół Nauk, 2010.

Dawkins, Richard. *The Selfish Gene.* Oxford: Oxford University Press, 1989.

Domańska, Ewa. *Historie niekonwencjonalne. Refleksja o przeszłości w nowej humanistyce.* Poznań: Wydawnictwo Poznańskie, 2006.

Franco, Barbara. "Public History and Memory: A Museum Perspective." *The Public Historian* 19, no. 2 (1997): 65–67.

Godziński, Bartosz. "Nosacz a sprawa polska. Dlaczego małpy stały się tłem do popularnych memów o Polakach?" *naTemat.pl.* Accessed February 23, 2021. https://natemat.pl/210833,co-ma-nosacz-do-polaka-malpa-z-borneo-bohaterem-przesmiewczej-serii-memow.

Jordanova, Ludmilla. "Approaching Visual Materials." In *Research Methods for History,* edited by Simon Gunn and Lucy Faire, 31–51. Edinburgh: Edinburgh University Press, 2012.

Kamińska Magdalena. *Niecne Memy: Dwanaście wykładów o kulturze Internetu.* Poznań: Galeria Miejska Arsenał, 2011.

Miodrag, Hannah. *Comics and Language: Reimagining Critical Discourse on the Form.* Jackson: University Press of Mississippi, 2013.

"Official Polandball Tutorial." Accessed February 23, 2021. https://imgur.com/dcW9rpR.

Oleksiak, Wojciech. "Polandball – A Case Study." *Culture.pl.* Accessed February 23, 2021. https://culture.pl/en/article/polandball-a-case-study.

Perkins, David. "A Definition of Caricature and Caricature and Recognition." *Studies in Visual Communication* 2, no. 1 (1975): 1–24.

"Polandball." Know Your Meme. Accessed February 23, 2021. https://knowyourmeme.com/memes/polandball.

"Reddit.com." SimilarWeb. Website Traffic – Check and Analyze any Website. Accessed February 22, 2021. https://www.similarweb.com/website/reddit.com/.

Regiewicz, Adam. *Mediewializm wobec zjawisk audiowizualnych i nowych mediów.* Warszawa: DiG, 2014.

Rose, Gillian. *Visual Methodologies: An Introduction to Researching with Visual Materials.* Los Angeles: Sage, 2016.

Sroka, Jakub. *#OBRAZKOWE #MEMY #INTERNETOWE.* Warszawa: CeDeWu, 2014.

Wiggins, Bradley E. *The Discursive Power of Memes in Digital Culture: Ideology, Semiotics, and Intertextuality.* New York: Routledge, 2019.

13 The Historical Reenactment Movement in Poland and Its Specificity

Filip Wolański

Over the last 40 years, various trends of historical reconstruction have developed dynamically in Poland, and they can be characterized both from the perspective of epochs and cultural circles which fascinate the enthusiasts involved in them and in connection with the forms of reenactment they practice. Transitions occurring in the characteristics of the historical reenactment movement in Poland are similar to the same processes taking place worldwide, but they are not devoid of their own characteristics. In Poland, several thousand people are concentrated in various types of reconstruction groups and organizations, along with the associations that support them. According to the Report prepared at the request of the Ministry of Culture and National Heritage by the Social Research Bureau "Question Mark," in 2016 there were at least 458 active reconstruction groups in Poland. The authors of the report concluded that due to the lack of specific information on some groups, their number may in fact be even twice as high. In this case, cautious estimates seem justified, given that 536 Polish reconstruction groups were registered in the voluntary online register for reenaction performers known as the *Great Registration of Robert Bagrit* in the years 2001–2015. Assuming that the average group consists of ten people, it was calculated that Poland could have over 5,000 historical reenactors.[1] Given the findings of the Report and the fact that its authors have adopted a similar assumption, the number of active actors may range from 5,000 to 10,000. The analysis of the scale on which events are organized in Poland shows their clear and dynamic growth. While in 2011 there were 110 events throughout the country, in 2016 this had grown to approximately 330.[2] The exact numbers seem to be less important in this case, as what is key is the fact that this type of activity is systematically growing in popularity.

The beginnings of the historical reenactment movement in Poland are associated with the activity of Zygmunt Kwiatkowski (who died in 2005), the president of the local branch of the Polish Tourist and Sightseeing Society, which has been organizing a knightly tournament at the castle in Golub-Dobrzyń since 1977. Golub-Dobrzyń is a small town located in northern Poland, the main tourist attraction of which is its medieval castle. In the

DOI: 10.4324/9781003165767-17

past, the city was located on the border of Poland and Prussia. The tournaments that have been organized at the castle for over 50 years have helped to develop the tradition of Polish historical reenactment of the Middle Ages.[3] The activity of the actors gathered in the community created by Zygmunt Kwiatkowski have also given rise to what can be described as introducing history into public space. On the other hand, the first reconstruction group which supported the organization of a large outdoor event was the "Brotherhood of the Sword and the Crossbow," which still exists in Warsaw to this day. In 1992, it co-organized a tournament in Stębark for the anniversary of the Battle of Grunwald.[4]

The movement of historical reenactment is of great interest to the Polish academic community, as reflected in the shaping of theoretical reflection on this subject and the related polemics. Using the concept of historical reenactment over historical reconstruction in Polish literature was proposed by Michał Bogacki, referring to the translation of the English term of "historical reenactment." In his articles, however, he emphasized the use of other names by Polish researchers and popularizers, e.g., the chivalry movement or historical recreation, which should not be used due to imprecision or too narrow a meaning.[5] There have also been views according to which historical reconstructions are "edutainment," understood as a form of historical education conducted through entertainment addressed not only to young people but also to adults.[6]

Considerations on the precise name of the phenomenon do not exhaust the theoretical reflection on it. Polish researchers have also proposed their own typologies of native reenactment. Bogacki divides the reenactment into two main streams: combat reenactment and living history.[7] Some people add experimental archaeology to the activity of reenactors of old epochs,[8] however, the dominant view is that this type of term can only be used for research activities carried out by professional archeologists working at universities.[9] Apart from the above-mentioned approaches, Adam Regiewicz emphasizes the role of historical reenactment in two plans: one centered around recreating artifacts of material culture, and the other, broader one, of visualizing the past.[10]

Typology is also carried out due to the degree of professionalization of the historical reenactors. In such approaches, attention is drawn to the degree of involvement of actors in living history tourism. Bogacki proposes a distinction relating to categorized actors, due to the level of historical knowledge and the level of involvement in the activities of the groups to which they belong. The researcher distinguishes professionals with very extensive historical knowledge and argues that: "In certain situations, actions taken at this level may have some potential for the development of the state of research."[11] This proposal corresponds to the opinions expressed by Igor Górewicz, who also tends to assess highly the capabilities of the performers whose reenactments can serve as a source of knowledge for experimental archaeology.[12] The second group is made up of performers with a good level of historical knowledge, which does not differ drastically from the state of knowledge about a given epoch. Finally, the third group consists of actors who differ in their approach to the state of research on the past, or are ignorant of it.[13] Using the above-described thought, it is also possible to propose a perspective on the movement of historical reenactment in Poland based on the types of practiced activity, which also define it. From this point of view, the trends in Poland can be divided primarily into: reenactment focused on the staging of military history; reenactment focused on everyday life; and sporting events. Assuming this division for historical reenactors, we can consider those who participate in these forms of activity because of their passion, and this may turn a hobby into a profession. Due to its social function, historical reenactments are an important way of disseminating history in public spaces.

Historical Reenactment in Poland – Military

Medieval Military

In Poland, the historical reenactment of the Middle Ages has enjoyed unflagging popularity for many years. Early medieval times seem particularly appealing, including references to the Viking and Piast tradition, connected with the Slavic one. This kind of reenactment refers to the history of the formation of the state ruled by the Piast dynasty, which in the tenth and eleventh centuries gave rise to the future Kingdom of Poland. The connections between Piasts and Vikings, who supported the Slavic princes as mercenaries, make it possible to combine reenactments referring to the history of Poland with Scandinavian elements, which are extremely popular all over the world. This advantage is eagerly used by reenactors in Poland. There is also an extremely dynamic reenactment movement focusing on late medieval times. It owes its importance largely to the memory of the Battle of Grunwald (in the German historical tradition – at Tannenberg), fought in 1410 between the troops of the Teutonic Order (the Order of the Hospital of Our Lady of the German House in Jerusalem) and the combined armies of the Kingdom of Poland and the Grand Duchy of Lithuania. The defeat of the Order, which resulted in a change of the balance of power in this part of Europe, appears in Polish historical memory as a symbol of the victorious struggle with the threat of German expansion to the East. It is also widely considered the most important battle in medieval Polish history. The impact of the Grunwald tradition can be seen as a major element of fourteenth- and fifteenth-century chivalry culture that has influenced the development of many reenactment groups.

When writing about the importance of the Grunwald tradition in Polish historical memory, one should clarify how different it is from the German one. The memory of the medieval battle competes with the memory of the German-Russian struggle in the same area during the First World War. The Battle of Tannenberg, in which the troops of Field Marshals Paul von

Hindenburg and Erich Ludendorff defeated the Russian armies in August 1914 was treated by German historiography before the Second World War as a kind of rematch for the defeat of the Teutonic Order.

Modern Military

The early modern period is less popular, although there are groups that recreate not only the military formations of the sixteenth and seventeenth centuries, but even the royal guards from the Saxon era. This trend of historical reenactment refers to the tradition of the Polish-Lithuanian Commonwealth. One of the difficulties faced by the enthusiasts involved in it is the fact that the majority of Polish troops at that time were cavalry, which entails high costs. Despite these issues, in 2010 groups specializing in recreating the cavalry formation appeared, including the Hussar banners used in the staging of the Battle of Kłuszyn, organized near Warsaw with about 60 riders participating. What is surprising is that there are groups reenacting the formations dating to the reign of the Saxon Wettin dynasty in Poland (1697–1763). In Polish historiography, this period is viewed as the complete collapse of the military in the country. During this time, the army was reduced to several thousand soldiers, and its organizational breakdown is considered by historians to be one of the reasons for the partitions of the First Polish Republic in the eighteenth century.

Other popular eras for reenactment groups are the Napoleonic era, the uprisings against the partitioning powers in the nineteenth century and the battles for independence after the end of the First World War. The Napoleonic period in the Polish historical tradition is associated with the first heroic attempts to regain independence after the partitions of Poland at the end of the eighteenth century. The Polish national anthem also has its origins in this period. Reenactors recall and recreate the participation of the Poles in wars on the side of Napoleon's army. On the other hand, references to the tradition of national uprisings concern tragic events in the history of the Polish struggle, primarily with Russia (the November Uprising 1830–1831 and the January Uprising 1863–1864). In 2018, much attention was paid to the Greater Poland Uprising of 1918 because of the centenary of its outbreak. It is worth adding that this fight against Germany, which was additionally defeated in the First World War, is widely considered the only victorious Polish uprising. Historical reenactments of the insurgent tradition are very often supported by state institutions. There are groups referring to the activity of Poles within the structures of the partitioning states. As a result, we can see references to the Austro-Hungarian monarchy in Kraków or to the Prussian or German military before the First World War in Poznań.

Military of the Second World War

The greatest numbers of historical reenactors are involved in groups preoccupied with the twentieth century, especially the period of the Second

World War. It should be emphasized, however, that this event is associated with extremely traumatic experiences from the perspective of Polish society. Most of the performers refer to the episodes of the war that are particularly relevant for the Polish people. This includes the Polish campaign of 1939 fought against Germany and the Soviet Union, actions of the underground army against both occupiers, combat of Polish military formations in the West in the structures of the Allied forces and finally the Polish formations fighting on the Eastern Front together with the Soviet Army. In this context, references to local traditions and regional history are also essential. For example, in Warsaw, references are made to the Warsaw Uprising started by the Polish underground Home Army in 1944, and in Wrocław to the siege of the city by the Soviet army in 1945. Closely connected to the events of the Second World War is the participation of historical reenactors in staging the anti-communist underground's battles against the new political order after the end of regular military operations.[14]

Living History in Polish Historical Reenactment

Activities concerning military and political events are connected with the performances of groups staging everyday life (living history). A lot of attention is given to this kind of reenactment by enthusiasts of ancient periods, especially of the Middle Ages and the early modern era. The question arises as to the scope of such activities. Recreating everyday life in the conditions of the Polish historical reenactment movement should be associated with a fascination with the past, but also with the commercial dimension of events related to military reenactments. People dealing with handicrafts and creating artifacts needed for the staging work are often members of the reenactment groups or cooperate with them. Their work goes to the performers or becomes available for sale. Occasional, and especially cyclical, events with performers from all over Poland and abroad provide opportunities for this type of commercial activity. Another sales opportunity appears on the occasion of workshops addressed to people interested in the history of craftsmanship, cuisine or simply everyday life in the past.

The above-mentioned creators, despite their knowledge and the professional nature of the undertaken activity, cannot be included in the current of experimental archaeology or, more broadly, experiments on learning about the conditions of life in the past. This is mainly due to the specificity of the production carried out as part of the activity of reconstruction groups, the aim of which is to popularize history and not to reconstruct artifacts with the use of scientific methods. Another problem is the lack of support from academia, which is an effect of the lack of a deeper understanding of historical reenactment as a social and research need. At the moment, in Poland, there are no formalized or institutionalized research directions in the field of experimental archaeology comparable with the likes of the British ones at the Universities of Exeter or Sheffield.[15]

The Most Important Cyclical Events in Poland
Attended by Historical Reenactors

Every year in Poland, there is an opportunity for historical reenactors to participate in various types of cyclical and occasional events, either directly addressed to their community or those in which their participation is considered indispensable. This activity can be perceived as a manifestation of their role as popularizers of history in public space.

The staging of the Battle of Grunwald held in July holds the status of the largest cyclical event (the anniversary of the battle falls on July 15). The event has been organized continuously since 1998, initially by a group of enthusiasts who received institutional support, among others, from the Museum of the Battle of Grunwald in Stębark (a branch of the Museum of Warmia and Mazury in Olsztyn) and local government authorities. The staging in 2021 was to be co-organized by a number of groups, including the local government authorities of the Warmian-Masurian Voivodeship, the Grunwald Foundation established specifically for this purpose and the Historical Theater of "*Chorągiew Komturstwa Gniewskiego*," responsible for the historical reenactment.[16] Additional co-organizers consist of the Museum of the Battle of Grunwald in Stębark and the National Cultural Center, which is a government agency operating at the Ministry of Culture and National Heritage. The invent was cancelled, however, due to the COVID-19 pandemic.[17]

Due to the level of success that the staging had reached at the beginning of the twenty-first century, it quickly gained an international ranking. In addition to the appeal of the spectacular outdoor event, the reasons for the aforementioned success should also be seen in the history shared between the inhabitants of this part of Europe (Poles, Germans, Lithuanians, Belarusians, Ukrainians). In this case, a common past does not mean a common memory, as there are significant differences in the interpretation of the battle's meaning in individual countries. The reasons behind it can be found in the perspectives adopted by individual national historiographies. There is no doubt that the battle is of the greatest importance for Poles, Lithuanians and Belarusians, and the axis of the dispute is the role of Polish and the Grand Duchy of Lithuania troops (Lithuanian-Belarusian) in the battle and the consequences of winning the battle. Despite these differences, Grunwald, as a symbol of identity, integrates rather than divides contemporary historical performers from different countries.

The "Grunwald Days," organized in connection with the staging, are an opportunity to meet Polish and foreign actors. They enable the meeting of enthusiasts who are not only interested in the military aspects of late medieval history, but also in recreating details of everyday life. The battle is preceded by several days of events that include workshops with craftsmanship demonstrations in the so-called craftsmen's camp, which is connected with the commercial dimension of this type of event. Creators of artifacts required by reconstruction groups have the opportunity not only to sell their products for several days, but also to collect future orders. Among the craftsmen operating on the fields of Grunwald, there are blacksmiths/ armorers, weavers, potters, black gunpowder producers, shoemakers, jewelers, brewers and makers of food products.[18] Some, such as a group/company called SPES Medieval Market, declare that they specialize in "the manufacture of items related to the recreation of everyday life in the Middle Ages," ensuring that they "try to make their products as compatible with the realities of those times as possible. The most important element of this work is the study of historical sources and, on their basis, the development of fully functional objects of reconstruction."[19] For this type of activity, the organizers charge fees depending on the scope of commercial and production activity, though some producers are exempt from fees.

During the "Days of Grunwald" there is also a tournament with the use of various types of medieval weapons, such as bows and long swords, as well as firearms. The competition is attended by representatives of reenactment groups from different countries, and it can be considered a sporting activity. An example can be the "Grunwald Sword and Shield Battle Tournament" which was granted the status of the Open Polish Championship in Knight Fighting.[20] There are also shows and competitions addressed to the general public. Examples include chess tournaments using medieval boards and rules of the game. Concerts and workshops are organized, during which visitors can listen to Gregorian chants and take part in the preparation of performing one of them for an audience.

Every year, up to 2,000 performers from various European countries are involved in the staging of the battle. The scale of this event is evidenced by the fact that, for example, in 2017 actors from Poland, Germany, Italy, France, Finland, the Czech Republic, Slovakia, Hungary, Russia, Belarus, Ukraine and the United States announced their participation in it. Before the battle, one can see the long list of participants of the staging, who are organized under Polish-Lithuanian and Teutonic banners (*chorągiew*) referring to the historical realities of the conflict.[21] The number of viewers arriving to watch the staging every year is estimated at around 100,000.[22]

Another cyclical event is the festival organized on the island of Wolin, as part of the activities carried out by the "Center of Slavs and Vikings Wolin-Jómsborg-Vineta," addressed to enthusiasts of the early Middle Ages. Wolin is a city located at the mouth of the Oder River to the Baltic Sea. In the early Middle Ages, it was an important trade center, inhabited by the Slavs, very strongly associated with Scandinavia, primarily with Denmark. Wolin was also mentioned in many Viking sagas. Polish princes from the Piast dynasty tried to conquer the city in the tenth and twelfth centuries, making it temporarily dependent on several occasions. The wealth of Wolin was the source of many legends, and contemporary archaeological and historical research confirms the great importance of this center in the western part of the Baltic Sea.[23]

In 2019, the 25th Festival of Slavs and Vikings was organized. The 2020 Festival had to be cancelled due to the pandemic. In Wolin, the Viking tradition is particularly strongly emphasized, although there are many references to early Piast or, more broadly, Slavic tradition as well. Much attention is paid to combat shows. In 2016, according to the organizers, a total of about 400 performers participated in them. In addition to fights, numerous workshops and shows are organized, including crafts or culinary shows. The event, lasting several days, abounds in lectures, meetings with authors and chronicle readings. One can watch a staging of everyday life, including rituals such as *swaćba*, meaning a wedding ceremony.[24]

The number of local events that are co-organized by historical actors is growing. An example of such initiatives may be events in Silesia referring to the tradition associated with the local fortresses, such as Kłodzko, Koźle or Srebrna Góra. The above mentioned festival organized in Wolin follows this trend. Reconstruction groups have good conditions for action, and often receive logistical assistance or accommodation, and a certain organizational, and to some extent, financial stabilization. The demand of local communities for this type of activity and popularization of history is systematically growing, and local governments are beginning to notice the benefits of promoting the city, commune or region in this way. The role of historical reenactment understood in this manner fits into the concept of cultural tourism, especially what is referred to as living history tourism[25] or archaeological tourism.[26] The importance of this type of activity is on a steady increase.

International Involvement of Polish Historical Reenactors

For many years, members of Polish reconstruction groups have taken part in great international events that can serve as models from which Polish historical reenactors can learn. The first international cooperation of this kind took place in the 1980s when, at the initiative of Zygmunt Kwiatkowski, a Polish-Italian knight tournament was fought in Arezzo.[27]

In the Czech Republic, the staging of the Battle of Austerlitz is organized periodically at the turn of November and December. It is attended by Napoleonic military enthusiasts from different countries, including Poland, and the number of Polish groups that participate has been rising. In 2019, almost 200 out of 1,000 performers gathered in the fields around Slavkov came from Poland.[28] The year 2015 marked the 200th anniversary of the Battle of Waterloo, which became the reason for organizing a spectacular performance, attended by numerous Polish actors who recreated an infantry unit that was even supported by a chaplain. Similar large-scale performances were planned as celebrations of anniversaries related to the remembrance of Napoleonic campaigns, such as the battles of Leipzig and Borodino. Poles were present during all the great anniversary stagings in 2012–2015, organized in Germany, Russia, the Czech Republic, Belgium and other countries.

In the context of cyclical, large-scale events addressed to historical reen-actors, it is necessary to mention perhaps the world's oldest staging of this type in Gettysburg in commemoration of the 1863 battle of the American Civil War. Polish actors have been joining the battle performance for years.[29] They are also present at the stagings that take place in Russia, which are characterized by a unique momentum and even by official support from public institutions. Events of this kind primarily reference the period of the two World Wars. For some time, they have been organized, for example, in the Patriot Park in Kubinka, located 80 km south-west of Moscow, which was created specifically for this purpose.

Historical Reenactment as a Sport

It would be challenging to present a complete picture of the historical reen-actment movement in Poland without recalling its competitive aspect. This element is present not only during traditional events of historical reconstruc-tions, but especially during events dedicated to people interested in sporting activities. Some of the enthusiasts involved in this type of recreation have made their hobby a profession that can be compared with competitive sport.

There is the "Polish League of Knight Fighting" which organizes a se-ries of tournaments to select the Polish champion in knight fighting.[30] It primarily involves fencing with various types of white weapons. Details on the activities of the League can be found on Facebook and Twitter.[31] Due to the situation caused by the pandemic, the league's activity was severely re-stricted in 2020. Another opportunity to engage in this type of competition is the Fire and Steel Olympics. These are Open Polish Championships in Extreme Knight Fighting organized in Fort Bema in Warsaw, and, among others, in Nowy Dwór Mazowiecki.

The Polish National Team of Medieval Combat (*Rycerska Kadra Polski*) is active in international competitions of similar groups from all over the world. On its website, we read that "[it] is a group of about 50 best fighting women and men selected in the Polish League of Knight Fighting." Repre-sentatives of this group have won medals at the Battle of the Nations world championships, organized by the HMBIA (Historical Medieval Battle International Association) and the IMCF (International Medieval Combat Federation) world championships.[32]

Criticism of Historical Reenactment in Poland

Historical reenactment, as a social phenomenon relevant to the cultivation of memory and images of the past, receives mixed opinions, ranging from enthusiastic to extremely unfavorable. The dangers that are most often cited in connection with the activities of reconstruction groups include superficial interpretation of staged events, potential commercialization of this type of activity and finally, the possibility of using it for political purposes.

Regarding the first issue, professional historians emphasize a simplified image of the past created as a result of the activity of reenactment groups. They observe a disproportion resulting from an excessive focus on details and a superficial approach to deeper processes that the historical events refer to. Among other accusations connected with the superficial treatment of history, we can find repeated comments on the overrepresentation of men and marginalization of women in the reconstruction movement. Women are viewed as playing only auxiliary functions in groups that are preoccupied with recreating events of a military nature. Excessive focus on the military is also criticized, stating that the reenactors favor elite units, e.g., the aforementioned old Polish hussars, or paratrooper and commando formations in the twentieth century. Superficial and, consequently, irresponsible interpretations of history are connected with the lack of understanding of the ban for using symbols of military units considered to be participants in genocide or war crimes. An example is the particularly controversial appearance of the markings of the Nazi SS formations during the Second World War.

The threat of commercialization must be connected with the phenomenon of superficial treatment of history, which results from treating the produced artifacts as an element of contemporary pop culture. The success of this activity may lead to the mass production of such items and the loss of its crucial asset, which is the uniqueness of a highly specialized handicraft. The participation of living history actors in numerous events and striving to turn their passion into a profession poses a risk of reducing the quality of manufactured products in order to meet the expectations of the mass audience.

Lastly, there is the question of the instrumental treatment of reconstruction groups by politicians. This is connected with how politicians tend to approach difficult topics in modern history and introduce them into public debate. Kamila Baraniecka-Olszewska has recently drawn attention to this type of threat in Poland, describing the instrumental treatment of the history of the Second World War by the ruling political elite in Poland.[33] Reenactment groups specializing in recreating the events of this period are used to popularize the image of history only from the perspective of one side of the political life. Such practices lead to a superficial, simplified depiction of tragic events, the historical interpretation of which is very complex. The question that should be asked is whether historical reenactors are prepared to take on such difficult and ambiguous challenges.

Conclusions

The popularity of historical reenactments in the world has been growing for many years, mainly resulting from the dynamic development of their forms and communities of practice.[34] Today, this type of movement cannot be limited to staging battles and military events, although it is these activities that make historical reenactment so iconic.[35] The complex nature of this phenomenon is evidenced by the existence of numerous groups of performers who are primarily involved in recreating everyday practices, including crafts, cuisine and rites of passage (e.g. weddings, funerals), but also ceremonial events, such as coronations.[36] Another side of this phenomenon are sporting events in which historical costumes and combat techniques are used in professional competitions or semi-amateur groups of actors competing in various leagues and championships, both on a national and international level. Historical reenactment understood in this way should be treated not only as a movement focused on military history, but more broadly on social history, or the history of material culture and even sport. It aims to popularize history in the public space. The number of associations and groups engaged in these activities proves the great social demand for learning about history where stress is put on the experience.[37] The popularity of historical reenactment is manifested by cyclical festivals and events organized by the milieu of historical reenactors. Moreover, such performances are welcomed by local communities and local government authorities at the municipal or city level, as well as by state-owned authorities at the highest levels. This is probably due to purely utilitarian reasons, such as the benefits of tourism promotion. Historical reenaction shapes the collective memory in an extremely vivid way, and the message sent by performers fits into various aspects of the historical narrative about the past of cities, regions and the state. In some cases, this form of creating historical memory is an expression of the politics of history.

Notes

1 Michał Bogacki, "Historical Reenactment jako nowy sposób prezentacji przeszłości," *Do broni! Magazyn Rekonstrukcji Historycznych* no. 4 (2006): 20.
2 https://www.nck.pl/badania/raporty/raport-grupy-rekonstrukcji-historycznych-dzialania-oddolne-na-rzecz-krzewienia-, accessed May 15, 2021.
3 http://zamekgolub.pl/turnieje.html, accessed May 15, 2021.
4 Małgorzata Skotnicka-Palka, "Powtarzamy powtórzone. Rekonstrukcje historyczne," *Pamięć i Przyszłość* 26, no. 4 (2014): 62.
5 Michał Bogacki, "O współczesnym 'ożywianiu' przeszłości – charakterystyka odtwórstwa historycznego," *Turystyka Kulturowa* no. 5 (2010): 4–6; Bogacki, "Historical Reenactment," 34–37.
6 Adam Regiewicz, "Rekonstrukcje historyczne jako edutainment. Przypadek powstania styczniowego," *Prace Naukowe Akademii im. Jana Długosza w Częstochowie, Filologia Polska. Historia i Teoria Literatury* 13 (2013): 90.
7 Bogacki, "O współczesnym" 2010: 17; Michał Pawleta, "Rekonstrukcje i inscenizacje przeszłości w perspektywie turystyki archeologicznej w Polsce," in *Skanseny archeologiczne i archeologia eksperymentalna*, ed. Jan Gancarski (Krosno: Muzeum Podkarpackie, 2012), 375.
8 Igor Górewicz, "Profesjonalizacja odtwórstwa historycznego. Wystawy edukacyjne jako poszerzenia instrumentarium popularyzacji historii," in *Gospodarka ludów Morza Bałtyckiego*, vol. I, *Starożytność i średniowiecze*, ed. Michał Bogacki, Maciej Franz, and Zbigniew Pilarczyk (Toruń: Adam Marszałek, 2009), 341–365.

9 Bogacki, "O współczesnym" 2010: 17–18. Cf. the chapter by Anna I. Zalewska in this volume.
10 Regiewicz, "Rekonstrukcje," 91.
11 Bogacki, "O współczesnym," 19.
12 Górewicz, "Profesjonalizacja," 341.
13 Bogacki, "O współczesnym," 18–19.
14 Kamila Baraniecka-Olszewska, "On the Performative Power of Stereotypes. WWII Historical Re-enactment and National Identities." *Revue des Études Sud-Est Européennes* 57, no. 1–4 (2019): 51–61.
15 https://web.archive.org/web/20111207075307/http://humanities.exeter.ac.uk/ archaeology/research/themes/experimentalarchaeology/, accessed May 15, 2021. https://web.archive.org/web/20101018055821/http://www.shef.ac.uk/archaeology/ prospectivepg/masters/experimental.html, accessed May 15, 2021.
16 http://teatrhistoryczny.pl/, accessed May 15, 2021.
17 http://www.grunwald1410.pl/index.php?cat=6, accessed May 30, 2021.
18 http://www.grunwald1410.pl/index.php?cat=151, accessed May 15, 2021.
19 http://www.grunwald1410.pl/index.php?mod=Rzemieslnik&rId=2129, accessed May 15, 2021.
20 http://www.grunwald1410.pl/index.php?art=9, accessed May 15, 2021.
21 http://www.grunwald1410.pl/index.php?art=1, accessed May 15, 2021.
22 www.muzeumgrunwald.fbrothers.com/inscenizacja-bitwy/#oinscenalizacji, accessed May 15, 2021.
23 Władysław Filipowiak, "Some Aspects of the Development of Wolin in the 8th–11th Centuries in the Light of the Results of New Research," in *Polish Lands at the Turn of the First and the Second Millennium*, ed. Przemysław Urbańczyk (Warszawa: IAiE PAN, 2004), 47–74.
24 https://wolinwsieci.jomsborg-vineta.com/, accessed May 15, 2021.
25 Bogacki, "O współczesnym," 4.
26 Pawleta, "Rekonstrukcje," 364–385.
27 https://historia.org.pl/2015/07/10/najstarszy-turniej-rycerski-in Poland/, accessed May 15, 2021.
28 https://www.segregatoraliny.pl/bitwa-pod-austerlitz-rekonstrukcja-2019/, accessed May 15, 2021.
29 https://www.gettysburgreenactment.com, accessed May 15, 2021.
30 https://www.facebook.com/sportowe.walki.rycerskie, accessed May 15, 2021.
31 www.facebook.com/sportowe.walki.rycerskie, accessed May 15, 2021.
32 https://rycerskakadra.pl, accessed May 15, 2021.
33 Baraniecka-Olszewska, "On the Performative," 52; Kamila Baraniecka-Olszewska, *Reko-rekonesans: praktyka autentyczności. Antropologiczne studium odtwórstwa drugiej wojny światowej w Polsce* (Kęty: Wydawnictwo Marek Derewiecki, 2018).
34 Vanessa Agnew, "Introduction. What Is Reeanctment?" *Criticism* 46, no. 3 (2004): 327–339; Rebecca Schneider, *Performing Remains: Art and War in Times of Theatrical Reenactment* (New York: Routledge, 2011), 2–4; Agnessa Vanessa, Jonathan Lamb, and Juliane Tomann, "Introduction: What Is Reenactment Studies?," in *The Routledge Handbook of Reenactment Studies. Key Terms in the Field*, ed. Vanessa Agnew, Jonathan Lamb, and Juliane Tomann (New York: Routledge, 2020), 1–11.
35 Mads Daugbjerg, "Battle," in *The Routledge Handbook*, 25–26.
36 David Dean, "Living history," in *The Routledge Handbook*, 120–124.
37 Piotr T. Kwiatkowski, *Pamięć zbiorowa społeczeństwa polskiego w okresie transformacji* (Warszawa: Scholar, 2008), 110–185.

Bibliography

Literature

Agnew, Vanessa. "Introduction. What Is Reeanctment?" *Criticism* 46, no. 3 (2004): 327–339.

Agnew, Vanessa, Jonathan Lamb, and Juliane Tomann. "Introduction: What Is Reenactment Studies?" In *The Routledge Handbook of Reenactment Studies. Key Terms in the Field*, edited by Vanessa Agnew, Jonathan Lamb, and Juliane Tomann, 1–11. New York: Routledge, 2020.

Baraniecka-Olszewska, Kamila. "Naprzód do przeszłości! Rekonstrukcje historyczne między historią a teraźniejszością." *Etnografia Polska*, 59, no. 1–2 (2015): 87–95.

Baraniecka-Olszewska, Kamila. "On the Performative Power of Stereotypes. WWII Historical Re-enactment and National Identities." *Revue des Études Sud-Est Européennes* 57, no. 1–4 (2019): 51–61.

Baraniecka-Olszewska, Kamila. *Reko-rekonesans: praktyka autentyczności. Antropologiczne studium odtwórstwa drugiej wojny światowej w Polsce*. Kęty: Wydawnictwo Marek Derewiecki, 2018.

Bogacki, Michał. "Historical Reenactment jako nowy sposób prezentacji przeszłości." *Do broni! Magazyn Rekonstrukcji Historycznych*, no. 4 (2006): 34–37.

Bogacki, Michał. "O współczesnym 'ożywianiu' przeszłości – charakterystyka odtwórstwa historycznego." *Turystyka Kulturowa*, no. 5 (2010): 4–25.

Daugbjerg, Mads. "Battle." In *The Routledge Handbook of Reenactment Studies. Key Terms in the Field*, edited by Vanessa Agnew, Jonathan Lamb, and Juliane Tomann, 25–29. New York: Routledge, 2020.

Dean, David. "Living history." In *The Routledge Handbook of Reenactment Studies. Key Terms in the Field*, edited by Vanessa Agnew, Jonathan Lamb, and Juliane Tomann, 120–125. New York: Routledge, 2020.

Filipowiak, Władysław. "Some Aspects of the Development of Wolin in the 8th–11th Centuries in the Light of the Results of New Research." In *Polish Lands at the Turn of the First and the Second Millennium*, edited by Przemysław Urbańczyk, 47–74. Warszawa: IAiE PAN, 2004.

Górewicz, Igor. "Profesjonalizacja odtwórstwa historycznego, Wystawy edukacyjne jako poszerzenia instrumentarium popularyzacji historii." In *Gospodarka ludów Morza Bałtyckiego*, vol. I, *Starożytność i średniowiecze*, edited by Michał Bogacki, Maciej Franz, and Zbigniew Pilarczyk, 341–365. Toruń: Adam Marszałek, 2009.

Kwiatkowski, Piotr T. *Pamięć zbiorowa społeczeństwa polskiego w okresie transformacji*. Warszawa: Scholar, 2008.

Pawleta, Michał. "Rekonstrukcje i inscenizacje przeszłości w perspektywie turystyki archeologicznej w Polsce." In *Skanseny archeologiczne i archeologia eksperymentalna*, edited by Jan Gancarski, 364–385. Krosno: Muzeum Podkarpackie, 2012.

Regiewicz, Adam. "Rekonstrukcje historyczne jako edutainment. Przypadek powstania styczniowego." *Prace Naukowe Akademii im. Jana Długosza w Częstochowie, Filologia Polska. Historia i Teoria Literatury*, 13 (2013): 87–104.

Schneider, Rebecca. *Performing Remains: Art and War in Times of Theatrical Reenactment*. New York: Routledge, 2011.

Skotnicka-Palka, Małgorzata. "Powtarzamy powtórzone. Rekonstrukcje historyczne." *Pamięć i Przyszłość*, 26, no. 4 (2014): 62–69.

Websites

https://www.nck.pl/badania/raporty/raport-grupy-rekonstrukcji-historycznych-dzialania-oddolne-na-rzecz-krzewienia-. Accessed May 15, 2021.

http://zamekgolub.pl/turnieje.html. Accessed May 15, 2021.

https://web.archive.org/web/20111207075307/http://humanities.exeter.ac.uk/archaeology/research/themes/experimentalarchaeology/. Accessed May 15, 2021.

https://web.archive.org/web/20101018055821/http://www.shef.ac.uk/archaeology/prospectivepg/masters/experimental.html. Accessed May 15, 2021.

http://teatrhistoryczny.pl. Accessed May 15, 2021.

http://www.grunwald1410.pl. Accessed May 15, 2021.

www.muzeumgrunwald.fbrothers.com/inscenizacja-bitwy/#o_inscenizacji. Accessed May 15, 2021.

https://wolinwsieci.jomsborg-vineta.com. Accessed May 15, 2021.

https://historia.org.pl/2015/07/10/najstarszy-turniej-rycerski-w-polsce. Accessed May 15, 2021.

https://www.segregatoraliny.pl/bitwa-pod-austerlitz-rekonstrukcja-2019. Accessed May 15, 2021.

https://www.gettysburgreenactment.com. Accessed May 15, 2021.

https://www.facebook.com/sportowe.walki.rycerskie. Accessed May 15, 2021.

https://rycerskakadra.pl. Accessed May 15, 2021.

14 Gaming the Polish Past

Case Study of *Kolejka* (*The Queue*)

Joanna Wojdon

In recent years, games have been included increasingly often in research on history-related entertainment. For some reasons, video games have been given priority over more traditional board games.[1] They use cutting-edge technologies that appeal to the "digitally native" generations, which per se seem to fulfill the notions of public history as addressed to large non-professional audiences with messages about the past. Their public includes millions of players worldwide, making the messages carried by games (including historical interpretations) truly transnational. Among the Polish game developers, CD-Projekt has gained worldwide recognition for its top-ranking *Witcher* series. A number of other IT companies operate in this segment of the market in Poland, too. None of their products is related to history, however, unless we regard quasi-medieval sceneries of the fantasy world of *Witcher* as historical.

On the other hand, a more than century-long tradition of history-related board games has been continued since the beginning of the twenty-first century. *Piast: Rzut kostką przez polskie dzieje* (*Piast: Roll of the Dice through the History of Poland*),[2] released in 2013 by the Ossoliński Institute of Wrocław, claims to be a reprint of the oldest game of this kind, developed at the turn of the nineteenth and twentieth century in the Polish community of Galicia – then part of the Habsburg empire. The game, based on the simple mechanics of "snakes and ladders," leads players through the dates of the history of Poland, starting from the baptism of Duke Mieszko I in 966 (regarded as the beginning of Polish statehood) up to the end of the nineteenth century. However, if a pawn stops at the spot marked with 1795 – the date of the third partition by Russia, Austria and Prussia, when Poland disappeared from the map of Europe for over a century – the player loses the game instantly.

The game which sparked the interest of the Polish public in history-related board games in the twenty-first century was *Kolejka* (*The Queue*, pronounced koh-ley-kah), developed in 2011 by Karol Madaj from the Office of Public Education of the Institute of National Remembrance.[3] This chapter uses *Kolejka* as a case study to present board games as a form of public history.[4]

DOI: 10.4324/9781003165767-18

Kolejka's Rules

Kolejka can be played by two to five people. Each player is a head of his/her "family" of five wooden pawns who are busy shopping in the neighborhood stores or at the outdoor market. There are five stores on the board, each specializing in one category of merchandise. The aim of each family is to acquire all the items on their shopping list (drawn at the very beginning of the game). Each list has a different number of goods to buy in various categories: food, clothes, furniture, household appliances and various small stuff from a kiosk. Each player, thus, has a different goal. One person is supposed to organize a first communion party (which requires four pieces of food, three household appliances, two pieces of furniture and one piece of clothing), another person is to furnish a newly acquired apartment (four pieces of furniture, three pieces of clothing, two minor items, one piece of food), another is to send the kids for a summer holiday, another to re-arrange the kitchen and yet another to spend a holiday in a cottage. The first family to acquire all the listed items wins.

Besides the shopping list and the pawns in one of the five colors, each player has a set of queuing cards which will help the family move towards the beginning of the queue in order to be able to pick up some goods as soon as the shop opens. The goods are represented by the cards with the pictures of typical products from the 1970s and 1980s, some of which have become iconic, partly due to the fact that the assortment of goods available for purchase was quite limited and many of them appeared only occasionally, becoming objects of dreams rather than of possession. It made the advertisements that started to appear in the Polish media in the 1980s somewhat absurd, which is reflected on the playing cards by the short ads, similar in style to those from the communist period, that accompany the pictures of goods.

At the beginning of each round the players take turns placing their pawns, one at a time, in front of the stores of their choice, until all the pawns are lined up. At the beginning of the game, once the queues are in place, a speculator (a black pawn) is put at the end of each one and remains in the queue for the whole gameplay.

Only at that point is there time for merchandise delivery – so in the first stage the players queue without even knowing if there will be anything to buy in a particular shop during that round. According to the information on special cards, so called delivery cards, the manager (a designated player) transfers an appropriate quantity of merchandise (usually between one and three pieces) from delivery trucks to the stores, as long as supplies last. There may be shops that receive up to six items and shops that receive none in a given round.

Once the merchandise is delivered, the opening player chooses one of the queuing cards in his/her hand, puts it face up on the designated spot in the center of the board and proceeds to carry out the action described on the card.

Some examples of actions are as follows:

Delivery error: A truck driver has delivered merchandise to the wrong store. Transfer one piece of merchandise to the neighboring store. – So the player will be able to buy, e.g., a sofa for their new apartment in a kiosk or in a clothes shop where he/she is (presumably) closer to the beginning of the queue.

Friend in the workers Party provincial committee. A friend has tipped you off about the delivery schedule. Peek at the top two delivery cards. – Thus, he or she will know to which two (of three) shops the merchandise will be delivered in the next round and thus, in which queues it is worthwhile to place his "family members."

Mother carrying a small child. You have borrowed someone else's baby and are entitled to being served without queueing. Move your pawn to the front of the queue. – The pawns in front of the queue are the first to take items once the shop opens.

Community list. A community list that entitles people to certain places in the queue has been drawn up. Pick up the whole queue between your fingers and turn it back to front so that the last pawn is now first. – This action is one of the most annoying for other players, second only to *Closed for stocktaking* which "closes" a particular shop so that nobody from the queue can take any merchandise for the whole round.

The next player in a clockwise direction plays a queuing card in a similar manner and the game proceeds this way for three rounds or when all the players say "pass."

Then the stores open. When it finally happens, each pawn can take only one item of merchandise, but the merchandise is distributed only while supplies last. This is why getting a good place in the queue is crucial. The pawn returns home with the shopping or remains in the queue empty-handed.

If an item of merchandise has been "purchased" (though there is no money in the game) by a speculator, it is placed on a special field representing the outdoor market, and the speculator is moved to the end of the same queue.

At the end of each "shopping day," the players who in the "queuing up" phase lined up their pawns in front of the outdoor market can exchange any number of purchased items for items available at the market. According to the *Instruction*,

Merchandise is exchanged at the ratio of 2:1, i.e., any two items from home are left in the market in exchange for one item taken from the market. Items which have the market trader marker sitting on top of them can be purchased at the preferential ratio of 1:1. After shopping at the market, the pawn returns home with the purchased merchandise cards. There is no rationing at the market so one pawn can return from the market with several items of merchandise.

The next day starts with the "queuing up" phase once more: the pawns that brought merchandise home can select shops and start queueing again.

Kolejka as Public History

Kolejka *Is a Historical Narrative*

If a narrative is defined as "a spoken or written account of connected events, a story,"[5] then, literally speaking, board games are not spoken or written accounts. Players cannot press a button and listen to a story, as happens with radio or TV shows. The text of the game instructions does not make a story, either. However, while playing the game according to the rules, players do create the narrative. They make/build/tell the story. In fact, there are at least two layers of game narratives.

The first one refers to the gameplay itself. What had been played, what decisions the players had made, how they had behaved while playing can be recorded and/or (re)told. Psychologists could analyze players' personalities, or the influence of certain mechanisms of the game rules on players' behavior.

Many games, *Kolejka* included, also offer some form of a narrative behind the game's rules. They set the gameplay in a certain story based on a real or invented world. We enjoy reading narratives (e.g. novels), listening to them, telling and viewing the stories. To paraphrase Hayden White, "Narration is a manner of speaking as universal as language itself, and narrative is a mode of verbal representation so seeming natural to human consciousness"[6] that it is also employed by game developers. While dominos is purely logical, chess originated from the story of a battle between two armies and "snakes and ladders"[7] have multiple "stories" behind the same rules: with trains and tracks, helping animals, firefighters and their ladders, or, as in the case of the *Throwing Dice through the Ages*, mentioned above – progressing in chronology. A good connection between the game mechanics and the story it conveys is appreciated by the players. The narrative dimension of games makes playing more enjoyable.

In the case of *Kolejka*, the game introduction and the gameplay itself prove without any doubt that the narrative was intended to be a historical one. The authors/developers of the game took on the role of public historians. According to the Introduction, the goal of *Kolejka* is "to reconstruct, in a vivid manner, the circumstances in which Poles lived for decades under an externally imposed communist system" (Łukasz Kamiński, then president of IPN) and "to show young people and remind the older ones what hard times these were..." (Karol Madaj, the author).

Sometimes, particularly in the case of video games, developers are not aware of their role as public historians. Their historical knowledge is rather superficial. Some studios hire professional advisors but playability is usually prioritized over historical accuracy, especially in the top-ranking commercial productions.[8] In the case of *Kolejka*, however, the creators were professionally trained historians, specializing in the history of the twentieth century and old enough to have been living under communism for some time. Moreover, Andrzej Zawistowski, who took part in the production process, has authored a book on the systems of rationing cards in post-war Poland.[9]

I have observed several hundred young people from various countries (Poland included) playing *Kolejka* since the beginning of its international career. I have been using it during classes on the post-WWII history of Poland, on public history and on the methodology of teaching history, as well as during Erasmus visits abroad, during the social part of the Public History Summer School in Wrocław, and on other occasions. After the gameplay I usually asked players to write anonymously if they enjoyed the game (the vast majority did) and what they learned from the gameplay. Their responses confirm that there is historical narrative behind the game and that the players are able to grasp it.

> It is hard to believe that buying goods back in communist times was so unpredictable.

> The game was an interesting representation of how lines operated during communist times. Sometimes unfair, sometimes easier if you have the right connections. If the game gets frustrating, I can only imagine how frustrating it could have been in real life.

Kolejka *Deals with Everyday Life of Ordinary People –*
It Is "about the Public"

According to its classical definition, public history is history *for* the public, *by* the public, *with* the public and *about* the public.[10] It has been proved above that *Kolejka* can be regarded as a historical narrative.

It refers to the shopping experiences in Poland in the so-called economy of "real socialism," or "economy of deficit," where restrained free-market mechanisms, ideological preferences for heavy industry and geo-political realities of dependence on the Soviet Union were among the factors that led to permanent shortages of supplies needed for everyday life (from food, clothing and medicines to house appliances, electronics and cars). The situation was also quite similar in some other countries of the Soviet bloc during the Cold War era. Governments were introducing various strategies to overcome those difficulties, from seeking foreign assistance in order to import goods (e.g. Poland, Hungary, the German Democratic Republic or GDR) to the temporary introduction of rationing cards (Poland, USSR in the 1980s), but the core of the problem remained unsolved until the collapse of the communist system. As a result, people living in those countries had to develop their own strategies for coping with everyday realities, where acquiring even basic goods often occupied much more attention and required more sophisticated skills than just earning money for

living. Jerzy Kochanowski called this "the back door" of socialist economy.[11] Some of them were large-scale projects, but many were performed
on a daily basis by ordinary people. The queuing cards of *Kolejka* reflect
some of them, such as using acquaintances in order to get knowledge of
when and where certain goods might be available (such information might
also be bought or bartered for other information or services) or performing various strategies, rather less elegant, to get promoted to closer to the
front of the queue.

Małgorzata Mazurek has claimed that only really big money allowed
some people to live without caring too much about such strategies because
they could afford to buy necessary goods outside of the official market
where the state regulations of socialist economy applied[12] – these aspects
are illustrated in *Kolejka* by the activities of "speculators" and the rules at
the "outdoor market" where exchange of unnecessary goods can be made.
In a special addition to *Kolejka*, called *Ogonek* ("tail" in English, which is
a synonym for a queue in the Polish language) and sold separately, alcohol
was introduced as a token of exchange which made it easier to acquire goods
or be promoted in the queue – yet another reflection of the realities of everyday life under communism.

The Public Plays a Crucial Role in Creating the Historical
Narrative of *Kolejka* – It Is Created by the Public

In the case of books, oral narratives, movies or TV programs, it is presumed
that the story is told by their authors/creators/developers while the audience
receives it passively, generally speaking, in a predictable way. The narrative is delivered in one shape to all the public. Its reception may depend on
the audience's background (e.g. education, previous experiences or beliefs),
it can be commented on, contested or supplemented, but at least for the
outside observer everyone receives the same content. In the case of games
(both traditional board games and video games), each gameplay is different. Developers provide a general framework, but the players play an active
role in creating the narrative itself. It cannot come into being without their
engagement. To cite Jeremiah McCall: "[...] the game does nothing without
a player, and so designer and player are in a sort of active, constructive dialogue about the past through gameplay."[13]

Adam Chapman in his book on digital games employs the findings of
ecological psychology in order to "understand how [...] historical games describe, and allow us to explore, past action by offering opportunities for
present action."[14] The games, he writes, "are especially concerned with what
the relationships of the past afforded (what could or could not be done)
rather than simply what things or events were" (174). "Games can structure
affordances that are in some way similar to the environments of the past
(e.g. those experienced by historical agents)."[15] "Players are forced to act
in historically meaningful ways in order to be successful and must learn to

perceive the information that the game argues was important to the systems and processes it represents and which it argues resemble the initial context of information."[16] Thus, Chapman argues that games can be interpreted as a form of historical reenactment.[17]

The same findings can also be applied to board games, such as *Kolejka*. After opening the game box, we can see a set of pawns, boards, cards and pictures – in part realistic, in part symbolic. The game "is happening" thanks to the engagement of the players who follow the rules, but players' intelligence, emotions, preferences and bad or good luck are necessary to make use of the potential provided by the developers and to develop the story about the past. This form of reenactment helps them to understand the motivations of the people in their dealing with the economic system of communism, which is reflected in one of the players' opinions:

> I have learnt that our nowadays' life is totally different from the past and things have changed completely. During the game it helped me to understand more clearly the hard period of that time even in the simplest things, because I felt it on my own.

Playing Is a Public Experience – It Does Not Happen without the Public

As in any multiplayer game, *Kolejka* requires social interactions. It is public, as opposed to private, single-player (or single-user) forms of entertainment. I used it both as an icebreaker and a starting point for serious discussions about the past, about human nature and about various forms of public history.

While observing the players, I noticed more than once young people who were initially skeptical or shy, or extremely nice and polite, but as the game progressed became more and more engaged, but also more selfish and ruthless in completing their shopping tasks and competing with other players – which proves their engagement in the gameplay.

Such emotions are also reflected in the post-play notes:

> Queuing can foster a certain sense of solidarity but also some hostility. I was frustrated when I couldn't get what I needed and happy when I finally got it.

> The feelings during the game have been frustrating and unfair but sometimes you had a feeling of success after you got a product. I think this is a great game to understand a little bit how the people felt in the communist times.

Jeffrey Byford has noted similar observations regarding his students playing *Kolejka*: "Observation of students becoming frustrated from limited and unpredictable deliveries was common. In addition, black market purchases and privileged players grabbing desired products provoked negative emotions, insensitive students and manifestations of malice."[18]

There were attempts to transfer *Kolejka* into a digital format, with an option of a single player playing versus computer-operated opponents. As of now (2021) this has not yet materialized.

Kolejka Attracts the Public – It Is Designed for the Public

Public history is often promoted as a more attractive, more interesting, engaging form of presenting the past if compared to traditional academic history, locked away in the "ivory towers" of academics who communicate only with one another (if at all) and concentrate on research rather than on presentation of their findings. For public history, reaching the audience is an entry level while deep interaction with the public or with multiple publics becomes a desired goal of most undertakings, from museum exhibitions to films, and from monuments to public celebrations.

While games are interactive by the very fact that they are played, their attractiveness varies. *Kolejka* is not one of the "serious" games preoccupied with an educational mission that pupils play when they have to.[19] People of different ages play it voluntarily, in their free time. One can find boxes with *Kolejka* in Polish libraries, but also in cafés and hotel lobbies. It has turned out to be the biggest commercial success of IPN. It has sold over 100,000 copies in the first two years, first in Polish, but then also in other languages, including English, French, Spanish, German and Japanese.[20] For legal and procedural reasons, the Institute could not fulfill the market demand and sold the license to a commercial company, *Trefl*.

After the success of *Kolejka*, multiple other games related to history, most often to communist times, have been produced in Poland. Karol Madaj himself developed more than a dozen of them. He claims that he is able to turn any historical topic into a game by adjusting one or more of the existing models of game mechanics.[21] He has used, for example, hexagonally shaped boards for strategic games related to the battles of the Second World War (*111* about the defense of Warsaw in 1939 and *303* about the Battle of England), while Doblo-like mechanics of recognizing common symbols on the playing cards has worked in the *ZnajZnak* (*Know-the-Sign*) series, with thematic releases related to specific periods or themes of history (i.e. the battle of Monte Cassino, Sports or Polish-Hungarian relations). None of them has been as successful as *Kolejka*, however. Most of them focus on educational aspects or on the promotion of institutions, such as *Across the Iron Curtain* developed for the European Platform of Memory and Conscience, where players implement various techniques of escaping from the countries behind the Iron Curtain to the Free World.

On the other hand, Madaj's productions have by and large surpassed most of the other games that have appeared on the market. There were the bridge/poker cards *Wspomnienia PRL-u* (*Reminiscences of the People's Po-land*) with pictures of 1980s rationing cards on the decks and photographs from the communist period on the faces. Drawings of merchandise from the communist period (such as packages of sugar, sewing machines, typical cupboards and radio receivers, or rolls of toilet paper, which was constantly in shortage under communism) were used on the bricks of *Domino PRL*. There were memory-type games with such objects and the *Monopoly*-like *PRL: Sentymentalna gra planszowa* (*PRL: Sentimental Board Game*). Their references to the communist period were rather superficial and they lacked any meaningful narratives. Some were too difficult,[22] others too easy and many needed better testing for inconsistences in the rules or more elaborate esthetics. Their weaknesses illustrate the factors that have contributed to the success of *Kolejka*, which thoughtfully combines playability with education, and leisure with commemoration.

Conclusions: The Public's Perception of the Gameplay

The question may arise as to whether the players who enjoy *Kolejka* perceive it as a (public) historical narrative. Do they understand and appreciate its message about the past or perhaps they simply ignore it and perceive the game as pure entertainment?

Even if some players ignore the history-related aspects of *Kolejka*, it would not necessarily prevent it from belonging to the realm of public history. Such a situation could be compared to a monument that is unrecognized or misinterpreted by passers-by, a street name whose patron is unknown to visitors or even inhabitants, or a museum artifact unnoticed by visitors. They do not carry their messages to everyone but only to those who are interested and prepared to read them. Yet, they are widely recognized as examples of public history.

I know of Americans who had no experience of living under communism who still play *Kolejka* for leisure.[23] Thus, it can be appreciated because the mechanics of the game work well and the story is enjoyable, not because of the shared historical experiences.

Reactions of adults who had lived in Eastern Europe in the 1970s and 1980s leave no doubt, though, that they notice and appreciate the historical narrative. In their case the gameplay often initiates stories of their (or their relatives') experiences of shopping under communism, partly funny and partly traumatic, that correspond with the mechanisms illustrated in the game.

The students' comments like

> Coming from an ex-Soviet country, the queuing up reminded me of my grandmother's stories about the lack of goods, bureaucracy, and always trying to know someone who knows someone in order to get better goods in less time and hassle

indicate that there exist shared memories of shopping in other countries of the Soviet bloc. More detailed analysis of the reactions of people from the former Soviet bloc compared to those from the rest of the world should help specify if their experiences or memories influence the way the game is perceived and the narratives it evokes. The fact that *Kolejka* was banned by the Russian authorities for spreading anti-Russian sentiments among the players[24] (in the Introduction, the Soviet dominance over Poland is blamed for the hardships of the economy of "real socialism") can serve as another proof of its potential for shaping public perceptions of the past, even if the creators did not necessarily predict such a reaction.

Observations of the students coming from the post-Soviet countries who visited a typical room of the 1960s–1980s in the museum of post-Second World War history in Wrocław (*Depot History Center*) indicate that they recognized the household items on display as similar or even identical to those that they or their relatives (usually grandparents) had possessed. Thus, even untranslated pieces of merchandise that appear on the cards with goods that *Kolejka* players acquire during the game can appeal to the memories of some international players.

Another possible comparison would be among the older and younger generations: those who lived under communism for whom the game refers to their personal experiences versus those who learn about communism from the game. My experience suggests that those who had experienced real hardships of shopping did not find the game as enjoyable as those who do not have this kind of first-hand experience. "And what is so funny about it?", one of them asked me while playing. However, one should take into consideration that the older generation in general does not enjoy playing as much as the youngsters.

Introductory knowledge about the historical background can also be taken into consideration in assessing the narrative potential of the game. I can hypothesize that those who are familiar with the communist realities in Poland or elsewhere in the world, would be able to grasp more nuances of the gameplay than total novices. However, I have used the game both as a summary of a semester-long course on the history of Poland under communism and as a form of social event during conferences and summer schools for novices in this area of history, and no easy generalizations can be made on the reception of the gameplay in those different settings, or at least I was not able to identify meaningful differences.

The types of sources of background knowledge could be researched more accurately, and their influence on understanding the gameplay: school history education, scholarly literature, popular culture (from movies to songs and articles in popular magazines), museum exhibitions, and other public history places and events. Other potential factors may include the political views of the players, their social status and social background, including the roles and positions of their family members under communism.

Some researchers attribute the popularity of the games that refer to the communist past to *"ostalgia"* – a term coined in Germany, meaning nostalgia for the "east," for the GDR ruled by the Communist Party, as opposed to the realities which were overwhelmed by the "west" and the free market economy. Some board games available on the market may indeed fall into this category, but not *Kolejka* which is far from shaping a positive image of "good old times" along with occasional fun at some of its drawbacks. To cite the introduction by Łukasz Kamiński, the president of IPN at the time when the game was released:

> As you will soon see, this game arouses various emotions, including laughter. But it is also worth taking a moment to consider the fate of those who were unable to escape the absurdity of communism, and had to endure the system for long years.

This kind of reflection was also present in the notes by student-players cited above, which proves that the public, or at least this part of it, is reading the narrative of *Kolejka* in the way in which it was designed by its creators. This is how public history should work.

Notes

1 Adam Chapman, *Digital Games as History: How Video Games Represent the Past and Offer Access to Historical Practice* (New York: Routledge, 2016); Jeremiah McCall, *Gaming the Past: Using Video Games to Teach Secondary History* (New York: Routledge, 2013); Jeremiah McCall, "Video Games as Participatory Public History," in *A Companion to Public History*, ed. David M. Dean (Hoboken: Wiley–Blackwell, 2018), 405–416; Scott A. Metzger, and Richard J. Paxton "Gaming History: A Framework for What Video Games Teach about the Past," *Theory & Research in Social Education* 44, no. 4 (2016): 532–564.
2 https://ossolineum.pl/index.php/piast-historyczna-gra-planszowa/   (accessed May 14, 2021).
3 Two other successful history-related games can be mentioned. *Pan tu nie stał* (*It was not your place, Sir*), like *Kolejka*, refers to the phenomenon of queuing in the realities of the shortages of goods on the market. It is based on the license of *The Great Wall of China* by Reiner Knizia – which per se is a fascinating example that a game's mechanics and contents can be treated separately. The gameplay is shorter and somewhat less sophisticated than in *Kolejka*, a player represents an individual, not a family, but "tricks" to be promoted in the queue are quite similar, as are some of the items of merchandise. *Pan tu nie stał* was commercially successful enough to have two sequels: *Cinkciarz* that focuses on illegal money exchange and *Demoludy* which provides an opportunity to acquire some goods (illegally) in other countries of the Soviet bloc. *Mali powstańcy* (*Little Insurgents*) was developed in 2011 by Filip Miłuński for the Warsaw Rising Museum. It deals with the role of the Polish scouts (both male and female) in operating a postal service for the insurgents and civilian population in occupied Warsaw during the uprising of 1944. Players compete in completing the tasks of transporting messages between given locations on the city map, but at the same time they have to take care that all the messages

have been delivered in order to prevent the failure of the rising in one or more districts of the city.

4 I have presented *Kolejka* during the 2018 annual meeting of the Association for Slavic, East European & Eurasian Studies: "The 'Queue' (Kolejka) Board Game as a Form of Historical Reenactment" and during the conference 'Narratives of Europe's Shared Past: Between Singularity of the Holocaust and Totalitarian Paradigm,' at the House of European History, Brussels, on May 16–17, 2019, as "The Polish game Kolejka (Queue) as a narrative of shared (Eastern) European Past," and published an article "Public History and Board Games," *Public History Weekly*, 7 (2019) 9, March 14, 2019, https://public-history-weekly.degruyter.com/7-2019-9/kolejka-history/.
5 "Narrative," in *Oxford English and Spanish Dictionary,* accessed May 25, 2021, https://www.lexico.com/en/definition/narrative.
6 Hayden White, "The Question of Narrative in Contemporary Historical Theory," *History and Theory* 23, no. 1 (1984): 1–33.
7 On the roots of this genre cf. Andrew Topsfield, "The Indian Game of Snakes and Ladders," *Artibus Asiae* 46, no. 3 (1985): 203–226.
8 Laurent Turcot and Anna Jenkin, "Meet the Historical Experts: Laurent Turcot on 'Assassins Creed: Unity," in *History Matters. History Brought alive by the University of Sheffield,* last modified April 16, 2015, accessed May 15, 2021, http://www.historymatters.group.shef.ac.uk/meet-historical-experts-laurentturcot-assassins-creed-unity/; María E. Navarro (interviewed by Manuel Saga), "What It's Like to Be an Architectural Consultant for Assassin's Creed II," *Archdaily,* last modified October 7, 2015, accessed March 20, 2020, https://www.archdaily.com/774210/maria-elisa-navarro-the-architecturalconsultant-for-assassins-creed-ii. Stéphanie-Anne Ruatta (interviewed by Andrew Reinhard), "Consulting for Ubisoft on Assassin's Creed: Odyssey," *Archeogaming,* last modified April 19, 2019, accessed March 20, 2020, https://archaeogaming.com/2019/04/19/consulting-for-ubisoft-on-assassinscreed-odyssey; Chad Sapieha, "How Ubisoft Montreal Used Historians to Make Ancient Egypt Authentic in Assassin's Creed Origins," *Financial Post*, last modified October 27, 2017, accessed March 20, 2020, https://business.financialpost.com/technology/gaming/how-ubisoft-montrealused-historians-to-make-ancient-egypt-authentic-in-assassins-creed-origins.
9 Andrzej Zawistowski, *Bilety do sklepu. Handel reglamentowany w PRL* (Warszawa: PWN, 2017).
10 Barbara Franco, "Public History and Memory: A Museum Perspective," *The Public Historian* 19, no. 2 (1997): 65.
11 Jerzy Kochanowski, *Through the Back Door. The Black Market in Poland 1944–1989* (Franfurt: Peter Lang, 2017).
12 Małgorzata Mazurek, *Społeczeństwo kolejki. O doświadczeniach niedoboru 1945–1989* (Warszawa: Trio, 2010).
13 McCall, "Video Games," 409.
14 Chapman, *Digital Games*, 173.
15 Ibid., 174.
16 Ibid., 187.
17 Ibid., 173–194. Cf. the chapter on historical reenactments by Filip Wolański in this volume.
18 Jeffrey Byford, "Kolejka: Teaching Daily Living in 1980s Poland," *International Journal of Historical Learning, Teaching and Research* 12, no. 2 (2014): 162.
19 Jeremiah McCall, *Gaming the Past: Using Video Games to Teach Secondary History* (New York: Routledge, 2011), 58–59.
20 Instruction and queuing cards are translated, and can be stuck onto the original Polish cards, but the descriptions and quasi-ads of the pieces of merchandise remain in Polish only.

21 Karol Madaj, "Proces projektowania gry historycznej z perspektywy autora," in *Historia w przestrzeni publicznej*, ed. Joanna Wojdon (Warszawa: PWN, 2018), 495–500.
22 For example, *Alternatywy 4*, the game based on the TV series by Stanisław Bareja, a comedy director who ridiculed many aspects of communist realities of the 1980s.
23 Discussion during the 2018 annual meeting of the Association for Slavic, East European & Eurasian Studies in Boston.
24 Damien Sharkov, "Russia Bans Poland's 'Communist Monopoly' Board Game," *Newsweek*, March 21, 2016, accessed May 29, 2021, https://www.newsweek.com/russia-bans-polands-communist-monopoly-being-anti-russian-438972.

Bibliography

Byford, Jeffrey. "Kolejka: Teaching Daily Living in 1980s Poland." *International Journal of Historical Learning, Teaching and Research* 12, no. 2 (2014): 162.

Chapman, Adam. *Digital Games as History: How Video Games Represent the Past and Offer Access to Historical Practice*. New York: Routledge, 2016.

Franco, Barbara. "Public History and Memory: A Museum Perspective." *The Public Historian* 19, no. 2 (1997): 65.

Kochanowski, Jerzy. *Through the Back Door. The Black Market in Poland 1944– 1989*. Frankfurt: Peter Lang, 2017.

Madaj, Karol. "Proces projektowania gry historycznej z perspektywy autora." In *Historia w przestrzeni publicznej*, edited by Joanna Wojdon, 495–500. Warszawa: PWN, 2018.

Mazurek, Małgorzata. *Społeczeństwo kolejki. O doświadczeniach niedoboru 1945– 1989*. Warszawa: Trio, 2010.

McCall, Jeremiah. *Gaming the Past: Using Video Games to Teach Secondary History*. New York: Routledge, 2013.

McCall, Jeremiah. "Video Games as Participatory Public History." In *A Companion to Public History*, edited by David Dean, 405–416. Hoboken: Wiley Blackwell, 2018.

Metzger, Scott A., and Richard J. Paxton. "Gaming History: A Framework for What Video Games Teach about the Past." *Theory & Research in Social Education* 44, no. 4 (2016): 532–564.

Navarro, María E. "What It's Like to Be an Architectural Consultant for Assassin's Creed II." *Archdaily*, last modified October 7, 2015. Accessed March 20, 2020. https://www.archdaily.com/774210/maria-elisa-navarro-the-architectural consultant-for-assassins-creed-ii.

Ruatta, Stéphanie-Anne, and Andrew Reinhard. "Consulting for Ubisoft on Assassin's Creed: Odyssey." *Archeogaming*, last modified April 19, 2019. Accessed March 20, 2020. https://archaeogaming.com/2019/04/19/consulting-for-ubisoft-on-assassinscreed-odyssey/.

Sapieha, Chad. "How Ubisoft Montreal Used Historians to Make Ancient Egypt Authentic in Assassin's Creed Origins." *Financial Post*, last modified October 27, 2017. Accessed March 20, 2020. https://financialpost.com/technology/gaming/how-ubisoft-montreal-used-historians-to-make-ancient-egypt-authentic-in-assassins-creed-origins.

Sharkov, Damien. "Russia Bans Poland's 'Communist Monopoly' Board Game." *Newsweek*, March 21, 2016, accessed May 29, 2021, https://www.newsweek.com/russia-bans-polands-communist-monopoly-being-anti-russian-438972.

Topsfield, Andrew. "The Indian Game of Snakes and Ladders." *Artibus Asiae* 46, no. 3 (1985): 203–226.

Turcot, Laurent, and Anna Jenkin. "Meet the Historical Experts: Laurent Turcot on 'Assassins Creed: Unity." In *History Matters. History Brought Alive by the University of Sheffield*, April 16, 2015. Accessed May 15, 2021. http://www.historymatters.group.shef.ac.uk/meet-historical-experts-laurent-turcot-assassins-creed-unity/.

White, Hayden. "The Question of Narrative in Contemporary Historical Theory." *History and Theory* 23, no. 1 (1984): 1–33.

Wojdon, Joanna. "Public History and Board Games." *Public History Weekly*, 7, no. 9 (2019), last modified March 14, 2019. Accessed May 15, 2021. https://public-history-weekly.degruyter.com/7-2019-9/kolejka-history/.

Zawistowski, Andrzej. *Bilety do sklepu: Handel reglamentowany w PRL*. Warszawa: PWN, 2017.

Games

111. Warszawa: IPN, 2013.

303. Warszawa: IPN, 2010.

7. W obronie Lwowa. Warszawa: IPN, 2014.

Across the Iron Curtain. Warszawa – Praha: IPN – Platform of European Memory and Conscience, 2017.

Alternatywy 4. Warszawa: TVP, 2014.

Domino PRL. Węgrów: Tupiko, 2014.

The Great Wall of China by Reiner Knizia. Roseville: Fantasy Flight Games, 2006.

Kolejka. Ogonek. Warszawa: IPN, 2011.

Kolejka. Warszawa: IPN, 2018.

Mali powstańcy. Warszawa: Muzeum Powstania Warszawskiego, 2011.

Pan tu nie stał. Cinkciarz. Warszawa: Egmont, 2016.

Pan tu nie stał. Demoludy. Warszawa: Egmont, 2015.

Pan tu nie stał. Warszawa: Egmont, 2012.

Piast: Rzut kostką przez polskie dzieje. Wrocław: Ossolineum, 2013

PRL: Sentymentalna gra planszowa. Węgrów: Tupiko, 2015.

Wspomnienia PRL-u. Sopot: Trefl, no date.

ZnajZnak. Felismered? Warszawa: IPN, 2018.

ZnajZnak. Monte Cassino. Warszawa: IPN, 2014.

ZnajZnak. Sport. Warszawa: IPN, 2015.

ZnajZnak. Warszawa: IPN, 2012.

Index